D0404365

PRAISE FOR

THE GREAT DETECTIVE

"For even the casual fan, the history of this deathless character is fascinating. Dundas does a fine job of tracing the roots of Holmes . . . [and] writes in a jovial, casual way that invites the reader to take part."

— *Boston Globe*

"Find[s] fresh ground . . . [Dundas's] scholarship is impressive . . . He's an amiable guide, placing more than a century of Sherlockiana into an appealing, modern frame." — Daniel Stashower, *Washington Post*

"Dundas weaves fascinating parallel histories of Holmes as literary creation, Holmes as broader cultural phenomenon, and the character's larger-than-life creator, Sir Arthur Conan Doyle . . . Incisive, well informed, and slyly witty (like Holmes himself), Dundas's book provides entertaining and irrefutable evidence that the game is still — and is likely to remain — afoot." — *Shelf Awareness*, starred review

"The first thing to note about *The Great Detective* is Dundas's stellar turn of phrase . . . Well polished, punchy." — *Weekly Standard*

"Charmingly eccentric . . . The reader who has met Sherlock Holmes only in film or on television, in comic books, or even in the original sixty stories is likely to be surprised and, yes, amazed at Dundas's skillful account of the rise of Sherlock Holmes and his appearances in other media . . . For all who enjoy the company of Sherlock Holmes, in any of his many forms, reading Dundas's book will be hours well spent. The book feels like a long conversation with a new friend."

— Leslie S. Klinger, *Los Angeles Review of Books*

"[A] sprightly, riveting exploration of Sherlock Holmes — and the character's thriving, eccentric subculture." — *Mental Floss*

"Sherlock Holmes means different things to different people: to die-hard readers, Sir Arthur Conan Doyle's original (who cracked his first case in 1887); to older filmgoers, Basil Rathbone and Peter Cushing; to children of the 1970s and pretty much no one else, Nicol Williamson and Robert Stephens; and to younger fans, Robert Downey Jr. and Benedict Cumberbatch. All of them turn up in *The Great Detective,* in which Zach Dundas traces Sherlock's evergreen celebrity. Such is Dundas's enthusiasm that one almost forgets Doyle's wary role in the legend. The author's resigned response to an extraordinarily rich $45,000 offer from *Collier's Weekly* to resurrect Holmes in 1903: 'Very well.'" — *Vanity Fair*

"A lighthearted blend of travelogue and cultural criticism." — *Oregon Humanities*

"The author of this wonderful book has crammed it with enough research — Holmesian, Watsonian, Doylean — to bulge the seams . . . [But] Dundas's matey writing style makes the details easy to absorb . . . A delight for Baker Streeters." — *Booklist*, starred review

"A lively look at the enduring detective . . . A cheerful romp . . . A bright read for Sherlock's fans." — *Kirkus Reviews*

THE
GREAT DETECTIVE

THE AMAZING RISE

and

IMMORTAL LIFE

of

SHERLOCK HOLMES

ZACH DUNDAS

Mariner Books
Houghton Mifflin Harcourt
BOSTON · NEW YORK

First Mariner Books edition 2016

Copyright © 2015 by Zach Dundas

ALL RIGHTS RESERVED

For information about permission to reproduce selections from this book,
write to trade.permissions@hmhco.com or to Permissions, Houghton Mifflin Harcourt
Publishing Company, 3 Park Avenue, 19th floor, New York, New York 10016.

www.hmhco.com

Library of Congress Cataloging-in-Publication Data
Dundas, Zach.
The great detective : the amazing rise and immortal life
of Sherlock Holmes / Zach Dundas.
pages cm
ISBN 978-0-544-21404-0 (hardback) — ISBN 978-0-544-22020-1 (ebook)
ISBN 978-0-544-70521-0 (pbk.)
1. Doyle, Arthur Conan, 1859–1930 — Characters — Sherlock Holmes.
2. Holmes, Sherlock — Influence. 3. Detective and mystery stories,
English — History and criticism. 4. Private investigators in literature.
5. Dundas, Zach. I. Title.
PR4624.D86 2015
823'.809 — dc23
2014039684

Book design by Chrissy Kurpeski
Typeset in Minion Pro

Printed in the United States of America
DOC 10 9 8 7 6 5 4 3 2 1

The spot illustrations are from the following sources: Title page, chapter 5, chapter 6: *2,000 Early Advertising Cuts,* edited by Clarence P. Hornung; Chapter 1: *3,800 Early Advertising Cuts: Deberny Type Foundry,* selected and arranged by Carol Belanger Grafton; Chapter 2, chapter 7: *Harter's Picture Archive for Collage and Illustration: Over 300 Nineteenth-Century Cuts,* edited by Jim Harter; Chapter 3: *Food and Drink: A Pictorial Archive from Nineteenth-Century Sources,* selected by Jim Harter; Chapter 4: *Scan This Book: Two,* compiled by John Mendenhall; Chapter 8: *Victorian Display Alphabets: 100 Complete Fonts,* selected and arranged by Dan X. Solo from the Solotype Typographers Catalog; Chapter 9: *Scan This Book: Three,* compiled by John Mendenhall; Chapter 10: *Scan This Book,* compiled by John Mendenhall.

C.E.M.
"How came he to have so singular a companion?"

·

C.V.D.
The stormy petrel of crime

·

G.C.H.
The Secret Weapon

CONTENTS

"Reality" is not the subject nor the object of true art which creates its own special reality having nothing to do with the average "reality" perceived by the communal eye.

— VLADIMIR NABOKOV, *PALE FIRE*

There are two kinds of truth: the truth that lights the way and the truth that warms the heart. The first of these is science, and the second is art. Neither is independent of the other or more important than the other. Without art science would be as useless as a pair of high forceps in the hands of a plumber. Without science art would become a crude mess of folklore and emotional quackery. The truth of art keeps science from becoming inhuman, and the truth of science keeps art from becoming ridiculous.

— RAYMOND CHANDLER, *NOTEBOOKS*

PRELUDE: 221B

I CLIMBED A NARROW staircase in an old house in London, trying to count the steps. *Eleven, twelve, thirteen* — but I was amid a large and constricted crowd, and its jostling interrupted my humble attempt at observation. We started and stopped as we climbed toward our shared destination, a small and dimly lit room furnished in a style out of time.

This chamber's walls bore florid, red-flocked paper, punctuated by shelves overflowing with dusty and battered books. A pair of fusty old chairs flanked the hearth. And everywhere, everywhere, clutter in its most elaborate form: old chemical instruments, exotic mementos, a violin, a curved pipe of intimidating size, a funny hat with bills on either side, a Persian slipper. Why just one Persian slipper?

I navigated a gigantic children's science museum, a place of glaring light and thousands of very young, very loud voices, in my adopted city, Portland, Oregon. The noise faded as I made my way into a series of vast half-darkened rooms. At last I entered a much smaller space — again, lined with ancient tomes and strange apparatuses, once more centered on a fire's hearth and mantel and two empty old armchairs, obviously placed for the cozy convenience of two intimates. Above the fire, a jackknife — a jackknife? — impaled a pile of disheveled papers to the mantelpiece.

In a far corner stood a life-size bust rendered (or so it appeared) in pale wax, depicting a tall man of aquiline features and commanding presence, his high forehead punctured by what looked — with just a little imagination — like a bullet wound.

On another day, I ducked out of the rainy streets of a neighborhood not far from my place of employment in Portland's city center, a sleepy pocket of old Masonic halls, dowager hotels, throwback cocktail lounges, and brick apartment blocks, almost all built before the Great War. I entered an empty theater. The stage had a familiar look to it. Flocked wallpaper. Fireplace. Jackknife. Persian slipper. Violin.

I climbed the stage and crossed an imaginary line into 221B Baker Street, Marylebone, London, the home of Sherlock Holmes, the world's only consulting detective, and John H. Watson, his companion and chronicler. This theatrical set contained an agglomeration of Victorian, pseudo-Victorian, exotic, and just eccentric ephemera, piled and nailed up everywhere to achieve the effect of the legendary bachelors' lair first depicted in the writing of Arthur Conan Doyle in the 1880s. A collection of masks and Japanese prints jumbled up against artfully precarious piles of old books and an incongruous stuffed armadillo. A sword stuck randomly from an ornate vase; an abacus perched on the mantelpiece. Seashells, skulls, and statuettes anchored piles of old newspapers, some real, some — I would learn from talking to the company's set designer — created on a large-format printer.

A curious sensation, standing in a slightly ersatz reconstruction of a place that never existed. The real nonreal place where I stood was just the latest in an endless series of reconstructions of the 221B sitting room, the starting point for most of Arthur Conan Doyle's detective adventures. In his stories, Holmes and Watson sit by that fireplace, awaiting the clients who come to tell them their peculiar and often deadly problems. Now, well over a century after the world's most famous tales of crime and deduction first appeared in print, a certain compulsion has developed around that room. Versions of 221B Baker Street crop up everywhere, all around the world. The creators often claim that their particular reconstruction is the most "authentic" or "accurate"— though compared to what, they never say. Not long before I climbed on that stage in Portland, a writer for *Smithsonian* magazine inventoried the oddity of this imaginary flat that real-life people keep building and rebuilding. He counted not one but two Baker Street sitting rooms in Switzerland, one of which boasts windows custom-made in England and shipped over. The University of Minnesota created a 221B in Minneapolis after its library accumulated a large Sherlockian archive. Or, more particularly, UM reassembled the room, originally constructed in a collector's private residence and donated and transported after his death — in other words, a reconstruction of a reconstruction. The writer also noted the "existence" of a virtual reconstruction of the Baker Street set created for the BBC television series *Sherlock,* made by a fan within the participatory video game Minecraft. And I knew of others down the years: the now-defunct Sherlock Holmes rooftop bar atop a Holiday Inn in San Francisco, for instance, and the member of a group known as the Baker Street Babes who emulated the BBC's Baker Street by dressing up her front door as "221B." And — as I would see myself — a commercial re-creation of Sherlock's home operates in the real Baker Street, in the real London (though in a completely wrong location), and an exhibit centered on a 221B would begin traveling the world's science museums in the improbable year of 2013, almost 130 years after Conan Doyle first portrayed that snug chamber.

The lair of Sherlock Holmes might be a unique phenomenon: the world's only viral *room.*

As I discreetly fondled the knife that impaled a stack of random papers on the Portland stage set, it seemed that I was not standing in a place so much as briefly inhabiting a revenant corner of Arthur Conan Doyle's mind — a fragment of a long-dead man's imagination that somehow detached itself from his physical brain. Why? I wondered. What combination of forces impelled so many people in the twentieth and twenty-first centuries to rebuild, often to obsessive detail, the headquarters of a Victorian detective who never existed? Why did so many people — people with jobs and families and the usual range of mundane concerns — feel called to the 221B hearthside? How had Arthur Conan Doyle created an illusory world so potent that it replicated itself in minds, and even actual spaces, all over the planet?

Deep waters. The strange case of 221B, that self-twinning room, seemed to hint at a much bigger mystery around Baker Street's central figure. Human beings tell lots of stories, with many characters. Why have Sherlock Holmes, John Watson, and the mysteries Conan Doyle challenged them to solve not only endured, but thrived?

These questions demanded investigation. Considering my immediate surroundings, that only made sense. This particular version of Baker Street, cobbled together from whatever evocative (or just odd) stuff a Portland set designer could find, achieved the desired illusion: that Sherlock Holmes himself could dash through the door at any moment, hot on the trail of some new and abstruse mystery plucked from the fog-bound, gaslit streets of an imagined Victorian London. There's always a new problem to solve at 221B Baker Street. That room, above all, is a place where adventures begin.

THE GREAT DETECTIVE

1

BOHEMIA

A DARK, COLD NIGHT in March, circa 1888. Dr. John H. Watson rides through London in a hansom cab. Watson is a married man, a working medico weary from a busy day on the rounds. Truth be told, he's bored out of his skull. He peeks out of the cab at an upper-story window of a familiar house. Above, he sees a skinny, hawk-nosed shadow pace behind a brilliantly illuminated blind. He orders his cab to stop, and he steps onto the gaslit pavement outside 221B Baker Street. (Or so I have always imagined. Watson doesn't actually specify his means of transport, but it seems so boring to picture him on foot. As we will see, with Sherlock Holmes, the reader is well advised to fill in the blank spots with her or his own invention.)

Arthur Conan Doyle wrote fifty-six short stories and four novels set in the world of Sherlock Holmes, consulting detective, and John H. Watson, his best friend and indefatigable chronicler. As Dr. Watson climbs the stairs to 221B, he sets in motion the first of the short stories, "A Scandal in Bohemia," which appeared in the *Strand Magazine*'s issue for July 1891. In the months that followed, one Sherlock Holmes adventure after another hit the bookstalls of Victorian Britain. The stories' young author, just barely in his thirties and working a desultory day job as an eye specialist, had used these two intriguing characters — a beaky superdetective and his pal, an ex–army doctor with underappreciated storytelling gifts — in a couple of earlier novels, with mixed commercial results. With "A Scandal in Bohemia," Conan Doyle truly (but accidentally) launched Sherlock Holmes and Watson into the literary cosmos.

Watson opens the door to the Baker Street sitting room. The chamber is bright but shadowed in the corners, where the gaslight and coal fire's glare dies away amid the startling array of detritus Sherlock Holmes accumulates in his adventures. Every corner overflows with crumpled newspapers, obscure and frightening books, strange chemical implements, and stray weapons. Sherlock is no mere cop grinding away in an office, but an exquisite self-creation who operates against the criminals that plague the world's most powerful city. Well, let's say he defends his own version of Victorian London — one besieged not by run-of-the-mill grifters and garden-variety psychopaths but by demented math professors, conspiracies of redheaded men, and cunning blackmailers who skulk about wearing astrakhan, whatever that is. Holmes doesn't live in our reality. He lives in a more interesting (if sinister) dimension.

Watson finds Holmes rampaging around the room, exuding his own personal, lurid atmosphere of tobacco funk and global intrigue. The good Watson has already warned his readers, in the second paragraph of "Scandal," about Holmes, his "Bohemian soul" and irregular habits. Sherlock has been off in Odessa dealing with a murderous (or maybe murdered) Trepoff. He's pondered a "singular tragedy" in Trincomalee (that's in Sri Lanka), and sorted out some nasty business involving the Dutch royal family. The detective gives his old pal a cigar. Drinks in hand (at Baker Street, a glass is never far away), Holmes produces a letter, lately delivered, written in broken English on thick pink stationery. The letter informs the detective that a man will call at a quarter to eight. The visitor will wear a mask. Holmes and Watson deduce, based on the writing paper's watermark and quick reference to a handy "European gazetteer," that this missive comes from "Bohemia." (That's in the Czech Republic these days. Victorian readers would have known it as one swatch in the crazy quilt of the Dual Monarchy, Austria-Hungary.) The mystery guest then sashays across the threshold.

The masked man is six feet six inches tall. As for the rest, we must defer to Watson:

Heavy bands of astrakhan were slashed across the sleeves and fronts of his double-breasted coat, while the deep blue cloak which was thrown over his shoulders was lined with a flame-coloured silk and secured at the neck with a brooch which consisted of a single flaming beryl. Boots which extended halfway up his calves, and which were trimmed at the tops with rich brown fur, completed the impression of barbaric opulence ... He wore across the upper part of his face, extending down past the cheekbones, a black vizard mask ...

Good Lord, is it the Marquis de Sade?

I discovered a thick, brick-red-covered, dog-eared book in my school library in Montana one suitably frigid winter's day when I was about eleven years old. The volume bore some pre-gender-equity title like *The Boys' Sherlock Holmes*. It smelled faintly of mold and many small hands. I opened to the first story, spied the exotic, very *adult* title "A Scandal in Bohemia," and tumbled in. In some sense, I suppose, I was never seen again.

I had heard of Holmes, of course, though the character was better known among my mid-'80s peers for the phrase "no shit, Sherlock" than as "the most energetic criminal agent in Europe." But I proved more susceptible to old Arthur Conan Doyle than most boys and girls. Raised by a pair of avid readers, grandson of a librarian, offshoot of a clan full of writers and English teachers (I have often wondered why my lineage didn't tend toward stock brokerage, electrical engineering, medicine, cobbling, or, really, anything more lucrative than literature), I read rather boldly for my age, as doting relatives and mildly alarmed teachers never ceased to remind me. I read the encyclopedia for fun. Furthermore, I was fascinated by the foreign — which in Missoula, at that time, meant just about anything with an accent — and the old-fashioned, which in the '80s meant anything not dyed hot pink. "A Scandal in Bohemia" met all requirements.

I sat, rapt, on the fraying shag carpet of the bedroom I shared with my younger brother, my spine riveted to the edge of our bunk beds, the Rocky Mountain winter in full howl outside a window insulated with a thick plastic sheet. I devoured one story after another: the Bohemian adventure, *The Sign of the Four*, "Silver Blaze." In retrospect, I can't say that I quite caught everything — and, in fact, I would soon discover that some 1950s bowdlerizer had weeded *The Boys' Sherlock Holmes* (or whatever it was) of Holmes's edgier moments. This caring editor had expunged the cocaine, toned down some bludgeonings. But that black mask! The astra-khan! The "flame-coloured" silk! The weird Victorian regalia, the secret worlds suggested by Baker Street's riotous mess of newspapers and urgent letters on pink stationery — all inflamed my boyhood mind. People often describe the Sherlock Holmes stories as "cozy," and I can see what they mean. It does feel snug there by the Baker Street coal fire. But I primarily think of these stories as exuberantly, beautifully strange artifacts — star-tling jewels set in gnarled brass, lit with the glow of a lost time. From the beginning, the Sherlockian saga has served me as an escape hatch into an intricately constructed alternate dimension.

It also acted as a gateway drug. Before long, I ditched the expurgated anthologies for the real thing: a hulking, ancient edition of the Double-day *Complete Sherlock Holmes* — very exciting, owning a book with "com-plete" right in the title. And as I worked through (and then back through) the sixty tales over the next few years, I also began to wander into more obscure corners of Missoula's libraries and bookstores, chasing more of the ghostly Victoriana the Holmesian adventures evoked. As years passed and my frontal cortex kept right on developing, the Victorians prodded me along. They took me into a lost world where men wore pre-tied cra-vats and frock coats and top hats, and the prevailing decorum contrasted with arch-ribaldry. I learned about the parliamentary system, the evolu-tion of newspapers, the roots of modern professional sport, and the cre-ation of urban transport. Given my own era's general attitude — viz., any-thing or anyone predating 1965 was a boring, pretechnological prude — I was startled to realize that the Victorians seemed, by many measures, more modern than I was. The barely functional computers that lurked in the back of my classrooms made a poor substitute for nineteenth-century London's seven or more daily postal deliveries and instantaneous global telegraph connections. The seemingly eternal Cold War face-off paled in interest compared to the imperial Great Game and the cosmopolitan ho-rizons of a mercantile, scientifically progressive age. And the sex! Before too many years passed, I discovered that a Sherlock Holmes obsession made an excellent cover for researching lush oddities like the Cremorne Gardens, Victorian London's open-air swingers' hangout, where young bucks mingled with sporting ladies to notorious effect.* Who knew? In one particularly intrepid adolescent archival dive, I discovered that the same culture that created my beloved, celibate Sherlock also produced a startling tract called *Lady Pokingham; or, They All Do It* — printed, according to the subtitle, for "The Society of Vice."

Over the decades that followed, Sherlock and I would have our ups and our downs. I would sometimes swim out of his ken, as Watson rather curiously put it one time, for a year or two. But I always found my way back to Baker Street. I considered the place a semiprivate domain, and Holmes an almost clandestine amusement, of scant interest to my peers and definitely to be played down when eligible young ladies made the scene. Sherlock might be many things, from expert single-stick fighter to medieval manuscript researcher, but "cool," in any recognized Reagan-era sense, he was not.

These days, however, one of those mysterious shifts in the spirit of the age has taken place. Nearly 130 years after he debuted in a disposable holiday magazine, Sherlock Holmes now seems to be everywhere. At least three different major on-screen reinterpretations of the character have gathered audiences of millions. In director Guy Ritchie's entertainingly bumptious movies for Warner Bros., Robert Downey Jr. and Jude Law ricochet around a grimy Victorian-ish London replete with slow-motion fight scenes and massive exploding fireballs. (Watching those movies is like huffing gasified cotton candy, but the world loves them. As of this writing, the first two *Sherlock Holmes* movies have grossed well over $1 billion globally.) In 2010, the BBC unveiled *Sherlock,* a modern re-up of the character, tense and moody and hilarious, starring a magnificent creature named Benedict Timothy Carlton Cumberbatch as the Great Detective and Martin Freeman as a brilliantly bemused Watson. Set in a semirealistic contemporary London of mobile phones and cheap cafés,

---

* "If our students, and learned clergy, and holy bishops write long articles about the Athenian Dionysia only held once a year, why should we not speak of ours which last all the summer, and the scene of which is Cremorne?" — J. Ewing Ritchie, *The Night Side of London* (W. Tweedie, 1857).

the series inspires almost audible gasps of adulation on every medium known to computerized man. (The Twitter hashtag #Sherlock can always yield some goody: just now, for example, I found a fan's fondant cakes made in Cumberbatch's and Freeman's images.)

Indeed, the 2010s have become an improbable golden age down Baker Street way. Sherlock and Watson prowl pop culture in many forms, familiar and strange. The American TV series *Elementary* embodies the duo in the heterodox pairing of Jonny Lee Miller and Lucy Liu. The Russians created a bespectacled, gun-toting, all-action Holmes not long ago. When I heard the sequel to the animated *Gnomeo and Juliet* might be none other than *Sherlock Gnomes,* I had to take some big yoga breaths.

In Conan Doyle's tales, Sherlock's brother, Mycroft, once remarks to Watson, "I hear of Sherlock everywhere since you became his chronicler." No kidding. Of course, though its popularity waxed and waned, this fictional world never stopped shaping real people's imaginative lives. I was long acquainted with the Sherlockians (or as some, particularly in Britain, prefer, Holmesians), an amiably eccentric global tribe of enthusiasts who gather to drink elaborate toasts to Conan Doyle characters, sometimes while wearing full Victorian costume. As we'll discover later on, this sub-sub-subculture traces its lineage to the 1930s, when some convivial New York bookmen founded the Baker Street Irregulars. By one estimate, about three hundred Sherlockian clubs are active now, from the Sydney Passengers of Australia to the Ural Holmesian Society of Ekaterinburg to the Baker Street Arabs, based at the US embassy in Baghdad.

But these clubby diehards are relatively few, and these days the Sherlock-addicted horde seems legion. A quick dive into the Internet reveals thousands of fans agnostic about whether their fix comes from Conan Doyle or from *The Great Mouse Detective.* They keep #221B percolating and can muster flash mobs under the slogan I BELIEVE IN SHERLOCK HOLMES. A New York mystery novelist and esteemed Sherlockian named Lyndsay Faye supplies the creed: "It is a widely accepted fact among our ranks that you can turn Sherlock Holmes into almost anything and he will still rock harder than David Bowie circa 1972." Faye, I would discover as I surveyed the sudden Sherlockian Renaissance (Faye's own term, in fact), is a leading light of the Baker Street Babes, an international coterie of young women who podcast, tweet, blog, and indie-publish on all things Holmes. Did I wish I could go back in time and tell the fourteen-year-old me that there would someday be Baker Street Babes? Badly.

What is going on? In a world of action heroes and cat-video memes, how does a 130-year-old detective in a velvet dressing gown hold his own? How, and why, has Sherlock Holmes — of all things — endured?

As I pondered these questions, a deeper mystery took shape. In Sherlock's debut, the novel *A Study in Scarlet,* Holmes tells incompetent police inspectors Gregson and Lestrade that "there's nothing new under the sun." Conan Doyle created a Baker Street HQ jam-packed with files, newspaper clippings, dossiers, privately printed monographs, obscure criminal histories — all so Holmes can recognize the characteristics of old cases hidden in fresh problems. It soon dawned on my Watson-like brain that this all happened before: Holmes keeps coming back with the relentlessness of Halley's Comet. The character anchored one of the most popular stage melodramas of the early 1900s. In the 1940s, Sherlock Holmes fought the Nazis. In the '70s, he went to therapy. In the '80s, he did way too much coke. Every generation remakes the Great Detective in its own image.

And *that,* to paraphrase Holmes himself, began to seem the really curious incident. I began to wonder what makes this character — which, as we'll see, Conan Doyle slapped together from previously published fictional detectives and an old professor from his school days, and very nearly named Sherrinford — not just immortal, but endlessly elastic. Why is there a Sherlockian society not just in London, but in Kyrgyzstan? How have Holmes and Watson managed to be memorialized not only in Sidney Paget's iconic ink-wash illustrations, but also in GIFs? How can Lucy Liu be Watson? It was time for a modest investigation of my own.

Holmes once declared that "no branch of detective science . . . is so important and so much neglected as the art of tracing footsteps." I decided to follow his and see where they might lead. I started back at Baker Street, once more, face to face with the masked King of Bohemia.

The target is a photograph. Irene Adler has it. The King of Bohemia wants it.

Irene Adler, you see, is a sexy opera star and well-known "adventuress," a prefeminist (or proto-feminist?) femme fatale. She and His Majesty enjoyed a certain interlude, a certain tête-à-tête, and certainly some other French words. The photo, a memento of their time together, shows both of them — *together*. His Majesty now plans to marry some stuck-up Scandinavian princess and needs to sanitize his old social media. He tried bribery. He tried theft. Yet the hot opera singer won't relent. The King needs Sherlock Holmes.

This all transpires over several propulsive pages of classic Conan Doyle dialogue: snip-snap verbal fencing matches that often oil and power his narratives with almost no extraneous exposition. The King slaps down "three hundred pounds in gold and seven hundred in notes." Cut to the next day. We see Holmes rollicking back to Baker Street disguised as a drunken horse groom, regaling Watson with a description of his surveillance of *la* Adler's abode. First, he cruised the neighborhood and formed an alcohol-based alliance with the grooms who work the carriages and stables, whom he lubricated into spilling many secrets. Second, he tailed Miss Adler to a church, where he was surprised to act as a witness for the lady's impromptu marriage to a lawyer, one Godfrey Norton. This marriage, obviously, complicates the matter. Holmes calls for "some cold beef and a glass of beer" and briefs Watson on the operation's next phase. Then the detective dons a second disguise, transforming into an idiotic-looking clergyman. The duo rattles off in a hansom cab to make some trouble for poor Irene.

When he created "A Scandal in Bohemia," Conan Doyle made strategic use of characters and a world he'd already sketched in two novels, *A Study in Scarlet* and *The Sign of the Four*. He intuited that in Sherlock Holmes and John Watson he had a pair of ready-made adventure machines, and he devised a commercially brilliant scheme to use them in separate but interlocking stories, each complete unto itself but connected to the rest. He began to amplify and enrich the Holmesian atmosphere and perfect Watson's storytelling voice. Because "Scandal" is the first Sherlock Holmes short story, it gives us a unique opportunity to peer over Conan Doyle's shoulder and look along with him as he builds the snug Baker Street chamber and its fog-swirled surrounding world — a setting and a cast of characters that he himself is still getting to know.

Some evidence suggests that Conan Doyle wrote "A Scandal in Bohemia" in an ambience that neatly paralleled, and maybe influenced, the story's own atmospherics. We can allow ourselves to imagine the young writer, a thirty-one-year-old Scotsman of Irish descent, sitting in a newly furnished medical office in London's Upper Wimpole Street, professional digs he'd recently rented. He grips a pen in his meaty paw. The rasp of metal on foolscap paper might be the only sound — certainly few patients ring the bell of this unknown and unheralded provincial attempting to set himself up as an eye specialist in the world's most competitive medical market.

We can assume it's pretty miserable outside. Britain has just emerged from a brutal winter that won't be beaten for cold and snow until 2010. A few weeks before, a "great blizzard" seized London and England, a blast of snow that paralyzed the capital for several days. (The *Times* reported: "no cabs or omnibuses at work for many hours, the streets first deep in muddy snow and then a pool of slush.") A fierce influenza is going around. A coal fire burns in a grate, perhaps. As he sits at his desk that day, Conan Doyle doesn't know he is making a land grab in eternity. He's just trying to drum up £35, given ophthalmology's rather glum prospects.

His journey to this moment makes a story of its own: one young man's epic traverse of Victorian Britain. Conan Doyle descended from a tribe of expatriate Irish artists. Tucked away on his father's side, a great-uncle named Michael Conan was a Paris-dwelling editor of the *Art Journal,* one of the era's most influential arts magazines. There was a sizable nest of London-connected Doyles, most tied, one way or another, to the early and middle nineteenth century's burgeoning visual and graphic arts industries. Many were notably prosperous by the time young Arthur came along in 1859. His paternal grandfather had been a leading social and political caricaturist of the early Victorian years. Conan Doyle's uncles included printers, illustrators, and gallery officials; Richard Doyle created a cover design the satirical magazine *Punch* used for decades.

Conan Doyle's father, Charles Altamont Doyle, was an artist himself, but lacked the family's commercial knack. His drawings tended toward fantastical, grotesque, and creepily naïve elements: a group of fairies lounge in a meadow, apparently about to be eaten by some giant rodent. A young woman clutches a huge butterfly, deep in conversation with a human-sized owl. In a self-portrait, drawn later in life, Charles Doyle seated himself in a gloomy room crawling with ghosts and demons. Nor were these strange visions the product of any gentle eccentricity: Arthur's father was a full-tilt alcoholic with florid psychological tendencies. The Doyle clan sent him off to semiexile in Edinburgh, where he worked sporadically at a dead-end job as a government clerk until, at last, when Arthur was still a young man, he couldn't work anymore.

Conan Doyle's mother, Mary, was an emigrant Irishwoman, with connections to both that island's Protestant aristocracy and Roman Catholicism. Her own circumstances were much reduced compared to those of some of her more high-flown ancestors, and certainly did not improve after she married Charles Doyle in 1855 and produced seven kids, of whom Arthur was the oldest boy. Undaunted, Mary Doyle cultivated lifelong interests in chivalry, heraldry, ancestry, and medieval nobility, which she passed on to her son. Even though the Doyle situation was chaotic — the family moved constantly, from one Edinburgh flat or house to another — Mary modeled erudition and bookish enthusiasm. Conan Doyle conjured her in an autobiographical piece of fiction: "I can see her . . . with the porridge stick in one hand, and the other holding her *Revue des Deux Mondes* within two inches of her dear nose." Conan Doyle would always call her "the Ma'am" — his most intimate counselor and final court of appeal.

Many of the Doyles were devout Catholics (Charles Altamont particularly), and the family packed Arthur off to horrific-sounding Jesuit boarding schools from the age of nine. He spent his formative years at an institution where the instrument of discipline was a hunk of India rubber used to beat the palm of an offending boy's hand until it was so swollen the lad couldn't turn a doorknob. (In his autobiography, Conan Doyle claimed: "I went out of my way to do really mischievous and outrageous things simply to show that my spirit was unbroken.") Meanwhile, he entertained the other boys with wild, extemporaneous stories. Eventually, after friends and family praised the limpid style of his letters, he began to harbor literary dreams. And so when he enrolled as a medical student at the University of Edinburgh, Conan Doyle had already hatched a plan for a dual career: doctoring for security, writing for fame and fortune. He often spent his lunch money on used books; "my way to the classes led past the most fascinating bookshop in the world," he would later recall. He read voraciously and widely—one could say his literary mind swept outward in concentric circles, starting from Thomas Babington Macaulay's sprawling collection of essays, an episodic, nearly encyclopedic examination of history, philosophy, literature, and politics that Conan Doyle would credit with "open[ing] a new world to me." Macaulay, a Scot who died when Conan Doyle was an infant, would write boldly about anything, and could "throw a glamour round the subject," no matter what. Conan Doyle would strive to do likewise.

From a fresh young age, he fired off short story and essay submissions to the magazines of the day; he scored his first paycheck for fiction at the age of nineteen. He made only three guineas (just over £3),* but he never forgot—decades later, he told an interviewer that he was "a beast that has once tasted blood, for I knew . . . I had once proved I could earn gold." By the time he begins to write "Scandal," he's a veteran professional twice over. As a doctor, he's worked as a GP in Southsea, near the maritime city of Portsmouth, and now migrated up to London to try his hand as an eye specialist. He's married, started a family, and otherwise acquired the outward trappings of middle-class solidity. He has also turned his mind into a steaming orchid house of fiction. He can write adventure stories, ghost stories, treasure-hunting stories, sea stories—any kind of story you want, basically, provided plot and intrigue. Throughout his career, he will maintain a gigantic "Ideas Book," a compendium of one- or two-line notes to seed future stories, checking them off as he plows them into print. He absorbs every form of narrative he encounters: the structural rituals of a genre short story, the cadence of a leading article, official history's steady drumbeat, adventure-romance's breathless gasp.

And he's had some success. Magazine editors know him. They even take him out and buy him dinner at times, a practice young writers may still recognize as a combination of professional perk and honey trap. He's propelled three novels into the world. Things are starting to happen—he just needs a few more big wins. And so, now, he returns to Sherlock Holmes.

The world's only consulting detective sits in rented rooms in Baker

---

* The guinea, equal to one pound plus one shilling, was the traditional denomination for calculating professional fees and services. It remains in notional use for racehorses.

Street, waiting for clients — not unlike his doctor-creator, one might say. The detective's manner oscillates between bitchy and suave; he lives for his work; he dabbles in cocaine and morphine and otherwise acts like a high-strung artist. He writes obsessive-compulsive articles about the "science of deduction"— how to identify tobacco brands by their ash, that sort of thing. He's aces on the violin and knows how to box, and his perception of minutiae reveals much. In the first pages of "A Scandal in Bohemia," Holmes asks Watson how many steps lead up from Baker Street's entry to the flat's sitting room. Watson has no idea. Sherlock knows: there are seventeen.

"You see, but you do not observe . . . I have both seen and observed."

This sentence and every other he writes this day will help transform Arthur Conan Doyle into one of the most elaborately documented people who ever lived: a fixture in the news of his day; a subject of scores of biographies; an imaginary character in his own right in novels, movies, and plays. His image will be captured in drawings, photographs, and films. In such portraiture, Conan Doyle bears a head that's an almost perfect rectangular block, ornamented with big ears and spectacularly lush mustachios. Though he's married to a girl named Mary Louise, whom he calls Touie, and has recently become a father, his beefy cheeks and sharp eyes retain something boyish and impish. He's ursine, big-boned — huge. He plays extraordinary amounts of cricket. A friend — a friend, mind you — describes Conan Doyle thus: "He was a great, burly, clumsy man, with an unwieldy-looking body that was meant for a farm bailiff, with hands like Westphalian hams." Another pal, *Prisoner of Zenda* author Anthony Hope, remarks, around the early 1890s, that Conan Doyle looks like a person who has never even heard of books, let alone written many. And yet from this stolid character, a much different profile would emanate:

"There was something in his masterly grasp of a situation, and his keen, incisive reasoning, which made it a pleasure to me to study his system of work."

Over the next few weeks, Conan Doyle will blast out the first series of Sherlock Holmes short stories. By summer he will have written a handful of the most influential crime stories in the world. (In the proper mood, Conan Doyle can hammer down eight thousand words a day and essentially send the bounty straight to the printers.) The stories will make him famous and rich, but there will, somehow, be even more to it than that. Within a year, newspapers will publish affectionate Sherlock Holmes parodies. By 1893, an actor named Charles Brookfield will impersonate the detective in an unauthorized stage satire. Before the turn of the new century, a duo billing itself as Conan & Doyle will tour British music halls. A bloody half century later, avid fan Marshal Tito, Red strongman of the Yugoslavs, will single out Conan Doyle's detective stories as ideal reading for young socialists. By 1953 there will be a Sherlock Holmes ballet; in the 1970s, a Muppet detective named Sherlock Hemlock will plumb the many mysteries of Sesame Street.

When he finishes "A Scandal in Bohemia," Conan Doyle will roll it up in a postal tube and send it off to the *Strand Magazine,* which will propagate it to thousands, then millions. Soon Holmes will belong to the world. For the moment, though, for just about the last time, the writer presides over Holmes and Watson as his own sole property. It's just him and them and the King of Bohemia by the fireside in Baker Street on a chilly spring night.

Here's the funny thing (well, one of them) about "A Scandal in Bohemia": the only people who commit actual crimes in the story are Sherlock Holmes and Dr. Watson. When they arrive at Irene Adler's house they find a bustling street scene, a cross between Damon Runyon and *The Canterbury Tales.* "There was a group of shabbily dressed men smoking and laughing in a corner," Watson relates, "a scissors grinder with his wheel, two guardsmen who were flirting with a nurse-girl, and several well-dressed young men who were lounging up and down with cigars in their mouths." This colorful assembly turns out to be a troupe of ne'er-do-well actors, hired by Holmes to stage a mini-riot as soon as Irene steps out of a cab at the curb. The disguised Sherlock wanders into the fray and feigns an injury to con his way into the house. Watson, acting upon instructions, hurls a small incendiary through the window for the purpose of forcing Adler to reveal the offending photograph's hiding place when she thinks her house is burning down.

Sherlock makes his escape, and he and Watson head for Baker Street, feeling rather cocky about this spree of felonies. As they mount the familiar doorstep, however, a disconcerting voice rings out from the darkening street: "Goodnight, Mister Sherlock Holmes!" A young man slips away around the corner. The detective and his stalwart friend find themselves peering into the gloom, wondering who the devil that could have been.

Soon enough, my contemplation of Sherlock Holmes and his renewed popularity metamorphosed — in the sinister way these things will — into "working on a book." And when I told people I was, indeed, working on a book about Sherlock Holmes, I got all kinds of interesting reactions.

In a gray-walled conference room, the eyes of two women in their late twenties lit up. "Sherlock Holmes is *so cool*," one of them said. Funny: I'd sometimes hoped for this reaction among young ladies in my adolescence, but never witnessed it. An enthusiastic discussion of Benedict Cumberbatch ensued.

I ran into a friend while we were both out Christmas shopping. "Sherlock Holmes," I said. His eyebrows cocked theatrically and he exclaimed: "Baritsu — the Japanese system of wrestling!" In Conan Doyle's stories, this martial art saves Sherlock's bacon at a key moment. (We'll return to this, of course.) We fell to discussing Alan Moore's *League of Extraordinary Gentlemen,* a strange comic book full of submarines and flying machines, set at the fringes of a reimagined Sherlockian world.

In a house surrounded by snow-draped Montana forest, a woman stopped fixing dinner, dodged around her two kids, and scampered to her bookshelf. "Now, this is *my* favorite Sherlock Holmes," she said, producing a couple of paperbacks by Laurie R. King, an American writer who has spun a long series of mystery novels around a character named Mary Russell. In these stories, set in the 1910s and '20s, young Mary meets an old beekeeper — who turns out to be Sherlock Holmes. The two start solving crimes together, then get married.

My acupuncturist, as she inserted a delicate needle near my ankle, explained the attributes ascribed to that spot by Chinese medicine, something about clearing perception. (I was face-down and off in a hazy trance, bristling with pins, not taking notes.) "Very Sherlock Holmes," she said.

Indeed, I found, as I reread Conan Doyle's original stories, there is far more to those tales than initially meets the eye. This time, I tried to read those old warhorses in a different frame of mind. I pretended as well as I could (which was not very well, but I tried) that I'd never read them before. I tried to forget the thirteen decades of Sherlockian kitsch and nostalgia layered over the stories, to encounter them fresh, as I imagined a bright young reader of 1891 would have experienced them in the *Strand*. And I found stuff that completely eluded me when I was twelve or twenty-two. For one thing, besides being ripping-good adventure yarns, the Sherlock Holmes stories are funny: often arch, sly parodies of themselves. Yet they can also manifest a sharp-edged darkness that Conan Doyle rarely gets credit for. In the ideological history of crime fiction, he's often cast as a lovably dotty uncle, who puttered off before no-nonsense moderns like Dashiell Hammett and Raymond Chandler came along. In fact, the Sherlock Holmes stories brim with weird lust and raw evil. In "The Adventure of the Copper Beeches," published in 1892, a poor young woman is financially suborned into a fetishistic relationship with a couple who hire her as governess at their isolated home. They force the girl to crop her beautiful hair, always to wear the same dress and sit in the same chair at the same time. A wing of their house is off limits, and it soon becomes clear to the young woman that she and possibly someone else are basically prisoners there. She finds a long coil of hair identical to her own locked in a drawer.

You don't have to be a literary theorist to find some psychosexual menace in all that.

Everyone acknowledges Conan Doyle as a highly competent storyteller, and that is true: the Sherlockian short stories, in particular, ratchet open and slam shut with Swiss-watch precision. (John le Carré described Conan Doyle's writing as "a kind of narrative perfection.") Simplicity, however, sometimes allows his writing to achieve a numinous power. In "The Five Orange Pips," bad weather hits: "The rain had beaten against the windows, so that even here in the heart of great, hand-made London we were forced to raise our minds for the instant from the routine of life and to recognize the presence of those great elemental forces which shriek at mankind through the bars of his civilization, like untamed beasts in a cage."

And while the writer himself would have made grumpy noises into his mustache at the notion of "symbolism" or "metaphor," I found stark images, dream-like in their intensity. In "The Adventure of the Red-Headed League," Holmes and Watson find themselves in a darkened underground vault awaiting an intruder. "Suddenly," Watson recounts, "my eyes caught the glint of light . . . At first, it was but a lurid spark upon the stone pavement. Then it lengthened out until it became a yellow line, and then, without any warning or sound, a gash seemed to open and a hand appeared, a white, almost womanly hand . . . For a minute or more the hand, with its writhing fingers, protruded out of the floor." What are we supposed to make of that, Dr. Jung?

And I was reminded of a curious phenomenon, remarked upon almost from the beginning of Sherlock Holmes. When people discuss the Great Detective and Dr. Watson, they slip into talking about them as if they are real. Over the years, some folk have simply taken Conan Doyle's stories as fact. The French seem interestingly prone to this error: in his 1930s book *The Private Life of Sherlock Holmes,* Vincent Starrett recounts the story of a party of French schoolboys who demanded, upon arrival in London, to be taken to "the house of Sherlock Holmes." During World War I, a French general allegedly asked Conan Doyle which British unit Holmes had joined. People around the world famously write to 221B Baker Street to seek the investigator's counsel.

But this same habit also steals up on those who know better. It happens imperceptibly. A conversation with the most knowledgeable Sherlockian I know glided from speculation about Conan Doyle's first impressions of London to an earnest discussion of Sherlock and his "experiences" in the capital. "He lived in Montague Street before Baker Street, of course," my friend said as I nodded sagely. "And then Baker Street would have had an obvious appeal. It was where many bachelor gentlemen lived." Well, of course. The effect can be eerie. It can feel as if Sherlock Holmes and John Watson aren't exactly characters in stories, but rather the leading citizens of a virtual reality just at the edge of our own. I began to think that this was Conan Doyle's real (accidental) artistic achievement: he invented a world in which people want to wander inside their own minds, and even physically re-create in our own pale universe.

And yet he was not the sole inventor. T. S. Eliot, who based his poetic mystery cat Macavity on Conan Doyle's villain Moriarty and once said that "every writer owes something to Holmes," also groused: "Arthur

Conan Doyle ... what has he to do with Sherlock Holmes?" It's actually a fair question, because Conan Doyle is not responsible for many essential aspects of the detective. The oldest trick in Sherlock-related sophistry is to point out that Holmes never actually says "Elementary, my dear Watson" in Conan Doyle's stories. Yet thanks in great part to Basil Rathbone's sleek film portrayal of the detective in the '30s and '40s, that phrase has become the character's unofficial motto. Conan Doyle never wrote about a double-billed deerstalker cap — that was the illustrator Sidney Paget's contribution to Sherlock's country attire, which somehow fused permanently to the detective's head in the mass mind's eye. Conan Doyle never described a huge calabash pipe, which seems to have attached itself to Holmes via the actor William Gillette, who may have used it for comic relief. Today, Amazon sells "Sexy Detective" Halloween costumes for women (or, hell, men — it's a new world) consisting of low-cut houndstooth minidresses, ersatz deerstalkers, and curved pipes. Slap a deerstalker on a pig, give that pig a magnifying glass and a pipe, and that pig becomes a master investigator (cf. *Freddy the Detective,* Walter Brooks, 1932). From the vantage of the early twenty-first century, it might be more accurate to say, with no disrespect, that Arthur Conan Doyle *originated* Sherlock Holmes. The rest of us, obviously, aren't yet finished creating him.

To witness this mass collaboration in action, look upon Irene Adler. She ghosts in and out of "A Scandal in Bohemia" in a matter of a few pages. Conan Doyle gives her precious few lines (though she gets the best ones). And yet how many men and women have read "A Scandal in Bohemia" and wondered at the fleeting image (mirage, more like) of the intrepid beauty who contends with kings and tangles with the Great Detective? A young lady whose capacity to slay monarchial hearts belies her origins in, of all places, New Jersey? Sherlock discovers that she is, indeed, quite lovely — "the daintiest thing under a bonnet," as he quaintly puts it to Watson. We learn she has sung at La Scala in prima donna roles. We learn she ventures out from her "bijou villa" in swanky St. John's Wood, about a mile from Baker Street in deeper northwest London, to grace small concerts around the metropolis. Sherlock will seldom mention any other girls. In his evidently monastic life, she will always figure as "the Woman," and he sighs after her, too.

For Sherlock Holmes fans, she's the Woman even now, the quicksilver wisp of sly femininity laced through Conan Doyle's masculine world. Irene has become more myth than character. Given the crazy speed at which he wrote, Conan Doyle probably created and dispensed with her in a matter of hours. No one else seems to want to let her go. A century after Irene's effervescent debut, the American writer Carole Nelson Douglas, author of such works as *Virtual Virgin* and *Vampire Sunrise,* will make her the star of an eight-novel series of her own. Between them, the actresses Rachel McAdams, in the Robert Downey Jr. films, and Lara Pulver, who traipses naked through bits of the BBC's ingenious "A Scandal in Belgravia," will turn Irene into a subcultural sex symbol in the twenty-first century.

At Sherlockian society meetings these days, someone often gets around to proposing a toast to the sexy antiheroine, possessor of racy photographs, singer of blood-drenched arias, Jersey girl. Someone stands up and recites what little we know of her. After that, it's all imagination. What was Irene Adler really like? What did she really do to earn that seductive scarlet-letter title of "adventuress"? Where does she go after she dissolves out of the Baker Street scene? Those of us who meet her can imagine her doing just about anything, and we hope it's something suitably grand. And then glasses are raised and the cry goes up: "The Woman!"

Why?

How did Sherlock Holmes become immortal? What makes him so adaptable? And why do we long to inhabit his imaginary world? And what *is* Sherlock Holmes anyway? A mild (but persistent) mass hallucination? These questions — no matter how many latter-day movies I watched or frantic hashtags I perused — kept leading me back to Arthur Conan Doyle and the original saga: the circumstances and progress of the sixty stories' creation, over forty-odd tumultuous years in which the Victorian era reached its zenith, and then, with a great traumatic wrench, transformed itself into the modern world. Everything anyone does with Sherlock, after all, is a reaction to or revision of words that emanated from Conan Doyle's mind.

And so this book operates in much the same way. In the chapters that follow, we'll trail Conan Doyle as he crafts Sherlock's saga in the heart of Victoriana. But we'll also see many other people — famous and anonymous — at work on this most famous fictional creation: collaborating, appropriating, mocking, celebrating, borrowing, and sometimes stealing outright. We'll visit places that shaped Conan Doyle's work in the first place, as well as scenes the author never could have imagined — like a media swarm in twenty-first-century Hollywood — but nonetheless inspired. During his own lifetime, as we'll see, Sherlock Holmes became a phenomenon that Conan Doyle could neither control nor fully understand. And after the author died, Holmes lived on to become one of the transcendent figures of the modern imagination. In ways subtle and lasting, the mythos of the Great Detective influenced not just specific entertaining inventions, but how popular culture itself functions now. And somehow it all began with that thickset Irish-Scottish doctor, alone in his consulting room, looking to make a few extra pounds.

In order to investigate this mystery, I decided to apply Holmes's own methods — his actual methods, as Conan Doyle actually portrayed them. Wily Arthur, a master of literary sleight of hand, loved to describe Sherlock as a "scientific" detective. He sequined his plots with elaborate vignettes in which Holmes tinkers with his chemistry set, declaring that if a vial of liquid turns red it means a man's life, or whatever. To the annoyance of Watson and Mrs. Hudson, 221B's eternally suffering landlady, Sherlock is forever doing something malodorous with a test tube. To this day, people talk about Holmes as a cofounder of forensics. But on close examination almost all of this proves to be mere atmosphere, with no substantive bearing on the narratives. In Conan Doyle's plots, science per se tends to play a minor role. Instead, art rules the day.

Yes, Holmes goes to the scene of the crime, pokes into everything, and interrogates witnesses. But he also reads this and that, sits around and stares into space, plays the violin, smokes lots of tobacco, goes to concerts, and plans dinner parties. He dresses up in funny outfits and wanders down the street. He buys people drinks and chats them up. He goes to the local pub and sees what the barman has to say, and fights anyone who takes exception. The difference between Sherlock Holmes and the official cops, in fact, is that while the Finest doggedly follow standard procedure and the obvious clues, the independent detective investigates trifling stuff he notices on the windowsill, what the groom said in between beers, something he remembers reading about once, or a dog that did or didn't bark in the night.

To put it another way, his methods are somewhat bohemian. Not to give myself airs, but I thought I could at least fake it.

2

THE SCIENCE OF DEDUCTION

OBVIOUSLY, I NEEDED to begin at the beginning. But where was the beginning? On a bright late-fall day, I asked Paul Collins to lunch.

Collins sometimes calls himself (on Twitter, for example) the Literary Detective. His several books include a narrative that traces the "career" of Shakespeare's First Folio, and a couple of deep dives into the most nefarious corners of nineteenth-century criminality and sensational news. In fact, it occurred to me as I waited for him outside his small office in a warren-like academic building at Portland State University, much of Paul's work fulfills a suggestion young Watson makes to Holmes early in their friendship: that the detective launch a newspaper called *Police News of the Past*. ("Very interesting reading it might be made, too," Holmes replies.)

When we met, Collins was at work on a biography of Edgar Allan Poe, on top of teaching at PSU (his courses include an in-depth survey of Sherlock Holmes) and contributions to magazines. (Of Poe, he told me: "People always focus on the drinking and the tragic child bride and all that. But if you look at what he actually did, he was a hardworking journeyman editor. He was the guy you called when you needed good copy for your magazine's front-of-the-book, fast.") He was about to publish a book on a forgotten murder-trial collaboration between Aaron Burr and Alexander

Hamilton, long before they dueled. Much of Collins's work is based on bloodhound missions into forgotten archives. As he dashed around the corner, waved, unwrapped his scarf, and unlocked the door of his book-crammed office, I felt I was meeting a genial descendant of the freewheeling nineteenth-century literary spirit.

About a year before our rendezvous, Collins had pulled off his own feat of detection, unveiling the shrouded authorship of *The Notting Hill Mystery,* the first fully fledged modern mystery novel. *The Notting Hill Mystery* appeared as a serial in a London magazine, starting in November 1862. The story presents itself as a voluminous case file of evidence regarding the death of a baroness who somehow managed to drink acid while sleepwalking. The "detective," saddled with the uninspiring name Ralph Henderson, is actually an insurance adjuster. Personally, even my somewhat severe Victoriaphilia doesn't always extend to more heavy-handed examples of the nineteenth-century insistence that every piece of fiction is really AN EXTRACT FROM THE DIARY OF MADAME _____, 185_, and I found *Notting Hill* rough going as bedside reading. But the book apparently made quite the sensation, and can be seen as a direct forebear of and inspiration to fictional crime fighters who came later.

Who wrote it? After considering a tantalizing suspect — *Prime Minister Benjamin Disraeli, where were you on the night of _____, 186_?* — and discarding him, Collins identified the pseudonymous "Charles Felix" as the book's publisher, Charles Warren Adams. The key clue was hidden in a single line in an 1864 "literary gossip" column in the *Manchester Times,* tying Adams to a different "Charles Felix" creation. Paul Collins will go to some lengths to get his man.

Collins and I walked to a Vietnamese restaurant near the Portland State campus, and, over lunch, we spun back the clock to the grotty middle of the nineteenth century. "When Charles Adams wrote *The Notting Hill Mystery,*" Collins said, "there was the beginning of a market for crime stories. Poe had written the first real detective short stories a couple of decades before, but there was no tradition, no real genre, no conventions. And *Notting Hill Mystery,* interestingly, is kind of a dead end: it has the logic and the clues but no real characters, and it reads like a recitation of evidence. It's like a puzzle you're supposed to solve rather than a narrative. But it remains significant because it shows there was an appetite for this kind of thing. The newspapers had cultivated a public knowledge of and interest in crime. There was a readership, but no one had done it in long form, in a novel. As much as anything, *The Notting Hill Mystery* shows you a genre that hasn't been worked out."

My conversation with Paul Collins was just the beginning of my examination of the forces and influences that led to *The Notting Hill Mystery* — and, come to think of it, to *CSI: Las Vegas* and *True Detective*. When and why did people all over the world decide that, given the chance, they'd really like to read about a good garroting?

Some claim biblical (or quasi-biblical) antecedents for the mystery genre. In an apocryphal addition to the Book of Daniel, Daniel scatters ashes on the floor of a chamber to prove that pagan priests and their families are secretly eating food offerings left out for Bel, a heathen idol. (Sherlock Holmes uses exactly the same method to solve 1904's "The Adventure of the Golden Pince-Nez," though he only catches an invalid professor of Coptic languages who is hiding a Russian dissident in his bookcase.) Entire priestly families are executed, and everyone lives happily ever after. The English essayist, mystery novelist, and hardcore Sherlock Holmes addict Dorothy L. Sayers located the earliest and best manifesto for detective fiction in *Poetics,* where Aristotle discusses tragedy: "It is also possible to discover whether someone has done something, or not done something." And, of course, *Macbeth* is a true-crime story, among other things.

In criminal literature, the signal year of 1776 is most notable for the first publication of *The Annals of Newgate; or, Malefactors Register,* a prison parson's account of the very worst people to whom he'd ministered in Newgate Prison. That dire hulk served as London's main gaol for most of a millennium, standing roughly between the Old Bailey criminal court and St. Bartholomew's Hospital, the future meeting place of Sherlock Holmes and John Watson. (We'll hit the neighborhood in chapter 3.) The popularity of this four-volume set — it inaugurated a long-running genre of real-life crime narratives that used the name Newgate as a de facto brand — presaged a large English-language readership for all things nasty and violent in the nineteenth century.

Throughout the century's early decades, low-class printers in London and other cities churned out an enormous body of one-sheet tales of murders and executions, sold cheaply and eagerly devoured by the British public. Many broadsides are branded as "dying speeches": the final words of the condemned, wherein he (or, more sensationally and in some cases better for business, she) repented of sin just before the rope went taut. The flaw was that these productions were often ready for sale *at* the hangings themselves, but audiences didn't seem to mind. These true(ish)-crime one-sheets make simultaneously fascinating and baleful reading, and remind you that they'd hang a person for just about anything in those days, from "dreadful and barbarous MURDER" to extorting 5 shillings.

The broadside genre reached its apogee with the 1828 popular smash "Last Dying Speech of William Corder." The associated case neatly captures the combination of domesticity and weirdness that would mark the crime news and fiction of the imminent Victorian era. Corder killed his lover in a country barn — commonplace enough — but, legend would have it, was captured only after the victim's stepmother experienced a prophetic dream about the crime. The hamlet where the victim died became a tourist attraction, and a huge volume of printed matter piled up. James Catnach, a no-brow printer based in London's Seven Dials — he once served six months for accusing local butchers of serving human meat — churned out "Last Dying Speech" and proceeded to sell 1.1 million copies when Great Britain's population was around 20 million.

In her 2013 book *The Invention of Murder,* social historian Judith Flanders tracks how the broadsides entwined with the era's growing newspaper industry and very popular melodramatic theater to create an early ecosystem of criminal-minded entertainment. Her examination of melodrama, in particular, shows how rapidly a juicy murder could saturate the public consciousness. In the 1860s, she notes, London alone held more than thirty thousand theater seats priced for lower- and working-class audiences; the fare on those stages overwhelmingly favored ripped-from-the-headlines crime dramas, produced from quickie scripts to allow typecast actors to bring the latest horrors to their audiences. The so-called Radlett Murder (amateur boxer shoots low-class lawyer over a £300 gambling debt, then slits his throat and bashes his brains out for good measure), for example, took place in late October 1823. Two prominent London theaters, the Coburg (later the Old Vic) and the Surrey, both staged plays based on the crime by mid-November. By that time, the newspapers overflowed with bloodcurdling copy on the murder, as did reams of broadsides.

Nothing invigorates in the morning quite like a transatlantic telephone call about lurid antique deeds, so I rang up Judith Flanders. She noted that the mass-media pattern of high-profile crime recurred throughout the nineteenth century, its exact form and tenor changing with technology and social mores but its basic outline remaining notably constant. "I looked at about fifty famous cases that occurred over seventy-five years," she told me. "Only four of them went unsolved — or, more accurately, without a killer being identified. In some cases it's quite clear now that the authorities convicted the wrong person. These are the cases that became popular. Random, sordid, anonymous killings, though there were many, of course, seldom attracted much of a following. And here you see the popular taste, in a way, forecasting the crime-fiction genre. There's a closed circle of suspects, and one of the satisfactions is going down the list. Could it be him? Could it be her? That is the same quality that readers of the newspapers and theatergoers responded to in those real stories.

"One crucial aspect of theatrical melodrama that we've lost as a culture is the sense of the working of divine providence," she continued. "In the melodramas of crime, the malefactor is always identified, sometimes through outlandish coincidence, because events are foreordained. This is why melodrama seems silly to us now. But crime fiction, as it evolved, would essentially serve the same function for a society that had lost its sense of the divine. Bad things happen, but they happen because of specific bad people, and you can catch them. This is the form that people found satisfying. There needed to be a solution. Crime fiction still provides that."

By the 1850s, Britain dropped its last taxes and stamp duties on printed material, after a series of populist campaigns. The prices of books, magazines, and newspapers plummeted. The grubby broadside aimed at a working-class market that previously could not afford newspapers faded away. Newspapers, in turn, seized the broadsides' bloody franchise with alacrity. "When you look at newspapers of the early nineteenth century, they don't really cover crime in any kind of narrative way," Paul Collins had told me. "There's the one-paragraph item when a shocking outrage occurs, the paragraph when they arrest someone, and the paragraph that says they hanged the guy. But slowly, you start to see papers turn crimes into actual stories, with interviews of witnesses and the bereaved family of the victim, with scenes and action. If you had a boring death, they wouldn't cover it. I think newspapers played a bigger role in seeding the fictional genre than anyone quite realizes. The broadsides almost always had a moral component: hear the wrongdoer repent as he goes to the scaffold, and do not do what he has done. The newspapers didn't do that. They realized that you could tell these stories and make the sale without being obliged to deliver a Christian moral lesson at the end."

In tandem with the fascination with the latest MURDER, a popular interest in police work slowly evolved — police work itself being a new idea. After the formation of France's Sûreté in 1812, the madcap (and largely made-up) autobiography of that agency's founder, the ex-thief and self-professed master of disguise Vidocq, became popular. Scotland Yard debuted in 1829, but the Detective Division wasn't started until 1842 — with all of two officers. Even this modest development was controversial in England, because paid detectives were seen as a Continental affectation, like garlic, and a possible threat to English liberty. (Prior to the formation of the Metropolitan Police, London — already the world's largest city in 1815, with its population destined to triple to more than three million by 1860 — made do with parish constables, night watchmen, and the Bow Street Runners, a small force run out of a single magistrate's office that served warrants and made arrests.) The acknowledged founding text of forensic investigation, the Austrian criminologist Hans Gross's *Handbook for Coroners, Police Officials, and Military Policemen,* wouldn't appear until 1893. Still, the notion of detection and crime fighting as a systematic (and entertaining) pursuit caught on. In the era just before Conan Doyle's birth in Scotland — *Chambers' Edinburgh Journal* ran police and lawyers' memoirs. And parallel to the respectable (or not so respectable) cops-and-crime coverage in middle-class newspapers and magazines, an enormous trade in "penny-bloods" supplied a down-market demo with serialized accounts of true, sort of true, and openly fantastical criminal sagas in eight- to sixteen-page installments. One series, as noted in *The*

Invention of Murder, ran for 12 years, 624 editions, and nearly 4.5 million words.

"The mass media made this discovery as the nineteenth century went on," Judith Flanders said. "The great discovery is that crime is fun. If it's not happening to you, it can be wildly entertaining. And it sells. Most importantly, it sells."

All these developments coalesced in a trio of short stories by one Mr. Edgar Allan Poe.

"With 'The Murders in the Rue Morgue,' 'The Purloined Letter,' and 'The Mystery of Marie Roget,'" Paul Collins told me, "Poe starts the tradition of the mystery that centers on a singular, charismatic detective, one who works outside the system and solves the mystery by observation and deduction rather than random chance." Poe's stories revolve around a Parisian oddball named Auguste Dupin. Significantly, his nameless and subservient roommate acts as narrator. When I later burrowed back into these numbers, all published in the 1840s, for the first time since high school, Dupin and his buddy struck me as obvious embryos of Holmes and Watson — though, this being Poe, they are significantly weirder. They live together in a giant, decaying mansion, keep the windows shuttered all day to produce artificial night, a.k.a. "the sable divinity," and lounge about reading creepy books and going into crackpot-Romantic trances. Mrs. Hudson would have to clean the place out with a flamethrower.

The stories themselves — no disrespect to the freak-chic sage of Baltimore, who wrote when readers harbored much different expectations about concision and plausibility — creak and groan a bit these days. "The Murders in the Rue Morgue" starts with a rambling essay, pages and pages long, about the nature of observation, completely disconnected from the plot itself. That plot involves a pair of killings far grislier than anything Conan Doyle would ever describe — one victim is beheaded, another is mangled and stuffed feet-first up the chimney. (The spoiler-sensitive should skip to the next paragraph, though if you can really have a literary landmark first published during the Van Buren administration "spoiled" for you, get down to the library.) The killer is a monkey — or, I'm sorry, an "Ouran-Outang."

"An aspect of the Poe stories that is fascinating now is that you see him trying out a couple of different ways of writing a detective story, because there was no such thing as a detective story," Collins said. "In 'The Murders in the Rue Morgue,' you see a full investigation in action. 'Marie Roget' basically consists of Dupin talking about how stupid all the journalists who covered the case are, and it's almost just a recitation of facts with very little in-scene action. It's like he shows you what *not* to do. And interestingly, I am pretty sure that in all of Poe's work, Dupin and his sidekick are the only characters that recur from one story to another. It's like he intuited that aspect of the genre: first you write one, and then you write another one."

This new fictional species, the Detective, began to creep out into the culture. In 1852, Dickens incorporated a detective subplot into *Bleak House*. At almost the same time *The Notting Hill Mystery* made its serial magazine debut, the Parisian literary jack-of-all-trades Émile Gaboriau began publishing long, digressive crime novels featuring Lecoq, a detective directly inspired by the real-life Vidocq's memoirs. Rapidly translated into English, Gaboriau mysteries like *The Widow Lerouge* found a large and enduring audience, to the point that Sherlock Holmes and Watson themselves debated Lecoq's merits in *A Study in Scarlet,* their own maiden voyage, published in 1887 (Watson *pro,* Sherlock *contra*).*

A readership and market grew. Parliament passed a landmark public-education act in 1870. In London and other British cities, new technical, administrative, manufacturing, mercantile, and service industries meant that throngs of commuters — the ultimate captive audience — packed suburban trains, omnibuses, and the Underground; the latter first rolled in 1863. Accounts of the time describe ubiquitous newsstands and seas of printed paper. Many people found all this reading by the masses very unnerving. Modern studies document much high-minded complaint about

---

* When I took a deep breath and dove into Gaboriau, I half expected that only dirty puns on Lecoq's name would keep me going. In fact, these chestnuts of mid-nineteenth-century Parisian trash fiction remain quite delightful, written with self-confident Gallic zest and spiked with racy plot details — an apparent ménage à trois, for example — that Conan Doyle might have judged too spicy for the public eye.

the spread of newspapers, magazines, and books. And it is true that readers of the 1860s, '70s, and '80s preferred their literary thrills cheap, inhaling "yellowback" novels (so called because they bore brightly colored, illustrated covers, in contrast to drably bound "serious" books) stuffed with crime, tragedy, and derring-do, often purchased to be consumed on the train and forgotten. "Even specialists in the field," Collins said, "sometimes don't quite grasp how much 'railway' literature was produced. Those books were published by the thousands, and they made the detective a standard character."

Some viewed this wanton reading for pleasure as the literary equivalent of the crack-den gin shops of 1700s London. In 1855, an anonymous Methodist penned a tract titled "What Is the Harm of Novel Reading?" Substantial, it turned out. Enthusiasm for fiction would lead innocent young girls straight to premarital sex. "Golden dreams of sinful pleasure," the pamphleteer writes, "ended in disgrace, ruin, disease, a broken heart, and an untimely grave!" Crime and "sensation" novels, in particular, came in for grumpy scrutiny. An Oxford don named Henry Longueville Mansel wrote an 1863 treatise, every bit as ponderous as his own name, for one of the leading smart-people's journals. Now somewhat notorious among scholars of the period, Mansel's screed tagged the emerging genre as an "indication of widespread corruption" fit only for "a diseased appetite." He knew whom to blame, too: magazines, libraries, and the railway bookstalls that so recklessly sold books to people who were not Oxford dons.

Even as it took shape, the crime and detective genre was perceived as a sign of accelerated times. In the same year that Mansel spouted off, an unnamed psychologist wrote a more nuanced appraisal in a specialist journal. This writer identified sensation literature as a byproduct of new industrial wealth, and the triumph of the famed Victorian morality over the raffish, lurid public fun of earlier eras. (Public execution, long a staple of entertainment particularly in London, was on its way out. The last in Britain took place in 1868, when a possibly innocent Irish separatist swung for his alleged role in a bombing, convicted on the hearsay evidence of a turncoat and a police informer.) "People with nothing to do," this anonymous psychologist opined, "have always had . . . a strong desire for 'sensations'—a desire that has invariably found gratification in the acts and sayings of conspicuous criminals.'"*

In 1868, Wilkie Collins stepped into that nascent market with *The Moonstone,* a doorstop of a novel serialized in a magazine founded by Wilkie's prime pal, Charles Dickens. (*The Notting Hill Mystery* had appeared in a competing magazine.) *The Moonstone* bound all the era's loose "sensational" threads into a gorgeous Bayeux Tapestry of mid-Victorian crime fantasy: sleepwalking, opium, sinister Indian conspirators, a gem of unfathomable value, financially ruined bounders, hypocritical lovers, fainting damsels, and—most crucially—a canny detective. *The Moonstone*'s multiple interlocking narrations, its shifts in tone and genre from rural Gothic to urban satire to lust-ridden confessional to police procedural, make it more "modern" than a lot of stuff written now. T. S. Eliot, who cultivated a mean eye for crime fiction, acclaimed Wilkie Collins the genre's true founder. (The richly bearded Dickens protégé was pretty sui generis overall: a proto-swinger who maintained lifelong, parallel relationships with two women.) Collins took the formulae first scratched out by Poe a quarter century before and turned them into art. He also helped establish a new model of pop authorship: fans could buy merchandising tie-ins to his various books, like *Woman in White* perfume.

Paul Collins (no relation) explained that *The Moonstone* marked a key intervention in crime fiction's path. "Collins went back to what Poe had done and created a narrative that the reader follows in which the clues are discovered through the experiences and insights of the detective and other characters," he said. "He set the template for the mystery that's less of a game, more of a story, all centered on the charismatic detective."

Conan Doyle worshiped Poe. He loved Gaboriau, too, whatever he had Sherlock say about him. *The Moonstone* would have been inescapable for him. He would later make Dr. Watson a devoted fan of yellowback novels and imbue Sherlock Holmes with expert knowledge of all that nineteenth-century true-crime pulp. (Early in their friendship, Watson would rate Holmes's knowledge of "sensational literature" as "immense," and re-

---

* I am indebted, for all these examples of commentary, to *Victorian Print Media* by Andrew King and John Plunkett (Oxford University Press, 2005).

mark that he "appears to know the details of every horror perpetrated in the century.") From the very beginning, the Sherlock Holmes stories don't just elaborate on the crime-themed entertainment of earlier decades of the nineteenth century, they comment upon it. And when Conan Doyle surveyed what came before — he was, for example, a fan of the American writer Anna Catherine Green's *The Leavenworth Case,* a socially vivid but somewhat slow-paced tale of murder and police detection published in 1878 — he also saw how to do it better.

"He was not an innovator, really," Paul Collins told me as our fortune cookies arrived. "Other writers developed the genre's conventions, down to the status and general behavior of the detective — he's an outsider, he's eccentric. Poe and Collins set up the template. But Conan Doyle worked at a slightly later moment, when the idea of using science to solve crimes was really gaining currency. And he took all those elements of prior crime fiction and merged them with this sense of the cutting edge, of new methods, and a breakthrough in detection. He took the forms that had evolved before and just about perfected them."

When Arthur Conan Doyle created Sherlock Holmes, he was twenty-six years old, several years into his general medical practice in Southsea, not long married to Touie. (Theirs was not the ideal courtship; they met when Mary Louise Hawkins's brother moved into Conan Doyle's medical establishment as a desperately ill resident patient, then promptly died.) Since his father had been committed, he viewed himself as the paterfamilias of a small clan, responsible for not only his wife and, as they arrived, their children, but his mother, brother, and sisters, too. At the same time, he lusted after adventure and action. In the midst of his days as a medical student at the University of Edinburgh, Conan Doyle impulsively signed on to an Arctic-bound whaling vessel as ship's surgeon. He went out with the harpooners and participated in bloody seal hunts on ice floes ("brutal work"). He almost died a couple of times when he slipped into the sea. He would later call the voyage his true coming-of-age. Already a creature of story, Conan Doyle recast this raw experience as a real-life epic adventure tale. It would not be his last.

Just out of university, he did a single jaunt as a doctor aboard an Africa-bound passenger liner that served dissipated colonials, earnest missionaries, and native chieftains enriched in the palm oil trade. Conan Doyle didn't like this crowd. Nor did he enjoy his first experience of Africa, where he encountered an endless, monotonous green coast and outposts of proto–Graham Greene characters, inhaling cocktails on their verandahs and trading complaints about the locals. The voyage both granted the young doctor a certain cosmopolitan exposure and helped Conan Doyle decide against a naval or colonial career.

He struck out on his own in 1882, setting up a general practice in the fashionable Portsmouth suburb of Southsea — about as far as one can get from Edinburgh, it might be noted, without falling into the Channel. (He would never live in Scotland again.) To keep up appearances, Conan Doyle initially furnished only the public sitting and examining rooms of his rented house, subsisting in camp-like conditions behind a curtain. He taught himself how to grill a single strip of bacon using a wall-mounted gas jet, and in lieu of an assistant, took in his kid brother, Innes, to live with him. But eventually he thrived, spurred by his own medical talent and natural gregariousness, which served him well in a male middle-class society that revolved around sport, clubs, and semipro intellectual pursuits.

Conan Doyle played bowls and billiards socially, cricket and football seriously — all good ways to land clients. On the football pitch, he played for Portsmouth AFC, a competitive amateur club, under the pseudonym A. C. Smith, featuring as a goalkeeper or a defensive back. In the latter position, he was noted for his tactical skill and his, shall we say, robust approach to a tackle. (Much later, a cricket teammate would comment that a particular Conan Doyle performance in that sport — always his favorite — caused a "surprisingly low death rate.") Some of his other pursuits likewise reflected macho zeal: on a few occasions, for example, he acted as a two-fisted street operative for the Liberal Unionists, his political party. On the more genteel side, he took part in various literary and philosophical clubs around Portsmouth.

Meanwhile, always, he wrote, securing publications (often anonymous) and fees (often minuscule) for short stories and articles. He would later call these "the days of very small things." As young writers will, Conan Doyle took on just about anything. A magazine would send him a woodcut illustration and ask him to write a story to go with it. For four guineas, he happily obliged. He wrote a story in the style of Henry James. He composed a bad novel that went out to publishers and returned, adorned with rejection notices, "with the precision of a homing pigeon."

His early stories now can seem somewhat maudlin and laborious, but still hint at ambition and scope. "John Huxford's Hiatus," for example, somehow spins globalization in the cork industry into a tale of violent shanghaiing, amnesia, lost identity, and a tearjerking — or gag-inducing — reunion of lovers separated for fifty years. That story and "J. Habakuk Jephson's Statement," a maritime thriller concocted from fictionalized eyewitness testimony and shipping-news reports, ran in the prestigious *Cornhill Magazine* with no byline. One reviewer mistook the latter for Robert Louis Stevenson's work. Conan Doyle liked that, but he liked the £30 fee better. (That sum would have equaled 10 percent of his most lucrative annual take as a doctor.)

He knew he could do better. "I realized that I could go on doing short stories for ever," the future master of short fiction later recalled, "and never make headway." Conan Doyle felt that most commonplace of youthful writerly urges: the desire to write and publish a book — or, more precisely, to see his name on said book. He peered at his first novel and shoved it into a drawer.

What kind of book would do the trick? Conan Doyle enjoyed a good detective story, and the genre had lately become so popular. Yet interesting detectives and credible plots were few and far between. And then his imagination summoned up a figure from his own past: an austere, high-cheekboned visage crowned with wiry white hair, an "eagle face." He heard memory's echo of a fierce, incisive, nasal voice, tool of an intelligence that could penetrate life's mysteries with scalpel precision. Conan Doyle remembered Joseph Bell.

Edinburgh, circa 1879. Gas lamps washed a huge lecture hall in murky light. The bodily warmth of scores of medical students packed into the galleries cut the stony cold, but only just. A man strode to the hall's focal point with a distinctively jerky gait, a hawk-nosed, gray-eyed wizard radiating an air of command. The students' chatter — burbling Scots mixed with stray foreign accents drawn to the world's most innovative medical school — subsided. They idolized this man, just in his forties but already a steel-haired icon known for his crisp style of prose and uncompromising pungency of speech. The Edinburgh medical school was home to the developer of antiseptic surgery, Joseph Lister, as well as innovators in military medicine, obstetrics, psychiatry, and other fields — but even there, Joseph Bell stood out. He had already written a significant surgery manual. He was a pioneering mentor to nurses and corresponded with Florence Nightingale. For all that, however, his students knew him best for the Method.

Just outside the hall, Bell's handpicked student clerk mustered a crowd of indigent patients who'd volunteered to serve as instructional specimens in exchange for treatment. Arthur Conan Doyle, age twenty, was an indifferent student in most ways — a "60 percent man," he later wrote. Perpetually poor, he had decided to cram in as much course work as possible to chop a full year off his time in med school: quantity over quality. And arguably he lacked a certain concentration, always distracted by sport, family concerns, and literature. Even so, he had forged a bond with Bell, who chose the youngster to run the mob scenes in his lecture hall. Conan Doyle lined up the patients — seventy or eighty at a time — and marshaled them in, one by one, for Bell's examination.

A patient wandered into the gaslight without speaking a word. Bell looked at him.

"I see you're suffering from drink," he rasped at the poor codger. "You even carry a flask in the inside breast pocket of your coat."

"Cobbler, I see," Bell curtly informed the next man. "Observe, gentlemen, the distinctive pattern of wear on the inside of the trouser knee. He rests his lapstone there."

A limping veteran took his turn. "Well, my man," Bell barked at him, "you've served in the army."

"Aye, sir."

"Not long discharged?"

"No, sir."

"A Highland regiment?"

"Aye, sir."

"A noncommissioned officer?"

"Aye, sir."

"Stationed at Barbados?"

"Aye, sir."

"Gentlemen!" Bell whipped around to face the students. "You see that this man has a respectful air about him but did not remove his hat. One does not do so in the army. If he'd been long discharged, he'd have learnt civilian ways. He displays an authoritative nature, and is obviously Scottish. As to Barbados, his complaint is elephantiasis, which is West Indian . . ."* Conan Doyle stood in the wings, riveted.

Bell had developed the Method from his youth and considered it a core medical skill. "All careful teachers have first to show the student how to recognize accurately the case," he would declare. This was best done with the doctor's own eyes, informed by experience. Patients, after all, could lie or misperceive their own symptoms. A man with a long-term injury might fail to recognize how his work did him damage; a drunkard might conceal his consumption. For Bell, observation sliced straight to the bone of diagnostic truth. It was all about trifles: "the accurate and rapid appreciation of *small* points in which the disease differs from the healthy state." Carpenters and masons developed different calluses. People acquired regionally peculiar tattoos as they traveled the world for trade and military service. Victorian Britons collected distinctive native baubles in the far-flung outposts of empire and wore them on their watch chains.

Bell saw *and* observed. Conan Doyle would never forget. (In later years, he kept a portrait of the surgeon on his mantel.) So when he decided to create his own detective, he returned to Bell and his lightning deductions. What if a detective did that? Bell's self-taught Method implied rigorous commitment to observed reality over abstract principle. This bright star among the medical profession's stars gave to Conan Doyle an appreciation for what science, awareness, practical knowledge, and quick

---

* The "Joseph Bell makes deductions" scene is a compulsory feature of all Arthur Conan Doyle biographies. There are many examples. I have adapted mine from two sources: Conan Doyle's own autobiography, the entertaining (if expurgated) *Memories and Adventures,* and an interview he gave the *Strand* journalist Harry How in 1892, which was supplemented by a lengthy explanatory letter from Bell himself. My description of the atmosphere of the Edinburgh infirmary relies upon a vivid essay of unknown research provenance, written by the mystery-genre scholar Howard Haycraft and published in the landmark Sherlockian anthology *Profile by Gaslight* (1946). Devotees of exacting historical accuracy, beware.

thinking could do when orchestrated by a master. From Bell, Sherlock Holmes inherited his signature trick. When a beefy pawnbroker named Jabez Wilson sits down at Baker Street, for instance, Holmes gives him a glance: "Beyond the obvious facts that he has at some time done manual labour, that he takes snuff, that he is a Freemason, that he has been in China, and that he has done a considerable amount of writing lately, I can deduce nothing else."

Et voilà. For Watson, for me, for you, for Mr. Jabez Wilson, the Method might as well be sorcery. For the Great Detective with the transfused essence of a canny old Scottish doctor, it is a matter of trifles: elementary.

Conan Doyle jotted out a page of rough notes for a mystery novel, *A Tangled Skein*. No, that wouldn't do: *A Study in Scarlet*, starring Sherrinford Holmes of Upper Baker Street and his friend and companion, Ormand Sacker. No! No! Terrible. (Sherrinford? *Ormand Sacker?*) But there was a cricketer named Sherlock . . . and an Edinburgh professor, Watson, an estimable expert in gunshot wounds. Now he was getting somewhere.

But not very fast. The completed manuscript of *A Study in Scarlet* made the publishing rounds, becoming more forlorn as it went. Finally, a relatively humble house offered young Conan Doyle £25 — yes, less than he got for short stories — for the entire copyright. Any writer can see why this was a terrible deal, and also why Conan Doyle said yes. The publisher then offhandedly told the writer that the market was flooded with "cheap fiction," so they'd be squirreling *Study* away. The slim novel appeared a year later, in the 1887 *Beeton's Christmas Annual*, a pulpy mini-anthology, packaged with two unrelated plays and sold for one shilling, basically a bargain stocking stuffer.*

---

* This might be as good a time as any to sort out the money. Throughout the Victorian era (and, in fact, until 1971), the British pound consisted of 20 shillings, each of which consisted of 12 pence. A single shilling therefore functioned roughly like an American nickel, though the Victorian pound was vastly more valuable than the US dollar. (The real-life buying power and function of money has changed so drastically from then until now that it is difficult to make fully valid comparisons. In the Sherlockian tales, small amounts of money exert an almost surreal power. One shilling buys a day's work from a street urchin. An annual income of a few hundred pounds is well worth staging elaborate felonies to control. A decent rule of thumb holds that £1 = $5 in

(Paul Collins told me: "The holiday annual was related to the railway yellowback, but distinct. They tended to be a way for publishers to make a fast buck off repackaged or really cheap content. A publisher would take a novel — or two — they'd already paid for and published separately and bundle it with whatever else they owned. Not a great moneymaking opportunity for writers, to say the least. But the annual was widely available. If you're someone like Conan Doyle, just trying to get started, these cheap publications made it possible.")

A Study in Scarlet — marketed as A STORY OF THRILLING INTEREST — didn't excite much comment in Britain. The Americans, who discovered *Study* in reprints for which neither Conan Doyle nor his publisher received a dime, rather liked it. The *Boston Home Journal* declared: "The lover of a good detective story will acknowledge it as one of the best of that class." Eventually, such encouraging words would prompt Conan Doyle to think of Sherlock Holmes and John H. Watson as more than just one-off characters. People seemed to like them. They might have further use. A few years later, the editor of an ambitious new American magazine asked for a ripping-good tale — a request made in the course of one of the most remarkable dinners in the history of publishing, but we'll get to that — and Conan Doyle came back to Sherlock Holmes for *The Sign of the Four*. Then, as he monitored the publishing industry's constant commercial shifts, he continued to think about how Holmes and Watson could help him earn bylines and cheques.

As the 1890s began, Conan Doyle judged that the golden age of the serial narrative had come and gone. The month-to-month format that sustained Dickens, Thackeray, and their fellow bull walruses of mid-Victorian fiction no longer suited the busy commuter and harassed homemaker. This was almost the twentieth century! Sooner or later you missed an issue of your magazine and lost the thread. But what about

---

Victorian values.) According to one handy online inflation calculator, that would make a single Victorian pound worth the 2015 equivalent of about $130, and the cover price of *Beeton's Christmas Annual* equivalent to about $6.50. In 2008, a single damaged copy of *Beeton's* turned up in a donation pile at the British charity shop Oxfam. It sold at auction for £18,600. In better condition, surviving copies have fetched more than $150,000.

a series of interlinked but self-contained narratives, repeating the same core characters, structured so they could be read in any order? Conan Doyle would later describe this idea, in one of his less humble moments, as "revolutionist." Whether or not he hit upon it first, the concept led him to retrofit Sherlock Holmes as a short story character, with one publication in mind.

In January of 1891, the first issue of the *Strand Magazine* appeared on British newsstands, the latest and most innovative popular magazine to appear in what may have been the greatest age of magazines, debuting with a circulation of 300,000. The publisher, George Newnes, cribbed the *Strand*'s format from a couple of his favorite American titles, especially *Harper's New Monthly*. The magazine would have a picture on more or less every page, unheard of at the time, and an editorial mix designed to be light but improving, broadly fit for family drawing room consumption. To perfect the formula, Newnes hired as editor one Herbert Greenhough Smith, a thirty-something failed novelist and known poker sharp, who'd somehow overcome the handicap of being an expert in French poetry to succeed in journalism.

Together, these men achieved a kind of genius as two of the best practitioners of publishing's dark arts ever to walk Fleet Street. (The Strand itself, in that era a fashionably raffish London thoroughfare, opens into Fleet at its eastern end. The eponymous magazine had its offices just off the Strand, in Southampton Street.) As long as sales prospered, Newnes stayed out of the way and paid the bills. Over about forty years, Smith became the rare magazine editor to raise his humble craft to something like an art, turning the *Strand* into a rich stew of reportage, consumer service, celebrity glamour, and original entertainment, publishing the best popular writers of his day. Essentially, he prototyped every magazine you and I have ever thumbed through at the dentist's office.

Smith published a Conan Doyle article at the very beginning of the magazine's run, so he would likely have opened the first two Sherlock Holmes stories sent to him, "A Scandal in Bohemia" and "The Red-Headed League," in a receptive mood. In retrospect, he remembered this as a moment of excitement. "I realized at once that here was the greatest short story writer since Edgar Allan Poe . . . To an editor jaded with wading through reams of impossible stuff, comes a gift from heaven." He even loved Conan Doyle's handwriting. He immediately signed the young author to a six-story deal, for the half-decent sum of £35 per piece.

You can read the *Strand*'s July 1891 issue on your iPad these days. The experience conjures up the uncanny fusion atmosphere — past, present, and future swirling together — that often hangs around things Sherlockian. Some of the material feels numbingly archaic: a writer named Irving Montagu contributes "Anecdotes from the War-Path," with that characteristic Victorian trick of making global conquest sound like an absent-minded lark, full of amusing foreign characters who must occasionally be killed. *Fine chaps, the Nubians* — that sort of thing. In another story, a grainy photograph shows military cyclists at attention, alongside some excellent diagrams demonstrating how to decapitate someone with a saber while riding a bike.

But other items speak to a sensibility we can recognize as ancestor to our own. The *Strand*'s role as a pioneer in *People*-style journalism manifests as "Portraits of Celebrities at Different Times of Their Lives"— though the Duke of Fife looks a poor reality show entrant. Most startlingly, there is actually *another* detective story in the issue besides "A Scandal in Bohemia." This tale tells of one George Markson, with a star-struck friend and companion — Markson's roommate, no less — acting as narrator to his pal's exceptional feats of perception. ("Talk about five senses, George had ten at least. He could see round a case, and through a man, and into your mind almost.") Stumbling upon this lost Holmesian doppelgänger is like learning that Elvis's stillborn twin brother lived just long enough to record a single.

But then there it is. "*Adventures of Sherlock Holmes.* ADVENTURE I. — A SCANDAL IN BOHEMIA." Over pages of stately double-columned type, Conan Doyle's agile prose flows around ink-wash drawings by Sidney Paget, beautiful in their smoky chiaroscuro and their combination of lifelike quickness, iconic gravity, and humor. Paget makes the King of Bohemia a big, sexy beast — with a faintly ridiculous waxed mustache. He portrays both of Holmes's disguises, that of the drunken groom and the "simple-minded" priest, to subtly hilarious effect. But as himself, Sherlock stands out as noble, stylish, handsome — too handsome, Conan Doyle himself thought.

The few previous illustrations of the two early Sherlock Holmes novels had tended to show the detective as a scruffy fringe-scene character.* Paget, in contrast, imbued Conan Doyle's investigator with saturnine elegance — sharply dressed, fresh and aquiline of face, lithe and muscular — the character would never lose. Paget gave Sherlock style. The thirty-year-old illustrator, a handsome youngster who peers out of period photographs with keen spectacled eyes, was well regarded within London's commercial-arts industry, but still an up-and-comer. An old legend says that Herbert Greenhough Smith intended to hire Paget's better-known brother, Walter, instead, but forgot the first name. Sidney Paget became the first to take Conan Doyle's words and engrave them as an image in the popular imagination. He was also the first person *not* named Arthur Conan Doyle who became professionally synonymous with Sherlock, but far from the last.

"A Scandal in Bohemia" thus landed with exceptional combined force: the hottest magazine, a terrific story, superb illustrations. The public reaction of the moment is hard to capture except in echoes. We know that the *Strand* would soon ascribe to Conan Doyle's byline the power to sell an extra 100,000 copies. (The publisher, Newnes, ran some Sherlockian adventures in his down-market jokes 'n' tales rag *Tit-Bits,* where they attracted an avid working-class following to complement the *Strand*'s middle-class crowd.) But there was more to it than that. As the present-day Sherlockian and mystery novelist Lyndsay Faye said the first time she and I spoke, "This character went viral right away, whatever that meant in 1891." Parodies and tributes commenced almost immediately. Less than a year after "Scandal" debuted, the *Idler* published the satirical adventures of "Sherlaw Kombs,"† and *Ludgate Weekly* devised "Sherwood Hoakes." *Tit-Bits* itself had "Shylock Oams" by 1892, and "Chubb-Lock Homes" was on the prowl by 1893. In November of that year, the actor/writer/theatri-

---

* Conan Doyle's nutty father, Charles Altamont, somehow got to illustrate one early edition of *A Study in Scarlet;* he made Sherlock a pointy-bearded portrait of himself.

† Sherlaw's boon companion, Whatson, finds him playing the violin, "a look of sweet peace and serenity on his face, which I had never noticed on the countenances of those within hearing distance." Affectionately done — Conan Doyle was *Idler* editor Jerome K. Jerome's pal — it's not a bad story. But a little of this sort of thing goes a long way.

cal jack-of-all-trades Charles Brookfield became the first known player to portray the detective — albeit in an unauthorized musical farce, staged at the fashionable Royal Court Theatre. The introduction to an opportunistic new edition of *A Study in Scarlet* — which, recall, its lucky publisher owned outright — described Holmes as "a household word and almost a public institution."

It happened fast. And when you read Sherlock here, in his original natural habitat, you can see why. Amid the *Strand*'s Victorian bric-a-brac, "A Scandal in Bohemia" gleams: a distinctly modernist achievement in design and execution. Watson's brisk introductory remarks establish the sense of reality and continuity that other authors laboriously chased by fashioning fake diary entries or imaginary letters. Edgar Allan Poe's digressive lecture on the nature of observation and deduction, from "The Murders in the Rue Morgue," begets a few lines of bright-edged conversation between Holmes and Watson.

> HOLMES: . . . in practice again, I observe. You did not tell me . . .
> WATSON: Then, how do you know?
> HOLMES: I see it, I deduce it.*

Bang! The plot then glides into motion, almost imperceptibly at first, quickly gathering steam as a huffy monarch in a mask storms into the room. Conan Doyle had devised his investigator's ideal format: seven or eight thousand words that drive a case — more properly, an *adventure* — from start to finish, ideally without a single wasted syllable.

The readers of 1891 demanded a reprise. Herbert Greenhough Smith, of course, couldn't have been happier. As he considered the *Strand*'s acute need for Sherlock, he offered Conan Doyle a contract for more stories. The author, for his part, seems to have caught the faint whiff of a trap, and demanded a massive raise. (Conan Doyle was among the first authors to employ a literary agent, the formidable A. P. Watt, who would soon represent most of the big guns of late-Victorian fiction, to handle the "hateful

---

* Or, as Sherlockian essayist J. L. Hitchings put it in a 1946 article in the *Baker Street Journal,* "If the logic of C. Auguste Dupin shines with the faultless purity of silver, that of Holmes gleams with the warm magic of gold."

bargaining.") When the first twelve commissioned stories, to be compiled as *The Adventures of Sherlock Holmes,* ran their course, Smith wanted another dozen. Conan Doyle wanted £1,000 — or more than triple his annual earnings in some of his best years as a general practitioner. Smith agreed without the slightest hesitation.

The arch-Sherlockian writer Vincent Starrett, in his book *The Private Life of Sherlock Holmes,* makes a case for "A Scandal in Bohemia" containing "all that is essentially important in the saga." Starrett, a Chicago bookman and journalist of high distinction whose life somehow spanned from 1886 to the disco inferno of 1974, was one of the crucial literary commentators to sustain the character's cause in the twentieth century. *Private Life,* published in 1933, remains a delightful rum cocktail of a book, definitive of merry highbrow enthusiasm; I have seen paperback editions handed around a meeting of a Sherlockian club like a holy text. Starrett points out that here Watson's storytelling formula snaps into place: the Baker Street scene-setter; sly references to matters too sensitive ever to be revealed (that naughty Dutch royal family!); the momentous arrival of a client bearing a problem that will keep Sherlock's mind off drugs and newspaper archiving for a while.

Apart from the use of Joe Bell's deductive method to spruce up the detective genre and his expert adoption of the short story format, "A Scandal in Bohemia" distills the third crucial, catalytic element in Conan Doyle's success. This far more intangible achievement is nothing less than the story's atmosphere: the all-important Holmesian vibe, which Starrett aptly describes as a "melancholy glamour." Edgar W. Smith, another pioneering Sherlockian writer, would gloss it as "the Baker Street scene." The milieu transcends any detail of Conan Doyle's plots, and creates a lingering, tantalizing sense that each of his stories is just a fragmentary glimpse of a full-fledged world. This world lives in the clip-clop of the horse that pulls Watson's hansom cab up to Baker Street; in the brilliant illumination of Sherlock's sitting room; in the thick pink notepaper made in Bohemia; in the King's vizard mask; in the gasogene and tantalus that hold the libations. It's a world fashioned from small touches of elegance and intrigue, powered by the tension between the sanctum-like quiet of Holmes and Watson's private lair and the tumult in the streets beyond, where an incognito king might bustle past a suburban family man disguised as a beggar. Conan Doyle conjured this world largely without meaning to, as he pushed stray pieces of imaginary window dressing onto his foolscap. He wanted to flesh out his detective yarns just enough to make them plausible, entertaining, and marketable. He accidentally made them virtually real.

Conan Doyle's private reality would prove not only durable, but capable of seducing people in times and places far removed from its creation. After I completed fifth grade, for instance, my mother, brother, and I moved to my grandmother's house in the dusty flatlands west of Missoula's center. This was the new part of town — much of it, in fact, subdivided chunks of my great-grandparents' former farm. In the early twentieth century, the family ran a grocery and orchard at the edge of town, but the "town" grew up. By my '70s and '80s childhood, the core of the old family spread had become a supermarket with an oceanic parking lot, framed by rubble-strewn vacant lots, along a howling road that would eventually breed Missoula's own big-box infestation. Unimaginatively wide streets and squared-off blocks gobbled up the fields, each block decked with squat, ranch-style houses, each house with its own vast yard. Grandma's place was a comfortable, spacious, resolutely unromantic postwar box offering no hint that her forebears had been lords of the manor in those parts.

The entire quarter manifested the 1950s dream, every distance elongated to automotive dimensions: Orange County under the Big Sky. And while I was a happy and well-cared-for kid, I remember a vague, pre-adolescent angst about my environs. One summer, I plunked myself in a backyard hammock with *The Complete Sherlock Holmes* and did my absolute best to do nothing else.

I stared into the broad, type-packed pages with monomaniacal intensity, as though I hoped white-hot focus (and complete obliviousness) could transport me into Conan Doyle's world. The luxurious physicality of the Baker Street scene made Missoula's version of '80s casual feel like a washed-out copy of a once-richer reality. Indeed, the old ancestral photos lovingly preserved by my grandmother suggested that just a few decades before, my people had dressed like off-duty members of the House of Windsor as they tootled about their spacious farm. I had arrived too late, doomed to be part of a generation clad in oversized Quiksilver T-shirts and sweatpants, fated to live behind a chain-link fence.

A gasogene? A tantalus? New Coke had just come out.

Conan Doyle offered an alternative culture in capsule form, less something to read than a place to go. I think now that this was what seduced me: Conan Doyle's trompe l'oeil effect, the ineffable but real-seeming world he created. He built up Baker Street's singular interior decor from story to story, constantly adding details — Holmes keeps his tobacco in a Persian slipper! He nails his unanswered letters to the mantelpiece with a knife! He shot the initials "VR" (Victoria Regina) into the wall in a fit of boredom! The author dressed his world with tantalizing hints around its edges: ragged "street arabs" performing secret missions, the covert hideaways around London — alluded to, never revealed — where Holmes could retreat to change his disguise. Astrakhan! I was certainly not the first to feel that this imaginary realm should, by rights, have been my home. Decades before I coiled myself in that hammock in the fleeting Montana summer, Vincent Starrett penned the most famous manifesto of Sherlockian longing:

> Here, though the world explode, these two survive,
> And it is always eighteen ninety-five.

Always 1895? I was too young to reflect on what that would actually mean, but just old enough to find the idea alluring.

And now, more than two decades removed from that hammock, I found myself beguiled by the detective and his scene again. This time, I wanted to figure out how Conan Doyle did it. He took the swirling Victorian fog of crime and detection, real and imagined, and distilled Sherlock Holmes via Joseph Bell, the tightly built *Strand Magazine* "adventure," and the signature Baker Street atmospherics. And then?

As I once again cracked Conan Doyle and the sprawling corpus of history, pseudohistory, literature, and quasi-literature that's accumulated around Sherlock Holmes, I noticed that I was, as I had planned, creating a working simulacrum of the Sherlockian method. I would find myself curled in an armchair, surrounded by notebooks, old paperbacks, photocopied texts dredged from the Library of Congress, grizzled hardcovers printed in bygone eras, and obscure periodicals. I don't think my "technique" would stand up to peer review, but in my defense it may be physically impossible to undertake a truly complete study of Sherlock Holmes. There's just too much stuff.* To survey Sherlockiana, at this late date, is like staring out over a wilderness — you finally have to pick a trail and start navigating.

I decided Conan Doyle's original saga would serve as my map. Imbibing the stories one after another, without the breaks of months or even years their first-generation Victorian, Edwardian, and post-Edwardian fans would have experienced, induces a distinct mental atmosphere of intrigue and perpetual alarm. You start to notice everything, including things that may not really be there. This reading campaign took me through a dark, grim fall and winter — the natural season for Holmes. After mornings and nights of immersion, I would ride my bicycle — that superb Victorian technology — into the moss-breeding rains of Portland's gloomy months, and sometimes feel my world blend with the Holmesian neverwhere. I'd cross the Steel Bridge, a black-steel-and-rust masterpiece built in 1912, and sense the ingenious people of Sherlock's era still helping me get to work. Dense fog often shrouds Portland in the winter, and in parts of the old city the streets remain cobbled, and the streetlights — while not gas, unfortunately — hulking, ornate throwbacks.

In fact, Portland made a weirdly apt backdrop. It may be closer to Tokyo than Baker Street and about one-tenth the size of modern London, but it is, at its heart, a Victorian-Edwardian city. Unlike London with its two thousand years of history, Portland was built by Conan Doyle's American contemporaries, and expresses both a progressive-minded, orderly zeitgeist and some of the era's more rococo leanings. Every day, I'd pass through a neat, tight, rational grid of streets platted in the 1840s, where gorgeously ornamental buildings dating to the 1870s and '80s still stand. I work in a downtown building constructed in 1914, just across the

---

* A Sherlockian scholar named Ronald Burt De Waal began compiling a "universal" bibliography of Holmes-related literary and scholarly materials in 1974 — now available as a $280 five-volume hardcover set from the University of Toronto, but also searchable online via the University of Minnesota's library.

street (named for a Civil War general) from Portland's Old Town and Chinatown districts. In those neighborhoods, you find old-fashioned doss houses, cheap cafés, down-and-dirty bars, and people still trading legends about shadowy nineteenth-century smuggling tunnels. Many of the city's brightest fashionable shops and zippiest tech start-ups have taken root there, too, which can foster the illusion that the twenty-first century just burst into flower in the husk of the nineteenth, with no twentieth century in between. At around this same time, young men had even taken to growing handlebar mustaches.

In fact, I developed a theory: the 2010s are a sort of neo-Victorian age, sharing more, in some ways, with the world of 1895 than with the middle-to-late twentieth century that birthed me. For instance, Holmes and Watson (and their real-life comrades) devoured reams of information and gossip from many different sources — Conan Doyle frequently portrays Baker Street as a riot of newspapers, dozens of titles lugged up by the long-suffering Mrs. Hudson every day. They would figure out our chaotic Internet/mobile/whatever milieu pretty quickly, and maybe find it more recognizable than, say, the monopoly daily newspapers and handful of broadcast TV stations that molded my media consciousness in the early 1980s. Texting and email would not surprise a detective who relied on high-speed telegrams and multiple same-day postal deliveries. (Conan Doyle's Holmes never wrote when he could wire; Benedict Cumberbatch's Sherlock never phones when he can text.) In his excellent revisionist book *Inventing the Victorians,* historian Matthew Sweet points out that in its day, the Victorian telegraph service was seen in almost exactly the same way we see email: highly convenient, often annoying. Spam telegrams blizzarded people with unwanted advertising, for example. Sweet also teases out the complexity of Victorian Britain's video culture — long before (and for a couple of decades after) the Lumières debuted the first cinema in 1895, people absorbed moving pictures via all kinds of now-vanished devices: "kinematographs, choreutoscopes, biophanascopes." The Victorians would grasp how we now traipse from grainy amateur YouTube videos to high-definition TV. I began to feel, in fact, that Sherlock Holmes and Doctor Watson could come to life, step into modern Portland, and adapt fairly quickly. They would certainly recognize our baroque geopolitics much more immediately than the austere, bipolar Cold War decades stalked by Ian Fleming's James Bond or le Carré's George Smiley.

The damp gloom of the Portland rain would glaze an ancient, time-grimed cast-iron façade. At three o'clock in the afternoon, the hulking streetlights would flicker on. It seemed an investigation into all things Sherlock would require me to tightrope-walk the border between actuality and fantasy. I had now pondered Baker Street's historical and imaginative foundations. It was time to see the (un)real thing.

3

THE WILDERNESS

PICTURE A MAN standing at a bar, drinking away his afternoon. The room stretches past him, a long, amber-lit rectangle with marble-columned arches down each wall and flecks of lapis lazuli in the gold mosaic ceiling. To be honest, he does not look good: his emaciated frame lost a third of its meat somewhere; his liverish skin oozes ill health. He's only in his twenties, but somehow he's no longer young. It's New Year's Day, and his head hurts.

The Criterion draws a buzzy gang of mustachioed horseplayers and fancy lads, but they leave our man alone with his drink and his morose stare. Outside, he can make out Piccadilly and its hansoms and buses on a whirligig, pavements mobbed by every species of grifter, wanderer, and tourist. London. What a cesspool — full of every idler and lounger in the Empire, including him. His shoulder aches where the Jezail bullet punched through it.

He joined the army fresh out of medical school. Before he reached India, war broke out in Afghanistan. He joined a convoy up to occupied Kandahar, to find the wards bloody and full. The army transferred him from the 5th Northumberland Fusiliers to the 66th Foot. In July, the regiment intercepted a huge Afghan force commanded by the governor of Herat, self-proclaimed emir. At the village of Maiwand, the young doctor's outfit of 2,500 British and Indian soldiers engaged 25,000 enemy troops. The Afghans tore apart the native Indian battalion on the left flank, then began rolling up the line. The 66th collapsed. Men fought with handspikes and knives. The medic commanded his orderly, Murray, to gather what supplies he could as the column began to fall back. And then a bullet struck him, grazing his subclavian artery. Young Murray threw him over a packhorse, and next he knew, he was at the base hospital in Peshawar.

Six months and a touch of enteric fever later, the doctor subsists in a cheerless, rapaciously expensive hotel in the Strand and liquidates his daily pension of 11 shillings 6 pence with great efficiency. He knows it cannot go on.

Suddenly, a familiar voice escapes the din. The doctor turns to see an old med school acquaintance — what the devil was his name? Stamford. Stamford! Good old fellow. (They'd never been very close, but in the great wilderness of London, any amiable face will do.) And Stamford — perhaps that cocktail in his hand is not his first of New Year's Day — seems positively giddy.

"Watson! John H. Watson. How wonderful to see you, old boy."

And so it begins. The opening scene of *A Study in Scarlet,* the first Sherlock Holmes novel, fades in not on a high-strung detective, but on John Watson, adrift and damaged, alone in the city. And the story opens not in a cozy imagined room on Baker Street, but in the very real Criterion Bar, in very real Piccadilly: elegant, jolly, ruthless London.

Conan Doyle starts in the only logical place for a British writer of his day to set a tale of intrigue, the effective capital of the Victorian world. He places his eyes and ears — that's what he will make Watson — deep in the city's frenetic center, and makes a chance encounter engage the gears of the Sherlock Holmes saga. It really couldn't have happened anywhere else. In the course of sixty tales, Conan Doyle's characters will become creatures of London. And his stories' cityscape — confected by the author from reality, fantasy, stereotype, urban legend, exacting description, and impressionistic imagery — will become essential to their appeal. Millions of people down through the decades will feel the pull of Conan Doyle's gaslit, fog-draped London. This city of the mind (where it's always 1895) will evolve into a strange hybrid: imaginary, but constructed from so many specific and actual places, it is also paradoxically real.

Or, let us say, it can be made real. Conan Doyle could not have created Sherlock Holmes without London as habitat and raw material. Conversely, Sherlock Holmes and the fictional atmosphere that swirls around him would come to saturate — and in some small but inescapable way, define — the real city. If you drift around the right neighborhoods in the right frame of mind, it takes only a slight blurring of the vision to sense the London of Sherlock Holmes: in the ceaseless pulse of cabs and buses, or the cryptic overheard mobile-phone conversation, whispered in some language unknown to you, that you catch as you duck into a Victorian-built Underground station. In today's London, you hear of Sherlock everywhere — if you listen.

A young man dressed like a Victorian cop peered down Baker Street, his face twitching to suppress mounting professional concern. His ears and cheeks pinked in the bitter wind. The wintry light, already choked by gray-black clouds, had begun to fade. To the north, gloom descended on Regent's Park, and I noticed more and more pedestrians making urgent moves for the Volunteer pub on the corner. I watched the young man in the retro police helmet mentally count the people in the queue that stretched from the door to the Sherlock Holmes Museum at 221B Baker Street, calculating whether he could herd at least fifty American, German, Japanese, Norwegian, Nigerian, and parts-unknown tourists into the premises before closing time. From my own place in line, I heard a chirpy ruckus behind me, and turned to see dozens of adolescent Russian school kids pouring across the street, £8 museum tickets clutched in hand. The faux bobby further narrowed his eyes.

My wife paced Baker Street with gloved hands clasped over her ears, eyes watering. I stood in line with my five-year-old son, wondering which new strain of pneumonia he would contract because his father insisted on visiting the world's most famous Sherlock Holmes tourist trap. In my defense, a multinational horde had the same idea. They (we) crowded the ground-floor shop below the museum, browsing the mother lode of Sherlock Holmes tchotchkes. Young Japanese women clutched souvenir magnifying glasses. German kids modeled £30 deerstalker caps. After several interventions to prevent my child from breaking a *Hound of the Baskervilles* chess piece or some damn thing, I'd forged my way to the sales counter. Was it always like this? "Oh, no, sir, never," the presiding young woman in a Victorian frock cheerfully said. "Ordinarily, you can go straight up. I couldn't say what's going on." She sold me tickets and an oversized postcard, which she tucked in a logo-adorned plastic bag, and sent me out of the shop to wait in the museum queue. "There, sir. The bag itself makes a fine souvenir!"

The Sherlock Holmes Museum opened in the present-day address 221B back in 1990, yet bases its trade in tours and knickknacks on the claim that the Great Detective's domicile "is still faithfully maintained for posterity as it was kept in Victorian times."* The building's exterior bears a blue plaque imitating those on London buildings where real people of historical interest once lived. (Benedict Arnold's plaque, not far from Baker Street, curiously describes him as "an American patriot.") In the 1880s, no actual 221B existed. The name Baker Street itself applied only to a completely different part of the thoroughfare to the south, and didn't extend to the museum's location until the 1930s. And — sorry to keep bringing this up — Sherlock Holmes did not exist, and therefore did not keep an actual residence of any kind.

As is generally the case with Holmes, his inconvenient imaginary status did not seem to trouble anyone in the queue. The youthful imitation cop judiciously allowed a few people at a time to step up to the supposedly famous door, pose for pictures while wearing a deerstalker cap and brandishing a calabash pipe kept ready for the purpose (the hygiene struck me as dubious), then climb to the museum itself. I distracted myself by looking up and down the line. The crowd's average age was probably twenty-five. I'd bet sterling that most had never read a Sherlock Holmes story. Here we all were nonetheless — hardly the strangest crew to visit Baker Street, in fiction or fact — paying good money to see a real

---

* In 2013, the family that runs the museum suffered a very public falling-out. The mother and daughter sued the son, claiming murky accounting of more than £2 million in revenue. Tales of £500,000 cash stuffed in a safe circulated in the press, while the son fired back with his own story of £400,000 gone astray on his mom's watch. According to the *London Evening Standard,* the matter was settled out of court.

version of a place that never existed, a self-proclaimed, for-profit Sherlockian space that couldn't be more inauthentic. Or really, in its own way,
more perfectly in tune with how Conan Doyle constructed his London.
He, too, liked to make the most of what people imagined about the place.

Conan Doyle did not actually know London very well when he started
creating Sherlock Holmes. He'd made a few youthful visits, and occasionally ran up from Southsea for professional reasons, or when he needed
furniture. But the whole culture had marinated in salacious and criminal London lore for centuries. In the 1750s, the city was called "a hydra
of villains," and early in the Victorian era, *Fraser's Magazine* warned its
readers of its "new and well-organized criminal class" who fancied themselves "patrons of crime." Beyond outright criminality, the capital was renowned (especially, maybe, among people who didn't live there) as the
ultimate magnet for would-be rakehells, hustlers, and those with more
money or time than sense. In 1888, a book titled *London To-Day* would
describe the city as "a pleasure lounge for the idlers of the globe," echoing
John H. Watson's description, in the first pages of *A Study in Scarlet,* of
"that cesspool into which every lounger and idler in the Empire is irresistibly drained."

Just as a modern novel or film can use "Las Vegas" as shorthand for bad
behavior, Conan Doyle tapped popular stereotype and the daily content
of newspapers to evoke a ready-made scene. The Criterion, Piccadilly, a
lonely hotel room in the Strand — most adult Britons likely to buy an urban murder story would carry their own versions of this world in mind:
the London of glamorous troublemakers, where money and mustache-
twirling amorality ruled. Conan Doyle recognized that he could put anyone into that world and have just about anything happen. Readers would
believe it. And so into that pop-mythological landscape he launched Watson.

And when he created Watson, the twenty-five-year-old writer fabricated a version of himself in some ways, giving the character the imperial
military career he declined, apparently making the fictional doctor just a
couple of years older to get him to Maiwand on time. (That battle loomed
large in British culture: the year Conan Doyle drafted *A Study in Scarlet,*
an iron statue of a lion was unveiled at Reading to commemorate Mai-

wand, and Kipling would soon write a maudlin poem about the carnage.) Some believe that he originally modeled Watson on a certain Alexander Francis Preston, an army surgeon wounded at Maiwand who survived the thirty-three-hour escape to Kandahar. Conan Doyle's notes show that he was also thinking about an episode from the *first* Afghan War, back in the 1830s and early '40s, in which an officer made a desperate escape. The Edinburgh medical school professor Patrick Heron Watson had pursued roughly the same professional course as his fictional namesake, serving as an army doctor in the Crimean War. Conan Doyle would likely have known of and treated injured and diseased servicemen through his practice near Portsmouth, a major military port, where he had his Watson disembark after being shipped home.

When I first read *A Study in Scarlet* as a kid, I missed Watson's desolation, sublimated in the novel's first matter-of-fact moments. Those few brief paragraphs reveal some of Conan Doyle's intentions for *A Study in Scarlet,* and that first tale's London backdrop, in ways that can escape a present-day reader but which would have resonated with the punters who bought *Beeton's Christmas Annual.*

Watson is living in an overpriced room in the Strand. Today, as you shoulder your way through the tourist throngs there, hulking palaces of entertainment and international commerce remind you, poor individual, just how insignificant you are to the global scheme. In the Victorian era, the avenue was just as bustling, and had not been sanitized. In the 1860s, the French social observer Hippolyte Taine claimed that "every hundred steps, one jostles twenty harlots." One can imagine what Conan Doyle himself might have imagined: that his wounded, unattached young war vet would eagerly seek lodging in the midst of this melee, then regret the move.

The Criterion, where Watson encounters young Stamford one afternoon,* also would have evoked a particular image. The "Cri" was a relatively new, hip bar opened just a few years before, known for new-fangled American cocktails, and figures frequently in the gossip and

---

* The idea that *A Study in Scarlet* opens on New Year's Day is something of a tradition among Sherlockian fans and, like most chronological elements of the stories, is subject to debate. Conan Doyle doesn't specify a date.

criminal news of the period. The neighborhood, Piccadilly, carried its own associations. The summer before Conan Doyle began writing *A Study in Scarlet,* a droll anonymous correspondent filed a story in the *Pall Mall Gazette,* under the headline "In Piccadilly Circus at Midnight." The journalist recorded a scene observed as he stood in the Criterion's door: "Three girls, all young and comely, in the Salvation Army uniform, were marching down Piccadilly, with about half a dozen prostitutes hanging very affectionately about them, and a motley crowd of street loafers in close attendance." To the first-generation *Study in Scarlet* reader, Piccadilly meant louche living, glamour, and sin.

After Watson runs into Stamford, the two school chums continue their revels. They head to lunch at the Holborn, a restaurant beloved by the party-hearty Prince of Wales, where mulligatawny soup might precede "calf's head in piquant sauce." Over a bottle of wine, they discuss Watson's desire to change his ways. He needs affordable digs. Stamford knows the perfect roommate. Now well fed and lubricated, the pals rattle off for the ancient City and St. Bartholomew's Hospital.

If it really ("really"— see how this happens?) was New Year's Day, Watson and Stamford might find the stony compound of St. Barts much as I found it on a recent wintry holiday weekend: forbidding, quiet, and austere, with its two hoary churches (St. Bart the Great and St. Bart the Less) and statue of Henry VIII, London's only one, conjuring a medieval aura. They venture into the hospital proper, to a laboratory, deserted except for a lone man crouched over a test tube. This lanky fellow with a hawk nose seems to be in a manic mood. The first words he speaks: "I've found it!" (Nice touch.) He regales them with a self-congratulatory speech about a scientific breakthrough, a chemical test that detects bloodstains, which he hopes will hang many guilty men. Watson finds the subject matter hard to take after several cocktails and a bottle of wine. But he's even more surprised when his new acquaintance gives him a single glance and tells him:

"You have been in Afghanistan, I perceive."

And where was Sherlock Holmes before Watson walked through the laboratory door? Like some mind-boggling thingy from quantum physics, he may or may not have been anywhere, depending on how you think of it. At the moment he portrayed the young detective tinkering in the laboratory,

Conan Doyle had no idea — at least of which we have record — where the character lived, where he grew up, who his family might have been. Some brainstorming notes survive, but they include little of later substance beyond the fact that Sherlock (originally Sherrinford) likes violins. Conan Doyle wouldn't invent Mycroft, Sherlock's smarter older brother and only family known by name, for years. Sherlock's pre-Watsonian existence must be puzzled out, inferred, or imagined.

Conan Doyle would eventually decide, in "The Adventure of the Musgrave Ritual," published years later, that young Holmes first established himself in Montague Street, right next to the British Museum. Happily enough, Montague Street's gorgeous terrace of brick Georgian townhouses has not changed much. This throwback quality has long given the place special status among Sherlockians trying to reconstruct Holmes's London. From about the middle of the twentieth century on, it became almost mandatory for anyone writing about the detective and his city to decry London's transformations — what must have looked and felt, at times, like the systematic dismantling of the Victorian (i.e., Sherlockian) city. Hitler blew up big chunks of the cityscape, of course, and the modernist planning regime that arose after the war did not rate compact brick-hewn districts or atmospheric gaslit streets. (Parliament passed the New Towns Act in 1946, codifying a strategy of dispersing humans from central London into exurban frontiers, where high-rise tower blocks of flats began to sprout in the early '50s.) In 1958, the Sherlockian scholar Michael Harrison indulged this tendency in *In the Footsteps of Sherlock Holmes*. The book packs in meticulous insights on the world Conan Doyle portrayed — that, for example, a particular Turkish bathhouse Holmes and Watson frequented occupied 12,000 square feet, and dropped its prices from 3s. 6d. to a flat 2 shillings after 7 p.m. (Behold, the detail Sherlockians crave.) Its author also launches many diatribes against architects, developers, planners, and government (or, as he styles it, "Government") bureaucrats. "Of all the superb hotels flanking the street," he writes of Northumberland Avenue, ". . . each has been commandeered by some department of the Civil Service, and the great public rooms have long since sunk into that grimy decay inevitably associated with Government ownership." One encounters a fair amount of nostalgic and/or reactionary harrumphing in works written by people who have searched for Sherlock Holmes and "his" London over the last 125 years. In the 1979 book *Sherlock Holmes: The Man and His World,* for instance, the late mystery novelist H.R.F. Keating goes so far as to bemoan public education and Darwin's theories.

I get it. I, too, become emotional when I see fine old buildings wrecked by utopian schemers and real estate profiteers. But these days, it seems those midcentury Sherlockians missed the real story. In Montague Street, when I most recently paid homage, the sun gleamed against brightly painted front doors set beneath characteristic fanlight windows. The serried rank of houses, now more than two hundred years old, looked chic, of the moment even. This reinforced my own perception of Sherlockian London, formed from visits to the capital over fifteen years: that the city Conan Doyle portrayed is actually in miraculously good shape. A modern-day Holmes replicant, generated by some fiendish science-fiction device, would still know where to find home.

Holmes and Watson promptly move in together. With his war wound and his miserly pension, Watson spends most of the early part of *A Study in Scarlet* sitting in a corner watching his weird new flatmate with inquiring eyes. They haven't talked about how Sherlock makes his living, and despite their encounter at St. Barts, he's definitely not a traditional medical student. (Stamford reports that Sherlock beats the cadavers in the dissecting room, just to see if the dead can bruise.) He attracts strange visitors. A "sallow, rat-faced, dark-eyed fellow" by the name of Mr. Lestrade pops by all the time. One day, Sherlock welcomes a fashionable young lady, followed by a tattered old peddler in a state of great excitement. Railway porters, old men — who are these people? Why does Holmes commandeer the sitting room to see them?

"Clients," Holmes brusquely explains. Clients? Clearly the youngster is running some kind of shade-tree business, with Baker Street as headquarters — a canny choice. In the 1880s, Baker Street was eminently respectable, but at least marginally affordable. (Harrison's *Footsteps* pegs the rent for a two-bedroom flat, including room, board, and optional indoor pistol practice and chemistry experiments, at between £3 and £4 per week. At that rate, Watson's share still would have gobbled up half his wound pension ... which reminds me of what an Australian lad once told me about living in London: "Every day, I wanted to vomit into my wallet.") The street's flat-fronted Georgian houses mixed commercial and residential uses, and served many independent artisans and freelancers. Pioneering professional photographers operated there — Messrs. Elliott and Fry, for example, shot portraits of theatrical celebrities. Small-time private schools offered classes. Furniture companies and piano shops blizzarded the newspapers with ads. Period photographs show brisk, but not overwhelming, traffic: hansom cabs, pedestrians pursuing their business at ground-floor shops. Maybe they're on their way to Madame Tussaud's Wax Museum, located in Baker Street since the 1830s. In other words, anyone could come and go. Who knew what people did in Baker Street, really, and who cared? It was precisely *not* Piccadilly Circus or the Strand — it would carry much less glamorous and charged associations in readers' minds. Baker Street would make a fine home for a confidential business.

Innumerable people have tried to unlock the identity of the "real" 221B, shrouded as it is by a chronologically impossible street number. Sherlockians are forever pacing Baker Street, armed with Conan Doyle's evocative but stingy descriptive details, ancient ordnance maps, and tiny notebooks. The modern scholar can combine Victorian-era maps with Google Street View to uncanny effect, but it's still more fun to go in the flesh, of course, to hunt the model for fiction's most famous address, which Conan Doyle refused all his life to reveal "for excellent reasons." How near was the closest streetlight? Where was the tobacconist? Clues abound, but in nearly a century of loitering with intent, Sherlock's fans have never reached a decisive verdict. This is one secret to the saga's long-term success: it invites endless speculation upon questions that can never be answered.

In my own wanderings, I began to feel that half the houses on the old "real" stretch of Baker Street, as so called in the 1880s, had duly received their nominations as 221B. In his sprightly 1959 book *Baker Street Byways,* James Edward Holroyd launches a gleefully demented numerological analysis of passages from Conan Doyle that he decodes as clues in favor of his choice, 109 Baker Street. Bernard Davies, an actor and scholar, composed a meticulous survey titled "The Back Yards of Baker Street," a boggling breakdown of streetlights, gates, alleyways, possible walking routes, and likely locations for a solitary backyard tree, mentioned once by Watson. Davies hoisted 31 Baker Street aloft.*

I stood at the latter chosen spot, at the corner of Baker and Blandford Streets. I found poor number 31 immured in a gleaming modernist office building, with the street-level shop occupied by Tossed, an oppressively jolly purveyor of "salads, smoothies, and wraps." I scurried over to the other side of the street, where the Georgian ambience survived. I craned my neck and iPhone up at 33 Baker Street's four floors, the stacks of three skinny windows, the stolid brown brick. This building houses an office of Hunters, an evocatively named real estate company. According to Davies's analysis, this would have been the model for "The Empty House," where Holmes and Watson lured Colonel Sebastian Moran — gunman, cardsharp, and, yes, big-game hunter — by using a wax bust of Sherlock, displayed in the window opposite, as bait.

Hunters stood mute before me, a swell piece of Sherlockian heritage. Could it be? It could! But here's the thing about this little puzzle: as you examine one possible location, another insistently suggests itself. You can walk Baker Street from one end to the other, and all you really find is Conan Doyle slyly grinning across the generations: "Oh, you think this might be it? Well, *perhaps.*" In the 1920s, Vincent Starrett satisfied himself with an "occult sense of rightness" as he stood on the pavement outside 66 Baker Street, about where a Subway sandwich shop stands today. In roughly the same era — days when Sherlock Holmes stories still occasionally ghosted into the pages of the *Strand* — a St. Louis doctor named Gray Chandler Briggs did the Baker Street pilgrimage, snapping photos and scrawling notes, and divined that 111 Baker Street, the longtime site of a post office, was the genuine holy ground. Perhaps uniquely in the annals of Sherlockian cryptogeography, Briggs presented his findings to Conan Doyle in person. Briggs's memory of the exchange survives in Starrett's *The Private Life of Sherlock Holmes.* "He told me, with such seriousness I

---

* The "Let's Find 221B" game also occasionally yields heretical theories that the sacred apartment was actually not in Baker Street at all, but rather some other part of London. We need not dignify such rank provocations.

could not doubt him," Briggs recounted, "that he did not believe he had ever been in Baker Street in his life . . .

"There is something spooky about Doyle, anyway."

Spooky, we can believe — by that time, Conan Doyle had aged into a silver-tipped eminence given to oracular pronouncements about life after death. He was also, obviously, full of mischief. Confronted with a medical colleague from across the pond, no doubt bearing documentary notes, Kodak snapshots, and a zealot's gleam, Conan Doyle took the opportunity to add a veil of fog. He certainly had been in Baker Street — in fact, curious connections linked him to the place and gave him reasons to think it special.

About a decade before he concocted Sherlock Holmes, the teenage Conan Doyle visited his London relatives, the artsy Doyles, and made the rounds. His devoutly Roman Catholic relations took him (probably under mild protest, as young Arthur had already drifted into nonconformity) to a chapel that served the French community, tucked near Baker Street. (When the street was originally developed in the Georgian era, many residents were aristocratic refugees from the French Revolution.) With more enthusiasm, he visited Madame Tussaud's waxworks, then housed in a complex called the Baker Street Bazaar. The old Madame and her descendants had traded in the likenesses of the famous and infamous for decades, with particular specialties in hanged murderers and severed heads. (Madame based her version of William Corder, the killer who inspired that most popular 1820s execution broadside, on the man's own death mask.) After touring taverns and exhibition houses for years, the Tussaud operation landed permanent digs in the Bazaar, a former military barracks that had become home to a mix of commercial ventures.

In the wax museum, young Conan Doyle found himself "irresistibly drawn to the images of the murderers" in the Chamber of Horrors. He ogled torture instruments and the severed heads of the Parisian Terror. He saw Burke and Hare, the infamous killers from his hometown of Edinburgh, who sold freshly slaughtered humans to a surgical instructor at the university's medical school for dissection before Conan Doyle's time. (This case would echo in a few of the Sherlockian tales. In "The Disappearance of the Lady Frances Carfax," Holmes and Watson pull a half-dead woman from a casket in which villains have concealed her. And one of Conan Doyle's own Edinburgh professors performed forensic work on the case: he'd beaten cadavers in the dissecting room to test the body snatchers' claims that their "product" suffered bruising after death.) Beyond the bloody Chamber, a young buck accustomed to bleak boarding school halls found the Tussauds had transformed the old barracks into a spectacular mirror-walled salon: towering ceilings, gilt and draperies, luxurious furniture. The fake but lifelike figures of kings and princes radiated elegance from every corner.

Imagine the brawny lad stepping back out into gloomy 1870s London, blinking at the hustle of tradesmen and hansom cabs in Baker Street. His natural storyteller's mind vibrates with a not-quite-articulated intuition. He's just absorbed a trade secret from Madame: the hallucinatory power of well-wrought illusion. And fresh from the Chamber of Horrors, young Conan Doyle may perceive a clandestine dimension within city life, his first inkling that a sharp observer could detect that secret world.* When he needed a home for a fictional seeker a few years later, he may have had the Bazaar itself in mind.

Over time, Baker Street has been heavily redeveloped — the Luftwaffe smashed the Bazaar on 8 December 1940, for example, and corporate offices now stand on the site where Conan Doyle ogled the waxen Burke and Hare. But the author created his London out of psychic atmosphere as much as physical detail. Wander into the side streets and byways of the old parish of St. Marylebone and you'll find the remnant Sherlockian world almost immediately. In Gloucester Place, just one street over, Georgian houses stand in packed rows, their crisply painted, fanlight-topped doors testifying to what George Orwell described as "the *privateness* of English life"— the sense that behind any of these doors, any life might be lived, and no one need ever know.

As I drifted toward the old neighborhood one morning, I emerged

---

* On a less mystical note, in the period when he wrote *A Study in Scarlet,* Conan Doyle was active in Portsmouth's local literary society. One of his comrades was H. Percy Boulnois, a talented civil engineer; Boulnois's family was responsible for the redevelopment of the Baker Street Bazaar property, and his brother Edmund managed it. The personal connection may have freshened Conan Doyle's not-very-distant memories of Madame Tussaud's and the Marylebone neighborhood.

from the Edgware Road Underground station and slipped down Homer Row, into a Sherlockian trapezoid of brick-clad terraces. One particular specimen, a rack of four attached houses at Rodmarton and Blandford, seduced me with its iron-railed balconies and subtly natty red-painted accents above each narrow window. Perhaps — there, that one, 104 Blandford. That could have been "Baker Street," or a model for Baker Street, or at least a mildly plausible simulacrum of an image in Conan Doyle's fertile mind in distant Southsea. Then I looked up: no bow window. Blast! Watson clearly describes a protruding bow window. The house before me — like just about every other house in the entire district — was bow window–free. That bow window, let me tell you, drives Sherlockians crazy. Where is it?

For my money, the less enervating way to explore the physical landscape of Sherlockian Baker Street is not to obsess over any one address but to wander. Dorset Street, Gloucester Place, Montagu Square: the loopy circuit takes in a preserve of brick-faced houses, a few of which do feature protruding upper-floor windows, if not the perfect bow window. Then: back up to modern Baker Street itself, whatever part of it suits you. Because Baker Street, despite the most diabolical efforts of the Third Reich and property developers, still has much to offer. The heterogeneous mix of shops, offices, cafés, hotels, and traffic of all varieties retains exactly the flow that Sherlock Holmes needed to launch and maintain his business. Today, this make-believe enterprise is woven into the real commerce of the street. At the Baker Street Underground station, which has whipped people in and out of the district since the 1860s, passengers stop to snap photos of tile work that shows the detective's instantly recognizable profile — deerstalker, hawk nose, pipe — repeated, Warhol-style, in groovy 1970s brown, white, black, and rust orange. Not one but two hotels bear the name Sherlock Holmes. The pipe and deerstalker recur on café signs and at souvenir shops. The detective has become his old neighborhood's talisman and mascot.

I had just about determined to rush the fake bobby on the museum's doorstep, even if it only got us out of the cold for a few minutes while he called the real authorities. At last, after two giggling Japanese fangirls took turns with the photo-prop deerstalker and pipe, he let us in.

The Sherlock Holmes Museum's exhibits are contained in tight, half-lit rooms, packed with Victorian disjecta and — in an unconscious but apt homage to Conan Doyle's visit to the Baker Street Bazaar — wax figures of characters from the saga. I could take or leave the obligatory vintage chemistry gear and dusty violin, but I found these effigies quite fun. Dr. Grimesby Roylott, the wicked stepfather and misguided exotic-animals enthusiast from "The Adventure of the Speckled Band," sat in a corner, wearing a toy snake wrapped around his head and a look of wild surmise. I was relieved to see that Bruton, a larcenous butler with a gift for historical code decryption, was still dead; in "The Musgrave Ritual," he found himself suffocated in a manor-house cellar. Good riddance. In the next room, Holmes and Watson themselves posed like trophy hunters with a stunned-looking Lady Frances Carfax, whom they'd just sprung from the coffin.

"Daddy, who are these people?" I turned from Lady Frances to find my son pointing at an endearingly vaudeville-esque rendition of the King of Bohemia, wearing a truly ridiculous mask, remonstrating with Irene Adler. "That's the King and the opera singer," I told him. (Not long before, I'd given him a carefully de-sexed oral retelling of the "Scandal.") And over there, the eerie-looking specimen with the unsunned, hairless dome of a head? "Oh, that's the evil mathematician, Professor Moriarty." My kid squinted at me. "An evil *mathematician?*"

We pawed through the museum's collection: Watson's rusty service revolver, a medal meant to evoke one planted on Holmes by some grateful, no doubt wayward royal, a Victorian toilet. On a side table, a binder held letters sent to 221B from people all over the world. A financial institution once located at 221B famously paid an employee to keep up with Sherlock's mailbag, and even though people have, generally speaking, ceased to write letters, they're still writing to Sherlock Holmes, requesting assistance with lost pets or asking for his autograph. As the Russian school kids herded through the rooms, I sidled up to their minder to give my terrible college Russian a spin. Communicating on the level of a bright two-year-old, I learned that the group hailed from Nizhny Novgorod, and (after she mercifully switched to English) that these fifteen minutes at Baker Street were hotly anticipated. "Russian people love Sherlock Holmes," this matron firmly told me, before hustling off to make sure no charge of hers was pocketing the gasogene. Closing time was upon us: the watery light through 221B's windows was beginning to fail. It was the hour when, in fiction, Holmes would stoke up the coal fire, break out the tantalus and have some brandy, and practice the violin. In reality, the twenty-something woman in a replica nineteenth-century dress stationed on the staircase looked positively desperate to leave. I hoped to beat her to the Volunteer.

Watson is a mess during his first weeks with Holmes. He barely sets foot outside, blaming his war wound and the weather. *A Study in Scarlet* is notionally an extract from Watson's own reminiscences, and in full dear-diary mode, the poor doctor confesses himself "objectless," living a bleak and bored life with nothing to engage his attention.

Well, except Sherlock Holmes. As he broods, Watson develops a fixation on the human whippet in the next bedroom. He composes private inventories of his housemate's "limits." Holmes's knowledge of philosophy and literature Watson summarizes as "nil." Sherlock knows nothing of astronomy — not even that the earth goes around the sun, a fact haughtily dismissed as useless to the man's work. (Whatever that is. Stalkerish list-making notwithstanding, Watson doesn't ask.) Sherlock is an expert fencer and single-stick fighter. Sherlock can identify London's varied soils by color. Sherlock knows how to cultivate poisonous plants, but not how to grow cucumbers.

Sherlock, Sherlock, Sherlock! Our Watson is ripening into a strong candidate for a restraining order. Then, one grim March day, the two get into a spat over an anonymous magazine article in which the author argues that a keen observer could see a drop of water and deduce the Atlantic Ocean. Watson scoffs, only to discover that Sherlock Holmes — Sherlock! — is the author. Holmes reveals that he is a "consulting detective," perhaps the only one. People bring him problems, and when the police are confused, as they usually are, they call in Sherlock Holmes. He is, if he doesn't mind saying so himself, quite brilliant.

Watson finds this news fairly annoying. But a few minutes later, a message conveniently arrives from Tobias Gregson, a Scotland Yard detective (as is, it turns out, that Lestrade fellow), reporting dark doings at Lauriston Gardens, off the Brixton Road. Empty room. Dead American. Who could ask for better on a cold March day? Holmes tells Watson to grab his hat. What? "If you have nothing better to do," Holmes replies. Thus Sherlock Holmes reaches a hand out into the churning sea and pulls Watson aboard the last lifeboat.

It's a nasty day, an early classic of Sherlockian meteorology, with a "dun-colored" sky mirroring mud-choked streets. Nor does number 3 Lauriston Gardens cheer the eye, sitting amid a weedy, half-abandoned block overlooking a teeming South London artery. "Three tiers of vacant melancholy windows . . . were blank and dreary, save that here and there a 'To Let' card had developed like a cataract upon the bleared panes." As Holmes and Watson step into the house, the reader feels the clammy chill, hears the floorboards' existential creak, smells the dust and stale drains. Sunlight dribbles into the murder room, while just beyond a soot-coated pane of glass, London life roars on.

Watson finds a stark tableau that mingles horror and grotesque comedy. The wallpaper, once a cheap and cheerful print, unravels in mildew-saturated strips. A fake-marble fireplace creates a parody of opulence. Gregson and Lestrade bustle about, trying to one-up each other like a deranged comedy team. In the middle of it all lies Enoch J. Drebber, dead, his top hat set neatly beside him. Watson, via Conan Doyle, reaches back to Poe to create a terrible still life in carved jet: "On his rigid face there stood an expression of horror, and, as it seemed to me, of hatred . . . This malignant and terrible contortion, combined with the low forehead, blunt nose, and prognathous jaw, gave the dead man a singularly simious and ape-like appearance."

Holmes couldn't be happier. He rifles the corpse with his long, precise fingers, scampers about the room, tosses out insights and criminal trivia. This first recorded opportunity to humiliate the police sends him into overdrive. There's blood, but not Drebber's blood. This reminds him of "the death of Van Jansen, in Utrecht, in the year '34." Gregson proves embarrassingly weak on fifty-year-old Dutch murders. The tobacco ash comes from a Trichinopoly cigar, of course. (Sherlock Holmes has written a monograph on the identification of ash — duh!) In a moment of ghoulish drama, Lestrade finds RACHE finger-painted on the wall in blood and immediately suggests a role for a woman named Rachel. Sherlock giggles, because he knows that *Rache* is German for "revenge." (And he knows this is a red herring, because the letter "R" is written in a non-German style—but useful for indicating the killer's height and the poor state of his manicure, all the same.) The amateur detective informs the professionals that their criminal is tall, red-faced, and arrived in a hansom cab.

This display leaves Watson smitten, and his delicate reluctance to set foot out in bad weather mysteriously vanishes. Soon he and Holmes cross rain-sodden South London to interview the beat cop who found Drebber's body. (They hurry, because Sherlock wants to check out some chamber music that afternoon.) Their search for the officer leads "through a long succession of dingy streets and dreary by-ways," and down a narrow passage into a courtyard lined with hovels. The bleary-eyed cop sits on his horsehair sofa and, in exchange for a 10-shilling bribe, recounts his night: a tavern brawl, rain, a dirty and lonely beat on the Brixton Road. He saw a light in 3 Lauriston Gardens—known to be empty, because the landlord refuses to fix the plumbing, and raw sewage killed the previous tenant. At one point, as he and the colleagues he summoned worked the crime scene, they ran into a tall drunk singing American songs. They let him go—which infuriates Sherlock, because that was the killer, you idiot.

A Study in Scarlet exemplifies how the common characterization of the Sherlock Holmes stories as "cozy" glimpses of picturesque olden times—gaslight, the clip-clop of hooves, et cetera—falls short. Here London glowers, devoid of charm, boggy and dank and violent—truly, as Watson called it at the outset, a "great wilderness" inhabited by four million treacherous beasts, a city of dirty work done in rented rooms. Holmes and Watson deal with whiskey-drinking cops, ragged street kids (whom they employ as spies), a crooked female impersonator. A man is stabbed to death in a miserable back-alley hotel. As Holmes says, a scarlet thread of murder runs through the colorless skein of ordinary life.

London outrages were the real-life newspapers' stock in trade. In 1881, the year in which Conan Doyle set his *Study*, the disappearance of an East End German baker sparked a celebrated case known as the St. Luke Mystery. Interested parties employed one Walter Scherer, a German emigrant who described himself in well-publicized court statements as "a professional *consulting* detective" (emphasis mine), an unusual phrase that apparently lodged itself in Conan Doyle's mind.* The author appropriated the idea of an independent investigator and molded it into a new figure: an urban knight-errant. By the tale's end, Holmes and Watson are partners, as it were, in crime. As they discover what happened to Enoch Drebber, the duo hits upon a less tangible but more essential truth: that the cold psychic void of the modern city—a place that will kill you in an abandoned room and grind on about its business—can be redeemed and enlivened only by friendship, by a spirit of shared adventure on its grimy streets.

The squat brick chimneys of the old villas off the Brixton Road jabbed at a (yes) dun-colored sky as I made my way from the Stockwell Underground station toward the scene—or alternate possible scenes—of *A Study in Scarlet*'s first killing. I was doing my best to re-create the proper Lauriston Gardens atmosphere, setting out in foul late March to skulk about the thoroughfare where the American met his end.

I knew little of Brixton. When I'd made a professional call at magazine offices in Dorset Street, just off Baker Street, a fellow journalist had observed, "Ah, Brixton. I lived there. It's where Conan Doyle set his murders. *Plus ça change.*" My only personal impression of the neighborhood derived from fruitless teenage hours spent trying to learn the bass line from the Clash song "Guns of Brixton." Still, my mission would put Conan Doyle to the test. All very well for a relative London novice to bang on about famous places like Piccadilly and St. Barts. But was there a "real" Lauriston Gardens? In his annotation of *The Oxford Sherlock Holmes,* the scholar Owen Dudley Edwards argues that Conan Doyle collaged many of his London venues from urban places he knew better, chiefly Edinburgh and Birmingham, where he'd done the Victorian medical equivalent of an unpaid internship. Edwards identifies possible architectural models for *A Study in Scarlet*'s locations far from London, and Conan Doyle himself

---

* In 1971, the Sherlockian writer Michael Harrison published an elaborate—overly elaborate, some might say—essay in *Ellery Queen's Mystery Magazine* attempting to establish textual links between *A Study in Scarlet* and the real-life St. Luke Mystery. He argued that Scherer, not Joseph Bell, was the true model for Sherlock Holmes. I found my way to this highly arguable argument, and the intriguing historical tidbit that underlies it, via an essay in Trevor H. Hall's 1977 book *Sherlock Holmes and His Creator.*

breezily said that he'd worked out much of his geography from post office maps. He lifted the name Lauriston Gardens from a street in central Edinburgh, not far from his university haunts. And he *could* be willfully reckless about accuracy—in his memoirs, Conan Doyle notes that in an early short story set in New Zealand, he precisely placed a farm twenty miles out to sea. "These little things will happen," he wrote. "There are times when accuracy is necessary and others when the idea is everything and the place quite immaterial."

Very good, sir. But the crime scene for Sherlock Holmes's debut can hardly be dismissed as immaterial. And I'd noticed that while reality's details might be obfuscated, disguised, or simply ignored, Conan Doyle rarely invented any place out of whole cloth. His style depended on rapier-like observations of physical detail—the weedy garden, the horsehair sofa. I wondered just how much of his Brixton Road could have been real. I would have my data soon.

In Brixton Road, traffic growled and random, scruffy shops stretched along. I stopped at a corner, looked north, looked south, looked across—and there stood a four-door block of Georgian houses. Iron railings and overgrown gardens bordered the complex, setting it back from ("off") the Brixton Road. The white-painted trim around the stolid brick fronts showed many chips and cracks. The windows stared out, baleful and blank. One unit's house number was scrawled in rough white paint in the half-moon glass arch above the front door. I was off to an excellent start.

I took out my phone and walked slowly south, rereading Watson's description on my tiny screen as I went. The good doctor captures Lauriston Gardens as—yes!—a block of four, its three tiers of windows "melancholy," fronted by sickly plants. "Ill-omened and minatory," he says. From my pocket, I retrieved a crumpled list of potential models identified, over many decades, by various researchers into Sherlockian arcana. As I walked, I scoped the general landscape. Apart from that exciting first offering, the side opposite me seemed to be dominated by squat midcentury apartment estates: 1950s social democracy, not aging well. Here and there, a nineteenth-century survivor poked out, like an ancient mustachioed colonel peering suspiciously at the contemporary scene through his monocle.

My side of the street, however, was replete with potential Lauriston Gardens.

I understood from a dip into a neighborhood history that Brixton Road was once lined with Georgian townhouses practically end to end. Along this stretch, enough survive that even today Enoch Drebber would have no shortage of places to die. But frankly, some potential Lauriston Gardens nominated by past searchers now had paint far too fresh, and a few showed signs of landscaping work. In an echo of Watson's description of the cataract-like To Let notices at Lauriston Gardens, property sale signs barnacled the road. Those signs, however, tended to have a sharp, smart look about them. The actual humans with whom I shared the street also looked as if they were on an upward trajectory; at the end of a working day, crisp business gear predominated. I could feel the Eye of the Great Real Estate Agent watching us all.

Brixton has fostered an ever more cosmopolitan and culturally fertile scene since at least 1948, when nearly five hundred Caribbean immigrants arrived in London aboard the *Empire Windrush,* many ending up in Brixton. These days the cachet that's developed over the ensuing decades of diversification — not to mention property values marginally less punishing than those of more upscale London districts — has begotten an entirely predictable gentrification. *Time Out London* and various blogs about ethnic cuisine told me so, and that standard hipster-imperialistic rebranding had dubbed the area Brixtonia. I had already passed a pub with artisanally distressed wood floors and Brooklyn Brewery ales on tap, and spied at least one guy on a fixed-gear bike. The crafty sameness of globalized urban style and the dynamics of a thermonuclear real estate market boded ill for future crime-fiction tourists.

Then, just as I was considering forming a fanatically retrograde Sherlockian Preservation Society, I found it: my ultimate Lauriston Gardens.

The houses numbered 314 to 320 had been marked as a candidate by the Sherlockian researcher H. W. Bell back in the 1930s. No one had visited with a scrub brush since about then. At one entrance, cracked white pillars stood ominous guard around a recessed portal, a great welt of peeled paint bruising the severe face the buildings presented to the world. A ragged garden grew — or, at least, survived — just as Watson described in his glance around before he and Sherlock plunged into the murder investigation. Of course, the place could be anything inside. But as far as I was concerned, the brick front concealed emptiness, dust, and the beginnings of adventure. A hansom cab could have materialized out of the Brixton Road traffic and disgorged some beefy-faced Scotland Yarders. Conan Doyle may have artfully faked his London now and again, but he could have built this grimy beauty before me. Whether he'd ever seen the place with his own eyes, or somehow simply channeled it, or confected it from some jaunt through Brixton, or transplanted a Birmingham house, or something, no one will ever know.

The sun broke through to bathe the street. A couple of joggers rambled past. I was about to issue a silent salute to bygone urban menace when a man in a black sweatshirt limped past, leading an enormous black pit bull with a nail-studded collar. He was just the sort of man I'd cross several streets to avoid, and just the sort Sherlock Holmes might approach with a cheery smile and the offer of a shilling in exchange for all he knew. Take that, Brixtonia!

Conan Doyle was still very young when he wrote *A Study in Scarlet,* but he was maturing apace. His medical practice in Southsea began from almost nothing. The local newspapers of the early '80s record a few exploits: Conan Doyle scurried out his front door to deal with riding accidents; he treated a jeweler who fell into a pub's cellar and cut his head; he testified in police court after patching up some drunken brawlers. He had become an established medico, with a consulting room decorated with seventeen paintings, many by his father. He did a bit of everything — forceps deliveries, cancer cases, odd jobs for insurance companies. It paid the bills. Conan Doyle would soon have Sherlock Holmes declare that "my mind rebels at stagnation . . . I abhor the dull routine of existence." Decades later, Holmes would compare his brain to an engine that could, if improperly used, "rack itself to pieces," and the detective would frequently bemoan the horror of a "commonplace" life. Make of it what you will.

He kept writing. As he came of age, he sensed great leaps in his literary skill. In 1883, he was messing around with anonymous political screeds and banging his head against various publishing industry walls. By the end of 1885, he had broken into the pages of several significant venues. The publishing world began to notice him — *Cornhill* invited him to a select Christmas rave-up in '84 at the Ship tavern in Greenwich, where he partied with George du Maurier (Daphne's grandfather) and several best-selling authors of the day. He would later write that his marriage, in the following summer of '85, unleashed new power in him as a writer.

Conan Doyle wrote his mother habitually and others voluminously, and his letters often dwelt on finances in a manner that now reads as weirdly indiscreet, telling anyone who'd listen how much money he was earning, how much he owed, about his tax situation. Five decades later, he would still remember that he earned *exactly* £154 one year. But one can hardly blame him. His preteen brother Innes lived with him in Southsea while his sisters were off in Portugal working as nannies. These arrangements all traced back to 1876, when Charles Altamont Doyle was forced to retire early from his government job; eventually he went into what his older son would euphemistically describe as a "convalescent home"—we would call it a secure residential rehab facility. He got his hands on alcohol even there, and accounts suggest a violent attempt to escape involving a smashed window. In 1885, the year Arthur Conan Doyle married, Charles Doyle transferred to the Royal Lunatic Asylum at Montrose, Scotland. There he doddered about, scrivening crazy sketchbooks and lamenting his fate with occasional flashes of black humor. In one note, he attributed his incarceration to "the narrow Scotch misconception of Jokes." In memoirs written almost half a century later, Conan Doyle brazenly misdated Charles Altamont's death to around this time period—maybe a dead father was less upsetting to imagine than a mad one. In fact, the old man lived into 1893.

His father's periodic, then permanent, absence stirred up other turbulence, too. In the '70s, his mother started taking in boarders to make ends meet in Edinburgh. One of them, a doctor named Charles Waller, became a close friend—perhaps too close, in Conan Doyle's view. Mary Doyle began spending time at the Waller family's estate in Yorkshire, and eventually moved there. People have speculated about the nature of this relationship ever since, but whatever it was, young Arthur didn't much like it. In the 1920s, the author would chop Waller out of his memoirs entirely. Waller was still very much alive to absorb the snub.

So, much was churning within young Arthur's outwardly placid middle-class existence when stray thoughts about Joseph Bell's deductions and the publishing market coalesced in *A Study in Scarlet*. He began writing in March 1886, producing a narrative that thrums with angst, incorporates barbed satire of police and press, hints at vile sexual crimes, and more or less excuses murderous vengeance. A strangely built book: the second half veers into a Wild West historical narrative, set in the Utah of the 1850s, with no Sherlock or Watson in sight, portraying the Mormon Church as a violent white-slavery racket. (This section, full of truly terrible writing, is probably one of the most frequently skipped in all of crime fiction. It also introduces Conan Doyle's bizarre outlook on the United States, which figures in the Holmes stories as a land of cults and secret societies, with Ku Klux Klan assassination teams practically tripping over Irish nationalist gangs and polygamist death squads.) Of more lasting import, Conan Doyle begins his deep sketch of Sherlock Holmes and John Watson — the reader can feel pulses beating in the characters already. But the landscape impresses most. Conan Doyle finds a dark and somber stage for his imagination, a London that suggests a hidden world of mystery. It was a city, but in Conan Doyle's hands it would become the City, an archetypal landscape of secret passages, low alleys, and sparkling halls where anything could happen. Conan Doyle's London would serve him (and many others) as a divine inspiration, but the gods who built it were mad.

For all of the hours I have spent trying to meld myself with Sherlock Holmes and his world, I am still a somewhat limited investigator. For example, I spent days out on the *Study in Scarlet* trail, scoping out possible grim South London murder manors and haunting Baker Street, before I remembered the most elementary — yes — dictum of the Sherlockian method: when looking into any matter, one's usual first move should be to go to where it all started and have a look around.

Fortunately, I was both near Piccadilly Circus and in need of a drink when this realization dawned. I pushed open a polished door and tucked myself into a nook at the Criterion Bar, where Watson ran into young Stamford and slipped, unknowing, into Holmes's sphere. The old Cri has seen some odd phases since then. The place was made over into something called a "milk bar" for a while at midcentury. Then, in the 1980s, it became a cheap place to drink in faded glamour and whatever else one could afford. A few years ago, some Georgian entrepreneurs gave it an upscale refresh. The fare is not well spoken of: a *Guardian* reviewer, mixing his Conan Doyle metaphors, not long ago wished that "Sherlock were still at one of the tables . . . He could set off after whosoever is guilty of the crimes against food now being committed at the Criterion."

Still, the old tart remains seductive. The curved, golden ceiling, oozy lighting, and Europolitan staff exude the atmosphere of modern central London, where one breathes not oxygen but money. When the sprightly young Slavic gentleman in a black waistcoat handed me the cocktail list, I steered my eyes past the prices.

I had given some thought to what Watson drank that afternoon. The doctor usually took his medicine straight and simple: brandy, whiskey with water or a soda blast from the gasogene, a bottle of claret (or two), maybe a pint of ale while out on the chase with Holmes. But the Criterion just isn't that kind of place. It owes its distinction in British drinking history to being one of the first "American bars" to introduce the proper cocktail to London. In the 1870s and '80s, the Cri employed a prototypical celebrity mixologist: Leo Engel, a New York import with a droll, puckish mouth and the requisite champion mustache. In '78, Engel wrote a book, *American & Other Drinks,* which could still challenge other cocktail manuals for both volume ("upwards of 200 of the most approved recipes for making the principal beverages used in the United States and elsewhere") and bantering panache. Practical recipes for impractical quaffs — "Norfolk Punch" starts with 20 quarts of brandy, 30 lemons, and 30 oranges, and eventually must "stand six weeks in a warm cellar" — interweave with observations of life as lived round the bar. Of eggnog, Engel writes that "in the East, the wise men imbibe it, in the West the egotist believes in it, and in the North it is a favourite at all seasons." Elsewhere, he quotes a devotee of mint juleps: "They are, like American ladies, irresistible."

The modern Criterion lists a few Leo Engel originals among its beverage options. One choice caught my eye. I summoned the lad and ordered the "Criterion Reviver."*

---

* In Engel's book, the recipe for the Reviver appears just before something called the "Bosom Caresser" — an unholy-sounding mash of strawberry syrup, brandy, and an egg. Try it sometime. Let me know.

CRITERION REVIVER.
Use a Soda-water tumbler.
Glass and a half of Encore whiskey; small block of ice; dash of brandy
bitters; bottle of Taunus water; drink while effervescing.

Simple! Strong! Watsonian! When the Reviver materialized at my elbow,
adorned with a heretical but welcome orange slice, pale gold whiskey re-
fracted the amber glow from gilded, seven-pronged light fixtures. The
first sip was frigid, fizzy, and faintly ginger-spiced. I sat back to share a
drink with Watson and observe the Criterion.

Hypnotic international dance music softly played while middle-aged
Americans talked about college admissions and medical conditions. A
party of cute French people took a table. At precisely 5:30, the lights and
music dropped a notch. The first pretheater diners wandered in. The
newspaper before me was full of a ministerial crisis, Afghanistan, and the
strange death of a Russian oligarch in a locked bathroom. I took the Reviver slowly. It's one of those cocktails that peel open your chakras, given
some time. As I considered the arched alcoves set in the marble-clad walls
and the glittering ceiling, Watson's world didn't feel far away at all.

I had become attached to thinking of Conan Doyle's first Holmes novel
as an urban noir before its time. But the Reviver helped me perceive at
least one alternative reading of *A Study in Scarlet,* requiring just a slight
change of perspective. (There's almost always more than one way to look
at Conan Doyle.) Let street grime, stabbings, and freaky death cults fade
to the background, and *Study* becomes the uplifting tale of How John
Watson Got His Groove Back. The newly discharged war vet was emotionally and financially bereft as he idled at the Criterion Bar. But maybe
a long draw at Leo Engel's Reviver, accompanied by a sly wink from Leo
Engel himself, revealed to him another facet of London life. A city that
could provide a drink this good couldn't be all bad.

His young mind would take a reflective turn as he imbibed. Should
he really rusticate in some country village? That path led to marrying
a parson's daughter or some equally dismal end. No. To paraphrase a
1950s calypso hit by Lord Kitchener, a Trinidadian blacksmith's son who
hitched a ride to the metropolis aboard the *Empire Windrush,* London
was the place for Watson. You never knew who would turn up, or what

unimagined new life might spin out of the churning tumult of four million souls. As Conan Doyle wove himself into Watson, the writer gave the character that part of his own soul that would never settle for grinding out life in Southsea, mending broken bones. Watson is often presented as Mr. Normal, Sherlock's arch-conventional foil. But at the beginning of A Study in Scarlet he is a man whom convention — professional training, the army, society — has failed. He needs a new life, new ideas. The city is a great generator of new lives and a fission reactor of ideas. Watson, completely imaginary though he, of course, was, would become one thread in this tapestry. And by creating his half-fantastical, half-concrete London, Conan Doyle added his own layer to the city's ancient/modern/futuristic palimpsest.

Holmes would brag of his "exact knowledge" of London. In contrast, I now carry around a highly unreliable (but fun) psychogeographical map of the place, plotted around Sherlock Holmes stories, literary trivia, '70s punk songs, and a few youthful misadventures of my own. My London is a place where Samuel Johnson is forever running into the Sex Pistols. On a recent visit, I was excited to note that the bistro where my family and I paid way too much for a late lunch stood around the corner from Bankrobber, a hot-pink avant-garde gallery named after a Clash song, just a few blocks from where George Orwell lived. It all comes together! My personal London is also the place where, in my heartier early twenties, I watched a fistfight in a gruesome Chinese restaurant in Camden Town, just before my consciousness faded out under the influence of about ten pints and an absinthe shot. In all, it is a hazy "faerie kingdom of romance"— which is how Arthur Conan Doyle described the world of Sherlock Holmes, his imaginary London, which has since merged with the real London. Above all, it's a place where things happen. One day, at an American bar, the city throws Watson together with an old acquaintance and spins the broken soldier in a new direction. The moral of A Study in Scarlet may be that sometimes we John Watsons of the world just need to let life's brilliant chaos do its work. Sit down. Have a Reviver. Drink while effervescing.

4

HOLMES & WATSON

A GOLDEN EVENING. Arthur Conan Doyle would always remember it. The end of August 1889.

He boarded a London-bound train, then a cab to the Langham Hotel. All the best people stayed at the Langham, a four-hundred-room velvet-cushioned fiefdom in Portland Place. Here one could buy railroad or steamship tickets to any place on earth and play billiards on the finest tables ever built. A telephone office linked the hotel to every other part of London (well, every other part of London that mattered, surely). Conan Doyle must have loved it. Just a few years earlier, he'd eked out a life in Southsea on a few pennies a day, and polished the brass nameplate on his door by night so the neighbors wouldn't see him doing it himself. Now look at him.

Joseph Stoddart, the American magazine editor, hailed Conan Doyle. Thanks to the United States' disregard for international copyright, British authors got plenty of attention over there — at least it was something. *A Study in Scarlet,* published about two years earlier to a somewhat muted domestic response,* achieved a respectable American readership. Stoddart represented a new magazine from Philadelphia called *Lippincott's*

---

* Not that *Study* went entirely unremarked upon in Britain. The *Hampshire Telegraph* for 3 December 1887, for instance, praised "Sherlock Holmes, a consulting detective of

Monthly, which aimed to recruit British talent. Hence the invite to Conan Doyle. The evening would revolve, however, around another writer of Irish extraction, a big-chinned and milky-eyed man with hair flopping off to both sides, resplendent in a necktie of fiendishly intricate construction: Oscar Wilde.

At the time, Wilde worked as the celebrated, talented, terminally bored editor of *The Woman's World.* He wanted out, to fulfill his obvious destiny for better things. The newspapers certainly rated him: Wilde made good copy. The previous February, the *Pall Mall Gazette* column "Today's Tittle-Tattle" giggled: "Here is Oscar Wilde's latest. He chanced to call upon a lady who had purchased a number of Japanese screens, which were standing in disorder in her drawing room. 'You have come just in time,' she said, 'and can arrange my screens for me.' But Oscar said, 'Don't arrange them. Let them *occur.*'"

Wilde charmed Conan Doyle with praise for *Micah Clarke,* a meticulous historical novel about Puritan rebels published earlier in the year — Conan Doyle's first substantial literary success. The conversation flowed in brilliant, desultory fashion. At one point, Wilde suggested that future wars would be fought by lonely chemists from opposing sides, each approaching the frontier with a bottle in his hand. Conan Doyle — new father, cricket fanatic, amateur footballer, Liberal Unionist — communed with Wilde's high bohemianism. The aesthete conveyed all he said with peculiar, subtle gestures and attitudes, unlike those of anyone else Conan Doyle had ever met. And as well as Wilde could talk, Conan Doyle remembered, he also listened with singular focus. Victorian machismo notwithstanding, Conan Doyle always preserved the Celtic art in his blood, and in this elaborate creature he must have recognized a distinct vibration of the age. Oscar Wilde saw *and* observed.

Stoddart handed both men contracts for short novels, which *Lippincott's* would publish as the centerpieces of future issues. Oscar Wilde would respond with *The Picture of Dorian Gray.* Arthur Conan Doyle decided to bring back one Mr. Sherlock Holmes.

. . .

---

the most amusing eccentricities and strangely balanced powers . . . an unrecognized prince among the detectives of London."

When *The Sign of the Four* appeared in *Lippincott's* the following February, the world rejoined Sherlock and John at an intimate Baker Street moment. Holmes opens a "neat morocco case," removes a syringe, fills it with a liquid "seven-percent solution of cocaine," and shoots up. Watson, who absorbed a skinful of French red wine with lunch, nags the detective about this filthy habit, but Holmes welcomes the debate: "He put his finger-tips together, and leaned his elbows on the arms of his chair, like one who has a relish for conversation."

Holmes insists that cocaine just barely keeps the World's Greatest Detective from dying of ennui. He needs a royal marital crisis, a cipher left on a sundial, a corpse, or a kidnapping — all this daily living gets him down. Sure, he can pour his energy into monographs of approximately zero general interest. (The shapes of workers' hands — illustrated!) He can use his photographic memory of criminal history to aid baffled French detectives. (By the way, here's a letter of thanks from a baffled French detective.) He can take one hard look at an old watch Watson just inherited and deduce that the doctor's late brother was a no-account drunkard. But otherwise? "I cannot live without brainwork," Sherlock vamps. "Was ever such a dreary, dismal, unprofitable world?" Oh, behave.

Conan Doyle does a few things in the opening of *The Sign of the Four.**

---

* The name of this novel fluctuates. The original *Lippincott's* publication in February 1890 used *The Sign of the Four,* hence my preference here. It often appears, however, as *The Sign of Four.* Considerable textual discrepancies exist among published editions of the Sherlockian tales. Titles shift, wording changes. Leslie Klinger's *New Annotated Sherlock Holmes* examines many such peculiarities. The 1893 short story "The Adventure of the Reigate Squires," for example, also appears as ". . . the Reigate Squire" and ". . . the Reigate Puzzle."

These bibliographic oddities, however, are nothing compared to the inconsistencies inherent in the stories. *The Sign,* for instance, is nominally set in 1888, while *A Study in Scarlet* was set in 1881 — yet in Watson's narration virtually no time seems to have passed between the episodes. More startlingly, the opening passages of *Sign* clearly state that it's July. A few pages later, the month has somehow changed to September. Temporal anomaly would prove to be a recurring problem (or perhaps, as they say, a feature, not a bug) in the Sherlockian saga. In "The Adventure of the Red-Headed League," Watson begins his tale with the emphatic statement that it is autumn, then refers to a newspaper item from April as "just two months ago," then once again returns the action to October. As Conan Doyle might put it, these little things happen.

It's tempting to focus on the drugs: that coke needle in Holmes's hands inadvertently gave the character some nihilistic street cred handy from the late 1960s onward. Conan Doyle could not have foreseen our somewhat shallow societal preoccupations, but he did use the needle as a device for portraying his detective in a fresh way. This opening scene zooms in on Holmes. Almost four years had passed since Conan Doyle had written *A Study in Scarlet*. In that time, he had subtly matured. Newfound confidence glows on the page. *A Study in Scarlet* introduced Sherlock but never showed him close-up, remaining somewhat schematic for all its excellent qualities. Now we see the sinewy forearm mottled with track marks, the febrile sensibility, the delicate and expressive gestures, the popinjay egotism and snappy way with a sentence. It hardly seems coincidental that Conan Doyle wrote this passage within weeks of meeting Oscar Wilde.

Conan Doyle — though he didn't know it yet and would have been horrified to learn — would spend almost forty more years constructing Holmes and Watson and their comradeship. This monumental (if unplanned) study in friendship provides the structure and soul for all the adventure to come. Conan Doyle could have taken his Hounds of Baskerville, his Signs of Four, his Bohemian scandals, and whatever else and chucked them, had he not created the Great Relationship. He needed both men. Watson, the upright (if sometimes indolent and wine-soaked) professional, argues for practicality, good sense, and healthy living. You can imagine him on the cricket team. Sherlock insists on art, sensation, fanatical work alternated with willful self-oblivion. *He* could arrange your Japanese screens to impressive effect. From this moment in *The Sign of the Four* onward, the push-pull continues: Watson stolid, Holmes volatile, each reliant on the other to attain any kind of life.* Sherlock is high, Watson's a bit drunk, and they share a desperate need for a case to animate a fully realized imaginary world centered on Baker Street.

Enter Mary Morstan.

I found my way to the third pillar from the left outside the Lyceum Theatre on a bright afternoon. The old showhouse tucks away just off the Strand;

---

* Late in his career, Conan Doyle wrote two stories with Holmes narrating directly and Watson absent. They are not considered successes. To put it mildly.

Conan Doyle came here on his teenage visit to London to see Henry Irving on the stage. (I found *The Lion King* running in apparent perpetuity.)
A rank of six slightly grimy pillars guards the entrance. In *The Sign of the
Four,* Miss Mary Morstan, a twenty-seven-year-old orphaned governess,
receives cryptic instructions to arrive at the third from the left, with two
friends who are not police officers. The space between the pillar's base
and the theater wall is narrow — three or four people would fill it. Alone
except for a rapidly disintegrating ice cream sandwich lying on the pavement, I stood there with a certain reverence. From here, the Sherlockian
scene began to throw its tentacles out into a wider world of intrigue.

Miss Morstan arrives at Baker Street, as one does, bearing a mystery.
Her father, an army officer stationed at an Indian Ocean prison colony,
rotated home on leave, then promptly disappeared. A few years later, his
daughter began receiving large pearls, one every year, via anonymous
post. Now, her benefactor summons her to the Lyceum, promising to reveal all.

As Mary tells her story, Conan Doyle allows Watson to linger over the
young lady — here's a new side to our John, too traumatized during *A
Study in Scarlet* to exhibit libido. (In any case, that novel's only female
characters are either dead or cross-dressed men.) Now he makes eye-
opening reference to "an experience of women which extends over many
nations and three separate continents." Watson! Mary, he notes, wears a
stylish but austere all-gray ensemble with a matching turban, adorned by
a "suspicion" of a white feather in the side. Her looks are plain but she possesses an appealing sensitive quality. (Conan Doyle could be describing
his own wife, Touie, in whom the author noted a simple spirituality and
retiring nature, in sharp contrast to his own extroversion and unsettled
religious views.) Watson is smitten. Holmes, of course, takes no interest
in matters hormonal except when they indicate motives for poisoning
or blackmail — but he finds this business of secret pearls and vanished
daddy stimulating. The three soon plunge into the London gloom, bound
for the Lyceum. A few sentences establish *The Sign of the Four*'s aesthetic
of smoky glamour shot through with philosophical musing:

A dense drizzly fog lay low upon the great city. Mud-coloured clouds
drooped sadly over the muddy streets. Down the Strand the lamps were

but misty splotches of diffused light which threw a feeble circular glimmer upon the slimy pavement. The yellow glare from the shop-windows streamed out into the steamy, vaporous air and threw a murky, shifting radiance across the crowded thoroughfare . . . The endless procession of faces . . . flitted across these narrow bars of light — sad faces and glad, haggard and merry. Like all humankind, they flitted from the gloom into the light and so back into the gloom once more.

With nothing to look at but a decomposing Magnum Bar during my visit to the Lyceum, I found myself wistful for this vivid world. When the three adventurers arrive at the theater, they find thick crowds, fancy carriages, men in evening wear, and women decked in diamonds.* In general, this story teems with humanity of every conceivable (or inconceivable) description. *The Sign of the Four* reminds me of that joke about why one joins the army: to go interesting places, meet fascinating people, and kill them. Conan Doyle finds both great humor and spikes of horror-movie thrill in our convoluted get-rich-quick schemes, health phobias, vengeful obsessions, and interior decorating whims. His novel mingles high civilization with archaic violence.

A brusque hired thug hustles Watson, Holmes, and Morstan into a waiting cab, and they ride out to a faceless suburb. There they find a man named Thaddeus Sholto, a fantastic oddball waited upon by a "Hindoo" servant outfitted in a yellow turban and sash. Sholto — a bald, spastic, jagged-toothed hypochondriac — holds court in a carpeted, incense-perfumed sanctum hung with tiger skins and tapestries, where he puffs a hookah and proudly describes his collection of art forgeries. (Another face of Oscar Wilde?) Sholto reveals the secret of Mary's father's disappearance. On his return to England, old Major Morstan tracked down Sholto's own dad, a military crony from the prison camp on the Andaman Islands. They quarreled, and the elder Morstan pitched over dead of a heart attack. Sholto *père* and an Indian servant surreptitiously buried him.

---

* The theater's programming for 1888 — if that's really when *Sign* is supposed to take place — included *Macbeth* and *Dr. Jekyll and Mr. Hyde,* based on the novel by Conan Doyle's fellow Edinburgh boy (and eventual pen pal) Robert Louis Stevenson. These details would have been fresh in theater fan Conan Doyle's mind as he wrote in late 1889.

As if this weren't enough to drop on poor Mary late at night in an Orientalist pleasure lounge, Thaddeus also explains why the two men argued: they'd heisted a huge cache of jewels from India and disagreed on how to divide the spoils. The elder Sholto died before he could reveal the fortune's hiding place to his twin sons, Thaddeus and Bartholomew, leaving them only a few pearls to hint at vast concealed riches. Thaddeus remitted pearls to Mary over Bartie's objections. But now the treasure has been found in a secret attic! Thaddeus proposes a showdown with brother Bartholomew at the old family manse, Pondicherry Lodge, to insist upon a three-way split. Mary will be rich! (And, Watson despairs, out of his league.)

The midnight scene shifts to Pondicherry Lodge, a morose South London mansion surrounded by desolate walled grounds heaped with dirt piles, evidence of the Sholto brothers' years of trying to find their dad's missing treasure.* Inside, the team discovers Bartholomew Sholto locked in his room, regrettably dead (though it sounds like a small loss), his face contorted into a grinning mask, a tiny thorn dipped in some unspeakable tropical poison stuck in his neck. The treasure box, pulled down from the secret attic just the night before, is gone.

The situation calls for some thinking over, especially after Scotland Yard über-buffoon Athelney Jones shows up and arrests poor Thaddeus and all the Pondicherry Lodge servants. But Sherlock Holmes, by various feats of research, soon identifies the real perpetrators: the One-Legged Man and the Cannibal Islander. The former: an escaped convict from the old penal colony, bent on revenge. The latter: a grotesque parody of a "native," diminutive and huge-headed, armed with poison blow darts. They're after a great treasure, stolen from an Indian fort by the One-Legged Man and three accomplices (the Four!) in times gone by, then bamboozled away by Morstan and Sholto. These two creatures have crept to London, like specters of far-flung colonial misdeeds, to reclaim the booty.

---

* Conan Doyle spent time in South London during his youthful visits to the city. Sherlockian scholar Bernard Davies suggested that he'd glimpsed Kilravock House, a stately early-nineteenth-century manse at the edge of a park, which he transposed into Pondicherry Lodge.

The novel quickly achieves the hurdy-gurdy rhythm of a prolonged chase scene, punctuated by bursts of surreal description. First, Holmes and Watson pursue the One-Legged Man and the Cannibal Islander through the London night on foot, following a bloodhound borrowed from a Dickensian menagerie. As that episode ends without success, Holmes looks up into the breaking dawn to remark upon how "one little cloud floats like a pink feather from some gigantic flamingo." (Conan Doyle's father often painted out-of-scale birds. Meanwhile, years later Conan Doyle would remark upon Oscar Wilde's propensity to splash his texts with odd swatches of vivid color.) The narrative otherwise seldom glimpses sunlight — *The Sign of the Four* is a novel of muggy nocturnal landscapes and shadowy machinations. Conan Doyle creates a psychic atmosphere of peculiar intensity, alternating riffs of dreamy stoner philosophy with hard, remorseless violence. Over three short paragraphs, for instance, Sherlock muses on Carlyle, Jean Paul Richter, and man's ability to perceive his own significance — then abruptly vows to shoot the Islander dead. The characters sometimes break from their grim hunt for jarringly convivial moments at table. "I have oysters and a brace of grouse, with something a little choice in white wines," Holmes chirps to Watson and the Scotland Yard imbecile, Jones, at one point. "Watson, you have never yet recognized my merits as a housekeeper."

The climax comes on the black and dirty Thames, as two boats weave through the night, deadly small-arms fire blazing between them. The Islander, Tonga, never gets to be much more than an animalistic savage — indeed, all the novel's portrayals of people from India, used as atmospheric props, could keep a conscientious graduate student up nights. (Actual people from India I consulted regarding their own affection for Sherlock Holmes seemed mildly amused.) But the story of stolen treasure and murderous vengeance can also be read as old imperial sins coming home to roost, with colonialist greed underlying all the crimes. (The tale eventually finds its way back to the Indian Mutiny of 1857–58, an all-out slaughter that saw white settler families butchered and sepoy mutineers strapped to cannons and blown to pieces. There's a scarlet thread of murder for you.)

The politically incorrect rough edges, in any case, only augment the impressionistic suggestion of secret worlds within the city, freak-show cast, and seductive but unsettling beat of nocturnal pursuit. In my mind, *The Sign of the Four* marks an artistic high-water mark in the Sherlockian tales — like a particularly successful hallucination, or maybe a REM episode after an overly long night on that red wine Watson prefers. Above all, though, this novel seals the tentative friendship of *A Study in Scarlet* into full-blown companionship. Sherlock now tenderly settles an exhausted Watson to sleep by playing him violin lullabies. Yes, as the final chapter closes, Watson proclaims his love for Mary Morstan. Holmes shakes his head and reaches for the cocaine bottle, with an implicit *You'll be back.* The engagement is on, but poor Mary — what chance does she really stand?

Sherlock Holmes does cut a magnetic figure, coiled in his armchair, wreathed in smoke: a gray-eyed whipcord of skinny muscle wrapped in a dressing gown. He's an exotic orchid of the imagination, delicately veined with different tones and shades. Conan Doyle sketched him in *A Study in Scarlet* and began fleshing him out in *The Sign of the Four*. Soon, in the two dozen stories that raced through the *Strand* from '91 to '93, he would carve Holmes into the popular consciousness. Those stories, bound together as *The Adventures of Sherlock Holmes* and *The Memoirs of Sherlock Holmes,* combine with the two early novels to form the core of Sherlockiana and establish a character that proved so durable, charismatic, and malleable.

So who is Holmes? Conan Doyle's original stories give us many alternate Sherlocks, from melancholic improv violin player to high-class drug fiend to top-tier amateur boxer to bizarre home economist — he bundles one day's tobacco remnants into a nasty wad and smokes them the next morning before breakfast. Anyone who watches Basil Rathbone or Benedict Cumberbatch may carry a particular image of an overdriven, hyperprecise mind expressed in staccato verbal bursts. Or our minds may harbor cartoonish stereotypes of a man with a big nose, weird hat, and magnifying glass leading a befuddled and often chubby companion. These impressions are fine as far as they go, but each merely glosses aspects of the prismatic figure Conan Doyle created. They all omit some essential element. Almost every stage or screen portrayal of Holmes, for example, ignores two qualities that Conan Doyle himself took pains to emphasize.

First — and maybe most surprisingly given his reputation as a caustic übermensch with no patience for mortal humans — Sherlock Holmes is basically a nice person. Again and again in the short stories of the *Adventures* and *Memoirs,* Conan Doyle describes the detective as genial, suave, friendly. Holmes possesses terrific manners and an "easy, soothing" way with people. In "The Adventure of the Beryl Coronet," a client arrives half mad with anxiety over a damaged royal treasure — the fellow begins pounding his head against the wall. Holmes calms him with smooth, low-key kindness: "You have come to tell me your story, have you not? You are fatigued with your haste . . . Pray compose yourself . . . and let me have a clear account of who you are and what it is that has befallen you." In "The Yellow Face," when another highly distressed client frets and babbles over a mystery that threatens to unravel his marriage, Sherlock cools him down. "My friend and I have listened to a good many strange secrets in this room," he says, "and . . . we have had the good fortune to bring peace to many troubled souls." He extends reassuring hospitality to anyone who needs it. When Watson shows up with a young engineer suffering a severed thumb, of all things (in the aptly named "Adventure of the Engineer's Thumb"), Holmes first sits the lad down for bacon and eggs.

Second, Sherlock Holmes approaches his work — which is to say, his art — with boyish enthusiasm and joy. When he hears something exciting about a case, he wriggles in his chair like a six-year-old. As we see at the start of *The Sign of the Four,* Sherlock craves action and stimulation. At times, this longing brings out the worst in him — his bitchiest behavior toward Watson tends to come just before a client arrives, when a bored Holmes often indulges in amateur literary criticism of Watson's writing: "You have degraded what should have been a course of lectures into a series of tales," and so on. As soon as a case begins, however, he transforms. Sherlock Holmes on the investigative trail defies sturdy Anglo-Saxon description and sends one diving into the Latinates. *Sprezzatura. La bella figura. Élan. Panache.* After capturing a murderer, Holmes will offer the man a cigar. For Sherlock, a clue isn't really a clue until it can be distilled into a diamond-edged epigram, most famously in the short story "Silver Blaze":

INSPECTOR GREGORY: Is there any point to which you would wish to draw my attention?

S.H.: To the curious incident of the dog in the night-time.

GREGORY: The dog did nothing in the night-time.

S.H.: That was the curious incident.

It is currently fashionable to portray Holmes as an all-action dynamo of fisticuffs and verbal gymnastics — stuff that translates into, say, international action-adventure blockbusters starring Robert Downey Jr. or tour de force monologues for Benedict Cumberbatch. But in truth (or in Conan Doyle's fiction, that is), Holmes is at his most intense and active when engaged in intellectual, not physical or dialectical, combat. As he pursues clues, Holmes can seem like a man in the grip of a transcendent psychedelic experience. In "The Boscombe Valley Mystery," as the detective arrives at the scene of a rural bludgeoning, "his face flushed and darkened. His brows were drawn into two hard black lines, while his eyes shone out from beneath them with a steely glitter . . . His nostrils seemed to dilate . . . Swiftly and silently he made his way along the track which ran through the meadows, and so by way of the woods to the Boscombe Pool."

He might as well be running naked through the jungle, chasing his own spirit animal. Holmes himself often equates his practice to archaic blood sport. He will describe an unknown malefactor as his "quarry." When he finally runs a criminal to ground, he prefers to make the catch himself, with the police and Watson as able seconds. ("I love to come to grips with my man," he declares in a later tale.) The chase justifies all life's boring afternoons. One early morning, he rouses Watson from bed with a terse manifesto: "Come, Watson, come! The game is afoot!"

And yet in Conan Doyle's most formative stories about him, Sherlock Holmes relies equally on deep contemplation. He knows how to sit still for a long time and let his consciousness drift. This tendency is admittedly less than cinematic, but it can still serve the cause of drama. In "The

Man with the Twisted Lip," one of Conan Doyle's early triumphs of atmosphere and surprise, Holmes and Watson investigate a particularly arcane missing-person case. The vanished gentleman seems to have evaporated from a room, and red herrings abound. The decisive breakthrough comes when Sherlock constructs a throne of five pillows — Watson calls it "a sort of Eastern divan"— sits cross-legged, and smokes. And smokes. And stares. And smokes. All through the night, he sits there motionless, pumping out tobacco haze, until he figures it all out.

Conan Doyle somehow makes this meditation as memorable as any fight scene, unspooling a single limber sentence to convey an indelible image of his Great Detective: "In the dim light of the lamp I saw him sitting there, an old briar pipe between his lips, his eyes fixed vacantly upon the corner of the ceiling, the blue smoke curling up from him, silent, motionless, with the light shining upon his strong-set aquiline features." Sherlock's inaction is as essential as his action. This elevation of mere thinking into drama is one of Conan Doyle's most distinctive sleights of hand.

It's entertaining to see how this fictional creation resonated with his first readers. From the beginning, Sherlock found champions. *A Study in Scarlet* survived the Ward & Lock slush pile thanks to an editor's wife, Jeannie Gwynne Bettany, an accomplished novelist who recognized a good thing. Shortly after *The Sign of the Four* appeared in *Lippincott's*, Conan Doyle received a letter written by a renowned surgeon, Lawson Tait, on behalf of himself and Baron Coleridge (of the poetic Coleridges), Lord Chief Justice of England. At a time when Sherlock Holmes was a minor fictional figure at best, the two eminences expressed their enthusiasm for the character and demanded more. The letter undoubtedly helped spark the *Strand* stories, and once that series got rolling, Sherlock's admirers grew legion. Newspapers up and down the land praised the character. The *Yorkshire Gazette* proclaimed that the *Adventures* "holds the highest position for imaginative writing." By February 1893, the *Lincolnshire Echo* could pay no higher tribute to the local constabulary than to compare their work on an ironworks robbery to Sherlockian detection. The *Daily Mail*, launched to capture a lower-middle-class commuter readership (and inspired by George Newnes's *Tit-Bits*), ran cute parodies, titled "Sherlock Holmes II," by one "Lady Charlotte."

For the tired office clerk riding the rails back to Stockwell from the West End, or the wrist-sore lady typist shunting homeward across Birmingham, Sherlock Holmes might have served as a bracing antidote to wage work and paying the gas rate. The Baker Street scene evolved into an alluring fantasy lifestyle based on irregular hours, self-determination, and tobacco. Holmes rarely speaks of money (except when he's taking £6,000 off a nobleman for returning his missing son). While his work ethic is legendary, so too is his lassitude — and with Mrs. Hudson, Baker Street's landlady, around to make curried chicken for breakfast and bring up coffee on demand, he rarely lifts a finger for his own keeping. Coupled with his lack of interest in romantic relations, this arrangement frees up a lot of time to mess around with dangerous chemicals, medieval manuscripts, and whatever else strikes his fancy. He is, in a word, free.

Unconsciously, Conan Doyle built Holmes into an idealized version of a distinct, emerging human type: the independent urban brainworker, essentially different from the foppish noble, the office drone, the capitalist baron, the small shopkeeper, the industrial laborer, or the farmer. In the online Jewish cultural magazine *Tablet*, the writer Liel Liebovitz (with nods to Isaac Deutscher and the historian Yuri Slezkine) has argued that Holmes fits in with the likes of Karl Marx and Sigmund Freud to embody "a radical new way of being in the world that ushered in the age of cosmopolitan globalism." Citing Slezkine's book *The Jewish Century*, Liebovitz argues that some of Sherlock's salient characteristics — "urban, mobile, literate, articulate, intellectually intricate . . . and occupationally flexible"— make him a "non-Jewish Jew." Several stories hinge on Holmes's status as the consummate cosmopolitan and man-about-town; for instance, in "The Adventure of the Noble Bachelor," a mystery's solution presents itself because Sherlock instantly recognizes how much a fancy hotel charges for sherry.

Academic literary analysis often makes Sherlock Holmes out as a symbolic force for law, order, empire, and Victorian morality.* While

---

* "Conan Doyle's fiction ratified the principles and ideologies of an imperial, patriarchal Britain" (Jon Thompson, *Fiction, Crime, and Empire: Clues to Modernity and Postmodernism*, 1993). "Holmes represents the Orientalist, the Westerner who utilises European study of the Orient with the result of revealing and outwitting the crimi-

I would not deny anyone on a tenure track the pleasures of subaltern theory and whatnot, this reading may have more to do with modern academic trends than with the spirit of the stories themselves. Holmes may well have delighted his Victorian readers, at least in part, because Conan Doyle made him a rebel. Sherlock uses his detecting powers on behalf of the system — when it suits him — but never within it. He rarely speaks of the state, per se, but repeatedly talks about "the community," which to me suggests loyalty to a deeper and more organic sovereignty. He adores the Queen — besides shooting her initials in the wall, he eventually takes tea with her — but he takes a delightfully high hand with cabinet ministers (he almost kicks the Prime Minister out of Baker Street at one point) and wayward aristocrats (he barely bothers to open letters bearing baronial crests). Capitalist achievements leave him cold. In the late-period "Problem of Thor Bridge," he treats an American "gold king," portrayed as one of the world's richest men, like the small-hearted thug he really is. Holmes admires self-reliant types, like Violet Hunter, the plucky and resourceful governess in "The Adventure of the Copper Beeches" (Watson rather hoped Holmes would fall for her — no dice), or, for that matter, Irene Adler. He expresses refined appreciation for brilliant criminals. He appears to regard official bureaucratic machinery as merely functional (or dysfunctional), and whenever legal procedures contradict his own notion of justice, he brushes them away like lint. (In "The Adventure of the Blue Carbuncle," he turns a rookie jewel thief loose and jauntily tells Watson, "I am not retained by the police to supply their deficiencies." Besides, it's Christmas.)

Is Sherlock Holmes some kind of anarchist? Not quite — in fact, he harbors all kinds of unclassifiable political opinions. So did Conan Doyle, who could write approvingly of a left-wing party's victory in London elections, then turn around and support whatever war-like imperial ad-

nally linked" (Nicholas Stewart, "A Post-colonial Canonical and Cultural Revision of Conan Doyle's Holmes Narratives," 1999). "While the Sherlock Holmes stories register anxiety about the possible inscrutability and unruliness of Britain's imperial territories, they also present a fictional solution to these perceived problems in the character and method of the detective. Holmes is a guarantor of stability and order" (Yumma Siddiqi, *Anxieties of Empire and the Fiction of Intrigue,* 2008). Et cetera!

venture of the moment. At one point, Sherlock voices the startling view that the United States and Great Britain should reunify — which is exactly what Conan Doyle believed.

Sherlock resists tidy definitions. Sometimes he seems an arch-materialist, bereft of any religious sentiment. Then he'll suddenly ramble on about the theological promise implicit in flowers. He is always simultaneously the single-stick fighter and the violinist. And yet he is always and only Sherlock Holmes, no matter what he's doing, an endlessly mutating character who somehow exudes a very distinct personality. He's almost like a real person in that sense. And while it's not entirely clear that our esteemed author intended this — he wrote the Holmes stories as fast as he could, for money, with scant regard for consistency — all this volatility and alternation between violence and calm, action and dream, science and art, manic and depressive, does suggest to me at least one real individual: Arthur Conan Doyle.

You can pit Sherlock Holmes against invading Martians (as has been done) and he remains Sherlock Holmes. But no matter how many times the character reappears on stage, screen, or radio, in comic book or video game (Minecraft players build some amazing Sherlockian mini-worlds), the *complete* Holmes resides only in Conan Doyle's original stories. The author built Holmes out of chunks of experience, impressions of his time, and components of his own complex personality. Conan Doyle channeled and amplified these influences, like a message resonating on a frequency only he could hear.

One recent day in London, the Internet-enabled quest for affordable accommodation led my family to a generic but serviceable chain hotel at the edge of Hyde Park. The building shared its ground floor with a gas station and convenience store — if that tells you anything. The view from our fifth-floor window, however, suitably impressed: the park, stripped and wintry but vast, deep green, and glimmering here and there with water. As I meditated on the vista (actually, ignored my five-year-old as he jumped from one twin bed to the other — long day), I suddenly fixed on a small gate separating the park from the sidewalk.

By God, it was Hattie Doran's escape route.

Our hotel, unprepossessing as it was, stood about a hundred yards from the scene of "The Adventure of the Noble Bachelor,"* a fizzy high-society comedy that entered the Sherlockian annals in the spring of 1892. "Noble Bachelor" does not quite enjoy classic status among its fifty-nine siblings, and contains none of the key mythos-of-Sherlock scenes — no cocaine, no nighttime chases on the Thames, no silent dogs in the night, no street urchin operatives. But it comes off with a distinctive metropolitan flourish and provides an excellent look at Conan Doyle's toolkit of tricks and stratagems. The story opens a window into the effervescent world of Holmes — and, not coincidentally, practically demands that the reader drink a cocktail (the characters drink plenty).

Watson has been reading the papers. Holmes receives a fancy letter, which, as noted, he regards with little enthusiasm — he prefers the correspondence of fishmongers. But the contents prove interesting: one Lord St. Simon has lost his wife, an American heiress named Hattie Doran, when she bolted from the wedding reception in Lancaster Gate (my temporary neighborhood by Hyde Park). Watson, the press coverage fresh in mind, briefs the detective. Not only did the wife vanish, but a dancing girl from the Allegro showed up at the party to cause trouble — a former "friend" of the groom. Meanwhile, the marriage itself has a *Downton Abbey*-style financial basis. St. Simon's father has been selling off the family pictures, but Hattie Doran's daddy struck it rich in the California goldfields. Everybody wins, or so it would seem.

St. Simon himself arrives — Holmes abuses the aristocrat subtly but deliciously — and describes the vanished Hattie as something of a sexy Wild West hellion. He shows a picture to Watson, and that old dog approves, but St. Simon bemoans the woman's free and easy republican manners. She was happy before the ceremony, but bumped into a strange man on the way to the altar, became distracted, then pulled her disappearing act, last seen walking through the park in the company of the distressed Allegro party girl. The nobleman's account leaves Holmes in need of an immediate midday whiskey and soda.

Before long, Inspector Lestrade shows up at 221B, in memorably goofy nautical garb, fresh from dredging the Serpentine, Hyde Park's long, crooked pond, in search of the girl's corpse. He grabs a tumbler of his

---

* Spoilers ahoy!

own and reports that he found only the soaked remains of Hattie's wedding dress and a note, addressed by an unknown party, scribbled on the back of a hotel receipt. Holmes tells him the receipt itself is the important thing, at which point Lestrade gets huffy and takes his pea coat elsewhere.

Holmes sets off into London, leaving Watson in command at Baker Street. Before long, to the good doctor's astonishment, a catering service shows up and lays out a feast: cold woodcock, pheasant, cobwebbed wine bottles. Holmes returns, as does Lord St. Simon — but then they are joined by surprise guests: Hattie, the missing wife, and her *real* husband, gold miner Francis Hay Moulton! The two married in secret years before! But then Frank was reported killed in an Apache raid! But now he's back! So Hattie and St. Simon were never really married! See? (Holmes, as noted earlier, tracked down the absconding pair by analyzing cocktail price structure reflected on that stray hotel receipt.)

It's all a blow to His Lordship (and his bank account), but high good times for everyone else. And aside from a general air of bibulous fun — with no real crime at hand, everyone except St. Simon just parties their way through — "The Adventure of the Noble Bachelor" shows Conan Doyle at work in his well-stocked storytelling laboratory. Though they're all ostensibly "mysteries," the Sherlock Holmes tales eventually sweep through just about every major pop-fiction genre. This one story alone shifts from comedy of manners to social satire (parodies of newspaper gossip columns convey big chunks of narrative) to Western, of all things. Over the sixty stories, Conan Doyle would jump from hard-boiled noir to romance to Gothic horror. (I know worldly adults who refuse to reread "The Adventure of the Speckled Band".) "Silver Blaze" and "The Adventure of the Missing Three-Quarter" are sporting tales, set within the worlds of horse racing and rugby, respectively. "The 'Gloria Scott'" and "The Adventure of Black Peter" smack of the sea — Conan Doyle expressed his appreciation for that genre by making Watson a fan of William Clark Russell, one of the era's preeminent nautical novelists. "The Musgrave Ritual" records a cozy manor-house treasure hunt. "The Crooked Man" provides a social-realist glimpse of garrison-town military life. Crackling espionage tales like "The Adventure of the Second Stain" sit alongside sci-fi experiments like "The Adventure of the Creeping Man," in which a lust-addled elderly professor becomes addicted to a rejuvenating extract of monkey gland, which transforms him into a human-simian hybrid. The full-hearted melodrama of "The Yellow Face" gives way to the flinty, David Mamet–ish scam caper of "The Stock Broker's Clerk." The almost self-parodying "Case of Identity" seems to be mostly about Watson's fashion sense,* but immediately gives way to the brutal country revenge tale of "The Boscombe Valley Mystery," which itself threads in another of Conan Doyle's Wild West sketches, this time set in Australia.

In this expansiveness, the Holmes stories echo Conan Doyle's larger career. Basically, he could do it all — or at least thought he could, and didn't mind trying. One of his least remembered novels, *A Duet; with an Occasional Chorus,* surprised his Sherlock-centric fans of 1899 with a sober, frank (and frankly rather boring) modern love story. Just the year before, he'd published *The Tragedy of the Korosko,* a ripped-from-the-headlines terrorism thriller featuring radical Islamists on the Nile. Conan Doyle could roam at will because, apart from his almost demonic work ethic, he'd mastered some adaptable tricks of highly efficient storytelling. In nearly every Sherlock Holmes story, he compacts and nests different narrative styles and formats. A long passage written as a newspaper report cues up a breathless all-dialogue update from a street urchin or a cop, which leads to a brief zing of Watson-narrated action, followed by pages of flashback told by a single character, bracketed by Sherlock's explanation of how he solved the case. *Rapido.* And Conan Doyle's skill at interlocking distinctly told, fast-paced mini-stories makes possible his most characteristic trick: he makes you think things are happening when really nothing is happening. Just as he can turn a scene in which Holmes does nothing but stare at the ceiling into a riveting vignette (as in "The Man with the Twisted Lip"), he can concoct a high-velocity narrative out of set pieces and collaged voices, not so much action as an illusion of action. In "Noble Bachelor," many vivid scenes unfold: a wedding, a disap-

---

* The client, a woman whose fiancé has vanished, receives the Watsonian once-over: "a large woman with a heavy fur boa round her neck, and a large curling red feather in a broad-brimmed hat which was tilted in a coquettish Duchess of Devonshire fashion over her ear." Whatever his other flaws as an observer, Watson is a major clotheshorse — in this story, Holmes even compliments his "quick eye for colour." Key clues to the tale's mystery hinge on eyewear.

pearance, a police investigation, a dinner party, a gold-rush picaresque, *an Apache raid,* if you please. You can enjoy this rumpus a half-dozen times without catching the joke: Watson, our narrator, never leaves the Baker Street sitting room. Almost the whole tale is a mirage, conjured by Watson from stories told by other people.

And those other people, in Conan Doyle, can be quite something. The author populated the Baker Street scene with unforgettable minor players, and the stories often belong to them — to the Hattie Dorans — as much as to the Great Detective.

In one corner, I give you one Mr. Jabez Wilson: a fat, dull, sweaty-faced pawnbroker with flaming red hair. In the other, John Clay: "murderer, thief, smasher, and forger," rated by Sherlock Holmes as "the fourth-smartest man in London," marked with a white acid splash on his forehead and pierced ears. Like Irene Adler, these two fellows flash in and out of the Sherlockian saga in a matter of a page or three, never to return. And yet they and the story in which they appear, "The Adventure of the Red-Headed League," demonstrate how Conan Doyle crafted his dramatis personae with freehanded blending of reality and fantasy.

Wilson shows up at Baker Street perplexed. He runs a marginal hock shop in a shabby City of London square — a business notable only for his assistant, a bright young man with pierced ears and an acid-scarred forehead so eager he works for half wages. A few weeks before, this assistant showed Wilson a newspaper ad that spoke of a Red-Headed League, endowed by a lunatic American millionaire. A properly carrot-topped man, it seems, can get himself four quid a week doing virtually nothing. Aspiring gingers need only apply at an office off Fleet Street. Wilson and his helpful helper bustle off to the appointed place. There they behold men plumed in "every shade of colour . . . straw, lemon, orange, brick, Irish-setter, liver, clay." But Wilson (surprise!) is chosen by the League's officers as the reddest of them all, and plunked down with orders to copy out the *Encyclopaedia Britannica* every day for four hours. And so he does, working his way through "Abbots and Archery and Armour and Architecture and Attica," until one day he shows up to find a cryptic notice proclaiming the League dissolved. (The only forwarding address turns out to belong to an artificial-kneecaps factory.)

Any Nigerian email scammer would love to stumble upon Jabez Wilson today. His look combines lumbering disrepair (baggy checked trousers, a dirty frock coat) and macho ostentation (brassy watch chain, Masonic ornament, Chinese tattoo). And yet there is a certain oafish dignity to him: all he really wants to know is what it's all about, and he's heard that Sherlock Holmes makes a specialty of divining such things. He presents the problem, then dutifully shuffles off into oblivion. The Sherlock Holmes stories are full of Jabez Wilsons: memorable characters from all walks of Victorian life, drawn to the last detail, who get only a scene or two as they drift into and out of the Great Detective's magnetic field. Conan Doyle invents them by the score (one could say, by the league) to people his dramas' sidelines.

That pawnshop assistant's description rings a bell with Holmes, and the detective finds Wilson's report that the man spends every spare moment in the cellar practicing "photography" suggestive. Upon investigation (with breaks for sandwiches and violin concerts), Holmes discovers that "Vincent Spaulding" is really John Clay, criminal genius. The League is an elaborate ruse to shift Jabez off the premises so Clay can tunnel into the adjacent vault at the City and Suburban Bank to steal thirty thousand French gold coins.

The capture of John Clay becomes a signal moment in the young Sherlockian epic — "The Red-Headed League" was just the second short story published by the *Strand*, in August 1891. Holmes, Watson, good old Jones of Scotland Yard, and a bank officer wait in the darkened subterranean vault as Clay and his accomplice chisel their way in from below. They snatch Clay as he clambers through a hole in the floor. After a brief struggle, the criminal (who, we've learned, descends from an old duke) assumes an air of high-camp hauteur. "I beg that you will not touch me with your filthy hands," he shrills. "Have the goodness, also, when you address me always to say 'sir' and 'please.'" His few lines spoken, he exits with a theatrical bow.

If Jabez Wilson is a Conan Doylean Everyman, Clay sheds some light on how Conan Doyle adapted real criminal history and lore. A wellborn thief endowed with class and style (and pierced ears, no less) played on an enduring Victorian idea of a parallel criminal aristocracy. A venerable tradition regarded burglars, in particular, as professionals of some substance. John Binny, one of social observer Henry Mayhew's collaborators on the epic 1850s document *London Labour and the London Poor*, paid tribute to "cracksmen" as the elite among metropolitan wrongdoers: "They have the look of high-class businessmen . . . groups of them are to be seen occasionally at the taverns beside the Elephant and Castle, where they regale themselves luxuriously on the choicest wines, and are lavish with their gold." Top cracksmen patronized specialist toolmakers, notably a Birmingham custom artisan whose wares, in the 1870s, included £200 diamond drills.* The use of unoccupied adjoining buildings was standard industry practice, and many notorious incidents featured audacious tunneling. In February 1865, a gang under the command of cracksman extraordinaire Thomas Caseley penetrated a supposedly invincible jeweler's vault in Cornhill Street by slipping into the tailor's shop next door on a Saturday, tunneling into the strongroom from below, then breaking the safe at their leisure. Caseley — ultimately betrayed by a jealous woman, convicted, and transported to Western Australia — attained a brief fame. His intelligence and gentility on the witness stand, in the words of a correspondent to the *Standard*, "produced in the minds of all who heard it the feeling 'What a pity such a man should be a thief.'"

But if John Clay's short and lively fictional existence shows Conan Doyle's debt to reality, the fantastical setup — Jabez Wilson's feverdream encounter with hordes of redheads, the absurd comedy of a fat man hand-copying the *Encyclopaedia* — makes the story distinctively his own. As often as he borrowed from the real criminal news or evoked well-known outrages, he gave himself complete freedom to ignore reality. There is no trace in the Sherlock Holmes stories of the violent rival Slavic-Jewish street gangs that roamed the real East End, the Bessarabians and the Odessians. Most fictional criminals of Conan Doyle are outstripped for cruelty by the likes of Kate Webster, a domestic servant and serial thief who, in 1879, killed and chopped up her employer and scattered body parts all over London. Most famously, Jack the Ripper, who tore his bloody swath through Whitechapel in 1888, smack in between

---

* This insight, and some others on the real-world criminal milieu of the Victorian era cited here, can be found in popular historian (and Sherlockian) Donald Thomas's book *The Victorian Underworld* (New York University Press, 1998).

the publication of *A Study in Scarlet* and *The Sign of the Four*, makes no appearance.

Often, in fact, Conan Doyle was happy enough to riff on other fiction. I once spent a long, cold, fruitless afternoon wandering the north bank of the Thames, searching for possible locations for the Bar of Gold, a deliciously foul opium den — a hive of scum, villainy, and Orientalism populated by "sallow" Malays and shifty lascars — described with gusto in the opening pages of "The Man with the Twisted Lip." Watson ventures to the Bar of Gold on a solo mission of mercy, trying to find a drug-addict friend, only to discover Sherlock Holmes disguised as a poppy smoker. Watson locates the Bar of Gold and its "vile alley," Upper Swandam Lane, with some precision amid a labyrinth of sleazy streets and wharves.

I'd armed myself with photocopies of Victorian survey maps in hopes of picking from a number of passageways that then connected the riverfront to Upper Thames Street, the district's major east-west thoroughfare. I found most of the old lanes long since entombed beneath modern buildings, though Sugar Quay Walk, where the brown Thames slopped over an old stone staircase, and Swan Lane, now occupied by various financial institutions (better or worse?), at least suggested a ghostly outline of the more intricate Victorian urban geography. A few skinny byways led up to pubs — the text prominently mentions one as a landmark. In Martin Lane, I found a wine bar dating to the 1860s, and at the top of Bush Lane stood an ancient place called the Bell. Mostly, however, I just got cold.

I tempered my disappointment in my Sherlockian wayfinding skills when I discovered that, while Conan Doyle surely referred to much the same maps as I did as he devised his locations, he probably airlifted his actual opium den from elsewhere. Specifically, from Dickens: the great novelist, whom Conan Doyle naturally admired, opened *The Mystery of Edwin Drood* with a hallucinatory scene in an opium den. Dickens's den also featured various Asian mystery men,[*] as well as an Englishwoman who'd "opium smoked herself into a strange likeness of the Chinaman."

---

[*] The Victorian cultural repertoire was only partly defined by yellow-peril Orientalism. In 1892, the year after "The Man with the Twisted Lip" first appeared, the Indian liberal Dadabhai Naoroji was elected the first Asian member of Parliament.

And *Drood,* which appeared in 1870, itself relied on a trope of popular journalism: the expedition to the East End, boldly reported by some fearless correspondent, featuring an inevitable visit to an opium den. In fact, as historian Matthew Sweet argues in *Inventing the Victorians,* all those writers kept visiting the *same* opium dens. "Nearly every account . . . in nineteenth-century journalism is a description of one of two establishments in New Court, Shadwell," Sweet writes, "and the shifting cast of characters that occupied their beds and floors."

All of which is to say that Conan Doyle didn't do true crime. Real-life inspiration came in handy, but the author did very little research for his detective stories, and blasted out copy with an obvious disregard for details and consistency. (In one letter, he casually mentions completing four Sherlock Holmes stories within two weeks.) In contrast, he lavished care upon his historical novels, reading hundreds of volumes on, say, English archery, or Napoleon. Those books still have their supporters, but frankly, they are just not much fun. They labor under the onerous burden of Fact.

Though the Sherlock Holmes stories, on the other hand, insistently claim to revolve around Fact, they're really about Art. "Silver Blaze," the horse-racing story in which the dog doesn't bark, is riddled with errors that render it ridiculous *qua* horse-racing story. Holmes, for example, leaves the titular missing racehorse in the custody of a rival owner without telling anyone, and ensures, in secret, that the horse makes the start of a big race. A wee advantage at the betting counter, you might say. As Conan Doyle himself noted later, such behavior would get all concerned in quite a lot of trouble. "Half would have been in jail," the amused author noted, "and the other half warned off the turf forever." But does anyone care? In the creepy "Adventure of the Speckled Band," the author ascribes biologically impossible actions to a snake: its murderous trainer controls it with a whistle and lures it with a saucer of milk. Snakes can't hear and don't drink milk. Does anyone care?

Conan Doyle did not aspire to create a social document, but rather impression and sensation. He was making mythology, not history. For every bank vault heist fabricated from newspaper archives, there must be an invented Red-Headed League. If Conan Doyle needed a Bar of Gold, he simply transplanted a scene from Dickens and sensational newspapers.

The stories don't unfold in our world, exactly. They take place, as Conan Doyle himself would say late in his life, in a "faerie kingdom of romance."

The irony, of course, is that this all can seem so very real to certain minds. Mine, for example.

One day when I was twelve years old, my uncle showed up at our house, his eyes alight with benign mischief. He slipped me a letter in a pale blue envelope.

The envelope's front bore my name and address, written in a florid scrawl of purple ink. In my world, the finely textured writing paper was as exotic as a shrunken head. I turned the envelope over and read the return address, in that same elaborate hand:

JOHN H. WATSON, M.D.
221B BAKER STREET, LONDON W1

The note within was brief, cordial, and, to me, astounding. It rang truly *Watsonian*. Given my flickering but powerful preadolescent belief in the fantastic, this seemed like a telegram from Santa. By that point, I read Sherlock Holmes morning to midnight. In my world, people drank Diet Coke, light beer, and 2 percent solutions of milk. In the Holmesian universe, lushly suited men frequented private clubs, playing baccarat. I could tell you where the real action was. I suspect I had become a somewhat alarming child.

Bless my uncle. Bless, especially, a clever friend of his, familiar with the symptoms. They had devised the perfect plan for delighting my twelve-year-old mind. I knew, of course, that Holmes and Watson weren't "real"—the sane part of me did anyway. But this knowledge seldom troubled a brain teeming, at that moment, with whatever hormones make humans that age such ready-made cultists. (Consider how much of big-budget twenty-first-century pop culture — with its languorous vampires, Hunger Games, and endlessly revolving Supermen — originates in the fascinations of twelve-year-olds.) To that least rational, most powerful slice of my brain, the gaslit world Watson portrayed, where the most evil men in London wore astrakhan, *was* real, or something better than real.

And here in my grubby hands was an apparent fragment of that world, made solid.

It would be easy enough to attribute my Holmesian affinity to the fact that I lived in a state popularly known as a fly-fishing destination or a place to retreat to if you believe that US currency is unconstitutional. But the Sherlock Holmes stories would probably have triggered the same monomania had I lived in New York, Tokyo, or exalted London itself. Looking back, I suspect that my imagination vibrated, like a just-struck tuning fork, to the Sherlockian cycle's atavistic quality: all those adventures, so skillfully (if inattentively) machined by Arthur Conan Doyle,* can wield the hypnotic force of parables told by an elder at the campfire. His style of storytelling exerts a special power over a person whose own adventures have not quite started yet.

I recognized that this artfully counterfeited letter was part of some elaborate game that I had only begun to play myself. I was eager to improve, so I quickly replied to "Watson." Without realizing it, I was engaging in an old tradition of half-serious playacting that has surrounded Sherlock Holmes almost from the beginning. The stories later collected as the *Adventures* and *Memoirs* were still running in the *Strand* when people began to badger Arthur Conan Doyle to sign autographs as "Sherlock Holmes." The author refused. His correspondence suggests he found the business rather nettlesome. Why? Perhaps he dimly perceived an unsettling power. (His mother, whose friends wanted S.H. autographs too, thought he was being too particular.) The character's rapidly growing financial potency may also have slightly unnerved its creator, even as it funded Conan Doyle's big house and cricket habit. As much as Conan Doyle loved making money, he hated being told what to do. In his negotiations with the *Strand,* the author continually raised the price of Holmes stories — and the magazine kept saying yes. If Sherlock Holmes could prompt a magazine publisher, of all creatures, to part cheerfully with £1,000, what chance did Conan Doyle have of getting rid of the detective?

---

* In an essay in his book *Maps and Legends,* Michael Chabon offers a perceptive metaphor for the Sherlock Holmes stories: a set of interlocking gears, each designed to set the next in motion, that function as "storytelling engines."

Conan Doyle must have felt, as perhaps some of the adults in my life did when I was in the first bloom of Holmesian obsession, that things were getting a bit out of hand.

The Reform Club stands in London's Pall Mall, looking like the world's biggest funerary monument from without and a Hogwarts for grown-ups within: after negotiating entry with a laconic, shaven-skulled doorman, I stood on the mosaic-tiled floor of the club's vaulted central atrium, gawping up at gray-tan columns, a shimmering skylight dome, and towering oil paintings of dead eminences. I felt very American, and made a conscious effort to keep my jaw shut and generally act like it wasn't my first rodeo.

"Right, you've a jacket on?" The crisp presence to my right snapped me back to reality. Simon Blundell, the Reform's librarian, had graciously offered a tour of this rectangular chunk of Victoriana. I ducked into the humid cloakroom — magnificently austere, with rows of fist-sized, numbered wooden knobs mounted on the wall — to deposit my things. Blundell, an incisive young fellow, launched right into it. "Did Conan Doyle have politics of any particular sort?" he asked. I gave a half-cogent account of his Liberal Unionism. "Ah. Well, he would have been in his element here, then. The club was and is a place for ambitious people to meet other ambitious people of a similar outlook. That's how it functioned then, and that's how it functions now."

Indeed, as the librarian led me down lushly carpeted halls, through tremendous dining rooms, and along verandahs outfitted with enormous red leather chairs and marble busts, it was easy to imagine Conan Doyle being downright giddy at the prospect of joining. In spring 1891, he had set up shop as a London eye doctor. By July, the *Strand* published "A Scandal in Bohemia." In October, he was nominated to the Reform, a club originally founded as a refuge for political progressives — radical parliamentarians, campaigning journalists — of the 1840s. By '91, the Reform had lost its outright partisan flavor and welcomed men from across the literary, professional, and political spectrum, though, as Blundell explained, it retained its appeal to elite liberals. Membership was not easy to obtain; Conan Doyle had to wait until June '92 for confirmation. In a cozy room stuffed with impressively bound records, Blundell flipped through a vast Ballot Book to find Conan Doyle's entry. There: member number 5402, his strong, neat signature alongside a self-description as "author & physician." The book recorded that Thomas Wemyss Reid nominated the new man for membership. A journalist with an impressive track record as both a parliamentary beat reporter for provincial papers and a London-based editor, Reid himself was on the cusp of a knighthood. In his own memoir, he would record that the Reform harbored a blackballing clique that fought to keep new nominees out. "Personal influence . . . goes further than anything else in securing admission to a club like the Reform." Such chaps now welcomed Conan Doyle, creator of Sherlock Holmes, into their circle.

Goodbye, Southsea! Even as he insinuated himself into the London scene, however, Conan Doyle never lost his outsider's gift for observation, or his penchant for a sharply ironic twist. In "The Adventure of the Greek Interpreter," published not long after Conan Doyle joined the Reform, Watson suddenly learns that Sherlock Holmes has a brother: a smarter, older brother, name of Mycroft. Mycroft does something vague for the government and seldom appears anywhere but the Diogenes Club, "the queerest club in London," a refuge for misanthropes where speaking is forbidden, except in the Strangers' Room. The doctor and detective hustle off for Pall Mall and silently enter this social tomb. "Through the glass paneling," Watson relates, "I caught a glimpse of a large and luxurious room in which a considerable number of men were sitting about and reading papers, each in his own little nook." Mycroft wobbles into the Strangers' Room, gray-eyed, distant, and oddly sinister. He soon reveals that he has a problem for Sherlock to solve, and the adventure ensues. It's not a very good one, to be honest. Like several Sherlockian stories, "Greek Interpreter" is most noteworthy for this atmospheric scene-setter, Conan Doyle's cheeky in-joke, perhaps, for his new friends at the Reform. In the Diogenes Club, the author creates the ultimate "blackballing clique," a cabal of unsociable hermits.

"Greek Interpreter" falls among the second run of stories Conan Doyle wrote for the *Strand,* that £1,000 payday that would take book form as *The Memoirs of Sherlock Holmes.* Those stories generally achieve a darker resonance than what's come before. The earliest *Adventures* allowed a few frolics, like the quizzical "Red-Headed League" and the fashion farce of

"A Case of Identity." These earlier stories contain, for crime tales, surprisingly little violence. As Sherlock hits maturity, Conan Doyle unleashes the hard stuff: grotesquely hanged men, suffocated butlers, brained horse trainers, foiled scam artists attempting suicide, colonial military vets subjected to torture and slavery, sexual betrayals unraveling in violence.

The man writing all this grim business had become a jolly suburbanite, bronzed from constant sport and richer than he'd ever dreamed. In the summer of '92, the *Strand* sent journalist Harry How to interview its newfound star. How found the Conan Doyle family comfortably ensconced in South Norwood — they'd escaped central London as soon as Arthur chucked his eye practice for full-time writing. A "happy, genial, homely man" greeted the journalist, "tall, broad-shouldered, with a hand that grips you heartily, and, in the sincerity of its welcome, hurts." Conan Doyle eagerly showed off his house to How and photographers from the prominent firm Elliott & Fry. (Remember them? Their shop was in Baker Street.) His wife and girl scampered off to let the men smoke cigars amid creative clutter: various Doyles' artwork, Arctic mementos, china looted from Egyptian palaces (given in payment for medical services back in Southsea), cricket souvenirs, a portrait of Joseph Bell, Sherlock's inspiration.

Conan Doyle must have been in a chipper mood. He rambled through his biography and expounded on his admiration for medieval English archers. He disclosed that he often devised his Sherlock Holmes plots while playing cricket, or riding with Touie on a two-person tricycle with enormous wheels, or on the tennis court. Meanwhile, the newly besotted public was bombarding him with curious (but useless) ideas for Sherlock. The recent post carried details of a New Zealand poisoning case, and a huge wad of documents concerning a disputed will in Bristol. He didn't need any of that, Conan Doyle assured his visitor; he had enough material in mind to keep Holmes going for some time. The next story, he vowed, would be the most puzzling yet!*

---

* Conan Doyle never lacked chutzpah. A few months before the How interview, he experimented with writing a one-act play — and sent the result straight to Henry Irving, one of the most famous actors of his day and an old Conan Doyle favorite. Irving and his manager, Bram Stoker, of later *Dracula* fame, loved the piece and bought

A few months after this convivial glimpse of Conan Doyle in his castle, the *Strand*'s readers absorbed "The Cardboard Box." An innocent elderly lady in the suburbs has received a gruesome parcel: two freshly severed human ears, one male, one female, roughly packed in salt. Sherlock Holmes takes a look at the box, a look at the recipient's ears, snoops gently into the family traumas, and deduces that the female item belongs to a sister. The perpetrator, when captured, tells a horrific tale, one of the grimmest extended verbatim quotes in the Holmes cycle. He married a girl, and they loved each other, but he took to drink, and boiled his mind in alcohol. Under the influence of a conniving fellow female, the wife entered into an adulterous affair. One afternoon, the drunken husband trailed the wife and her lover to a seaside resort, where they rented a pleasure boat and paddled off into a hazy afternoon. The husband followed, tracking them through a gauzy mist that soon isolated the two boats, well out to sea. There, the drunkard beat the lovers to death and slashed off one ear apiece as revenge tokens. "You can hang me," the killer says, "but you cannot punish me as I've been punished already."

Stark stuff. When it came time to publish *Memoirs* as a collection, Conan Doyle couldn't quite embrace the sordid tale. He cut "Cardboard Box" out of the anthology, and the book appeared with just eleven stories. The author often oscillated between brutal honesty and a well-honed, almost reflexive suppressive instinct — think of him brazenly misdating his father's death in his own memoirs — and while he cited the story's sexual misdeeds as the reason for its omission, it's not hard to imagine that its portrait of hardcore alcoholism troubled Conan Doyle just as much. In December 1892, his mother wrote to the superintendent of the Crichton

---

it outright. *Waterloo,* a glimpse of an old Napoleonic veteran, became an Irving staple. The following year, Conan Doyle and his friend J. M. Barrie (*Peter Pan,* etc.) collaborated on a musical. It flopped. Barrie then wrote an affectionate Sherlockian parody titled "The Adventure of the Two Collaborators," in which Barrie and Conan Doyle themselves descend on Baker Street for a face-to-face with Sherlock Holmes. The two real-life writers demand that Holmes attend their failed play to help them figure out why it turned out such a disaster. Holmes refuses. Conan Doyle threatens him. Holmes remains steadfast. Conan Doyle draws a knife. Holmes magically melts away, finally dwindling to nothing more than a ring of smoke floating by the ceiling, taunting Conan Doyle in a ghostly voice: "Fool, fool!" Perceptive fellow, J. M. Barrie.

asylum, where Charles Altamont Doyle had resided for most of the year after being diagnosed with dementia and getting booted from his previous institution for general incorrigibility. (Arthur had signed the transfer certificate.) "My poor husband's condition was brought on by drink," Mary wrote the institution. "Using the most awful expedients, many times putting himself within reach of the law — to get drink — every article of value he or I possessed carried off secretly . . . There is a public house in Edinburgh where I am told they have a most valuable collection of his sketches, given for drink . . . He would strip himself of all his underclothing, take the very bed linen, climb down the water spout at risk of his life, break open the children's money boxes. He even drank furniture varnish . . . If he were free again I believe he would kill himself in a few weeks."

At roughly the time Mary Doyle wrote these lines, her son would have been at work on "The Cardboard Box." He was the cheerful clubman, the literary star, the suburban cyclist — but also a person who wondered if the cosmos had any purpose. He'd rejected Roman Catholicism. The Anglican faith of his mother and wife was, perhaps, not hot-blooded enough for him. For years he'd been reading books about Spiritualism, the pseudoscientific pursuit of evidence for life beyond death. He had convened séances and sought out wizened mediums. He saw things in those sessions that fed his curiosity and his very particular and peculiar sense of morality. "Let every inquirer bear in mind that phenomena are only a means to an end," he wrote to the Spiritualist magazine *Light* in 1887, ". . . simply useful as giving us assurance of an after existence for which we are to prepare by refining away our grosser animal feelings and cultivating our higher, nobler impulses." Yes, refine away those grosser animal feelings, by all means. "The Cardboard Box" had to vanish. Of his father's decline, he once wrote in a letter, "better to keep it in Scotland." But there was a lot churning inside that big brain and body that couldn't be addressed by sociable afternoons at the Reform Club or a tennis game. Those passions and doubts had to surface somewhere — in the final lines of "The Cardboard Box," for instance. "'What is the meaning of it, Watson?' said Sherlock Holmes solemnly . . . 'What object is served by this circle of misery and violence and fear? It must tend to some end, or else our universe is ruled by chance, which is unthinkable. But what end?'"

· · ·

Yes, it's a rotten vale of tears. You need a friend to get through it, someone who has your back, someone to pry the coke needle out of your hand when things get too weird, someone to help you listen to all . . . those . . . people's . . . bloody . . . problems.

Sherlock has his Watson, and he'd be lost without him. John H. Watson becomes the dark matter of the Sherlockian universe, the force that mysteriously holds the whole thing together. Only he, among the four million souls in Conan Doyle's semi-imaginary London, can unlock the hermetic personality of that brilliant detective, who, left to his own devices, would smoke himself into oblivion while alphabetizing help-wanted ads from the *Standard.* We would be lost without him, too. So thank the muses that Conan Doyle created such a good guy — a rock, a chum, a man of action with an eye for the ladies, occasionally a depressive bastard, but above all someone modern culture doesn't mind hanging out with for 130 years or so.

Sherlock can be rather abusive toward John, what with all those digs on his literary output and incessant demands that he abandon hearth and home to chase criminals. We can all treat people we love that way, I suppose. Deep down, the arch-investigator knows the truth. By "The Adventure of the Red-Headed League"— early days in Conan Doyle's creation of the saga — Holmes describes the army doctor, once his random roommate, as his "partner and helper." Just as Watson has somehow figured out how to live with and (though he would never put it like this) adore the prickly detective, Holmes has discovered something very surprising in Watson, who masquerades as the embodiment of Normal. "You share my love of all that is bizarre and outside the convention and humdrum routine of everyday life," Holmes says with confidence. (One can imagine Watson thinking, *I do?* But he does.) Of more practical moment, Holmes knows that he can trust Watson with his life. He will always clean and load his old service revolver and stand ready for battle. He's the man you want sitting next to you as you wait in a darkened room for a highly trained poisonous snake or the fourth-most-dangerous man in London. In "The Adventure of the Copper Beeches," when a wild mastiff leaps upon his master and begins mauling his throat (he frankly deserves it), Watson is the man to step forward and coolly pump bullets into the beast. He's an old campaigner, a rough-and-ready traveler who can throw a toothbrush and a pulp novel in a bag and zip across the country by train at a minute's notice.

Conan Doyle no doubt had many people in mind, at various times, as he shaped Watson (himself, among others). More than any one specific model, though, it seems that the author envisioned Watson as a certain *type* of man: the energetic all-rounder. Conan Doyle's occasional glimpses of Watson's world beyond Baker Street add up. In *The Sign of the Four*, Watson reveals he's been to Australia's gold-mining country, for example. Australia? When? How? But then the author himself, despite the modesty of his upbringing, had seen Paris, the Arctic, and Africa by the time he wrote that novel. Conan Doyle's sort of chap went out and did things in the world. Much later, Watson mentions in passing that he'd played rugby for Blackheath Football Club. This seems a throwaway line now, but Conan Doyle's contemporary readers would have recognized Blackheath as not just any rugby club, but the third-oldest team in the world, one that played a crucial role in the sport's evolution.* To play for Blackheath in the mid-to-late 1870s, when Watson would have been a sporty young buck studying medicine in London, was to battle with rugby's elite. A man like Lennard Stokes might have crossed Conan Doyle's mind as he dropped this Watsonian tidbit: a mustachioed three-quarter back who starred for Blackheath and England while he pursued a distinguished medical career, in precisely the years in which Watson would have played his rugby. Men like Stokes — serious amateur sportsmen who also achieved merit far from the playing fields — populated Victorian life. Conan Doyle was one of them himself, and he crafted a part of Watson in that bluff and hearty image.

Yet Watson is not all rugby and man-of-the-world machismo. We often find him brooding in a "brown study," restlessly shuffling through boring newspapers, staring at Baker Street's decorative pictures of war heroes, and meditating on human folly. We feel the throb of an inner pain and loneliness. (In *A Study in Scarlet*, he declares that he has neither "kith nor kin in England.") He may also have self-destructive tendencies.

---

* Blackheath led the breakaway that separated infant rugby from its equally formative twin, soccer. A club member disdained the other football's less violent rules as fit only for "a lot of Frenchmen." Arsenal fans, take note.

Sherlock keeps Watson's chequebook locked in a drawer, in some form of financial protective custody. The doctor at times displays a propensity toward excessive self-medication with claret. He sinks into laziness — in "A Scandal in Bohemia," Holmes notes that the newly married John has larded on seven pounds since his last appearance at Baker Street. Sometimes Watson reports himself "fleet of foot," but at others he notes his own "complete lack of training."

A bit of a moody yo-yo, dear Watson, perhaps always slightly dissatisfied. When he's batched-up at Baker Street, he craves a wife and a sturdy medical practice. When he's married and making the rounds of patients, he longs for Sherlock Holmes and crime. He must be difficult to live with in either mode; his wife* seems oddly eager to be rid of him every time an "urgent" note arrives from Holmes. "Oh, Anstruther would do your work for you," she blithely says one time — a comment I've come to worry might conceal some fairly dire happenings in the Watsonian marital scene. Watson, for his part, seems to find ordinary domesticity somehow soul-sucking; it leaves him physically "pale" and in need of a solid dose of deadly adventure. Like Sherlock Holmes, he rebels at stagnation.

Thus he needs Sherlock, and remains faithful long after most people would have told the bloodhound of Baker Street to take his acerbic comments and indoor revolver practice elsewhere. Over the cycle of stories, Watson's service — he actually uses that word — to Holmes attains an almost ministerial quality. For all his many pursuits, Watson finds his true vocation lies simply in being around Sherlock Holmes, in an equal partnership with the ultimate difficult-but-brilliant personality. He's faithful to his friend even when his friend is insufferable — he can see beyond all that. At some early point, Watson decides that, whatever other aspects of his life he may have screwed up, he can do *this:* he can be Sherlock Holmes's friend.

In Watson, Conan Doyle crafts one of literature's great studies in devotion. In return, Holmes comes to need Watson, though usually that need

---

* Okay, all I will say on the subject of Watson's wives is that it's commonly assumed, among Sherlockians, that he had more than one, maybe three, perhaps as many as five. Mary Morstan from *The Sign of the Four* is *probably* the first, but . . . it's a can of worms. Leave it. Just leave it.

is unacknowledged. Going down to a major university town to study ancient English charters? Better bring Watson. Running a long con against a ring of German spies? Better bring Watson. Need someone to race over to the library and learn everything there is to know about Chinese pottery (because Holmes *says so,* that's why)? Watson is your man. Above all, Watson's long career becomes an exemplar of sustained love, one we can all heed. Who couldn't use a manual on how to conduct a thick-and-thin committed relationship?

Of course, the doctor was not alone. By the time the stories of the *Memoirs* rolled through the *Strand* in their self-assured glory, Sherlock Holmes had become a very popular figure indeed. The newspapers used him as a byword for excellence. Women wrote asking to become his "housekeeper." Everyone, it seemed, loved the Great Detective, the scintillating sage of Baker Street.

Or, almost everyone.

5

MORIARTY & FRIENDS

THE HAIR ALMOST impaled me. Dark brunette ringlets cascaded from an eruption of feathers — bristling strata of quills protruding from a young woman's head at aggressive angles, swerving at me in the cash-bar line. A second before, I'd worried about snagging on the massive bustle attached to the back of her dress like a silken crustacean, possibly garnering a citation under some New York City ordinance not enforced in a century. I backed away. Such are the risks, it seems, among Sherlockians.

I removed myself to a safe distance. The lady in question wore elaborate layers of lace and light and dark olive green. And while she may have been the most impressively arrayed personage among the seventy-five or so at the Salmagundi Club that January night, she was hardly out of place. Men wearing top hats intended to evoke 1891 strolled the creaky floors of the antique artists' fraternity founded in 1871, on Manhattan's Fifth Avenue. Bowler hats and tweeds were in heavy use, likewise walking sticks and deerstalkers. Off to one side, a three-piece band sawed out a magnificently Gothic dirge.

I had come to New York at the beginning of 2013 in answer to a Sherlockian homing signal of sorts. The Baker Street Irregulars, the eight-decade-old mother ship of a small, dedicated subculture of Holmes enthusiasts, hold an annual New York meeting on or around 6 January of every year.* The event traces back to some convivial evenings in the 1930s, when a few New York literary chaps gathered to raise a post-Prohibition toast to Sherlock Holmes. This heritage makes the annual conclave one of the oldest manifestations of what we now recognize as fan culture. Sure, people always went nutty for the boxer, singer, fainting literary heroine, artistically suicidal young poet, or racehorse of the moment. But the Baker Street Irregulars date to the era when lovers of particular pop-cultural and literary phenomena began to organize as a self-conscious force. While it's a long way from a cocktail hour in 1934 to a Frodo cosplayer at Comic Con, the Irregulars form a thread that ties together decades of pop-cultural celebration and obsession.

If the BSI itself represents something old, the event at the Salmagundi represented something new. The annual Sherlockian rendezvous in New York spiraled out of hand long ago, into a full weekend (Weekend) of spin-off events, sideline dinners, and informal cocktail sessions alongside the flagship (and invite-only) BSI dinner. This particular gathering, the Daintiest Thing Under a Bonnet Ball — the title, a tribute to Irene Adler — arose from the young women known as the Baker Street Babes. The Babes had never staged an Irregulars Weekend event, and as a first attempt, the ball looked decidedly impressive. Tables stacked deep with Sherlockian books, art, and collectibles lined the walls, holding such delights as teas in flavors inspired by the BBC's *Sherlock* series and a tower of pastiche novels bearing titles like *Sherlock Holmes: Séance for a Vampire*. Silent and live auctions would raise money to benefit wounded military veterans, in a nod to Watson's Afghan misadventures.

Amid the crowd I met Ardy, a German-born, England-living librarian and one of the Baker Street Babes — who, as a group, tend to favor Internet-friendly handles. In a short two years, they'd developed a twenty-first-century remix of the Sherlockian folkways that began with those bygone New York bookmen. "We staged a flash mob on Trafalgar Square," Ardy said by way of example. (The previous April, scores of peo-

---

* This frigid scheduling owes to the conceit — invented by Sherlock fans, eons ago, because the detective twice quotes *Twelfth Night,* and seems to be slightly hungover on 7 January in *The Valley of Fear,* and other random reasons — that 6 January is Sherlock's birthday. Roll with it!

ple assumed frozen poses beneath signs calling for the preservation of Undershaw, one of Conan Doyle's former homes, threatened by redevelopment.) "And these two fifteen-year-old twin girls from Chicago, of all places, came over to be part of it. They were so cute, and so earnest. They told us that, of course, they are the only kids in their school who are into Sherlock Holmes. No one back home gets it at all. They seemed so happy just to be there, and we all just wanted to hug them. So many people have a different version of that same story."

I knew it well: the geeky but pure thrill of finding other people who share your *thing*. I patrolled the gallery's fringe and marveled at the room filled with eccentric evening wear evoking an imaginary nineteenth-century world. This is how we enjoy culture now. There must be *Mad Men*–themed cocktail parties, Westeros-inspired bridal-party dresses (I've seen the video), and fan-written fiction detailing every imaginable erotic recombination of the Hogwarts student body. Though some of that behavior horrifies a faction of Sherlockians devoted to more reserved Old Ways, the subculture's long history anticipated what fans of every pop medium do all the time now.

The Daintiest Thing Ball expressed some truly exuberant Sherlock love. Fan-created paintings and drawings, including dramatic renderings of Benedict Cumberbatch and Martin Freeman in their BBC roles, figured prominently. At one table I discovered a most wonderful oddity: a framed drawing depicting a selection of Holmesian characters — Irene Adler, Mrs. Hudson, Holmes and Watson, others — as grinning skulls. Macabre, but appropriate in its way. It was quite possible that none of us would have gathered that evening if our beloved Great Detective hadn't once tumbled into the Great Beyond. The skulls recalled one of the strangest plot twists in the Sherlock Holmes saga, from 1886 to circa right now, when nice young people sip cocktails in neo-Victorian headdresses: the death of Sherlock Holmes.

Arthur Conan Doyle had a cold.

He sat by the fire on an April day, nursing his misery, reading *Pride and Prejudice* for the first time, murdering the Great Detective. He was in the middle of composing a final Sherlock Holmes story, he wrote his mother, "after which the gentleman vanishes, never to reappear."

Oh, everyone begged him not to do it. He'd almost terminated the detective as the twelve-story *Adventures* cycle neared its conclusion, but his mother intervened. ("You won't! You can't! You mustn't!") The gents at the *Strand* found the prospect of Sherlock's end very alarming — they were selling 500,000 copies a month, and it's not hard to imagine Sherlock Holmes as the chief reason. The author would not be dissuaded. "I am weary," he informed the Ma'am, "of his name."

People say all sorts of things about this. They say Conan Doyle "hated" Holmes, et cetera. I think he was simply irritated. Conan Doyle was a human perpetual motion machine. Around the time he plotted Holmes's demise, he was getting his house painted, helping his sister prepare for her wedding, practicing for his first major London speech, and remonstrating with his mother over financial matters. In a word, busy. In his voluminous letters, he seldom mentioned Holmes except in passing. Cricket, yes. Thirty-mile tandem bike rides, yes. Partying with his fellow literati, yes. Holmes, not so much — let alone any evidence of pathological rage. The killing was a professional, not psychological, decision. By 1893, Conan Doyle wanted more attention paid to his historical novels and was eager to begin a lecture career and continue writing for the stage. Considering the letters streaming in asking for him to sign autographs *as* Sherlock Holmes, it's not hard to imagine he felt trapped on Baker Street. "It was still the Sherlock Holmes stories for which the public clamoured," he would recall. "I was in danger of having my hand forced."

Of course, he couldn't just shank Holmes in some Limehouse alley, or have him bludgeoned by your average malignant country squire. A phenomenon's end demanded a setting with flair. And on a recent hiking vacation in Switzerland, Conan Doyle had espied just the place. As he tromped through the mountains near the hamlet of Meiringen with friends, the party neared Reichenbach Falls, a 250-meter Alpine cascade. According to one account, Conan Doyle and his pals were already lightheartedly debating his determination to slay Sherlock. Seeing his unswerving intent, one companion pointed to the waterfall: behold, a fitting grave for the master of Baker Street. Conan Doyle agreed. Now he just needed a killer.

. . .

Readers of the December 1893 issue of the *Strand* became the first (but not the last) startled to find John Watson striking ominous tones: "It is with a heavy heart that I take up my pen to write these the last words in which I shall ever record the singular gifts by which my friend Sherlock Holmes was distinguished." What the hell is this? And then, the title: "The Final Problem." And the gorgeous (but alarming) Sidney Paget frontispiece, depicting Holmes enwrapped with some old codger on the lip of a jagged precipice, foamy spray misting the background.

Things only get weirder from there. After some emoting (". . . a void in my life"), Watson lets slip the unknown name Professor Moriarty, and vows that at last (?) he will reveal what transpired between this mysterious personage and Sherlock Holmes. The nascent Baker Street Babe finds herself adrift here. Watson abandons his usual formulae: no 221B fireside, no Holmes grumbling over a test tube, no worried client. Instead, Sherlock appears at Watson's married-life abode one April night (in April, recall, Conan Doyle sat sneezing homicidally over his Jane Austen) with bloody knuckles and a nervy vibe. He closes the shutters, babbling about the risk of "air-guns" (??), and suggests, out of the blue, that he and Watson bolt for the Continent.

The good doctor is as befuddled as anyone, and Sherlock's explanation does nothing to lift the fog. It seems Holmes is engaged in a climactic struggle of wits against an arch-criminal, "the Napoleon of Crime" no less: James Moriarty, a professor of mathematics (???) gone terribly wrong, now supposedly running criminal London. "For years past I have continually been conscious of . . . some deep organizing power which forever stands in the way of the law, and throws its shield over the wrongdoer," Holmes proclaims. "He is the organizer of half that is evil and of nearly all that is undetected in this great city."

Well, this is news.

On the upside, Holmes explains that he stands mere days away from rolling up the Moriarty *apparat*. The rub is, the cops can't act until Monday (for some reason), and the professor's thugs are on the prowl, looking to kill Holmes before he can close his case. They're waylaying him on street corners, and shortly attempt to burn down 221B. (Projecting much, Arthur?) Moriarty even paid a personal call, which Sherlock recounts with memorable descriptive flourish: the reptilian professor, skeletally thin and huge of skull, his head oscillating in a most sinister way, threatens his rival in cadences worthy of Churchill, fifty years on. "You hope to place me in the dock," Moriarty declares. "I tell you that I never will stand in the dock. You hope to beat me. I tell you that you will never beat me."

Thus this hasty jaunt abroad. Watson naturally agrees, and after some mumbo-jumbo involving a masked cab driver and Holmes skulking about a train station disguised as an elderly Italian priest, they're off. The trip proves one of literature's most miserable European vacations. The duo wanders forlornly into the Swiss mountains, somehow ending up at Reichenbach: "a fearful place," "a tremendous abyss," a "boiling pit of incalculable depth," and then an "abyss" again, in case the inattentive reader hasn't grasped that if one, say, lucklessly plummeted into this chasm, one would be dead, kaput, finito, no inquest necessary.

At this point, a screamingly transparent subterfuge lures Watson away, leaving Holmes alone, brooding at the cliff's edge, completely at Arthur Conan Doyle's mercy. Watson returns to find the scene deserted. Many signs of struggle (and an annoyingly calm farewell note from Holmes) suggest that Moriarty tracked the detective down, and they both tumbled into the Reichenbach after a mano-a-mano wrestling match.

While "The Final Problem" is quite gripping when one first reads it, a step back reveals a deed hastily done. An evil (but unarmed) math professor? A waterfall? In bloody Switzerland? It's as if Conan Doyle bellows at you from the beyond: *I know, it's not great, and I don't care. Sherlock Holmes is dead! Dead! Dead!* We hear you, man. Watson signs off in a soggy jumble of confused detail and heartbreaking sentiment, echoing Aristotle to eulogize "the best and wisest man I have ever known." And so ends the Sherlockian saga. Apparently.

My New York adventure with the Baker Street Irregulars and their accomplices began in a midtown conference room filled with attentive people, many in deerstalker caps, listening to a man in a tan-vested tuxedo discuss the nature of evil. The BSI Lecture stood out as one of few Weekend events organized around discourse rather than highballs. At the podium, Kim Newman, a mustachioed British writer responsible for an admirably strange oeuvre of speculative, genre-warping fiction — in his novel *Anno Dracula,* the vampiric Transylvanian count has become ruler of England — considered the curious case of Professor Moriarty.

"With international banking in the shape it is now," Newman said, "with massacres in every corner of the globe, with our culture reduced to kibble — there must be a Moriarty." Newman limned the professor — who appears directly only in "The Final Problem," as a distant figure spotted on a speeding train, like a witch on a broomstick — as an archetype. "The diabolical mastermind," he offered. "Literally a race apart. Perhaps genuinely unkillable . . . Our recent past has been overloaded with them . . . Moriarty has lived many lives." His lecture wove fiction and reality, connecting Moriarty to organizations ranging from SPECTRE to Lehman Brothers. Look at the world, Newman insisted; the "mathematician of murder" must still be at large. And even though "falling from high places seems to be an occupational hazard for diabolical masterminds" — witness Lucifer — he noted, with eyebrows cocked, "his body was never found."

As I sat in the back of the room, Newman's talk recalled an old question. Where did Moriarty come from? In "The Final Problem" the professor emerges (and then submerges) fully formed, a heat-seeking missile aimed at Sherlock Holmes. Conan Doyle's construction of the Napoleon of Crime has occasioned much speculation. In the spectacularly nutty 1970s treatise *Naked Is the Best Disguise,* Samuel Rosenberg argued at length that Conan Doyle intended Moriarty as a symbolic incarnation of Friedrich Nietzsche, for whom the upright Scotsman did not care one bit.* I doubt that the author had to dig that deep. For one thing, the real criminal scene provided several models. Adam Worth, a German-born American, conveniently dubbed "the Napoleon of Crime" by London police during an outrageous career of high-society robberies and scams, stood trial in the spring of 1893, just as Conan Doyle wrote "The Final

---

* Rosenberg's thesis, audacious in its wild-eyed post-Freudian swagger, is that the entire Sherlockian saga is an elaborate allegory, strewn with coded images of deviant sex and mass murder by an obsessively repressed Conan Doyle. Well, whatever. His book was a pretty big hit back in '74, and remains worth tracking down despite some notable inaccuracies and rampant homophobia. It's an entertaining glimpse of 1970s cogitation in action, and proves — if nothing else — that there's more to Holmes than meets the eye.

Problem." Other antique malefactors suggest themselves. James Saward, alias "Jem the Penman," a criminal defense lawyer (and hapless gambler with large debts), ran a network of forgers and crooks out of his Inner Temple chambers for decades before the authorities caught him and transported him to Australia in 1857. "Barrister Saward" came to grief because he became entangled with the Great Bullion Robbery of '55, an extraordinarily complex (ultimately foiled) railway heist of £12,000 in gold. It was an age of criminal ambition. According to the *London City Press* of 1 August 1857, the government packed a single Australia-bound convict ship with an all-star cast: a trio of "fraudulent bankers" (including a baronet); "Robson, the Crystal Palace forger"; "Redpath, who committed the forgeries on the Great Northern Railway"; and Edgar Agar, the Bullion Robbery's mastermind.

Saward stood out even among these luminaries, according to the newspaper, as "the putter-up of all the great robberies in the metropolis for the last twenty years." A short imaginative skip gets you to Conan Doyle's "organizer of half that is evil and nearly all that is undetected in this great city." Saward's legend endured into Sherlockian times: a popular, frequently revived play recast the bent barrister as a (yes) diabolical mastermind atop an international ring of ne'er-do-wells.

In fiction, the figure of the all-seeing overlord of evil goes back at least to Hecate, the moonstruck Greek goddess whom Shakespeare deployed in *Macbeth* as the Weird Sisters' spiritual adviser, "the close contriver of all harms." In Victorian culture's "psychic underworld" (to borrow an evocative term from a modern academic), criminal conspiracies loomed large, particularly in the "sensation" fiction of midcentury, which did so much to lay the groundwork for Sherlock Holmes.

And inspirations aside, Conan Doyle already owned the perfect prototype: Holmes. To destroy the Great Detective, the author simply reversed the character's polarities. He endowed the professor with eccentric scientific talent (math, versus Holmes's medico-chemistry). Just as Holmes sat snug in Baker Street, attuned to the secret affairs of London, Conan Doyle placed his cracked academic "motionless, like a spider in the centre of its web, but that web has a thousand radiations, and he knows well every quiver of each of them." He made Moriarty as famous among crooks as the detective was among cops. Holmes acknowledged Moriarty as an intellectual equal. He might have said evil twin.

And like Sherlock Holmes, Moriarty provokes the imagination. In light of what Conan Doyle thought he wanted in 1893, this was a huge mistake. By adding a rival of truly mythic proportions, he gave people one more reason to keep thinking about Sherlock Holmes—another figure, like Irene Adler, that invites speculation. Here we were in 2013, speculating. Kim Newman himself stood as a good example of a now-long-established urge to mess with Moriarty. His 2011 novel *The Hound of the D'Urbervilles* gives the basic Holmesian setup a merrily perverse flip: it makes Moriarty the protagonist, with thuggish henchman Colonel Moran serving as a bizarre-world Watson. With Moran narrating like a rabid pit bull, the pair engages in criminal adventures with names like "A Shambles in Belgravia" and "The Red Planet League." Throughout, Newman furiously twists together various strains of Victorian fiction, as the title's Thomas Hardy reference suggests. "You want to create a sense of a populated universe, where everyone's paths cross," he told the room of Irregulars of his own work. "Maybe it goes back to when Hercules joined up with the Argonauts ... You can create a sense that all these people from different stories know each other. Maybe they don't like each other very much."

A populated universe: that's what Conan Doyle created while he thought he was writing mere detective stories. Moriarty completed the cosmology, adding the ever-necessary incarnation of evil. And when he threw his villain and his detective into that Swiss waterfall, the author permanently lost his role as this crowded world's sole diabolical mastermind.

People wore black armbands in the streets of the city when Sherlock Holmes "died." Or at least that was the story. For decades—generations, really—a legend circulated that the *Strand*'s fatal issue inspired London lads to don mourning clothes. It's a good story, reflecting the enthusiasm for a character that had climbed from obscurity to iconhood in just a few years. It doesn't seem to be true, unfortunately. Recently, Sherlockians have searched high and low for documentary evidence that someone—anyone—wore a black armband, in public, in London, for any

Holmes-related reason. So far, nothing. I commissioned an investigation of my own, hiring a real historian to complement my own asystematic, pseudo-Sherlock research methods. (Hiring an investigator, by the way, is really fun.) His digging suggested that the Adventure of the Phantom Armbands began with John Dickson Carr's 1949 biography of Conan Doyle. Carr, an eminent mystery writer in his own right, spent some time professionally entangled with one of Conan Doyle's sons. A certain hagiographical project may have been in the works. (Others have reached the same conclusion.)

The real reaction to Sherlock's odd Swiss assassination appears more subtle. (Well, not in the case of one female reader, who blasted Conan Doyle with "YOU BRUTE.") The press columns of December 1893 reverberate with disappointment and bemusement. The *Guernsey Star* opines: "Dr. Conan Doyle has crowned his achievements . . . by killing Sherlock Holmes . . . We cannot say that this culmination of the famous detective's career is particularly impressive." More in sorrow than in anger, the editorialist continues that the story simply beggars belief. (Presciently, the *Star* wonders: "How does Watson know exactly what happened when he was not present?") The *Leeds Times* mourns "the most famous detective probably of any age or any country . . . one of the most interesting creatures of contemporary literature." The *Times* journalist also points out the inconvenient truth that Sherlock Holmes made Conan Doyle famous, not vice versa. "This murder at the ledge of the gorge is surely a scurvy return for all that the great detective has done for his friend and, if I may be permitted to say so, it is bad art." The *Strand* replaces Holmes with a series called "Stories from the Diary of a Doctor," which one reviewer finds small consolation for "the lamented and violent death of that gentleman."

By the time "The Final Problem" dropped the Reichenbach bombshell, Conan Doyle had more serious problems on his hands. His father died in October 1893, at the Crichton asylum. (In swooping calligraphy, the official record of his demise lists Charles Altamont's occupation as "Artist" and the cause of death as epilepsy.) Around that time, Conan Doyle's wife, Touie, began complaining of pain and cough. A doctor diagnosed irreversible tuberculosis — "consumption," as they quaintly called this not very quaint illness. The case might have festered for years before discovery, a fact that has raised some eyebrows, given that Conan Doyle had made a special study of the illness during his medical career. If he'd been a bit oblivious, however, Arthur reacted with zeal, planning an aggressive campaign to preserve his wife's life: a long-term sojourn back in Switzerland, where the Conan Doyles now knew Davos and St. Moritz, followed by the dry climes of Egypt. Meanwhile, Conan Doyle felt the stress acutely. "What with Connie's wedding, Papa's death, and Touie's illness," he wrote, "it is a little overwhelming."

The Conan Doyle brood transformed into a "migratory tribe," as he once described it, circulating between Swiss mountains, Cairene deserts, and England, where the author commissioned the building of Undershaw, a country home where he hoped Touie could be comfortable during her permanent convalescence. As always, he wrote and wrote — the Napoleonic adventures of Brigadier Gerard, his novel of terrorism on the Nile, and a lightly fictionalized story cycle about his early medical career were merely highlights. He dabbled in politics, delivering speeches against Irish home rule, and in cricket, taking on some of the game's top players. He sat in the Reform Club, popping off letters to the press on the latest literary controversies.

A taxing business, being Arthur Conan Doyle, requiring a steady influx of capital. He made plenty of money. I once reviewed a random cross-section of his royalty statements from the mid-1890s, from an archive that did not by any means amount to a comprehensive look at his financial status but which demonstrated that he was constantly cashing fat checks. A single day's business in 1896 might bring, for example, $1,488.31 (over $40,000 by today's valuations) from America, for his medical short stories alone. By 1897, the Canadian royalties on a single minor novel, *The Doings of Raffles Haw,* amounted to more than he'd made in a year in the previous decade.

Still, he had a sick wife, two kids, an expanding clan to which he played financial paterfamilias, and a cricket habit to support. Conan Doyle counted every penny as he built and furnished Undershaw to the tune of some £7,000. And he knew that among his literary creations he had one guaranteed moneymaker — inconveniently submerged in a Swiss waterfall. By the fall of 1897, just four years after doing the deed at Reichenbach, Conan Doyle landed upon a device to revive Holmes, at least as a business proposition: the stage.

Actors and playwrights had toyed with Sherlock, in unauthorized oddments that made little impression on either theater history or the Conan Doyle bank account. Charles Brookfield's satirical music-hall impersonation, the first recorded stage Sherlock, supposedly enraged Conan Doyle; it may have been a bit camp for his taste. (The Watson character is recorded as repeatedly exclaiming, "Oh, Sherlock, you wonderful man!") The same year, a Glasgow theater staged *Sherlock Holmes, Private Detective,* in which a homicidal maniac kidnaps Watson. The *Glasgow Herald* praised actor John Webb's Holmes, but observed, "It is mostly a weird play." Sherlock had still other afterlives on stage: *Claude Duval,* a farce created for the comedian Arthur Roberts, featured a detective character named "Sherlock Holmes-Spotter." An actor named Max Goldberg prospered in the provinces and suburbs with a play titled *The Bank of England, an Adventure in the Life of Sherlock Holmes.*

Conan Doyle's thoughts on these efforts are unknown but easy to guess: someone was making money off the old franchise, and it wasn't him. An *authorized* theatrical Holmes, with the character's creator running the show (or, even better, just collecting the royalties), began to seem the most excellent possible use for a dead detective.

William Hooker Gillette, the American actor, mused upon a script by Arthur Conan Doyle, landed in his hands via theatrical business channels. Would he do it? Gillette — renowned for the ripping melodramas *Secret Service* and *Held by the Enemy* — descended from old Connecticut grandees. William became stage-besotted as a youth — he and a pal forged a printed playbill to con Gillette's killjoy father into believing that a touring melodrama was a Shakespearean play, suitable for their eyes. Starting as a young man, he climbed the ranks, from unpaid walk-on at Ben de Barr's theater in St. Louis and in New Orleans to starring roles in New York and the West End, where he scored a success in *Coriolanus.*

Fresh off a London hit with his Civil War rouser *Secret Service,* he needed a new vehicle. Sherlock Holmes — now here was an idea. Gillette stood regally tall and bore a hawkish face chiseled from granite. Even though he starred in melodramas, he'd pioneered theatrical restraint: "coolness and resource . . . nonchalance at moments of extreme physical peril," in the words of the *Illustrated Sporting and Dramatic News.* (Gertrude Stein once paid tribute to his "silence stillness and quick movement," arguing that Gillette invented the style of acting best suited to cinema.) Surely the detective would be perfect for him, even if, at forty-five, he was arguably a bit old for the role. (Publicity gave him an 1855 birthday, but he'd been born in '53. He would also be said to have "studied" at Yale, MIT, Boston University, and Harvard, a statement crafted with care, because he had no college degree.) The character, blending dash and gravitas, appealed.

This Conan Doyle script, however, would not do at all. Gillette wrote his most popular scripts himself, always ready to chop, change, and revise anything that failed to connect with audiences. If *Sherlock Holmes* was to fulfill its destiny as a hit, it needed his practiced hand.

A deal was made. Gillette set to work. Using a common blue-backed, clothbound 1895 edition of *The Adventures of Sherlock Holmes,* he pored over the stories, pencil in hand, annotating key scenes in spidery handwriting, underlining, highlighting huge swaths of dialogue, slashing through phrases for which he had no use. He razored Sidney Paget illustrations straight out of the volume for future reference. He paid particular attention to Conan Doyle's descriptions of Sherlock's mannerisms: how the detective curls up in his armchair, how his face bears a look of "infinite languor." In "The Boscombe Valley Mystery," he highlighted a description of Holmes as a "gaunt figure . . . in a cloth cap." He dog-eared pages and picked out singular "good scenes" amid long passages he otherwise ignored.

Gillette's copy of the *Adventures* survives in the New York Public Library, its worked-over pages providing a glimpse of a key moment in the history of Sherlock Holmes: an independent, keen, and utilitarian storytelling mind hacking at the Conan Doyle source code, stripping the stories down to their plot architecture and atmospheric essentials. Gillette noted "good, effective investigative material" in "The Adventure of the Red-Headed League," for example, and delicately extracted filaments of the Holmesian ambience for reuse. On the volume's endpapers he assembled long lists of notes, indexed to pages, building a Sherlockian shopping list: "uses *cigars* too . . . have pipe, cigars, cigarettes, cocaine . . . wore pea jacket . . . night work." He dissected Sherlock Holmes as a character: "respects women's intuition." He combed the text for scenes with theatrical potential. In "The Man with the Twisted Lip," when Holmes builds that "Eastern divan" of pillows for his climactic meditation on the case, Gillette scrawled, "Can I get this tableau in Act II, make it right?"

But above all, the blue book reveals Gillette seizing upon what he found in the text and making it his own. In "The Adventure of the Copper Beeches," Conan Doyle's Holmes complains about giving "advice to young ladies from boarding schools." But what, the actor wondered in pencil script, would William Gillette's Holmes do? ("Can young couple want advise [*sic*] about each other?") As the American sliced out pages and scribbled in the margins, he reanimated the dead, discarded Sherlock Holmes into a subtly different creative entity: a sort of collaborative project, passed to him by Conan Doyle like a relay runner's baton. Gillette pulled Sherlock up on his own workbench to overhaul him. This would work. That would not. Put this bit over there, bolt it to that. And let's have something new here.

At one point, Gillette fired an important question for Conan Doyle across the Atlantic: "May I marry Holmes?"

Conan Doyle replied: "You may marry or murder or do what you like with him."

I can't say, at this remove, how I came to learn of the Sherlockian subculture as it existed, in fact and lore, in the 1980s. How did one learn before the Internet? Well, let us hereby memorialize a time, not long ago, when people printed addresses in the backs of magazines, and you wrote to their post office boxes, and they answered you. You went to the library and looked up articles in *The Readers' Guide to Periodical Literature.* You made like Holmes and checked the index. I say this not out of Luddite conviction — I love a good hashtag — but because it's bracing to remember that such enterprise was necessary, and within the abilities of twelve-year-olds.

However I did it, I learned of the Baker Street Irregulars and the world they made. Here's some idea of how it works:

The BSI serves as the lodestar for organized Sherlockians in the United States. Membership is by invitation ("investiture") only, and is thus quirkily exclusive and laden with a certain Skull and Bones–ish mystery. For those outside the elect, there are many spin-off ("scion") societies, mostly geographical. In Portland, for example, we have the Noble and Most Singular Order of the Blue Carbuncle, a charming group of folk who eat goose every Christmas. The list of scion locations and names runs long and exotic, from the Disreputable Little Scarecrows of the Shoals (in Alabama) to the Afghanistan Perceivers of Oklahoma to the Merripit House Guests of Sheboygan. There are also dedicated Sherlockian societies for psychologists, funeral directors, poets, and mathematicians — the last named for Moriarty, of course.

Outside the United States, the big name is, quite naturally, the Sherlock Holmes Society of London, the equal, collaborator, and undeclared alternative to the BSI. (For instance, though the SHSL's membership rules have varied over the years, it currently stands open to all. Viz., they let me in.) Many countries have flagship national societies, like the Sydney Passengers in Australia, the Bootmakers of Toronto, and the Czech Sherlock Holmes Society of Prague. Indeed, Sherlockian societies — large, small, and microscopic — map the world like a parallel United Nations. My current sentimental favorite: the Seventeen Steppes of Kyrgyzstan.

But wherever they are, these current clubs almost all nod to a titan of early-century publishing and literary culture named Christopher Morley. Born in 1890 of America-transplanted English parents, raised in Bryn Mawr and Baltimore, Morley led one of those astonishing literary careers that leave a modern observer vicariously exhausted. He could write about anything. He wrote novels and essays and poems — he published his first verse collection when he was twenty-two, fresh from a Rhodes Scholarship. By the age of thirty-six, he'd written more than twenty books. He wrote essays on cider, and finance, and bookstores, and New York geography. He staged plays and edited anthologies. He labored for newspapers and started magazines. Later on, he became a radio personality. For years, he wrote several, concurrent weekly columns of national influence.

But Morley's truly peculiar genius lay in his mania for clubs. Everywhere he went, from boyhood on, he started clubs — usually several simultaneously. The more nonsensically constituted, the better. He formed a two-person club at college, then a separate three-person club in which he and the other two members, for some reason, pretended to be sons of a wool magnate named McGill. As a columnist for the *New York Evening Post* and then the *Saturday Review of Literature,* he regaled readers about his Three Hours for Lunch Club. Morley took socializing seriously. In the early 1950s, Morley claimed that he'd inducted his three friends into the very first Sherlockian society, dubbed the Sign of the Four, way back in 1902, when he himself would have been twelve years old.

And so, in the early 1930s, when a by-then-middle-aged Morley began to muse publicly on his lifelong love of Sherlock Holmes, what followed was inevitable. On 7 January 1933, his *Evening Post* column offhandedly noted that Sherlock Holmes's birthday had just passed. (Aside from the aforementioned reasons for 6 January's nomination: it was also the birthday of Morley's brother Felix.) Readers began writing in with their own Holmesian thoughts. The same time the following year, Morley wrote in the *Saturday Review*, "The 'Baker Street Irregulars,' a club of Holmes-and-Watson devotees, held its first meeting on January 6." In February '34, a consitution appeared in Morley's column, proclaiming that the BSI's officers would be "a Gasogene, a Tantalus, and a Commissionaire" and establishing, as one of several "Buy Laws," that any member who failed to identify a given quote from the "Sacred Writings" upon demand would be liable for the next round. In May, the magazine ran a Sherlock Holmes–themed crossword (prepared on a boring Atlantic crossing by Felix, but presented as the work of "Tobias Gregson"); Morley offered Irregulars membership to anyone who completed it correctly. In June 1934, eight men gathered at Christ Cella's famed restaurant (in Morley's formulation, a "speakeasy," even though Prohibition had just ended) on East 44th Street. They ate. They drank. They talked Sherlock. As they rose from the table, the gentlemen knew they had shared an interlude of easy comradeship, crackling thought, and highbrow good cheer worthy almost of Baker Street itself. They knew they'd do it again soon.

The BSI wasn't born in a vacuum. In the late 1920s, a time when original Sherlock Holmes stories still appeared in the *Strand* and *Collier's* on occasion, an embryonic tradition began to grow: books and essays *about* Sherlock Holmes. The years before and around Morley's creation of the Irregulars saw one curious tome after another, such as the Cambridge scholar S. C. Roberts's *Dr. Watson: Prolegomena to the Study of a Biographical Problem* and T. S. Blakeney's *Sherlock Holmes: Fact or Fiction?* An archaeologist and bibliophile with the spectacular name Harold Wilmerding Bell had written *Sherlock Holmes and Dr. Watson: The Chronology of Their Adventures,* attempting to untangle Watson's habitual shifts from spring to fall and so forth. Nor were these efforts particularly obscure. In 1933, Macmillan published Vincent Starrett's *The Private Life of Sherlock Holmes* to prominent reviews in the national press. The *Los Angeles Times* declaimed that "Starrett's volume, breezy and casual, sparkling and informative, will prove an indispensable companion — a Baedeker for a land of unforgettable enchantment." The year after the first BSI meetings, the eminent G. K. Chesterton wrote an essay on the Great Detective's seeming immortality: "Sherlock the God."

A deeper shift was also happening in the popular culture. The fan — short for "fanatic," some say, or perhaps (more agreeably) derived from "the Fancy," boxing's eighteenth-century following — was finding his (or her, but then mostly his) voice. In 1926, the entrepreneurial editor-publisher Hugo Gernsback launched *Amazing Stories,* a pulp dedicated to "scientifiction." Gernsback, easily the most interesting person ever born in Luxembourg, cultivated a community through the magazine's letters section, in which lovers of the newly declared sci-fi genre commiserated and confederated. In the densely printed "Discussions" columns, fans fiercely debated the relative merits of Jules Verne or "the possibilities of germs."

These exchanges spawned international correspondence groups, then real-world connection. A few months after that early Irregulars dinner at Christ Cella's in Manhattan, for example, the Los Angeles Science Fiction League held its first meeting in a founding member's garage. The Chicago Science Correspondence Club launched the *Comet,* possibly the first fanzine (a word coined in 1940), beginning a tradition of scruffy samizdat that flourishes even now. In 1946, the *Baker Street Journal* — the fanzine to end all fanzines, beautifully printed, stately in design, written at a high literary pitch — began under the aegis of Edgar W. Smith, a skillful General Motors executive.

A slippery business, re-creating the sensibilities of prewar sci-fi and Sherlock readers. My pseudo-Holmesian investigative methods led me to a cultural historian named Michael Saler, and his recent book *As If: Modern Enchantment and the Literary History of Virtual Reality. As If* proved the rare academic treatise with verve and style. (Or maybe just pitched right at my humble level. Saler prominently quotes the gypsy-punk band Gogol Bordello: "It's more than true / It actually happened.") Saler argues that modern fandom began as readers embraced books like *Treasure Island, 20,000 Leagues Under the Sea, She,* and *Dracula,* which used quasi-scientific storytelling apparatuses — maps, confabulated documents, fictional correspondence, charts — to create "enchanted" visions of modern life. These novels yoked fairy-tale wonder to the nineteenth-century imperium of science, archaeology, and exploration. They invited readers to imagine themselves within the meticulous alternate realities they spun. And in Saler's words, Sherlock Holmes strode into this "New Romance" genre to become fiction's "first virtual reality character," the one that most thoroughly seduced readers and beckoned them to explore and inhabit an invented world.

The early newspaper and magazine parodies hinted at this fascination. By the 1930s, it had ripened into the Irregulars' desire — somehow archly self-conscious and boyishly earnest at the same time — to bring imaginary Sherlockiana and their real lives into communion. By gathering in cozy, all-male corners of Manhattan and drifting off into long, boozy conversations* about an imaginary London, the Irregulars created a combined simulation of the Baker Street fireside and the chatty Diogenes Club Strangers' Room: a virtual reality, to borrow Michael Saler's term, where romance and adventure held sway.

After those off-the-cuff beginnings in '34, the Irregulars grew and grew, and began to sprout offshoots around the country and the world. By the time Edgar Smith founded the *Baker Street Journal* in 1946, Sherlockian tidings ran plentiful. From the first issue, the magazine bustled with correspondence from the Speckled Band of Boston, the Five Orange Pips of Westchester County, the Hounds of the Baskerville (clever!) of Chicago. The latter, particularly august cell featured the likes of Vincent Starrett and Charles Collins, a *Tribune* columnist who turned his corner of the newspaper into "a sort of clearinghouse for Sherlockian notes and queries." The Hounds met at Schlogl's, Chicago's premier journalistic wa-

---

* A consumption tally from a 1946 BSI gathering, by which time the organization had grown much larger than those original one-table affairs: "96 cocktails, 243 scotches, 98 ryes, and 2 beers."

tering hole, under the care of "Richard, the literary waiter." The new Sherlockian fraternity could thrive even in harsh circumstances. In one 1946 issue of the *BSJ*, a group called the West of Tokyo Interpreters reported in from aboard the USS *W. W. Burrows* in the Pacific: "We went through plenty of Kamikaze and both of those terrific typhoons last fall . . . We intend to remain active."

Not everyone found this behavior so charming. In the *New Yorker*, literary critic Edmund Wilson denounced the BSI and "the cult of Sherlock Holmes" as "infantile." (Wilson spent the mid-'40s on a crusade against detective fiction in general.) But naysayers faced not just a small group of devotees but a sociological current: the BSI both reflected and pioneered a way of responding to fictional characters and worlds that would become commonplace, almost standard.

I called Michael Saler at his University of California–Davis office to sound him out on the birth of modern fandom. "There had been brief eruptions of interest in particular characters before, certainly," he told me. "But they were not sustained, let alone so strong decades after the character's creation. And I'm not aware of anyone having *dinners* in their honor. It's not just that the Irregulars were the first, or among the first — it's how influential the early BSI members were. Morley's friends tended to be journalists or other people with extraordinary access to the media, and he and others were able to shape the way fandom was perceived. They were respectable people — very eminent, in some cases. And while science-fiction fans tended to be seen as grubby teenagers and working-class hobbyists,* any time newspapers wrote about the Baker Street Irregulars, they made the point that, hey, these guys are not stupid. It legitimized the whole practice of fandom. They could fight the likes of Edmund Wilson on his own terms."

---

* The beautifully garish ads in early issues of *Amazing Stories* generally offer trade instruction: "Learn Electricity in 13 Months! Make $200 to $800 a Month!" or "3 Drafting Lessons Actually Free!" or "Buried Treasure Can Still Be Found in Chemistry!" By contrast, the '46 issues of the *BSJ* (never intended as a profit-making concern) tend toward decorous and muted pitches for mystery novels and the Murray Hill Hotel, the "elegantly appointed . . . establishment . . . secluded from noise and uproar" that had become the BSI's unofficial headquarters.

When I was a Holmes-besotted kid, the Sherlockian scene sounded like the greatest thing man's mind could conceive. (It helped that I belonged to the infinitesimally small faction of preteens to whom a wood-paneled rendezvous with a bunch of tweed-clad beardies sounded like fun.) I was eager to don my figurative deerstalker (in Missoula, country shooting attire tended to hunter's orange) and join in. The problem, I discovered, was that I lived on one of the few patches of earth with no Sherlock Holmes fan club. The East Coast crawled with them; San Francisco and Seattle had their stars on the map of Pax Sherlockiana. Minnesota had its Norwegian Explorers. Even the frozen wastes of Alberta boasted a Singular Society of the Baker Street Dozen. But I appeared to be surrounded by an "arid and repulsive desert," as Conan Doyle described the interior West in *A Study in Scarlet*. I was too young for whiskey highballs, but desperate to commune with other obsessives. And here I was, alone.

Sherlock Holmes came back to life in Buffalo, of all places, on 23 October 1899. Once again, a cheerful red glow emanated from the Baker Street hearth (situated stage left). Mrs. Hudson's rented room, decorated with green silk curtains lit by the flickering blue flame of a spirit lamp on the chemistry bench tucked in an alcove, reverberated once more with the detective's acerbic tones. The figure himself stepped forth: "tall, pale, smooth-shaven . . . restrained." William Gillette, to judge by photographs taken of him in Holmesian guise, embodied the character as a paradox of elegance and austerity, sumptuous dressing gown offset by a flinty, square-jawed mien, simultaneously regal, languid, and forbidding. A correspondent to the *Era*, London's theatrical newspaper, reported that the Buffalo crowd demanded curtain calls after each of the four acts. Gillette had just unwittingly stepped into the role that would define his career. "Nobody who ever saw him as Sherlock Holmes will think of him first in any role but that," a journalist wrote thirty years later. "The impersonation was one of those rare and unforgettable marriages between a player and his part which occur but seldom." Gillette had fused with the character even before the play was completed: for his first-ever meeting with Conan Doyle, Gillette materialized on an English train platform wearing a deerstalker cap, whipped out a magnifying glass, and declared, "Unquestionably an author!"

Sherlock Holmes's journey to the stage had not been entirely smooth. The year before, a raging hotel fire in San Francisco consumed what Gillette claimed was the only draft of the script. (Gillette, the star, stayed at a fancier place than the rest of his touring company. His secretary, fresh from the blaze, roused the actor in the middle of the night. Gillette reportedly responded, "Well, is *this* hotel on fire?") But Gillette swiftly re-created, cast, and staged not so much a translation of Conan Doyle's detective to the stage as a freehanded reinterpretation. The actor-playwright snagged bits and bobs from several Conan Doyle stories, notably "A Scandal in Bohemia" and "The Final Problem," to stitch together a greatest-hits compilation of Holmes dialogue. He confabulated a crazed plot featuring an imprisoned girl, a mysterious packet of papers, scheming kidnappers, Professor Moriarty (operating from a superbly creepy underground lair outfitted with both telephones and speaking tubes), a gas chamber in Stepney ("as uncanny and gruesome in appearance as possible," per Gillette's stage directions), and cues for "characteristic music." The script hits a madcap pace, one scene of derring-do after another calling for incessant musical accompaniment: "Music. Danger. Melodramatic. Very low. Agitato. B String . . . A weird bar or two . . . a strange pulsation . . . melodramatic and pathetic."

Speaking of melodramatic (and arguably pathetic), Gillette made good on his request to Conan Doyle and gave Holmes a love interest, complete with the most awkward (and oddly punctuated) dialogue in the Sherlockian universe:

ALICE: From the way you speak — from the way you — look — from all sorts of things! (*With a very slight smile.*) You're not the only one — who can tell things — from small details.*

HOLMES (*coming a step closer to her*): Your faculty — of observation is — is somewhat remarkable, Miss Faulkner — and your deduction is quite correct! I suppose — indeed I know — that I love you. I love you . . .

---

* One actress who uttered these lines, Peg Entwistle, later leapt to her death from the "H" of the Hollywood — then the Hollywoodland — sign.

Within a few more lines, Alice has her right hand on Holmes's breast, he has his arms around the girl, and they're gazing at each other meaningfully as the lights fade. It's enough to send any right-thinking person scurrying to the Swandam Lane opium den, but Gillette knew his market. After its Buffalo trial, the play ran on Broadway for more than 250 performances, toured the States, and crossed to England in 1901. After a Liverpool warm-up, *Sherlock Holmes* opened at the Lyceum Theatre, where Sherlock and Watson had met Mary Morstan at the yellowing third pillar from the left in *The Sign of the Four.*

The London press was not exactly unanimous in praise: "the majority of the audience leave the theatre with a feeling savouring of disappointment," ran one of several wan assessments. The public ignored the critics. The production thrived for months, then spawned a sturdy touring franchise, with other actors taking the lead role. H. A. Saintsbury, notably, would parlay the job into well over a thousand appearances as Holmes on stage and screen, and was reckoned even better than Gillette by some. ("Saintsbury . . . was a living replica of the *Strand Magazine* illustrations," wrote one knowledgeable firsthand observer — Charlie Chaplin, who played Billy the Page in *Sherlock Holmes* as one of his earliest gigs.) Years after its debut, *Sherlock Holmes* continued to enjoy a lucrative provincial afterlife. Night after night through the first decade of the new century, the play proved and quickened the public's appetite for Holmes.

Whether or not they liked the play, theatrical journalists recognized that Gillette had surrounded his wacky plot and corny romance with true stage innovation. He was known for techniques that presaged the cinematic storytelling to come. The play opened in an almost pitch-black theater, with the curtain drawn up noiselessly. The lights then faded in to reveal the scene. His fade-outs proved as memorable: "the image remains with us — like the recollection of some striking, yes even beautiful pictures," in the words of the *Cheltenham Looker-On,* which noted that the stage managers and technicians at all the other London theaters were deeply impressed. The photographs of the sets show extraordinary depth of texture and detail, and the script demanded lightning-quick turns from elaborate, high-class drawing rooms to Baker Street to the moldering dungeon of the Stepney gas chamber, where Gillette's Holmes outwits

Moriarty's henchmen by dousing the lights and decoying them with the glow of a cigar.

Gillette's play marked the detective's first decisive success beyond the printed page, and just as entertainment was poised to explode into the realm of cinema, then radio, the actor became the first person famous for remaking Sherlock Holmes. The detective now had a real-world face, which usually happened to look like William Gillette, but which could also transform into the longer, more hound-like countenance of H. A. Saintsbury — or whatever form. Holmes could live again, and again, any-where. He could fall in love. He could defeat Moriarty in countless ways. (The professor, too, would always be back.) He could do anything, re-ally, provided a deerstalker and pipe were involved. (Conan Doyle re-ported himself delighted, particularly with the "pecuniary" result.) A characteristic moment came in May 1902 as Gillette toured England. The *Northants Evening Telegraph* reported a "packed and fashionable" audi-ence at the Theatre Royal, drawn by "the magic title of *Sherlock Holmes.*" And an uncanny trick unfolded on the stage: "The strange lighting and scenic effects . . . make the doings of the famous detective still more weird and realistic, combined with the likeness of Mr. Gillette to the character which has almost grown to be a real figure in the public mind."

Holmes had climbed out of his watery grave.

If I had no Sherlock Holmes society to join, the answer was obvious: I had to start one. I didn't feel like combing my hometown for stray Sherlock-ians; if they existed (I was pretty sure they did not), they might find the approach of an avid-eyed child clutching a battered Doubleday anthology unnerving. I decided to combine close-to-home recruitment with global outreach. I started the Street Arabs, which I proclaimed (without check-ing) the world's first club for young Sherlockians, open to anyone under twenty-one. The name, an oblique tribute to the Baker Street Irregulars themselves, referenced Holmes's gutter-urchin assistants in *A Study in Scarlet* and *The Sign of the Four.* (It did not strike me as at all racially prob-lematic, which perhaps speaks to Montana's demographics.) As for what would happen when *I* turned twenty-one, I couldn't imagine such a thing transpiring before the heat-death of the universe, so I didn't worry about it. I press-ganged my brother and my two cousins, all slightly younger than me, whom I had already tormented plenty about Sherlock Holmes. In imitation of the BSI, I gave everyone a Sherlockian alias — my cousin Ali, I recall, got "Laura Lyons," from *The Hound of the Baskervilles.* As for what we would actually *do* as a club, I had no idea. The important thing was simply to have a club.

Then the strangest thing happened: the gray aluminum mailbox atop the chain-link fence outside our boxy house on the unfashionable side of town began to fill with exotic envelopes. Italy. England — *England itself!* Australia. Japan. Kids from all over the world, cribbing my address out of the *Baker Street Journal*'s back pages and other Sherlockian listing services, started writing to me about Sherlock Holmes. A young man named Mattias wrote from Sweden, and he and my brother struck up a correspondence. I soon had pen-pal relationships going with boys in Florence and girls in Tokyo. Using our household's now-historic PC, I painstakingly assembled a typescript journal. (Sherlockians don't really do the word "zine"; it's "journals" all the way down.) I titled it *Wiggins's Report* in honor of the chieftain of Holmes's semihomeless detection commando, and filled it with whatever I could glean from my fellow Street Arabs, enlisting my family in marathon photocopying, stapling, and folding sessions.

I have a very patient family.

I began to view airmail reply coupons and that delicate, tissue-papery stationery everyone used for international correspondence as alternative currencies. I didn't realize that I was living in the last days of analog. If I'd had the Internet at my disposal, the enterprise would have been easier — but also, I can't help but think, much less fun. When I would throw on my puffy winter coat and troop to that dull gray mailbox, my fingertips would quiver with anticipation. The box's hatch wrenched open with a frozen metallic squawk. Inside, I would find cosmopolitan stamped envelopes, rain-stained and battered from an incomprehensible adventure across the seas and skies. I took them inside and sorted them on the sofa.

My romance with Sherlock Holmes had both enlivened my appreciation of my snug Missoula existence — for months, I saved the daily newspaper, thinking I might assemble something like Sherlock's vast index of clippings on the local scene, until the collection became a serious fire hazard — and put it in sharp perspective. The world could feel so far away.

The Sherlockian confederacy brought it closer. The Street Arabs sent me pieces of their lives. I sent them little pieces of mine. Under the cover of a fantasized Baker Street, we crafted an ephemeral reality of our own, companionship amid the equinoctial gales of early adolescence. At home, we were the kids with a peculiar interest in an antique fictional character. Together, we were something else entirely: an underage literary posse comitatus, playing a game of our own devising. The appeal, if I may say so, was elementary.

After music and cocktails, the Salmagundi Club crowd streamed into the old manse's basement, where slightly cockeyed chandeliers cast a romantic glow on stout, dark ceiling beams and an ample buffet. As I loaded my plate with chicken and mashed potatoes, it dawned on me: everyone else at the Daintiest Thing Under a Bonnet Ball traveled with an established Sherlockian pod. I faced the High School Cafeteria Vortex: I had no one with whom to sit.

I plunked myself at a forlorn two-top, feeling about as festive as Banquo's ghost. After two decades of journalism, I should be immune to social disgrace, but I was later told that I chewed my buffet-line chicken with the expression of a just-orphaned puppy. I soon looked up to see a six-foot-tall woman approaching me with concern. "Would you like to join us?" she asked, with an English-accented gentleness that might have served her well in soothing some street corner maniac. She gestured to the table behind her, already crowded with women. I do know when to say yes.

I found myself, then, a singular male ringed by seven Baker Street Babes: a fantasy/anxiety attack scenario for Street Arabs–era Zach. All appeared to be well under thirty (a gentleman doesn't ask), and I would learn that they found their way to 221B in the most wonderfully odd ways. My savior, Kafers, first discovered Sherlock via *Basil of Baker Street,* the animated version of an old children's favorite featuring the adventures of a mouse detective; by her own account, she didn't read Conan Doyle until after Robert Downey Jr.'s *Sherlock Holmes* came out in 2010. At my other elbow sat Melinda, a Brooklynite whose introduction to the character came in the unlikely form of a *Star Trek* android: in an episode of *The Next Generation,* Commanders Data and Geordi La Forge venture to the *Enter-*

prise's handy holodeck dressed as Holmes and Watson. Across the table sat Kristina Manente, a.k.a. Curly Four-Eyes, founder of the Baker Street Babes, who also started with the animated rodent as a youth, later to have Robert Downey Jr. and Benedict Cumberbatch revive her enthusiasm.

The wine began to flow.

The Babes originated when Kristina Manente, two years before, started musing publicly on Sherlock Holmes, just as Christopher Morley had eight decades earlier. Lacking a column in a widely circulated literary weekly, Kristina launched a podcast, which quickly garnered polish, followers, and coconspirators. "It was a little bit dizzying," Kristina would tell me later. "I was hearing from amazing people. I hadn't really known a lot about the traditional Sherlockian world before — the old-school Sherlockian world — until I started to hear from people who'd heard the podcast. It just kind of exploded."

Her homemade talk show hit the Internet at an opportune historical moment. Thanks largely to *Sherlock,* the web was alight with dynamic new Sherlockian energy. *Sherlock* fans ravenously pursued details about plots, costumes, actors, sets, producers — anything. Kristina and her Babes generated a full amateur-media lineup — podcast, blog, and a Tumblr site that became an era-bending trove of imagery and text, skipping from Lucy Liu to Arthur Conan Doyle within a half-second scroll. To the Babes, disparate fragments of the Sherlockian world happily jumble together. Podcast episodes have featured Daniel Stashower, author of a highly respected Conan Doyle biography — and pseudonymous authors of sexually explicit fanfiction. The vibe is exuberantly youthful and feminine (it's the web's "only all-female Sherlock Holmes podcast"), as far from a pipe-smoking 1930s Sherlockian fraternity as possible.

Lyndsay Faye joined the BSB gang early. Lyndsay grew up in Longview, Washington, not far from my adopted city of Portland. Now an established mystery novelist — her series set in pre–Civil War New York City has been nominated for an Edgar Award, the genre's Oscar — she debuted with a well-regarded pastiche pitting Holmes and Watson against Jack the Ripper. She'd first become a Baker Street Irregular largely through the force of her own sparkly will. "When I first started hanging out at BSI events, it was definitely not by invitation," she told me. "I just showed up. It was before the Robert Downey Jr. movies, before *Sherlock,* and there wasn't much going on in the mass media. By walking into the room, I marked myself as a legit Sherlockian. Otherwise, how the hell would I have known this event existed?"

Lyndsay evolved into a sort of diplomatic channel between the Baker Street Babes and the older Irregulars culture. "It takes all kinds, in my opinion," she said. "A lot of folk ten or fifteen years younger than me are very adept at finding great storytelling across all media. If they like storytelling in one format — film, TV, video game, whatever — they go back and find the source material, or variations on the theme in other media. I'm not saying everyone does this, but a lot of people do. Right now, a lot of great, bright young people are reading Conan Doyle for the first time because of Robert Downey Jr. or Benedict Cumberbatch, which I think is brilliant.

"People in the traditional Sherlockian subculture can be micro-focused. Some people only want to talk about Conan Doyle. Some people only want to talk about Gillette. I know a person who can tell you everything there is to know about Basil Rathbone, and others who can do the same about Sidney Paget. And I'm like, rock on. But the Baker Street Babes are coming at things from a completely different direction. We're trying to introduce everyone to everyone else. Because otherwise, how can we all shoot tequila together?"

I thought the Babes* seemed like great news for Sherlockiana. Yet surprisingly — then again, perhaps not — the Babes' integration into the scene had not proven painless. Kristina Manente told me of her first foray to a traditional Sherlockian event: "I felt like I was the only person under forty — like the most awkward human being on earth." She added that, after a time of suffering, a prominent Canadian Sherlockian came over to break the ice. Still: "Some people were excited I was there. Others were not. Some people wouldn't even look me in the eye, and someone said that the Baker Street Babes weren't 'serious.' That was my first clue that there might be some kind of divide."

---

* Women have been involved, in some cases quite prominently, in the Sherlockian fan world since the beginning, but not without some tension. In the 1960s, the all-female Adventuresses of Sherlock Holmes even picketed all-male BSI gatherings. The two organizations are now coed, with overlapping memberships.

Not long after the New York gatherings I attended, talk of a "Sherlockian civil war" surfaced, even catching the eye of the *New York Times*. In a small Sherlockian magazine, a longtime Irregular named Philip Shreffler published an essay bemoaning the rising influence of Internet-enabled fan culture, which he contrasted unfavorably to a more contemplative breed of "elite devotee." "Elite devotion to Holmes does not refer to one's economic wealth, rather to one's intellectual wealth," Shreffler wrote. He waxed onward, displeased that anyone might conflate the Baker Street Irregulars with the likes of the Baker Street Babes. He went so far as to quote Manente herself in an unflattering light — the extract, from an interview, was riddled with twenty-something verbal tics — and, generally, bemoan the Fall. "Organized Sherlockiana itself seems to be devolving when it should be evolving, growing in size but shrinking in influence," he wrote. As for the warming détente between the Babes and more venerable traditions: "There does seem to be occurring a sort of molecular recombination between the two that wants discouraging. The Island of Doctor Moreau is not a very pleasant place."

The essay sparked a frenzy of derisive online comments and outraged tweets forever known — within the Sherlockian microverse, at least — as "Shreffgate." Teeth gnashed. Invective sizzled. The president ("Wiggins") of the BSI issued a peacemaking statement, calling for an inclusive "world of Sherlockians." The most lasting effect on the Baker Street Babes, it seemed, was a notable increase in social-media following. "Ninety percent of what you might call 'traditional' Sherlockians are excited and welcoming towards anyone who's finding their way into the character," Faye told me. "Maybe ten percent are somewhat wary: Hmm, is this young lady a proper Sherlockian, or is she a Benedict Cumberbatch fanatic? The same thing has happened before; it'll happen again.* It works itself out."

The Salmagundi Club event, certainly, suggested that rearguard ac-

---

* When Shreffgate erupted in March 2013, I thrilled with recognition: the same writer had penned a very similar polemic in 1988, when I was a thirteen-year-old subscriber to the *Baker Street Journal* and newly minted fans of Jeremy Brett were rampant. Though I must respectfully take issue with Shreffler's outlook on the question of whether there's a "correct" way to be a Sherlockian, I do owe him a debt: he was the first editor who ever published my writing, in the *BSJ*.

tions would accomplish little. A full-scale dinner during the BSI Weekend was, in its context, rather audacious, and the impulse to turn it into a veterans' benefit reflected an outward-looking spirit. "There are so many events during the Weekend," Faye told me. "People come from all over the world. Some of them obviously have fairly robust pocketbooks. But traditionally the only charitable cause has been what's called the Dr. Watson Fund, which helps people who *don't* have robust pocketbooks attend. That's beautiful, obviously, and helps a lot of younger people make the trip, but it's still entirely within the community.

"I was idly thinking about what we could do that would have some larger meaning. And it hit me: no Watson, no Sherlock Holmes stories. And Watson's origin is bound up in, guess where, Afghanistan. The guy basically has PTSD at the start of *A Study in Scarlet.* Afghanistan, Iraq—125 years later and we're still doing this bullshit! Doing something that would help veterans just made so much sense."

Serious fandom can seem a delicate hothouse flower, but the passions it stirs can become muscular and vital. On the Baker Street Babes' website, Kristina Manente writes movingly about how her love of Sherlock Holmes helped combat dark times. "People see fandom . . . as being silly and frivolous, full of nerdy teenagers and introverted adults who hide away from the real world," she wrote. "They see fandom as a bizarre and ridiculous culture . . . Do these parts exist? Yes. Is that what fandom is? No. Fandom is family."

As the evening wore on, it did assume the giddy air of grown kids at Thanksgiving after the parents shove off to bed. Melinda Caric rose to offer an official toast to Altamont, Sherlock Holmes's World War I espionage identity, in a hilarious German accent. A quiz began — an absolutely diabolical quiz, devised by a Philadelphia Sherlockian named Nick Martorelli, with questions concerning not only the original Holmes stories but also several cinematic, television, and radio adaptations. Even at a table populated by eight rock-ribbed Sherlockians, it was hard. Very hard.* But each of us had our own storehouse of nerdy know-how. I chipped in one right answer. (Q: In the Basil Rathbone film *The Hound of the Basker-*

---

* The final question: Name each Sherlockian story, of the 60 total, that does *not* begin with a scene set in Baker Street, in order. I mean!

villes, how does Sir Henry Baskerville receive the famous note warning him to "keep away from the moor"? A: It was thrown through the window of his cab.) I felt an inner glow of validation. And this, I reflected, was the sentiment that makes fandom (or elite devotion!) vital enough to work for and fight over: the knowledge that you are not alone, that the beauty that speaks to you also speaks to others.

"I shall never forget the lean and agile Gillette in his deer-stalker's cap"—so wrote the Pulitzer Prize–winning playwright and journalist Elmer Davis, many years after William Gillette's *Sherlock Holmes* aged from innovation to franchise to throwback. Gillette and his producers drilled touring companies and dispatched them to Russia, Sweden, Australia, South Africa, and anywhere else that would have them—by 1904, the play had been performed more than four thousand times. Over the next decades, the actor revived the show repeatedly, to the point that the notion of a Gillette "farewell tour" evolved into a standing joke. In contrast to Conan Doyle, the American actor never seemed to mind Holmes surpassing and overshadowing his other work. Even when he was well beyond the plausible middle age at which he first played the character, he could almost always be persuaded to take up the pipe and don the deer-stalker for another round. And why not? Sherlock treated him very well. In 1916, Gillette built himself a full-scale castle in Connecticut. Over the years, Gillette cured into a cranky (but admired) veteran of the stage. (He always refused to join Actors' Equity, but the union waived its requirements to make his tours possible.) He, in turn, was good to Sherlock. Gillette plucked the talismanic word "elementary" from Conan Doyle, addressed it specifically to Watson, and made it a catchphrase. Gillette's Holmes donned the country deerstalker of Paget's drawings, making it all-purpose. He inflated Holmes's pipe to gargantuan proportions. He became so tightly identified with the character that when *Collier's* hired the American graphic artist Frederic Dorr Steele to illustrate Conan Doyle's stories, Steele simply drew Gillette—and his versions of the detective, which often assumed the stiff majesty of a totem pole carving, became almost as famous as Paget's work.

Gillette cultivated an air of mystery, even misdirection, about himself. In a 1903 cover-story profile for *Ladies' Home Journal,* Gustav

Kobbe commented: "Less is publicly known of the personality of William Gillette than of any prominent actor on the American stage of today . . . He is as close-shelled as an oyster." Gillette carried a preprinted card to hand to journalists, refusing interviews. The press of his day chronicled his stage performances, but Gillette became one of those personae about whom we simultaneously know a lot and not much. He was married early in his career, but his wife died suddenly; his grief drove him to a shack in the North Carolina mountains for a while, peeling years off his theatrical career. He never remarried, though he conducted some lavish platonic friendships with women. In later years, some remarked upon his habit of frequenting big-city parks after nightfall. A keen sailor, he would dock his boat, *Aunt Polly,* at Provincetown, go ashore, and lead troops of admiring lads around town. A couple of biographers have attempted portraits of the man, but those accounts' central figure stubbornly retains his murkiness. Gillette obviously wanted it that way. In the 1930s, the elderly Gillette roared around Manhattan on a motorcycle, elegantly attired. Throughout his life, he took refuge in the guise of a whimsical eccentric, a public role he played to the last. What remained (and remains) was Sherlock Holmes. Gillette retained his hold over the role long enough to play it on film and radio, and though his play's melodrama rapidly became a historical curiosity, audiences still loved it. In 1929, the *New York Sun* reviewed one of those farewell performances, at the New Amsterdam Theater. "It was not the old play that counted — it was the old master himself," critic Edwin Hill wrote. "Throughout the play the applause was like the firing of heavy guns."

Not long ago, a friend played for me a crackling, echo-flawed recording of Gillette in his signature part, made when the actor was eighty-two years old. (The clip can be found online.) The first famous flesh-and-blood Sherlock Holmes acts the role with no attempt at an English accent — that was not the naturalistic Gillette's style — delivering the detective's deductions in a wry mid-Atlantic drawl, at a staccato pace that would become the model for many an actor to come. He skillfully modulates his intensity, alternating the languid dressing-gown-clad dreamer with the incisive intelligence that sees what others do not. "The child's play of deduction," his Holmes coolly tells Watson. "I'm only doing it for your amusement, you know." But as Gillette describes Professor Moriarty, his voice locks into a hypnotic singsong, a lost nineteenth-century cadence of peaks and valleys, sway and rhythm: "The Napoleon of Crime . . . the Napoleon! Sitting motionless like an ugly venomous spider in the center of his web, but that web having a thousand radiations, and the spider knowing every quiver of every one of them." As the recording played, my companion handed me a sepia photo — Gillette's final publicity headshot, with copy on the back dating it to 13 January 1930, when he would have been seventy-six years old. The old master loomed out of a blurry background fog, a great nose surging at me like a battleship's prow, watery eyes gray and glittering amid the image's chill.

On the recording's static haze, Watson spoke of the danger of tangling with such a character as the evil professor.

"My dear fellow," Gillette replied, "it is perfectly delightful. My whole life is spent in a series of frantic endeavours to escape from the dreary commonplaces of existence . . . You should congratulate me."

To get to the first really big Baker Street Irregulars dinner, in 1934, Vincent Starrett and the *New Yorker* writer Alexander Woollcott scrounged up the last two horse-drawn hansom cabs in Manhattan. They let the first one roll away from the curb empty — Holmes once instructed Watson not to take the first cab he saw, as it might be a ruse — and rode in style through roaring midtown traffic in the second, to the bemusement of New York's Finest.

Myself, I just walked from some friends' apartment in Hell's Kitchen to the final event of the 2013 BSI Weekend, a luncheon at Delmonico's Kitchen. The place was riotous with humanity for an event open to both sworn and sealed Irregulars and anyone else (like me) who signed up. A vile flu had the run of New York just then, and a subpopulation spending days and nights eating, drinking, and talking in large groups proved quite vulnerable. Many Sherlockians looked a bit pale around the gills, and one Irregular elder made the rounds in a surgical mask. After collecting a nametag and paying $15 for a bourbon, I found a spot at a large corner table, opposite a Dallas Sherlockian named Joe Frey, who I reckoned to be about my own age. Joe seemed like a nice fellow, but at the moment looked like something Sherlock might pummel experimentally in a morgue, to gauge its ability to form bruises.

"I think all my blood is in my liver, trying to figure out what happened," he said.

Various Baker Street Babes began to arrive in cocktail finery, and Kafers and Kristina Manente settled at our table. Kristina kept sagging as if she might nap in the soup bowl, periodically perking up to call for cough medicine. We were joined by Ashley Polasek, a PhD candidate in a discipline called adaptation studies, with Sherlock Holmes as her subject. This makes sense, I said, given that the detective is probably the single most adapted character ever.

"I keep writing stuff and thinking, My God, someone in this field must have done this already," Ashley said. "But then I don't find it, so I keep going. Sherlock Holmes is like the North Star of the culture. Everything else swirls around and changes, but he's always up there."

The spot next to Joe Frey went to a genial man, again about my age, sporting a trophy beard and a masterpiece among Victorian waistcoats: Mattias Boström, arguably Sweden's leading Sherlockian — and the same Mattias who once corresponded with my brother and me as a member of the Street Arabs. We clinked glasses in honor of the old regiment. Across the room, a woman stood with a feedback-ridden microphone and recited a poem that somehow knit together Sherlock Holmes, Pussy Riot, and "Gangnam Style."

This is not how they did it in 1934, precisely. After the ride in the hansom cab(s) through an appropriately windy and foggy night, Starrett and Woollcott pitched up at Cella's. Elmer Davis, the journalist and playwright who would go on to lead the US Office of War Information in 1941, greeted Starrett at the entrance "with a highball in each hand." Starrett had already consumed a few Sidecars at Wit's End, Woollcott's apartment on East 52nd. His rendering of the affair, tucked into later editions of *The Private Life of Sherlock Holmes,* consequently grows fuzzy around the edges. Then again, he argues, every account of the evening that survives is "more plausible than true"— he denies, for example, the prevalent rumor that at some point, he went on all fours to imitate the Hound of the Baskervilles.

A few weeks later, the *New Yorker* ran Woollcott's version, which would be the most prominent piece of mythmaking about this affair. Published on the last page of the magazine's issue of 29 December 1934, Woollcott's

"Shouts & Murmurs" column is a beautiful distillate of Olde New York cheer. He recounts that boxing champion Gene Tunney was in attendance, that Davis read "what is known as a 'paper,'" and that he himself turned out for the occasion in a plaid hunting cap approximating a deerstalker. (In perhaps the first instance of Sherlockian infighting, Christopher Morley allegedly found Woollcott's presence and report highly irritating. They were old rivals. And Morley, being a journalist, probably saw the Baker Street Irregulars as *his* story, damn it.) Meanwhile, the befogged Starrett settled into a "coma" (his own word) between Morley and Frederic Dorr Steele, the famed Sherlock Holmes illustrator.

Seventy-nine years later at Delmonico's Kitchen, we did not blaze with such intense alcoholic energy or society-column flair. It was only noon, after all. Still, our table became quite lively. After a few minutes of conversation, it proved that Ashley, Mattias, and I were all at work on essentially the same writing project. Mattias was writing a history of the Sherlock Holmes phenomenon in Swedish; *Från Holmes till Sherlock* would appear later in the year. Ashley explained the Great Detective's metamorphic existence to academics. (One of her essays, for example, bears the title "Winning the 'Grand Game': *Sherlock* and the Fragmentation of Fan Discourse.") The three of us had much to discuss, and we soon landed upon William Gillette. Mattias had sleuthed in some of the same archives I had, and we all agreed that the most decisive sentence in the history of Sherlock Holmes was Conan Doyle's brief communication to the actor-playwright: "You may marry or murder or do what you like with him."

"In my world, we call that 'abandonment of authorship,'" said Ashley, who owed her own Sherlock obsession to a stint studying in Scotland, when she traded reading lists with fellow students to speed along friendships. "It's the moment when he gives Gillette — and by extension, everyone else — permission to muck around with the character." As I looked around the packed room, I offered silent thanks to Gillette and his kooky romance, and to Professor Moriarty and his skulking appearance at the Reichenbach Falls.* Real and imaginary, they'd both done their part to

---

* Lyndsay Faye's comment to me, re Moriarty and "The Final Problem": "And *then,* when Arthur Conan Doyle killed Holmes, he accidentally created this Jesus Christ–Harry Potter figure, and Joseph Campbell had nine orgasms."

shape the virtual reality in which everyone at this banquet spent so much time. And Arthur Conan Doyle, when he turned Sherlock over to the work of other minds, committed a pioneering creative act, unleashing the vast collective project of Sherlock Holmes. I was glad I had come to New York to see one important piece of that endeavor. The Baker Street Irregulars say they "keep green the memory" of the Great Detective. Poetic, but perhaps not emphatic enough to describe the vital role the tiny but avid Sherlockian fan movement has played in the much larger story of the Holmesian world: nurturing and sustaining the characters always, and offering guidance to the uninitiated at a time, like circa 2013, when their image suddenly waxed in popular culture.

A chance to play this game was all Mattias and I wanted when we started writing to each other from across the world in the late '80s, and all Kristina Manente sought when she started the Baker Street Babes podcast. The impulse could lead to impetuous and socially awkward moments. (Joe Frey, the chap from Dallas, recounted his effort to start a Sherlock Holmes society at college: "I put up posters and held two meetings. I was the only one who showed up.") But really, we were all just trying to have some fun, same as Christopher Morley and the boys back in '34. That afternoon, our table took its place in an obscure but grand tradition. It felt good.

Of course, we latter-day enthusiasts couldn't top that first grand Baker Street Irregulars gathering at Cella's for a dramatic finale. Deep into the evening, a commotion erupted in the corridor. "I came out of my coma with what is described by novelists as a start," Starrett recalled. A flurry of attendants briefly obscured the figure emerging into the smoke-fogged chamber. But then the assembled Irregulars saw him.

"Vague, abstracted, changeless, and inexpressibly charming," Woollcott reported, "an enchanting blend of slinking gazelle and Roman Senator." The chiseled profile. The regal bearing. The infinite languor. It was William Gillette. More than that, it was Sherlock Holmes — the detective who would not die.

6

THE CURSE OF THE BASKERVILLES

THE ENGLISH SEA seemed to rise up to swallow the train car. A wave erupted over the rocky embankment that separated the Great Western Railway tracks from the North Atlantic and smashed over the side and roof of our carriage. Salty droplets fizzed through ventilation openings, and the car rocked to one side. I involuntarily calculated my odds of rescuing my wife (four months pregnant, innocently reading a magazine) and my five-year-old boy (listening to some maniacal nonsense on Leap-Pad headphones) should our train be sucked into the ocean. I am a terrible swimmer.

The wave subsided and the sea went back to brooding hideously off to our left: a ragged, foam-flecked, sewage-colored churn. "I told you," a teenage girl — two rows in front of us, among otherwise sullen and withdrawn Englishmen — chirped to her companion. "We picked the weekend of the Apocalypse!"

A record bout of miserable weather indeed gripped that green and pleasant land. Every newspaper front page read something like COLD CRISIS PUTS FRIGID HANDS OF DEATH ON SUFFERING BRITAIN. In Wales, farmers found themselves exhuming herds of sheep from fatal snow dumps. A luckless partyer outside Manchester froze to death walking home from his pub. A kingdom situated near a massive undersea oil field was on the verge of running out of natural gas. And here we were, embarked on a family outing to England's most treacherous chunk of wind-blasted wilderness: Dartmoor.

After a lengthy delay (an earlier train had flattened some poor suburban Londoner), we reached the fabled English countryside and the island's southwestern coast. The torrential rain flooded fields in a coppery muck. Pleasure craft (unmanned, one hoped) bobbed pathetically in raging, brown bays and estuaries. I sat next to a malodorous youth whose iPhone and iPad put his media technology several centuries ahead of his hygiene. Christina, my wife, kept looking narrowly at me across the aisle, whole brochures on Mexican beach getaways writ behind her eyes. Cash, my son, periodically removed his earbuds to ask if we were there yet. I could only shrug and smile idiotically. We were on the trail of the Hound of the Baskervilles.

Sometime in the fictional 1880s, Dr. John Watson takes pretty much the same train trip, from London Paddington to Dartmoor, in the company of one Sir Henry Baskerville, heir to Baskerville Hall. Watson travels under orders from Holmes, as the partners commence an investigation into whether Sir Henry is fated to die horribly in the slavering jaws of a supernatural Demon Dog afire with lust for the blood of the Baskervilles. A Dartmoor physician named Mortimer, the rather creepy author of medical treatises titled "Some Freaks of Atavism" and "Do We Progress?," engaged the Baker Street duo. (At one point early in the client-detective relationship, Mortimer pauses to admire Sherlock's skull.) Mortimer recounts a hoary Dartmoor legend: centuries before, a wicked country baron named Hugo Baskerville met the end of a jolly life of rape and pillage when a gigantic, spectral hound interrupted his nocturnal pursuit of a peasant girl by ripping out his throat. Ever since, a fearful curse has pursued the Baskervilles. Many die young; others sensibly shove off for the New World.

The most recent incumbent, Sir Charles Baskerville, tried to rehabilitate the family name through good works and social improvements. But he, too, met a grim fate, not long before: found stone dead at the end of Baskerville Hall's yew alley, not a mark on him. The official investigation ascribed Sir Charles's death to a dodgy heart. But Mortimer, the neighborhood doctor, conducted his own search and found a singular clue — a clue so ominous and portent-laden he suppressed it during the inquest. It was . . . it was . . .

> "Footprints."
> "A man's or a woman's?"
> Dr. Mortimer looked strangely at us for an instant, and his voice sank almost to a whisper as he answered.
> "Mr. Holmes, they were the footprints of a gigantic hound!"

Yoinks! Now a final heir, a square-jawed young Canadian named Sir Henry, has been induced to claim Baskerville Hall. An atmosphere of menace already gathers round him. After some shenanigans in London — someone steals Sir Henry's boots; he receives a blackmail-style note warning him to KEEP AWAY FROM THE MOOR; Holmes and Watson fruitlessly pursue a sinister figure they spy tailing the young nobleman — the detective mysteriously appoints Watson as chaperone and sends the party on its way to Dartmoor. Thus begins the most famous Sherlock Holmes story of them all.

The Hound of the Baskervilles debuted in the August 1901 issue of the *Strand*, nearly eight years after the detective's death-tango with Moriarty at the Reichenbach Falls. The novel — compact in form but epic in feel — ran in serial installments through the fall, in the same months that William Gillette coolly strode the Lyceum Theatre's stage in *Sherlock Holmes*. For a fictional corpse, Holmes had a sensational year. The press hailed his return to the page, welcoming his "pristine clearness of perception." Soon American publishers, always hungry for Holmes, clamored to buy the *Hound*'s rights. The story would enjoy a big, pop-folkloric future. There would be dozens of radio, film, and television adaptations. The Germans, with their uncanny sense of timing, would produce versions of *Der Hund von Baskerville* in both 1914 and 1937, not otherwise banner years for Anglo-Teutonic cultural exchange.* Today, there's even

---

* A notable German use of the story is the pop duo Cindy & Bert's "Der Hund von Baskerville," featuring the tune from Black Sabbath's "Paranoid." I recommend the YouTube clip of Cindy & Bert performing this chestnut for a 1969 audience in groovy

a psychological phenomenon called the Hound of the Baskervilles Effect, documented in research that shows that heart attack mortality among Chinese and Japanese people spikes on the fourth of each month — the number four being unlucky in both cultures.

It was, all told, quite a coup.

Because he'd craftily set this new story in the pre-Moriarty 1880s, Conan Doyle could have it both ways: Sherlock remained safely dead, but Watson's archives stood open for lucrative business. The author had been — guess what? — busy. The turn of the century, in fact, roughly marks the moment when Conan Doyle's biography whirs into an uncontrollable Rube Goldberg engine. In 1899, war broke out in South Africa between Britain and the Boers, snarly descendants of Dutch colonists. With the benefit of post-twentieth-century hindsight, the Boer War's history unfolds like a cheesy horror film: *Don't open that door!* (They always open the door.) An overconfident imperial power dispatched troops to battle highly mobile, ideologically excited backwoods fighters: we know how that goes. The Boers inflicted one bloody comeuppance after another in the early months of the campaign. Conan Doyle longed to volunteer; he even imagined that he might inspire younger Englishmen to serve. His mother Mary was, shall we say, strongly opposed: "There are hundreds of thousands who can fight for *one* who can make a Sherlock Holmes . . . & you would suffer, my own dear one . . . *No living soul* would be one bit the better & thousands be for all time sadder & duller, for your loss — Your family would be *ruined,* your Mother heartbroken — your children left without a father."

Well, after that, of course he had to go. In a concession to his mother (and the fact that the army didn't actually want middle-aged civilians), Conan Doyle joined a volunteer civilian hospital unit and shipped off to South Africa in the spring of 1900. His outfit set up in a cricket pavilion in Bloemfontein, soon flooded with the wounded, sick, and dying. The Boers knocked out the town's water supply, and typhoid swept the

---

German party gear. This can lead, algorithmically, to the hour-long English-language cartoon version of the *Hound* from 1983 (with an incredibly fat Watson), not to mention a funky fan-made remix of clips from the splendid 1981 Soviet film adaptation. Be careful. You can do this all day.

wards. Conan Doyle worked "in the midst of death — and death in its vilest, filthiest form" (as he recalled in his memoirs). By all accounts he performed heroically, working round the clock, at constant risk of infection, close enough to the front to come under shellfire, until regular army medical services could be brought to bear.

And then, in typical Conan Doyle fashion, he was off, back home to Britain, steaming with vim. He'd already largely written a huge history of the Boer War, which would become a bestseller. (As the conflict dragged on, the Boers resorted to increasingly desperate guerrilla tactics, and the British herded Boer civilians into concentration camps, a new idea. This aroused international ire, and Conan Doyle would hammer out a separate, impassioned sixty-thousand-word defense of Britain's conduct, written in under two weeks and distributed at cost in many languages.) By September, he was running for Parliament as a long-shot Liberal Unionist candidate in an Edinburgh constituency, delivering a half-dozen speeches a day to raucous crowds in his old hometown, physically about as far away from South Africa as one could get without tripping over the North Pole. He almost won, too, but in the final hours of the campaign, a Protestant fanatic distributed a pamphlet implicating Conan Doyle in the grand Papist conspiracy. He then made a rare appearance home at Undershaw, where he promptly organized a hundred-strong volunteer rifle company and commenced a barrage of letters, essays, and public appearances in favor of a national civilian reserve force.

Most people would then have drawn a hot bath and submerged themselves for a year or two. But Conan Doyle always needed a project. After a 1900 devoted to unpaid medical, political, and paramilitary work, he wanted to recharge his coffers. En route from South Africa, he'd met a congenial journalist, Bertram Fletcher Robinson, and the two spent the voyage talking over lore of Robinson's native Dartmoor, a place rife with spectral beasts and mythical curses — the sort of material Conan Doyle had drawn on many times for short stories outside the Sherlockian saga. (His 1892 story "Lot No. 249," for example, spun the contemporary fascination with ancient Egypt into a tale of mummy-haunted terror — a story that later makers of certain famed horror films would essentially steal.) Robinson and Conan Doyle agreed to collaborate on what the latter described as "a real Creeper," taking Dartmoor's folktales as its basis.

Conan Doyle traveled to Dartmoor in April 1901, and he and Robinson commenced a regime of fourteen-mile walks over the moor and long outlining sessions in hotel lounges. In Dartmoor, Conan Doyle found all he could hope for in the way of foreboding menace: "a great place," he wrote his mother, "very sad & wild, dotted with the dwellings of prehistoric man, strange monoliths and huts and graves." The scrub-clad landscape jutted up into lonely, broody rock pinnacles called tors. Vast marshes of quicksand threatened to consume the unwary wanderer, who might spend a day tromping through the wastes without seeing a single other person. Setting: check. The tale would, however, require a strong central character. Luckily, Conan Doyle just happened to have one.

Christina, curled into a protective ball around our unborn child, cowered in the passenger seat of our rented blue Nissan Mitra. We'd procured this singularly unromantic vehicle in Newton Abbot, a big town near Dartmoor's edge. Back in Portland, when we booked our travel arrangements, I'd proclaimed an easy confidence in my British-style driving abilities. Man of the world and all that. But I had only driven left-sided in Australia, an automotive paradise of broad, smooth highways. Dartmoor is veined with fiendishly narrow dogcart tracks, many sunken into claustrophobic furrows in the earth. The Mitra hurtled through these terror tunnels just inches away from jagged stone walls, dense thorn-armed hedgerows, and icy creeks. I had requested manual transmission — because who doesn't like a sporting challenge? — and each time I tried to downshift, I instinctively smacked the driver's side door with my right hand, swore, then fumbled at the gearshift with my left. This, in turn, caused repeated swerves toward those ancient walls and fearful plunges.

Enormous freight trucks, teetering farm vehicles, careering tourists, and hell-for-leather locals came toward us, meanwhile, often forcing me to whip the Mitra into tiny shelters between sheer rock walls and the car-eating bramble. A queue of tailgaters gathered in my rearview mirror. I kept screaming at my wife to calm down. From the backseat, Cash offered bemused commentary. "You guys are stressing each other out," he observed. "Oh, there's a narrow-road warning sign, Dad. Let me watch for those. You just drive."

Upon their own arrival, Watson and Sir Henry Baskerville (accompanied by the redoubtable Dr. Mortimer, who spends the train journey describing Baskerville's skull in detail — a thing for skulls, that guy) gaze upon "a gray, melancholy hill, with a strange, jagged summit, dim and vague in the distance, like some fantastic landscape in a dream." Bully for them. When I briefly looked up from the half-flooded tarmac, I saw only a thick, low, freezing fog and the occasional onrushing truck. By the time we arrived in the village of Moretonhampstead, the base for our Dartmoor expedition, my hands quivered like a stoutly struck tuning fork and I was pretty sure several years of marital counseling lay in my future. I gingerly steered the Mitra up to the door of the White Hart Hotel. This squared-off, whitewashed seventeenth-century building started life as an inn for coachmen and their passengers. I understood it housed a bar.

Watson's party alights from its train to find a less frenetic but altogether more sinister scene. Armed troops guard the railway station and important road junctions. A convict (Selden, the Notting Hill Murderer!), escaped from the prison at Princetown, now lurks in the countryside. To add to the festive feeling, Watson spies Baskerville Hall looming over a gnarly grove of stunted and skeletal trees, its two towers glowering out over the moor, "a ruin of black granite and bared ribs of rafters." The party passes through stone and iron gates festooned with the family's signature boar's head. Sir Henry immediately starts babbling about busybody Western Hemisphere modernizations like electric lights, but his optimism only emphasizes the doom-laden character of his family abode.

Conan Doyle outdoes himself on Baskerville Hall, one of the saga's most striking atmospheric set pieces — all coats of arms obscured by overgrown ivy, crenellated towers, blackened oak, and ancient arrow slits. You half expect Lurch from *The Addams Family* to open the door. In any event, the greeting from the Barrymores, the lugubrious couple who serve as the only staff, proves hardly cheerful: five minutes into the relationship, the butler gives their notice. Sir Henry and Watson find themselves dining amid the Hall's dense shadows, beneath the baleful glare of many cursed Baskerville generations in oil portraiture.

The experience leaves Watson gasping for a cigarette. At least Afghanistan was sunny. By bedtime, the doctor sinks into depression as he stares out his bedroom window onto the forsaken moor — and as he lies sleepless, he hears the distant sob of a distraught woman.

Good times. For my part, I almost envied Watson and Sir Henry's comparatively quiet welcome as we assayed Moretonhampstead. A quaint and lovely place, Moreton (as the locals call it) — an impression only slightly dimmed by the dust-cobbed, out-of-business pub across the street from the White Hart, the howling wind exploding villagers' umbrellas, and mud-caked Land Rovers speeding down narrow lanes within inches of my son. Cash decided to discover Moreton his own way: by jumping off every low (or not low) stone wall in town. English villages come well equipped with stone walls. My luggage had chosen to spend an extra day in San Francisco, our layover, so I wore a thin sport coat and a silky purple scarf borrowed from my wife, no doubt producing the effect of a genteel lunatic. Christina looked a bit blue — not sad, literally blue — so retreat to the White Hart seemed in order.

We found a cozy fire blazing in the lounge, a jolly crowd in the bar, an amazing pot-roasted lamb shank, and a couple of pints of locally brewed Hunters Ale for daddy. A redoubtable South African woman ran the place, and the mostly Eastern European staff bore a competent look. We retired up the creaky stairs to our room. Cash and I parted the curtains. One hundred yards away, Moreton's rooftops gave out in favor of rising moorland. Thick, sodden mist choked out most of the view, but for a single lonely homestead jutting from a horizon treeline.

"That's a mysterious house," Cash said. "Sherlock Holmes should check it out."

The infusion of Gothic atmosphere isn't the only significant development in *The Hound of the Baskervilles*. With this novel, Conan Doyle makes an unwitting but critical alteration to the essences of Sherlock Holmes and John Watson: he turns them into nostalgic figures.

Queen Victoria died in January 1901, a few months after Conan Doyle's political campaign in Edinburgh. (Her grandson, Emperor Wilhelm II of Germany, was on hand to close Her Majesty's eyes.) Her funeral in London, with fifty thousand troops and a pantheon of global leaders in attendance, made a blindingly obvious end-of-an-era metaphor. Conan Doyle bore witness, on assignment for the *New York World*: "The Great Mother has gone down alone upon the dreary road which leads to the black portal . . . We watched in helpless sorrow while through the black banks of the mourners, down the valley of white faces, the Great Queen swept onward out of the sunlight into the gloom." Others sounded, if possible, even more ominous; Henry James proclaimed that "the wild waters are upon us now." The Queen's death closed an epoch — she had been born in 1819 — and she seemed to take a time-honored solidity with her. The new King, meaty Edward VII, liked to roar around the provinces shooting birds and shagging the nearest likely female, and favored the company of flashy new money and racing enthusiasts.

Conan Doyle repaired to Dartmoor with his friend Fletcher Robinson in this unsettled atmosphere, the hinge between two eras. *The Hound of the Baskervilles* would ultimately build much of its tension as modern characters — men of science and rationality, like Watson and Holmes — confront the moor's archaic desolation and myths. Conan Doyle's portrayal of Sir Henry Baskerville, young heir to a cursed feudal house, also channels, wittingly or not, turbulent social change. Several characters in the novel express the hope that Sir Henry's mere presence will improve the lot of Dartmoor. In real life, the landed British nobility was in the midst of a slow-motion collapse, caused by the very globalization and technology Britain had created and evangelized. Refrigerated ships, introduced in the 1870s and '80s, opened the British market to cheap foodstuffs from the New World. Demand for domestic agricultural products plummeted, and so too did the income base of the aristocracy. Liberal governments instituted death duties on inherited wealth. In 1900, about fourteen thousand estates had been mortgaged, the vast majority in arrears, and over the next decade, British nobles would liquidate millions of acres. Call it *Downton Abbey* Syndrome: the upper crust could no longer afford to be upper crust. The character of young Sir Henry is as much of a relic as the dusty, bloody legend of the spectral Hound.

Sherlock Holmes returned to this fast-forward world subtly transformed. Conan Doyle conceived the Holmes of *A Study in Scarlet* and *The Sign of the Four* as almost radically modern, with his free-form scientific researches, cocaine reveries, and self-made urban existence. As the stories of the *Adventures* and *Memoirs* appeared, Conan Doyle softened the character's edges, but kept his detective at the heart of the cosmopolitan bustle of the world's most essential city. As Holmes and Watson sleuthed around in hansom cabs and steamed across the countryside by train in those classic tales, they replicated the lives of their most connected readers. For the most part, those stories take place just a few years before they were printed in the *Strand,* in the early '90s.

Now Holmes was, of course, dead. *The Hound of the Baskervilles* takes place in the 1880s, two decades before its publication. In a Britain on the cusp of the automotive and aviation ages, Holmes and Watson still chase hansom cabs and rattle across the countryside in horse-drawn carts. The early portions of the novel portray a London already receding into the past — and the narrative's shift to Dartmoor, with its fate-doomed feudal manses and ruined prehistoric huts, only accentuates the gap between the *Hound* and the real-life present, whether that present is 1901 or today. Sherlock Holmes becomes retro. This development, motivated by Conan Doyle's self-interest in eking profit out of a character he'd killed off, adds a new quality to the saga. After the *Hound,* as the twentieth century hurtled on, Sherlock Holmes would become an incarnation of the good old days when Victoria was on her throne and the brass buttons on the commissionaire's uniform sparkled as he delivered your urgent telegram. The early Holmes was the anarchic invention of an unknown young buck in his twenties. After the *Hound,* written by a forty-two-year-old international celebrity, Holmes could be seen as a fictional consort to the old Queen herself and the certainty she represented. Once bracing doses of modernity, the Great Detective's adventures would increasingly serve as glimpses of a steam-fitted past.

Baskerville Hall lies isolated amid the moorlands like a marooned freighter ship. Everything is far away, cut off by sere expanses dotted with ruins. Rock tors stand as witchy sentries on the horizon. A nearby bog known as the Great Grimpen Mire periodically devours a wandering moor pony.

Neither does the social environment offer much pep. The local peasantry — or so it seems from Watson's narrative, presented as a series of journal entries and letters back to Baker Street — is too lumpen to dwell upon. Their social superiors make periodic reference to "the poor folk upon the moor," and make it known that everyone looks to Sir Henry, the new feudal lord, to use the Baskerville fortune to revive the countryside's economy. The people within Watson's immediate orbit assume an ominous cast. The Barrymores, Baskerville Hall's grumpy *domestiques,* are clearly embroiled in a plot of some sort. Mrs. Barrymore serves breakfast with eyes reddened by that nocturnal weeping Watson heard. The good doctor soon spots her husband creeping about the Hall in the dead of night. Besides Dr. Mortimer and his cranial obsessions, the neighbors are an insular, peculiar lot. The Stapletons, Jack and Beryl, the brother-sister team of nearby Merripit House, arrived not long before. He's a nutty butterfly collector, she's a morose character who issues cryptic warnings about the dangers of Dartmoor. And, my, does Jack seem mighty protective of Beryl. It's almost not even fraternal.

Around the way, there's Frankland, a top-drawer nutcase who occupies himself with crank lawsuits and spying on the parish through his telescope. Watson soon discovers that Frankland's estranged daughter, known as Laura Lyons after a loveless marriage, conducted some kind of covert relationship with the late Sir Charles — he planned to meet her on the night he dropped dead. Meanwhile, everyone keeps hearing inhuman howls in the distance, and the Notting Hill Murderer remains at large. Late one night (never mind how; read the book), Watson and Sir Henry set out to pursue the escaped convict across the moor. After a breathless chase, the criminal slips away into the wilds — but wait! Who's that? High up on a tor, outlined against the moon? It's . . . a mysterious figure! Over a few chapters — John Watson's longest solo outing of the Sherlockian saga — Conan Doyle expertly conjures a world of lies, murky relationships, and veiled motivations. Everyone is up to something out here. It's tempting to conclude that Conan Doyle did this so well because he was up to something himself.

In 1897, after a few years of nursing the tubercular Touie, Conan Doyle met Jean Leckie at a social occasion. She was fourteen years younger. To judge by her best surviving photo from the period, she was also a stone-cold knockout: stung lips, modish hair, big beguiling eyes, given to flirty tilts of the head and plunging necklines. They fell in love. While Touie lived, Conan Doyle maintained appearances — at least to a degree — and, it would seem, retained some pat-on-the-hand affection for his wife. In truth, their relationship never really sparked: one of those "companionable" marriages. Given the medical thinking of the time, the consensus is that Touie's consumption diagnosis meant no sex, for years. And Conan

Doyle did occasionally voice annoyance with plain-faced, plodding, shut-in Touie; as he rather casually and cuttingly put it in one letter, she would always be "dear," never "darling." She was a living link to his days as a struggling doctor in Southsea, when his life was very different. Jean was fresh, exciting, full of youthful ardor, and instantly devoted to her new boyfriend.

They conducted one of the stranger affairs in history. For a decade, Jean and Arthur contrived implausible social coincidences, coordinated vacation plans, made assignations at London hotels. Conan Doyle usually invited his mother along. He insisted, always, that while Touie survived his relations with Jean remained "honourable"— platonic — and made a great show of ensuring that he and his love were properly chaperoned. (We're going to have to take his word on this one. Sure, things were different back then, but — I mean, this went on for *years*.) With the connivance of his mother, Jean's mother, and various other friends and relations, Conan Doyle turned his life into a madcap covert operation. He was forever departing Undershaw for this golfing vacation or that London outing, meanwhile frantically planning the next one in flurries of letters to his mother. In those letters, Conan Doyle shows the strain: no matter how many vacations he takes, he constantly describes himself as in desperate need of a change, a rest, a walk in the woods, et cetera. It wore him down.

Not everyone looked on with sympathy. Shortly after his return from South Africa, he squired Jean to a cricket match at Lord's, the sport's premier ground in London, where the couple unexpectedly encountered Conan Doyle's sister and brother-in-law. He found himself compelled to explain the situation in all its intricate complication. They did not approve, and mutual bad feelings took some time to blow over. And then, writers never forget. Years later, in 1910, Conan Doyle would write a Sherlock Holmes story titled "The Adventure of the Devil's Foot," in which a great African explorer harbors a forbidden love thwarted by his legal inability to divorce an estranged wife. (Conan Doyle would also campaign for divorce-law reform.) A scheming sibling of his mistress intervenes against him, and poisonings with an unknown hallucinogen from the Dark Continent ensue. The author's sister's impressions of this tale are not recorded.

I will admit that when I first learned of the Conan Doyle–Jean Leckie romance, at a tender age at which I was unabashedly hero-worshiping the man, I found it appalling. The business makes Conan Doyle look a monstrous hypocrite, banging on endlessly about "honour" while he tootles around the cricket grounds and golf resorts with a woman conspicuously not his dying wife. In the thick of the affair, he wrote his oddball modern romantic novel, *A Duet; with an Occasional Chorus,* which he apparently intended as instructive uplift for young married couples. Chutzpah! Beyond the icky ethical dynamics, this episode becomes exhausting to observe. Was he ever actually at home? How much "fresh air" does one man need, anyway? How could his wife not have known? (I would guess that she did know, but curiously, almost none of her correspondence survives.) As a character in the mind's eye, the author begins to travel at the slapstick speed of a silent-movie gag, zooming manically about the landscape. (Conan Doyle was, no surprise, an early automobile enthusiast and a collector of some of England's first speeding tickets. He crashed into turnip carts and nearly killed himself in a 1904 rollover accident.) Conan Doyle found himself caught between his own insatiable energy and stagnation at home, in an age of sudden acceleration. Everything was changing. He wanted to be out in the world, experiencing it all. He wanted to buy motorcycles and take hot-air-balloon rides. The new century left behind anyone who did not sprint to keep up.

While I had not exactly received any anonymous, cut-and-paste notes warning me to KEEP AWAY FROM THE MOOR, several knowledgeable parties had expressed, shall we say, concern about my plan to take my pregnant wife and five-year-old kid to Dartmoor. The 368-square-mile expanse is a national park these days; I found no end of websites depicting happy families gamboling about. Eleven million people go there every year. And this being England, the countryside lives a life of its own, completely different from an American-style wilderness: dotted with villages and farmsteads, much of the open land a commons for grazing sheep and horses.

At the same time, Dartmoor remains treacherous. The British military uses vast tracts of moorland as a firing and training range, so live ordnance comes smashing down from time to time. The high tors and rocky outcroppings that dot the landscape attract climbers and hikers but, of course, pose their dangers. I did several ill-advised Google searches for variations of "death on dartmoor," which, combined with the *Hound*'s description of "this most God-forsaken corner of the world," created the impression of a disorienting fastness capable of devouring the unwary wanderer. In our first day or so in Moretonhampstead, conversations with locals wound their way to just how easy it would be to become lost on some remote stretch, which, in the prevailing conditions, would mean quick transformation into a human ice cube.

But, all the same, in two days we'd squeezed all the family entertainment possible out of a frozen Moretonhampstead. We'd been to the church. (Lovely Eastertide service — until an electric coffeepot shorted out and caught fire.) We'd done the (surviving) pubs. It was time to get out of there. In a rare stroke of practical intelligence, I had arranged an expert guide to show us the sights and keep us from getting killed. Tom Soby awaited us in the White Hart's lounge one morning: tall, white-haired, exuding ruddy, outdoorsy cheer. I had found Tom, who works for the national park service and hires out as a guide in his spare time, through a crosshatch of guidebook recommendations (he'd squired Rick Steves around) and Internet searches. He and I had exchanged a lively correspondence on the advisability of taking young Cash out on the moors. (SUMMARY: Tom: "Mmmmmmm . . ." The boy's father: "He'll be fine! I'm from Montana!") Tom would prove to be a man whose services I can recommend. After a few preliminaries — he presented old national park posters for Cash and a photocopied portrait of Henry Baskerville, the coachman for Fletcher Robinson, Conan Doyle's guide to Dartmoor, and unwitting source of the novel's title — Tom led us to his small, boxy red car.

"Are you a nervous passenger, Zach?" he asked as I strapped myself in. I said no. "You will be by the end of today."

Sherlockians have long debated the true identities or inspirations for the *Hound*'s locations.* In his usual way, Conan Doyle captured particular places with great feeling and precision, but freely remixed larger ge-

---

* Leslie Klinger's notes to the novel in his *Annotated Sherlock Holmes* make a useful point of departure for anyone interested in the particulars, though even they do not track every thread of the decades-old argument.

ographies to suit his plot, expanding distances and creating aliases. Tom had developed his own itinerary around the novel, which proved evocative enough. The first point of interest, he told us as he smoothly steered around blind corners that would have reduced my wife and me to tears, if not statistics, would be "the huts of the old folk," a stone encampment of Dartmoor's Bronze Age citizens.

Fog shrouded the landscape, reducing visibility to about ten yards. Tom pulled the car to a mossy roadside and hopped out. He outfitted himself with an enormous pack. (Tom would find himself obliged to supply all three of us with one piece of essential gear or another, even extra child-sized mittens for the foreseeable but inevitable moment when Cash lost his.) He forged up a steep hill, into the fog.

The trail threaded along a gushing creek, over frost-tipped heather and a carpet of boggy, yellow-green vegetation. We crossed several "clapper" bridges: small stone slabs laid across the creek bed, worn flush to the surrounding soil by eons of use. Each felt freshly oil-slicked, and my mind filled with visions of my son sliding off into the frigid water below. Cash scampered like a human-goat hybrid, leaping off every stony outcropping he encountered and cantering into every dense fogbank that came his way.

"We'll have no trouble with him, I see," Tom observed.

Four thousand years ago, Dartmoor was quite the bustling place: bits and pieces of at least five thousand stone houses remain, and many more wooden structures must have rotted away in the rugged weather and acidic soil. After being ignored for centuries bar the occasional looter, in Conan Doyle's time these ruins attracted the newly formalized discipline of archaeology. A major dig and reconstruction of our destination, Grimspound, the largest and most famous single site, took place only a few years before the author banged around the countryside with Robinson.* (In his letters, Conan Doyle noted the eerie fact that Dartmoor

---

* This project was initiated by Sabine Baring-Gould, a remarkable freelance scholar, novelist, folklorist, songwriter, priest, et cetera, et cetera, in that hyperactive Victorian vein; he wrote one of the great books on werewolves, for example, and composed "Onward, Christian Soldiers." His grandson, William S. Baring-Gould, would be a prominent midcentury Sherlockian, compiler of the first major annotation of the saga.

was more thickly populated thousands of years before than in his own day.) Reasonable enough, then, to suppose that Conan Doyle had in mind the gray stone fortress that materialized before us as we reached the high ground commanding the ravine below.

It felt a fearsome place. A wall fashioned from piled boulders described a wobbly oblong around a sloping expanse of high moorland, once home to about five hundred Bronze Age people. Round depressions bounded by enormous lumps of gray, frost-etched rock marked about two dozen of their dwellings, which would have had roofs of turf or thatch. This day, pools of frozen water filled the bottom of the huts; Cash quickly hopped into the biggest and most treacherous-looking of them. This would have been the metropole for a considerable stretch of countryside, but at the best of times it would have been raked by the elements. Over time the climate changed, the soil proved unsuitable for crop cultivation, and the people of Grimspound moved on (or died out). *Sic transit gloria,* or whatever it may have been.

In the *Hound,* Watson and other characters make several references to Dartmoor's stone huts, many riddled with anthropological inaccuracy (they attribute the structures to *Neolithic* man, for example), all foreboding. The presence of hundreds of abandoned hovels accentuates the feeling that unseen forces must be at work. It soon becomes evident that one or more shadowy figures are abroad in the countryside: the escaped convict, for one, but also the lonely watcher on the high tor whom Watson and Sir Henry spied during their nocturnal romp. With the help of cranky Frankland's telescope, Watson learns that a messenger boy now and again creeps across the scene, apparently bound for the stone huts. The intrepid doctor decides to investigate.

As Tom led us around Grimspound, I kept trying to think deep thoughts about how Conan Doyle's allusion to a distant past lends his commercial thriller a primal sense of the archaic. Mostly I thought about how I was freezing. On a clear day, Grimspound affords views of two high tors; we could see nothing beyond the compound's perimeter. As we wandered the site, people clad in bright, all-weather technical gear kept bounding out of the fog, hurtling over rocks in nimble leaps as they consulted handheld GPS units and exhaled great clouds of healthy breath.

"Ah," Tom said as we encountered one of these wraiths, "the Chagford Challenge." This annual race sends a couple of hundred hearty souls out onto the moor from the village of Chagford; I'd later read, on the organization's website, a promise that the event offers "Dartmoor at its springtime best." I marveled at the fact that these hale, skinny creatures in petroleum-based neon fabrics somehow belonged to the same species as those who lugged the building stones up Grimspound several millennia before.

We began our descent, picking our way down the sketchy path. Almost all the hiker-dead-on-Dartmoor stories I'd heard involved some variation on the theme of bearings lost amid confusing moorland geography. The place is full of towns and roads and landmarks, yet it can swallow you up in its big, sometimes fatal expanses of nothing. Tom had hiked Grimspound countless times. Left to my own devices, I probably would have led my family off into the void.

About halfway down, we heard a rustling in the mist. A half-dozen moor ponies materialized: squat, implacable figures, their coats and manes covered in ice crystals. We stood still as the horses passed, almost too perfectly ghostly and time-lost, back into the haze. Cash silently held Tom's hand as he watched. Farther along, we stopped to examine hawthorn trees and brambly bushes thick with ice crystals. And finally, the thin strip of asphalt and Tom's red car: I've never been so grateful for internal combustion, roadbuilding, and the global oil industry. I repented all the bad things I'd said about them.

John Watson, in his own sortie to the huts of the ancient folk, tracks the suspicious messenger boy to one stone domicile in particular, where "the barren scene, the sense of loneliness, and the mystery and urgency of my task all struck a chill to my heart." By the time he reaches the hut — a fine one, too, complete with roof — the boy has vanished and all is dark within. Watson throws aside his cigarette (forgetting that he always patronizes the same London tobacconist, and thus the brand will identify him to anyone with, let's say, highly developed observational faculties), grasps his revolver, and plunges into the gloom. No one is home, but he finds blankets, a waterproof Victorian forebear of a Chagford Challenger's jacket, tins of tongue and peaches (yum!), half a bottle of booze, and a sinister note: "Dr. Watson has gone to Coombe Tracey." By Jove, someone's been tracking his movements! As Watson ponders the implications of this evidence, he hears a boot striking rock outside. He slinks into a dark corner, cocking his revolver, awaiting a fateful interview in the antediluvian murk.

A moment later, a cool voice speaks: "It is a lovely evening, my dear Watson. I really think that you will be more comfortable outside than in."

When the wind was not gnawing my face, and when Tom's capable hands manned the steering wheel, I began to enjoy Dartmoor. The landscape alternates between plunging gorges, moss-banked rivers, and expanses of austere highland. Even on this miserable day, the settlements and back roads were surprisingly flush with outdoors folk and lumbering tour buses hauling loads of foreign tourists. "Germans love it here," Tom remarked as we pulled aside to inspect the enormous stone-slab bridge at Postbridge, his day-job station with the national park. "We check thousands of them through a year."

We stopped in Princetown at the moor's southern edge to inspect Her Majesty's Prison, whence Selden, the Notting Hill Murderer, escapes in the *Hound*. (Jonathan Small, the One-Legged Man of *The Sign of the Four*, predicted that he, too, would spend his final days here, "digging drains.") The penal compound lay in a thick haze, its stone gates stoically facing the trim village beyond. "Who's in there?" my son asked. "Six hundred of the nastiest men in England," Tom replied. Conan Doyle stayed at what was then the Duchy Hotel, now a visitors' center operated by the national park. We entered via a small columned portico to find an elegantly tiled former lobby, presided over by a life-size cardboard figure of Arthur Conan Doyle and a hilarious sculpture of a crazy-faced black dog. The center's small exhibit hall explained some latter-day issues. Average summer temperatures could rise 4 degrees Celsius by 2080, for example, and bracken and gorse are already growing in excess thanks to warmer weather. The national park attracts massive numbers of visitors, who exert ecological pressures of their own. Meanwhile, conservationists armed with lidar and biodiversity goals work to restore and preserve mires and bogs.

Out in the cold, however, the landscape's ancient dread still felt bony and strong. Tom's car wound through treacherous hairpins and in and out of blinding mists. At one point, as we crossed a small bridge, he recounted the legend of Hairy Hands, a phantom pair of fur-clad mitts said to materialize out of thin air at just this point and wrest control of vehicles from their luckless drivers, usually with fatal results. ("Hasn't happened in a while, it must be said," Tom noted.) In the compact village of Widecombe-in-the-Moor, Tom led us into the Gothic church of St. Pancras, where panels inscribed in seventeenth-century English told the tale of the day the Devil crashed through the church roof to incinerate some ne'er-do-wells playing cards in the back during divine service. St. Pancras's ceiling, since repaired, is decorated with the Green Man, Tinners' Hares (three rabbits circling one another in profile, sharing three ears between them), and other signs and symbols descended from pagan and folk tradition. (The three hares can be found in Chinese oasis towns on the Silk Road and on old synagogues in Europe.) We heard tell of depraved squires — clear models for the wicked Hugo Baskerville, original victim of the novel's curse — and of packs of rabid dogs long said to roam the moors by night.

I had taken along a curious book, dating to 1972, titled *Witchcraft and Folklore of Dartmoor*. The author, Ruth E. St. Leger-Gordon, drew upon both old-time oral tradition and a faint dose of Age of Aquarius grooviness. "On Dartmoor, the Wish Hounds, like the pixies, have caught the popular imagination and remain firmly enshrined among the tors. Here, on wild stormy nights ... they may be heard galloping over the moor cheered on by their huntsman ... the Devil himself. Whoever is unlucky enough to meet the pack will die within the year." St. Leger-Gordon considers such tales holdouts of a pre-Christian culture, bound up with Odin and Pan and that crowd, folded into the superstitious lore of an isolated country people. In the frigid and dimly lit confines of St. Pancras, it was easy to understand how the uncanny edge of nature — a ball-lighting strike on a church, for example — can become myth.

There's a reason that *The Hound of the Baskervilles* is the most famous Sherlock Holmes story, known to people who could not name "The Adventure of the Engineer's Thumb" if their lives depended on it. It is the one that's not like the others. The adventures published in the 1880s and '90s usually employ London as a backdrop; in the likes of *A Study in Scarlet* and "The Adventure of the Blue Carbuncle," plots hang on big-city anonymity and infinite social possibilities. Even countrified stories, like the horse-racing tale "Silver Blaze"— also set on Dartmoor but completely different in atmosphere — remain firmly within the modern world of railway timetables, telegraph connections, and mobile commerce. (A London dressmaker's receipt provides a key clue in "Silver Blaze.") The *Hound* steps out into the middle of nowhere and back in time. The cast of characters is sharply limited; if someone is plotting against Sir Henry Baskerville, the guilty party *must* be among the moody servants and few kooky neighbors, circling each other in a miserably medieval social scene. Conan Doyle infused this classic country-house-mystery structure with a chilly tincture of folklore and the tropes of classic horror: the shattered castle, the bleak countryside, the ambiguous curse upon an entire bloodline.

Thus the *Hound* lights up those neurons that fire when floorboards creak in the night. The novel reprises the process Conan Doyle had previously applied to the urban, criminal lore of late-Victorian London — just as "The Adventure of the Red-Headed League" opportunistically snatched details of a few celebrated heists and remixed them into a single caper, Conan Doyle synthesized those hoary Dartmoor myths into a pervading atmosphere. Conan Doyle's vow to create "a real Creeper" pays off. As Watson explores the moors, he hears an unearthly howl in the distance. You, dear reader, hear it, too.[*]

Against his grim backdrop, Conan Doyle turns *The Hound of the Baskervilles* into a philosophical battle of reason versus unreason. From the beginning, there's a debate on: could the hound (sorry, the Hound) really be some kind of demon from beyond, tasked to gnaw on the nearest available Baskerville? Or must there be some earthbound explanation? Are we dealing with ghosts here, or human agency? The promise of Sherlock Holmes, always, is that rationality, evidence, questions, and logic can

---

[*] Which is not to say that *The Hound of the Baskervilles* is perfect. In fact, the plot is full of inconsistencies — flaws perceptive readers noticed immediately. In January 1902, in the middle of the *Hound*'s original serial run in the *Strand*, the *Cambridge Review* published "An Open Letter to Dr. Watson" from a young publishing professional named Frank Sidgwick. Sidgwick makes a detailed analysis of the novel's internal chronology; to summarize, the story makes no sense whatsoever. The letter is generally considered the founding document of the Sherlockian "Great Game," about which, more anon.

win the day. In the *Hound,* Holmes faces the possibility of forces beyond rationality. Can his craft, which he describes in the novel as "the scientific use of the imagination,"* banish the dark fate that haunts the Baskerville clan?

Two ways of behaving in the world collide. The Dartmoor peasantry tells tales of the Hound of the Baskervilles every time a bog makes a funny noise. Beryl Stapleton goes around issuing baleful, Goth-eyed warnings about Sir Henry's safety. Even the scientific fanatic Dr. Mortimer allows for the possibility of some sort of supernatural force at play. Watson, that hardheaded ex–army man, gets so enwrapped in the cuckoo vibes as he works alone, he doesn't know what to think or whom to suspect. As he sits in the stone hut with his revolver in hand, his doubts and fears escalate to a crisis point.

And then Sherlock Holmes reappears, and the novel's tenor subtly changes: a shaft of light through darkness, a sunny morning after a stormy night — choose a metaphor. The detective has closely followed Watson's written reports, delivered by his messenger boy. And he's done some sleuthing out in the real world, combing public records for dirt on the neighbors. For all the drama out on the moor, *The Hound of the Baskervilles* turns out to pivot on, of all things, primary document research: a mundane Investigation 101 chore that yields a decisive clue to the evildoer. While everyone else runs around getting the vapors over the Demon Dog, Holmes sits back and takes in the drama at a cool remove, painstakingly checking rumor and half-truth against empirical sources. An inimitable Sherlockian crispness returns to Conan Doyle's narrative. Good job, Watson, but the Great Detective is on the scene now. Superstition had a nice run, but now it's up against observation and deduction. Time to bring a bad doggie to heel.

Tom drove us past his choice for Baskerville Hall — a forlorn and unromantic hulk, disappointingly bereft of gates and teetering towers, but

---

* A phrase Conan Doyle seems to have borrowed from an 1870 essay by the physicist John Tyndall. Tyndall's epigraph to an anthologized version of the essay, quoting Sir Benjamin Brodie, could be a Sherlockian manifesto: "physical investigation more than anything besides helps to teach us the actual value and right use of the Imagination."

with a full complement of gloom — and parked in a muddy turnout. We aimed to reenact the novel's climactic moorland episode, when Holmes and Watson (and the ever-handy Inspector Lestrade, who comes down from London with a pistol in his hip pocket) send poor, unwitting Sir Henry out into the wilds as Hound bait.

We four left the car and started on a ragged track up a broad, barren ridge. I immediately concurred with Lestrade's initial judgment: "My word, it does not seem a very cheerful place." No. The gray sky curdled above and the crosswind made a mockery of our jackets. The ground beneath our feet was a slurry of ice, mud, and hypothermic pools of standing water, which Cash instantly walked through, soaking his shoes and socks. We soldiered on. I looked to my left.

Over the Great Grimpen Mire there hung a dense, white fog. It was drifting slowly in our direction and banked itself up like a wall on that side of us, low but thick and well defined.

Fog concealed the isolated farmstead, analog to the villain's headquarters in the novel, toward which Tom led us. Our world became very small. By the time we'd walked two hundred yards, it felt as if we were doing one of those Sherpa-freezing Himalayan vanity expeditions.

"It's moving toward us, Watson."

"Is that serious?"

"Very serious . . . the one thing upon earth which could have disarranged my plans."

Holmes, Watson, and Lestrade soon take refuge in a rocky nook, from which they watch the path for Sir Henry and any assailants, canine or human, spectral or corporeal. Our party had no such luck. As microscopic hail began to blow, we were exposed.

"In half an hour we won't be able to see our hands in front of us."

Cash is a mighty little hiker, but at this point he began to protest, even as he obeyed the five-year-old's prime directive and stomped through more puddles. As the father who dragged his kindergartner out on a forced march across a windswept wasteland on a foreign island, I was naturally very upset. With him. Tom calmly attempted to explain the principles of frostbite to the boy. Christina volunteered to guide her firstborn back to safety. I thought that sounded dandy.

Still that dense white sea . . . swept slowly and inexorably on.

"Sorry, I can't let them go," Tom said. "If they wander off the track into this fog, they could be hopelessly lost."

"They'll be fine!" I was anxious to continue, to reach the point (or just the imaginative state) where Holmes and Watson and Lestrade heard footsteps in the fog and watched the bewildered Sir Henry emerge from the mist.

"Hist!" cried Holmes . . . "Look out! It's coming."

Because up here, on this ridge (or one like it, in Arthur Conan Doyle's mind), they saw it.

A hound it was, an enormous coal-black hound, but not such a hound as mortal eyes have ever seen. Fire burst from its own mouth, its eyes glowed with a smouldering glare, its muzzle and dewlap were outlined in flickering flame. Never in the delirious dream of a disordered brain could anything more savage, more appalling, more hellish be conceived than that dark form and savage face which broke upon us out of the wall of fog.

I was chasing the Hound, too — or the mystique of the *Hound*, a skinny novel originally run in installments in a consumer magazine that had somehow grown in my mind into a magical key to understanding the whole Holmesian phenomenon. This was different from wandering around Baker Street looking at the shops and houses. The *Hound* hauled me out here into the freezing wastes with my wife, kid, and unborn child. The *Hound* impelled me to employ dear Tom Soby on a day he would probably have preferred to spend with his own family. The *Hound* inspired me to drive down suicidal roads, through ice and miasma. What was I after? Confirmation that, in most cases, fictional danger is best appreciated from a snug armchair, with a mug of tea or something stronger at hand? Got it. Meanwhile, as we continued to scramble into the face-freezing cold, I was acting like the numbskulled peasantry in *The Hound of the Baskervilles*. I had only a shivering child on my hands, but in fact my challenge was not entirely different from the fear that momentarily paralyzes Sherlock Holmes and John Watson as the beast of legend erupts from the gloom. The doctor and detective confront the impossible: a supernatural predator with a taste for a particular family's jugulars. As for me, I had almost sent my wife and kid off into a treacherous fog so I could continue a hike to an imaginary destination. Like Holmes and Watson as the Hound bore down upon helpless Sir Henry Baskerville, I needed to come to my senses. Immediately.

Holmes and I both fired together, and the creature gave a hideous howl.

"Yes. We should turn back."

That cry of pain from the hound had blown all our fears to the winds. If he was vulnerable he was mortal, and if we could wound him we could kill him.

Tom, Christina, and Cash enthusiastically agreed, and we retreated down the track. In the novel, Holmes and Watson save lives with a combination of methodical thinking and decisive action. On the real Dartmoor, we just got warm and dry and rescued our day. Intact and unfrozen, we went on to discover many pleasant places in that high, wild place. (When the fog lifts, Dartmoor becomes quite beautiful.) That is the ultimate moral of *The Hound of the Baskervilles:* dark fantasy clouds the judgment. It will lead you off on deadly tracks, and leave you vulnerable to misjudgment and poorly trained mastiffs covered in glow-in-the-dark paint. We all hear the howl of the Hound sometimes. The trick is to listen more closely, think clearly, and get out of the fog.

7

SECRET HISTORIES

A MASKED FIGURE STANDS at a table in an ornately furnished room, furtively stuffing objects into a sack. A door to this sinister person's left opens. In walks a handsome, dark-haired, cigar-smoking fellow in a signature dressing gown — we know *him*. He nonchalantly approaches the thief and gives him a friendly tap on the shoulder.

And then the criminal vanishes! Into thin air! Sherlock Holmes knits his brow, shrugs, and takes a seat to light his cigar. But the cigar explodes! And the criminal instantly reappears, sitting cockily on the table! Up they leap. Holmes draws a revolver from his dressing gown pocket, aims — but the thief vanishes again! Then reappears on the other side of the room! Holmes chases him, but this most slippery felon ducks under the table and disappears. The confused detective turns to examine the bag of loot. But the bag dematerializes in his very hand, magically crossing the room to end up . . . in the clutches of the thief! The robber gives a saucy wave and bolts out the window, leaving only . . .

Sherlock Holmes Baffled: forty seconds of flickering, gray-and-black, silent action, originally watched by a single customer at a time on a whirring peep-show Mutoscope, shot in a rooftop studio in New York City with actors now unknown. Made in 1900, this curio occupies an outsized place in cinema history: the first known detective movie, and the first portrayal of a character that would become one of the most frequently conjured figures on film. Sherlock Holmes doesn't do much, admittedly — he's *Baffled!* — but the detective is surveying new fields of adventure. He and the camera will come to understand each other very well. A new century begins on Baker Street.

In the end, the United States resuscitated Sherlock Holmes. In the spring of 1903, with *The Hound of the Baskervilles* and Gillette's *Sherlock Holmes* fresh in many enterprising minds, *Collier's Weekly* made Arthur Conan Doyle a colossal offer: as much as $45,000 for a new series of Sherlockian short stories. (Call up your inflation calculators. I get $1.13 million in modern dollars with mine.) The author acquiesced via postcard: "Very well."

"I don't see why I should not have another go at them and earn three times as much money as I can by any other form of work," Conan Doyle wrote to his mother, who worried that New Sherlock wouldn't match the quality of Sherlock Classic. "You will find that Holmes was never dead, and that he is now very much alive."

So in another spring — this, in a fictional 1894 — John Watson loiters outside the Park Lane manse of a murdered aristocrat, Ronald Adair, who somehow took a revolver bullet through his brain while alone in a locked room. The mournful Watson confesses, as "The Adventure of the Empty House" begins, that in the nearly three years since Holmes's disappearance he has followed the criminal news, to no avail. As he turns to leave the scene, he jostles a stooped, whiskered old creature laden with rare books, who snarls at him. When Watson returns to his new medical practice and home in Kensington (where he lives alone because, we learn almost in passing, Mary Morstan has also died), he discovers that the weird bibliophile followed him. Tête-à-tête in Watson's study, the bookseller distracts the doctor. When Watson turns, Sherlock Holmes stands before him, alive and well. Watson — understandably — faints.

Sherlock brings his long-suffering friend back round with a dose of brandy and proceeds to spin a remarkable yarn. In fact, his story makes approximately zero sense. Holmes tells Watson that when Moriarty came for him at Reichenbach, he believed himself finished. But — aha! Sherlock happens to know baritsu, "the Japanese system of wrestling," and an elderly math professor turns out to be less than formidable. Moriarty goes into the falls.

Holmes then spies an opportunity: Moriarty's henchmen remain at large. If everyone believes Sherlock dead, he can work against them in secret. Unfortunately, it means breaking Watson's heart, but business is business, and up the cliff Holmes goes — menaced, as he climbs, by an unfriendly third party who chucks boulders. He scampers over the mountains to Italy, then vanishes. Only Mycroft knows he's alive — he funnels Sherlock money and maintains the Baker Street rooms. The detective disguises himself as a Norwegian explorer named Sigerson (as you do) and wanders forbidden Tibet for two years, "spending some days with the head lama" (as you do). He then tours the Islamic world — Persia, Mecca, Khartoum — and stops in the south of France to conduct some chemistry research. News of the Adair murder, which presents a chance to strike against the rump Moriarty regime, brings him back to London and the dumbstruck Watson's study.

By the way, should they get dinner?

Holmes may be lucky that Watson feels a bit faint. His account of "the Great Hiatus" (as Sherlockians call it) is packed with historical and logistical non sequiturs; the mechanics of the Swiss cliff-climb, alone, barely withstand scrutiny. ("That Sherlock should have been living for three years with hardly anyone noticing is remarkable," noted the *Whitstable Times and Herne Bay Herald*.) But far from detracting from "The Empty House," the murky account would become another selling point to generations of imaginative readers. What *was* Holmes doing during those three years? Acting as a secret agent under Mycroft's control? Becoming a Buddhist? How did he smuggle himself into Tibet and Mecca, not known for their hospitality to nonbelievers? Or . . . did any of it happen at all?

For the moment, Sherlock's tall tale suffices to explain away his absence and move us into the actual plot. An old-school nocturnal adventure across London ensues, culminating in a classic Holmesian ruse and the requisite tense vigil, the details of which we need not muck about with here. The jaunt ends in the capture of the wicked Colonel Sebastian Mo-

ran, Moriarty's chief thug and a crack shot with a cunning silent air rifle*
custom-made by a blind German mechanic. Moran used this weapon,
Holmes reveals to a suitably astonished Lestrade, to kill the unfortunate
Ronald Adair, who was about to blow Moran's cover as a high-stakes card
cheat.

And we're back! The October 1903 issue of *Collier's* appeared with
a sensational Frederic Dorr Steele color picture on its cover depicting a deerstalker-wearing Sherlock peering thoughtfully down into the
Reichenbach Falls, beneath a red-lettered headline proclaiming THE RE-
TURN OF SHERLOCK HOLMES. (Steele's style was much bolder than Paget's moody ink washes, with bright colors and sharp, heavy lines reminis-
cent of poster design.) The *Strand,* for its part, ran a puckish promotional
ad the previous month: "The news of [Holmes's] death was received with
regret as at the loss of a personal friend. Fortunately, that news, though
based on circumstantial evidence which at the time seemed conclusive,
turns out to be erroneous." That is fortunate, especially when you're a
magazine editor in possession of the first Sherlock Holmes short story
since 1893. Even the *Strand*'s competitors joined in the fun. *Punch* celebrated in verse:

> Oh, Sherlock Holmes lay hidden more than half a dozen years.
> He left his loving London in a whirl of doubts and fears.
> > For we thought a wicked party
> > Of the name of Moriarty
> Had dispatched him (in a manner fit to freeze one) . . .
> > But the very latest news is
> > That he merely got some bruises.
> If there is a man who's hard to kill, why he's one . . .
> > > > (The poet: P. G. Wodehouse)

---

* Curious: as you may remember, early in "The Final Problem," Holmes makes an inexplicable remark to Watson re his anxiety about "air-guns." Conan Doyle wrote that
story a decade before he created "The Empty House" and summoned an air-gun-wield-
ing military murderer to help put Sherlock Holmes back into action. Either Conan
Doyle's 1893 self unconsciously left a present for his 1903 self, or the older Conan Doyle
found a loose end and made a knot.

On both sides of the Atlantic, Holmes reanimated in magazines right abreast of the times. *Collier's* began its year with a special issue on automobiles, and an article in the *Strand* that carried "The Empty House" noted the presence of twenty thousand motorcars on Britain's roads. But Holmes himself would remain in his classical 1890s, his clients fretting on the train on their way to Baker Street, poor Watson freezing in a hansom cab in the "opalescent reek" of a London winter morning. The thirteen stories collected as *The Return of Sherlock Holmes* contain the purest distillate of Sherlockiana, as if some secret corner of Conan Doyle's mental laboratory had never ceased working to hone the old formulae. They run sleek and true, full of glinting talk and ironic humor. ("'From the point of view of the criminal expert,' said Mr. Sherlock Holmes, 'London has become a singularly uninteresting place since the death of the late lamented Professor Moriarty.'") Watson returns to Baker Street, where sharply etched set pieces weave the proper atmosphere, as when a fat schoolmaster barges into the 221B sitting room and promptly collapses on the bearskin rug to open "The Adventure of the Priory School," or when Sherlock strolls in to breakfast one morning with a harpoon under one arm, in "The Adventure of Black Peter," fresh from spearing hog carcasses. The tales are marbled with incident and weird glamour. While investigating "The Adventure of the Solitary Cyclist," Sherlock interrupts a chat at a country pub to exercise his scientific boxing talents upon a brawling ne'er-do-well. ("I emerged as you see me. Mr. Woodley went home in a cart.") "The Adventure of the Dancing Men" includes the cutest life-threatening hieroglyphic cryptograms ever drawn. "The Adventure of the Missing Three-Quarter" forces Holmes to think about rugby football. Smashed busts of Napoleon, impaled sea captains, sinister Russians, offended dukes, a vile blackmailer in astrakhan, a revenge-mad veiled noblewoman — the stories pitch the beloved Sherlockian world back into action.

The *Return* reaches a conclusion, in "The Adventure of the Second Stain," with the unexpected announcement that Holmes has retired to Sussex to keep bees. But never mind that: the story itself sizzles with intrigue and espresso-strength repartee. The Prime Minister himself must sit on a Baker Street sofa littered with old newspapers and explain that a vital state document has gone missing because a diplomatic minister, brought along to 221B for the sake of humiliation, took it home and lost it. When this august duo refuse to explain the document, they get the Holmesian high hand: "I regret exceedingly that I cannot help you in this matter, and any continuation of this interview would be a waste of time."

The chastened premier reveals that a highly offensive note from a Continental potentate has gone astray, its publication threatening geo-political disaster. "Consider the European situation . . . ," he bids the doctor and detective. "The whole of Europe is an armed camp. There is a double league which makes a fair balance of military power. Great Britain holds the scales." If this letter from Johnny Foreigner* gets out, every red-blooded Englishman will jolly well demand satisfaction upon the field of honour, et cetera, and 100,000 men may die in battle — the Prime Minister's offhand estimate. Sherlock Holmes certainly must investigate.

A jaunt through a world of champagne-society espionage follows, expertly stage-managed by Conan Doyle wielding all his old tricks: newspaper extracts, dramatic appearances at Baker Street, Sherlock darting off into the London streets leaving Watson at 221B, whence he spins a tale of great ferment and bustle without actually crossing the threshold until two-thirds of the way through. A gigolo secret agent ends up at the wrong end of an Oriental dagger. Holmes must weigh the "inscrutable" motives of a beautiful woman. Inspector Lestrade even gets a cameo. And in the end, of course, Holmes tracks down that incendiary letter. "You will be relieved to hear there will be no war," he tells Watson in triumph, ". . . that the indiscreet Sovereign will receive no punishment . . . that the Prime Minister will have no European complication to deal with, and that with a little tact and management upon our part nobody will be a penny worse for what might have been a very ugly incident."

Watson is beside himself with admiration. And aren't we all? With Sherlock Holmes back in action, London and the world stand safe.

The Return of Sherlock Holmes hit it big: legends come down of huge queues at newsstands, of libraries extending their hours. The character

---

* At the height of the Boer War, Kaiser Wilhelm inflamed British rage by sending a congratulatory telegram to a Boer commander. No doubt Conan Doyle kept the incident in mind.

was once again a cultural byword. When police arrested the perpetrators of a jewel theft in Conduit Street by using fingerprint identification, the press immediately thought of the brand-new "Adventure of the Norwood Builder," with one paper noting that Conan Doyle's story featured the technique just two weeks before police deployed it in the case. When a constable bagged a boot thief in Devonshire, he was proclaimed — that's right! — a local "Sherlock Holmes." A maid who solved a domestic conundrum was a "kitchen Sherlock Holmes." Anyone who figured out anything, just about, was proclaimed a Sherlock Holmes.

Even so, Conan Doyle struggled behind the scenes. His letters to Herbert Greenhough Smith reflect the *Strand* editor's uncharacteristic criticism of installments he found boring. Conan Doyle defends his work, at one point lamely arguing that, as far as decent Sherlock stories went, two out of three wasn't bad. He sulks a bit. At one point, he passive-aggressively declares that, in view of the editor's remarks, he plans to cut the series from the forecast twelve stories to eight. (In the event, he wrote thirteen; the full *Collier's* payout appears to have been contingent upon his doing so.) This exchange may be the first intimation that Sherlock's revival would sometimes tax Conan Doyle's creative resources — a strain he recognized himself. In his later years, he retailed an anecdote of a Cornish boatman who allegedly told him that Sherlock Holmes was never quite the same man after that fall from the cliff.

The author came away from the new series that much richer and, in keeping with his pattern, quite happy to forget the Great Detective. In 1905, he told an interviewer, "I am tired of Sherlock Holmes." He would never again write a sustained series of Sherlockian short stories, and would never revise his estimation that they represented a lower tier of literature than his other work. He may have shied from one aspect of his accomplishment in particular: Sherlock Holmes was no longer just a character, but an archetype, all the more inescapable.

All the quality magazines now filled their pages with eccentric crime solvers, it seemed. Arthur Morrison, a hardworking London journalist and popular fiction author, rolled out his investigators, Martin Hewitt and Horace Dorrington, during the post-Reichenbach interregnum, providing suave, archly observed glimpses of late Victoriana. Hewitt debuted in the *Strand* in March 1894, right when the magazine found itself short one great detective, and would prove a fairly serviceable replacement. Dorrington, who appeared in just six stories from *Windsor Magazine,* anthologized in 1897, cuts perhaps the more interesting figure: a "detective" whose investigations serve as cover for scams and blackmails perpetrated against his clients. This dark, knowing flip on the Conan Doyle formula* turns out to be fun; I particularly recommend "The Affair of the 'Avalanche Bicycle and Tyre Co., Limited,'" which revolves around bike-racing fraud and a high-tech speculative bubble in cycling gear.

Conan Doyle's friends got in on the act. Max Pemberton, a high-society dandy and journalist, wrote many mysteries; his urbane heist caper "The Ripening Rubies" avails itself of a little of that high-velocity dash that propels the best Sherlock Holmes stories.† Fletcher Robinson, Conan Doyle's collaborator on the *Hound,* cranked out adventures of a Scotland Yard detective named Addington Peace. (Robinson and Pemberton joined Conan Doyle and a few other writers of criminological bent in an informal club, Our Society.) Conan Doyle's own brother-in-law E. W. Hornung did likewise in his renowned stories of Raffles, the cricket-playing gentleman thief, and Bunny, his adoring roommate and accomplice. (Hornung dedicated these polished narratives to Conan Doyle as a "form of flattery," though Raffles's combination of sexy charisma and unrepentant criminality made the latter distinctly uncomfortable.)‡ Meanwhile,

---

* For a fascinating academic deconstruction of the Dorrington stories, see Clare Clarke's 2010 essay "Horace Dorrington, Criminal-Detective," published in *Clues: A Journal of Detection,* possibly the world's only interesting peer-reviewed journal.

† This story joins two of Morrison's in *The Rivals of Sherlock Holmes,* a useful and entertaining 1970 Penguin anthology edited by Hugh Greene.

‡ While Raffles continues to enjoy a small following today, the period's other imaginary detectives have all faded into history. An intriguing sidelight on the question of why Sherlock Holmes so decisively surpassed his fictional rivals comes from the Stanford literature professor Franco Moretti, renowned for his statistical analysis of literature. Moretti's research team compared Conan Doyle's stories to scores of other Victorian detective fictions and concluded that of them all, the Sherlock Holmes saga made the most consistent and effective use of clues. Moretti does note, however, that Conan Doyle's clues are not always fully decipherable to readers — unlike the puzzle-oriented mysteries that would become popular in the 1920s, you can't really beat Sherlock Holmes. This rigged game is less a science and more — yes — an art.

any publication seeking instant brand recognition could "borrow" the Great Detective and concoct imitations, from the Angus, Scotland, *Evening Telegraph's* unimaginatively named "Dundee's Sherlock Holmes," in 1904, to "Sherlock Guck, the Eskimo Detective."

Conan Doyle longed to be known for work less formulaic. After the triumphant 1903–04 *Return,* he could have churned out Holmes stories full time. But he saw himself as a great actor upon the stage of life, protagonist of grand missions and consuming projects. He ran hard, as always. The new King knighted him, officially as a Boer War propagandist, unofficially for Sherlock Holmes, apparently the joy of Edward the Caresser's literary hours. (Conan Doyle disdained the honor as "the badge of a provincial mayor," but his mother nagged him into it.) He staged a second unsuccessful run for Parliament. He nursed Touie through her final decline. Whatever else he did in that marriage, Conan Doyle worked tirelessly and spent liberally to extend his wife's life, and her death in 1906 brought on a pronounced depression as he whiled away a year of mourning before he could decently marry Jean Leckie.

He escaped these doldrums through an unlikely inspiration: a mostly blind, half-Indian lawyer convicted of animal mutilation. George Edalji, a young man who had authored a book on railway law, wrote to Conan Doyle. Conan Doyle took an interest, and the more he learned, the more outraged he became. It seemed that racist goons in the Staffordshire parish where Edalji's father served as Anglican vicar had framed him, abetted by lazy police and pliable courts, after a series of nighttime attacks on livestock. Conan Doyle launched a campaign to rehabilitate Edalji with long investigative articles in the *Daily Telegraph* and the *New York Times* in early 1907.

The case's details are technical (not to mention appalling), but these essays remain notably startling to any Sherlock Holmes fan: *Good Lord, he can really do it.* For Edalji, Conan Doyle brought the full range of Sherlockian technique into reality. He digested case files, analyzed old letters, tromped around the Staffordshire countryside, debriefed witnesses, reconstructed chains of events dating back decades. He once put these words in Sherlock's mouth: "You know my methods. Apply them." And so Conan Doyle did, even deploying the always valuable arcane knowledge: his brief experience in ophthalmology helped demonstrate that the young solicitor could barely see in daylight, rendering him an unlikely perpetrator of nocturnal open-air butchery.

Conan Doyle vests his published investigation with all the masterly intensity of Holmes, systematically unstitching the prosecution's case. Bloodstains, mud stains, handwriting, railway chronologies: he parses it all. His conclusions could come from Sherlock himself. "The upshot of my whole research," he writes, "has been to introduce me to a chain of circumstances which seem so extraordinary that they are far beyond the invention of the writer of fiction. At all times ... I have kept before my mind the supreme necessity of following truth rather than any preconceived theory, and I was always prepared to examine any point against the accused with as much care as if it made for his innocence." But if he used the investigative system of Holmes, a downright Watsonian instinct drove him: he had met Edalji and simply decided he was a decent chap. Authorities did finally, grudgingly, exonerate Edalji, who went back to practicing law and lived until 1953.* When he and Jean tied the knot in 1907, Conan Doyle invited Edalji to the wedding.

The case marked a new phase: Sir Arthur the Crusader. His perennial habit of writing letters to the press kicked into high gear, on a mind-boggling range of subjects, from the Olympic Games to "the traffic in skins and wild birds." Then, shortly after the Edalji case, Conan Doyle became incensed with the situation in the Congo, at the time a personal satrapy of the King of Belgium where millions had been murdered, mutilated, or starved in forced-labor rubber harvests. Cycling and motorcars created voracious demand, which the Belgians satisfied by chopping off the limbs of less productive workers. Chilling photographs and well-audited statistics shocked otherwise politically orthodox people in Europe and America: Hold on, *this* was imperialism? Who knew?† Conan Doyle pitched himself into a growing international pressure campaign, alongside other

---

* The case, and the relationship between Conan Doyle and Edalji, informs numerous nonfictional and fictional accounts, notably Julian Barnes's 2005 novel *Arthur & George*.

† In his book *Late Victorian Holocausts,* Mike Davis highlights famines in India and other British possessions during the final decades of the nineteenth century, which killed millions while exports in grain and other commodities continued apace.

prominent activists of the moment. In a letter to the London *Times*, published 18 August 1909, he wrote: "We live in the presence of the greatest crime which has ever been committed in the history of the world, and we who not only could stop it but who are bound by our sworn oath to stop it do nothing."

His Congo activism shows Conan Doyle at his absolute best. He hammered out *The Crime of the Congo*, a meticulous book-length indictment of Belgian policy, in a matter of days—his one full-fledged attempt to apply Sherlockian investigation to real-life politics. He and his fellow Congo campaigners set in motion the international humanitarian movement of the twentieth century. The results proved less than decisive: the King gave up personal rule of the Congo, but Belgian colonial government and many abuses continued, and global events soon conspired to make the *causes célèbres* of 1909–10 seem like ancient history. Still, in this and other public campaigns—he would help to free a wrongly convicted murderer, for instance—Conan Doyle made plain his dedication to the ideas implicit in Sherlock Holmes: the systematic accumulation of evidence, analysis, synthesis, and the revelation of truth and its translation into action.

Conan Doyle possessed such great passion, such a robust voice. The affairs of the world seemed to orbit around him. If anything, he was just waiting for his singular, defining mission.

As my train neared the Gloucester Road tube station one bright morning, sun streamed down between the back sides of terraced houses above. The London Underground emerges here as it threads through posh Kensington. I looked up at the residential windows, knowing one of them—which one?—played a critical role in "The Adventure of the Bruce-Partington Plans," a Sherlock Holmes adventure published in 1908, after Conan Doyle judged this an excellent place to dispose of a freshly bludgeoned corpse. My train stopped, and I ascended to the beautifully frumpy brick Victorian station, stepping into roughly the spot where—in that Sherlockian dimension which overlays our own in London—Holmes and his comrades gathered one foggy evening to catch a spy.

Conan Doyle had decided that Sherlock might still have his occasional uses. For most of the rest of his life, he would publish short-form Holmesian adventures periodically in the *Strand*. He uncorked "The Bruce-Partington Plans" as a Christmas treat for the magazine's December issue. It is something like the perfect Sherlock Holmes story.

A dense yellow fog settles upon London, leaving Watson bored and Sherlock nothing better to do than study medieval music and complain that the London criminal has lost his verve. Baker Street then has a notable visitor: Mycroft Holmes, last seen disguised as a coach driver during the getaway from London in "The Final Problem" (yes, that was him), and only really portrayed in 1893's "Adventure of the Greek Interpreter." Mycroft, Sherlock reveals fifteen real-world years later, is hardly a minor bureaucrat with an eccentric taste in social clubs. He is the secret power center of the British government, a one-man intelligence bureau and human analytical machine whose word repeatedly determines national policy.

We barely come to grips with Mycroft's newfound status as an *illuminatus* before the man himself arrives, Lestrade glumly in tow, to report that blueprints for a steampunky supersubmarine—"the most jealously guarded of all government secrets," Mycroft proclaims; ". . . naval warfare becomes impossible within the radius of a Bruce-Partington's operation"—vanished from the Woolwich Arsenal. The plans reappeared in the pockets of an arsenal employee found dead on a stretch of Underground track. Except the three most important pages remain missing.

The game is afoot, and Conan Doyle is in championship form. More than twenty years after two newly minted roommates dashed up the weedy path to a Brixton murder site, Holmes and Watson hurtle from drab government offices and suburban family homes to high-society houses to the guts of the Underground system. They consult lists of spies. They scan the *Telegraph*'s agony column for coded messages. At one point, Sherlock instructs his ever-game helpmeet to pack a kit of burglary tools and venture through the "fog-draped" streets to an Italian restaurant in the Gloucester Road, where the pals enjoy cigars with coffee and curaçao. Refreshed, they set off for some gentlemanly housebreaking at one of the "flat-faced pillared and porticoed houses which are so prominent a product of the middle Victorian epoch in the West End of London." Oberstein, a cosmopolitan operator, appears to have scampered to the Continent with the submarine plans. Holmes and Watson find their way into his vacated lair via the subterranean areaway and shake the place down for clues.

I walked the streets that day not in search of 13 Caulfield Gardens, Oberstein's manse — the address is fictional, and various theories compete as to its true identity — but rather in pursuit of the old Conan Doyle essence. The Kensington station environs, like Montague Street and the rundown bits of Brixton Road, remain notably Sherlockian. Strip away the chain coffee bars and fast-food restaurants, and the neighborhood looks just as described in "The Bruce-Partington Plans": endless rows of discreetly grand houses, each marked by whitewashed pillars, each smugly mute behind its firmly locked door. Thanks to Conan Doyle, I could imagine myself hopping down into one of the many open-topped basement areaways to jimmy a door. Cheerfully crass Italian restaurants still line the high streets, and Kensington would still make a plausible base for a modern-day Oberstein. (The 2011 British census revealed that the Royal Borough of Kensington and Chelsea, one of the most desirable districts on the planet, has lost population since 2001, a circumstance attributed to absentee foreign owners — your notorious Kazakh mini-oligarch, your generic Arab billionaire, what have you.)

I was smack in Sherlock's fictional footsteps, seeing the very locations and sensing the social resonances that triggered Conan Doyle's instinct for amplifying the capital's covert romance. "The Bruce-Partington Plans" hints at hidden dramas and endlessly tangled skeins of possibilities amid London's multitudes. As Watson puts it in the story's final passages, this adventure evokes "that secret history of a nation which is often so much more intimate and interesting than its public chronicles." The doctor could be describing all his best adventures with Sherlock Holmes.

Misgivings aside, Conan Doyle would continue to rely on Sherlock. A year after this story appeared, for example, the author got himself into theatrical trouble: he'd written a play about bare-knuckle boxing, which no professional producer would touch for the good reason that not a single woman would watch such a thing. Conan Doyle booked the Adelphi Theatre and mounted the play at his own expense. Box office lagged from the beginning, and then boisterous old King Edward VII died. All the West End theaters closed in mourning, leaving Conan Doyle custodian of a very expensive flop. At top speed, he whipped together a play based on "The Adventure of the Speckled Band," that gripping (if biologically impossible) Holmesian Gothic horror classic from back in '92, with its lonely house, wicked stepfather, oppressed daughter, and trained snake. He recruited H. A. Saintsbury, veteran of *Sherlock Holmes* touring productions, cast a stunningly beautiful actress named Christine Silver as his damsel in distress, and solicited script advice from his old friend J. M. Barrie, creator of *Peter Pan*. The Adelphi reopened with *The Speckled Band*. Surprise: huge hit, rave reviews, curtain calls, hundreds of pounds of profit every week. Holmes remained bankable.

In "The Bruce-Partington Plans," Conan Doyle used Sherlock as a political vehicle. He was becoming increasingly preoccupied by military technology. In particular, Conan Doyle obsessed over submarines and their threat to sea-locked Britain. The fictional high-tech vessel alluded to in this adventure, with its "automatic self-adjusting slots" and vaguely fearsome operational capacities, only hinted at his eventual interest. In July 1914, the *Strand* published "Danger!," a technically detailed near-future science fiction in which Conan Doyle invented a small European power that brings Britain to its knees with just eight submarines. Earlier that same year, Conan Doyle released an essay titled "Great Britain and the Next War," responding directly to a German general's book outlining the Kaiser's military imperatives. "I still think it would be an insane action for Germany to deliberately plan an attack upon Great Britain," he wrote. ". . . May it prove that the title [of this article] is an absurdity and the war an imaginative hypothesis."

These premonitions rattle around "The Bruce-Partington Plans," set in 1895 but a capsule dose of the world before the Great War in all its metropolitan flair, technological confidence, nationalist politics, and mounting unease. As Holmes and Watson enjoy coffee and curaçao at Goldini's Italian restaurant in 1895 (and as Conan Doyle's readers relax over their fresh copies of the *Strand* at Christmas 1908), all Europe is an armed camp. Germany races to challenge British naval superiority. France assembles a new force of colonial troops. Austria-Hungary bumbles around the Balkans. Everyone's playing for the slightest advantage. Everyone wants the Bruce-Partington Plans.

· · ·

In 1946, the founding editor of the *Baker Street Journal,* Edgar W. Smith, wrote: "What is it that we love in Sherlock Holmes? We love the times in which he lived . . . the half-remembered, half-forgotten times of snug Victorian illusion, of gaslit comfort and contentment, of perfect dignity and grace." Smith wrote lovely Sherlockian essays, but, all due respect, this is pure projection. When you actually look at the decades in which Sherlock Holmes appeared and matured as a pop-cultural figure, you find mere contentment in short supply.

In his own essay about Sherlock Holmes, the character he inspired, old Dr. Joseph Bell complained of a "weary, worn-out century." Others found the era's whirlwind change — "disruption," in the trendy current lingo — quite energizing. By roughly the time Holmes and Watson pursued Oberstein through the London fog, untamed new forces were on the loose. In 1911 and 1912, a Parisian anarchist gang led by one Jules Bonnot shocked the world with the first-ever use of a getaway car in an armed robbery, inaugurating a new epoch of crime. (A persistent tradition insists that Bonnot once worked as Conan Doyle's chauffeur, though that appears uncertain at best.) Just two months after the technothriller-ish "Bruce-Partington Plans," *Le Figaro* published quite another vision of high technology in the form of the Futurist Manifesto, wacky passion from some Italian kids with "electric hearts" ("We declare that the splendor of the world has been enriched by a new beauty: the beauty of speed"). The world found itself at a crux, a moment of mingled excitement and unease.

But what next? In spring 1914, Arthur and Jean Conan Doyle sailed for North America — his first time in twenty years, her first time ever. When the White Star liner *Olympic* (sister to *Titanic*) docked in New York, reporters crowded the famous author. CONAN DOYLE HERE, proclaimed the *New York Times,* EXPECTS IRISH WAR. The home rule issue consumed British attention that year. "Ulster will certainly fight," Conan Doyle told the journalists. ". . . They mean business up there in the North of Ireland." The reporters went on to ask him about British suffragettes — Conan Doyle expected one to be lynched any time now — about Teddy Roosevelt, a mysterious case in Atlanta, and his lunch plans. No word of any "European complication" arose.

I looped back through Kensington — Oberstein Land — and grabbed a coffee at one of six thousand Caffè Neros. On these streets, I could just about step into Conan Doyle's fictional world. When I first read the saga as a kid, the stories' distant Victorian-Edwardian paraphernalia fascinated me: hansom cabs, commissionaires, the gasogene, the tantalus. I love it all, still, but now I also see that Conan Doyle created a character too powerful and alluring for any one era to contain. Times change, just as they changed around Conan Doyle. Sherlock and Watson remain ever Victorian, but not *only* Victorian — as the century that followed "The Bruce-Partington Plans" and all of Conan Doyle's other gorgeous stories would prove.

So Oberstein Land made a good place to raise a cappuccino (no curaçao, sadly) to salute and say farewell to the birth-era of Sherlock Holmes. In some ways, the Victorians seem very different from us. They had generally better manners, even worse foreign policies, far more laissez-faire erotica,* and in some privileged cases, now-unimaginable amounts of time on their hands. Consider Conan Doyle, smashing out several books a year and playing untold innings of cricket while someone else looked after the kids. And yet our distance from the Sherlockian era is insignificant in the grander scheme of history. In five hundred years, people will no doubt lump us all together, as laymen now don't really distinguish between the Rome of Caesar and the Rome of Vespasian. (They'll know us all as the Age of the Coal-Burning Idiots, perhaps.) I felt a chill there at the Gloucester Road station, surrounded by multinational London — like Conan Doyle and his contemporaries, good people, steeped in the problems of the day, globalized, modern. The Europeans of 1914 accidentally devised a hair-trigger booby trap of diplomatic alliances and escalating military competition. We've accidentally (let's be charitable) filled the air with heat-trapping carbon. Or maybe it will be something else — just as it could have been "Irish war" or any number of great disruptions for them. Things change. It's seldom pretty.

Say you're a famous author, creator of the most popular fictional character of your time. Everyone asks your opinion on everything. You're enmeshed in all the big questions: fielding a united British Empire team for

---

* In *Inventing the Victorians,* Matthew Sweet writes: "The 1890s were the high noon of erotic ambiguity, the last moment of freedom before the system of personae and pathologies through which we have come to view our own sexualities became fixed."

the 1916 Berlin Olympics, for example — surely, that's very, very important. Then one day while you and your wife are on vacation in Canada, a Serbian terrorist shoots an Austrian archduke in Sarajevo. The Austrians issue an ultimatum, the Serbs reject it, the Russians mobilize to help the Serbs, the Germans mobilize to help the Austrians. The French mobilize on general principle. The Belgians look at the map and say, Uh-oh.

Who's going to sort it all out? Mycroft?

On a winter morning at 221B, Holmes and Watson puzzle over a coded message from an informant. "Porlock," a pseudonymous traitor in the Moriarty organization, has sent an alphanumeric sequence broken by the names Douglas and Birlstone. (Yes, we are back in the 1880s, pre-Reichenbach, and suddenly Watson knows all about Moriarty. And Watson lives at Baker Street? Wasn't he married? Continuity? Chronology? Elementary?) Sherlock needs a particular book to unlock the code. But which book? Young Billy the Page — a character lifted from William Gillette's play — bustles in with a second Porlock letter. The turncoat now refuses to reveal the source key, and advises Holmes to forget the whole thing, because "he suspects me. I can see that he suspects me. He came to me quite unexpectedly . . . I read suspicion in his eyes."

"He" is Moriarty, of course. Holmes remarks: "When you have one of the first brains of Europe up against you, and all the powers of darkness at his back, there are infinite possibilities."

But the Baker Street duo won't be stopped. They quickly deduce which book Porlock intended and crack the code, which portends danger for a rich man named Douglas at a country house called Birlstone. Enter a Scotland Yard man named Inspector MacDonald, bearing news — well, a wee dram of whiskey wouldn't hurt — that . . . drumroll, please . . . "Mr. Douglas of Birlstone Manor House was horribly murdered last night!"

Conan Doyle's British fans absorbed this fleet overture to classic Victorian detection in the *Strand* for September 1914. By the time many of them began *The Valley of Fear,* the final Sherlock Holmes novel, more than a quarter of a million French soldiers lay dead or wounded from Alsace to Flanders. After a chaotic series of clashes collectively known as the Battle of the Frontiers, the Germans threatened to roll on Paris. Authorities set demolition charges at the base of the Eiffel Tower and prepared to evacuate the government. From 5 September, the French and the still relatively small British Expeditionary Force pulled together along the Marne River — the French, famously, reinforced via Paris taxicabs. The Allies counterattacked through a gap in the German line and, amid horrendous carnage, flung the invaders back some seventy kilometers. The Germans began digging trenches.

In the imaginary 1880s, Holmes and Watson venture to a country manor built over the ruins of a medieval castle and girdled by a protective moat. The drawbridge works and the residents, the Douglases man and wife, raise it every night. Somehow, in that snug fortress, John Douglas ended up at the wrong end of a double-barreled shotgun, his head nearly obliterated, his face erased. A card lies beside him with a cryptic inscription. The murderer seems to have vanished. So matters stand when Sherlock Holmes arrives and begins ferreting around — he senses right away that testimony offered by the people of Birlstone Manor doesn't quite compute.

The small cast of characters — Watson/Conan Doyle titles one chapter "The People of the Drama" — includes the grief-stricken (but only sometimes) wife, a strapping best friend (and what are those two up to?), the mandatory hand-wringing housekeeper, and the standard-issue reserved and secretive butler. The novel thus becomes something like a prototype for the soon-to-be-classic English country-house murder mystery, which would shortly make the career of Agatha Christie and many other detective novelists. This genre had not yet congealed into formula in 1914 — Christie started writing her first Hercule Poirot novel in 1916, and the country-house plot would become standard in the interwar golden age of British crime writing. Colonel Mustard wouldn't kill anyone with the candlestick in the conservatory until 1944. So Conan Doyle was, once again, a pioneer, right down to the climactic scene when the detective gathers everyone in the study to reveal the solution. (It's pretty good.)

The author really only does two things that would strike discordant notes in any of the charming, forgettable minuets of genteel detection Christie and others would produce in the '20s and '30s. As in *A Study in Scarlet,* Conan Doyle pads the main Sherlockian narrative with a multichapter flashback set in the United States, again memorable for hilarious "American" slang. And then there is that shattered head, spattering the murder room with more viscera than the true country-house writer could stomach. Amid a jaunty, lightweight tale — the key clue is a missing dumbbell — the mutilated corpse is just too real: a wet, fleshy totem of human-on-human horror.

The Valley of Fear serialized through the fall, winter, and spring of 1914–15, as people in Britain and around the world woke up to even grimmer reality. Just after war broke out, Conan Doyle wrote his mother: "There is a good deal of nobility in it too and it will give Europe a chastening for which she will be the better. I don't think it can be a very long war. A year should see it through." To his brother Innes, a career army officer, he mused about joining up himself, at the age of fifty-five: "I have only one life to live and here is this grand chance of a wonderful experience."

A lot of similar nonsense made the rounds, of course. By midautumn, the nature of the beast began to reveal itself, by degrees grand and small. In October and November, Britain alone suffered about sixty thousand casualties in the first Battle of Ypres, essentially wiping out the original expeditionary force and triggering a vast mobilization. By then, Conan Doyle's brother-in-law Malcolm was already dead. His son Kingsley was in the army medical corps. He and Jean had twelve Belgian refugees living with them, and Conan Doyle was pushing an ambitious plan to organize a national civilian reserve. He had also, even at that early date, begun writing an epic history of the war, which he would continue, tracking the conflict at a near-real-time pace, resorting to huge troves of official and unofficial information, for five years.

By the time the final installments of *The Valley of Fear* appeared, in April and May 1915, poison gas, aerial dogfights, machine-gun nests, U-boats, zeppelin raids, and civilian massacres saturated the popular consciousness. Traumatized British boys were being shot for "cowardice" after rudimentary trials at the front. Troops from Australia and New Zealand landed in Turkey. It was as if Conan Doyle wrote his story in one civilization and the *Strand* published it in another.

The contrast between the mystery story's intimate, old-fashioned violence and values — a single man's death brings down the force of the state and, for God's sake, *Sherlock Holmes* — and the anonymous slaughter in the trenches could ring absurd, or obscene. At the time, though, many welcomed the distraction. "It is quite a relief to turn away ... from all the horrors of war, and to find a few hours' pleasant recreation in the pages of our ever-welcome old friend, *The Strand Magazine*," opined the *Grantham Journal* on 3 October 1914. ". . . Not least engrossing among its many good features being a further installment of Arthur Conan Doyle's 'Sherlock Holmes' serial, *The Valley of Fear,* a story which is proving even more exciting than any previous adventure of the great detective." As it progressed (if that's the word), the Great War lent Holmes new dimensions: as a touchstone from the old days and perhaps as an icon of British character and cleverness. In 1915, the *Bookman* wryly noted: "It has been suggested that since last August Mr. Sherlock Holmes has been at the head of the British system of espionage." (The journal also repeated an oft-told tale, perhaps apocryphal but hopefully not, that a real-life army doctor named Watson was captured early in the war, only to be freed by a German officer who told him, with a wink, that he'd soon see him back in Baker Street.) By mid-1915, Canadian troops read Holmes stories as a sort of primer on how to think.* Scottish soldiers snapped up cut-rate copies of *The Return of Sherlock Holmes.* At just sixpence, the Great Detective was a bargain to take to war.

Of course, Holmes was hardly exclusively British property. Conan Doyle's stories had been translated into just about every language spoken on the battlefields. The Ottoman Emperor himself, Abdul Hamid II, loved the Sherlockian tales. German actor Alwin Neuss, already renowned for playing Holmes on the screen, starred in a multi-installment silent serial spun off 1914's *Der Hund von Baskerville,* with scripts by Austrian filmmaker Richard Oswald, which continued production straight through the war. But given the circumstances, it was only a matter of time before the detective did his bit for King and Country.

I would wake up at night, paralytic with fright, staring up at the ceiling of our 1950s-style ranch house but seeing only the exploded face and rup-

---

* Sherlock found instructional employment in civilian life, too. A 1917 *Yale Law Journal* article used "The Adventure of the Empty House" as a case study in "Act, Intention, and Motive in the Criminal Law."

tured skull. I would then see the cavernous barrels of a sawed-off shotgun swinging my way — slowly, slowly. I would wait for the flash of fire and volley of lacerating shot.

After a few minutes, I would climb down from the top bunk, trying not to wake my little brother, leave our room, and pad down the long, carpeted hall in the darkness, making for my mom and stepdad's room. I must have looked like a wild-eyed urchin, half entranced, the pajamas I was rapidly outgrowing askew.

This happened night after night. I was twelve. Again and again, I woke up to that vision of spilled brain and pulped bone. Again and again, the shotgun loomed toward me.

I never told the long-suffering adults what scared me, because I didn't want them to confiscate my Sherlock Holmes. They were not stupid, however, and soon did exactly that. It was time to give old Sherlock a rest, they reasonably explained as I went into full foot-stomping mode. They extracted my battered Doubleday *Complete Sherlock Holmes* from my room and removed it to a secure location, and no doubt hoped I would develop a clandestine sedative habit to cope.

The nightmares dwindled away. I was, of course, relieved — not that I would ever tell *them* that. When I felt fully recovered, I began to reconnoiter the basement storage areas. How much time could I get away with down there, unmissed? I was only halfway through the story.

On an August evening in 1914, "the most terrible August in the history of the world," a German spy meets a somewhat elderly Irish-American operative at an English country house to take final delivery of stolen naval intelligence. Von Bork — what a great "German" name — feels pretty pleased with himself. After years of clandestine machinations in England, he has a safe full of British military documents and a place in the German embassy's evacuation plans. It only remains to deal with Altamont, a prickly character with a bristly goatee and a taciturn, heavyset chauffeur. Von Bork writes a cheque for £500, and Altamont hands over a wrapped book. The spy opens the package — to find something called *Practical Handbook of Bee Culture.* A choloroform sponge interrupts Von Bork's surprise.

A moment later, Holmes and Watson relax over a glass of Von Bork's wine. Sherlock reveals that he has spent two years on a deep-cover assignment worthy of le Carré: establishing "Altamont" (of course, the middle name of Arthur Conan Doyle's late father) in Irish activist circles in Chicago and Buffalo, then joining in some political mischief in County Cork, all in hopes that the Germans would make contact. (If Mycroft planned that one, hats off.) He contrived to plant Mrs. Hudson, of all people, within Von Bork's household staff, which allowed him to pick off German agents one by one. He stuffed Von Bork full of ersatz intelligence, and now has stuffed Von Bork himself into the backseat of the car piloted by trusty Watson.

The old boys of Baker Street, portrayed in their sixties for the first and last time, stand out on the house's terrace to enjoy the summer evening. Chronologically, this moment — "the last quiet talk we shall ever have," Holmes predicts — concludes the saga launched when Watson ran into his old medical-school chum Stanford at the Criterion Bar, back in the lost world of 1881.

> "There's an east wind coming, Watson."
>
> "I think not, Holmes. It is very warm."
>
> "Good old Watson! You are the one fixed point in a changing age. There's an east wind coming all the same, such a wind as never blew on England yet. It will be cold and bitter, Watson, and a good many of us may wither before its blast. But it's God's own wind none the less, and a cleaner, better, stronger land will lie in the sunshine when the storm has cleared."

"His Last Bow," published in September 1917 by both the *Strand* and *Collier's* in the United States — which had declared war on Germany the prior spring — is a pretty decent, if oddball, Sherlock Holmes story. (For one thing, it's told in the third person, rather than narrated by Watson.) It's fun to speculate about Holmes's secret mission in America and all the hardboiled characters he would have encountered in tumultuous Irish Chicago circa 1912. Once he drops his Altamont identity, Sherlock's dialogue is at its snappy best — he suggests that Von Bork's legacy will be a pub called the Dangling Prussian, should the German call out for help. The final exchange on the terrace could serve as the valedictory statement of an era.

All the same, I can't help wishing that Holmes was doing . . . something else. Working to save a shell-shocked seventeen-year-old private accused of desertion. Exposing a war profiteer. Teaming up with Irene Adler to blackmail the Kaiser into suing for peace. Anything. Nothing wrong with entertainment, of course; Conan Doyle was just trying to do his part for morale. But by 1917, Holmes's dreamy view of the war as a form of national renewal was quaint at best, cynically propagandistic at worst. When one considers that the publication of "His Last Bow" coincided almost exactly with the writing of Wilfred Owen's poison-gas poem "Dulce et Decorum Est"—"But someone still was yelling out and stumbling / And floundering like a man in fire or lime. — / Dim through the misty panes and thick green light, / As under a green sea, I saw him drowning." — Conan Doyle begins to seem . . . out of touch.

He visited the battlefield as a uniformed observer and saw some horrible things. He wrote long letters to the press condemning German atrocities and urging British forces to adopt new technologies, like body armor for the infantry and life preservers for naval personnel. He could sometimes hear the guns in Flanders as he stood in his own garden in Sussex. But the full scope of the thing — mechanized slaughter, systematic violence against civilians, gathering political chaos in Germany, Austria-Hungary, Russia, and elsewhere — exceeded his moral imagination. As artists in Berlin and Zurich went half mental with revulsion in the early spasms of Dada, Conan Doyle applied the techniques of Sir Walter Scott, and never abandoned his boyish view of combat as an especially vigorous form of exercise. His history of the war reads like a football match report: shopping lists of regimental names, every action "gallant," "splendid," "heroic," "gallant" again. At times he sounds almost loopy. "Yet from general to private," he writes in his volume on 1916, "there was universal joy that the long stagnant trench life should be at an end, and that the days of action, even if they should prove to be the days of death, should at last have come." Right! No doubt men in the trenches experienced the full range of human emotions, but this makes a strange overture to the Battle of the Somme.

Yet even as Conan Doyle showed himself mismatched to the moment, his detective proved highly adaptable. In the trenches and prisoner camps, British soldiers created their own alternative Sherlock Holmes. Throughout the war, officers and enlisted men produced an extraordinary array of DIY newspapers and magazines, cobbled together with whatever equipment could be salvaged, printed in tiny runs and passed from hand to hand.

The most famous was the *Wipers Times,* first produced on the Ypres salient, but there were many. The soldier-writers filled these publications with a wild collage of maudlin poetry, ferocious satire, friendly commiseration, and absurdist humor — an underground history of the Western Front's collective consciousness. "Take a wilderness of ruin," one anonymous (it's all anonymous) poem in the *Wipers Times* runs, "Spread with mud quite six feet deep; / In this mud now cut some channels, / Then you have the line we keep. / Now you get some wire that's spiky, / Throw it round outside the line, / Get some pickles, drive in tightly, / And round these your wire entwine." In particular, the *Wipers*'s many sham ads (they're all sham ads) display humor at its most arch and deadpan.

HAS YOUR BOY A MECHANICAL TURN OF MIND? Yes!

THEN BUY HIM A

FLAMMENWERFER*

INSTRUCTIVE — AMUSING.

Both young and old enjoy,

This natty little toy.

GUARANTEED ABSOLUTELY HARMLESS.

THOUSANDS HAVE BEEN SOLD.

The Great Detective played his role. At a POW camp in Mainz, Germany, British prisoners published the *Queue,* featuring the adventures of Barlock Jones. A regimental magazine titled the *Scarlet Drop* offered Spitlock Phones and Wonson. Chublock Bones, the mordantly named Mereluck Tombs — the detective assumed many aliases. The *Wipers Times* published nonsensical sagas of Herlock Shomes (or Sholmes) and

---

* A German flamethrower.

"his admirer," Dr. Hotsam. Produced under incredible conditions — the ad hoc staff often operated its printing press within a kilometer of the German line, and enemy fire destroyed the equipment twice — the *Wipers* began its Sherlockian misadventure with *Herlock Shomes at It Again, Shot in the Culvert,* set at the front, plotted with illogical abandon, and manically punctuated.*

A girl, startled upon seeing a soldier's corpse, has fallen into a river:

But this was not to pass unnoticed — Holmes was in the district, and whipping out his vermoral sprayer with his right hand, he gave three rounds rapid into his forearm, while with his left he proceeded to tune up his violin. Dr Flotsam, who had been walking in his shadow, hearing the haunting strains of the violin, rushed forward to his side, exclaiming "What is it, Sholmes?"—Sholmes with that grandiloquent gesture for which he is justly famed, said "You know my methods, Flotsam!" and fell into the Bec — Flotsam not to [be] outdone, seized the vermoral sprayer, and fell in also — the water of the Bec flowed on. — (To be Continued.)

N.B. Next week: — A fresh supply of characters, and another thrilling installment.

Through multiple chapters, Shomes (or Sholmes or Holmes) and Hotsam (or Flotsam or Plotsam) pursue a series of violent, disconnected episodes that end when shelling, machine-gun fire, bombing, gas, and "liquid fire" abruptly kill the entire cast of characters, including them. Like his official incarnation, Sholmes returned from the dead for another *Wipers* serial, investigating stolen rum rations. A third, the amazingly titled *Zero! The Bound of the Baskershires,* sadly never concluded owing to real German shelling.

A generation — men and boys raised on Sherlock Holmes, whether they read Conan Doyle or not, as a staple of popular culture — flashes an ironical smile as it goes down in the mud. The war destroyed "half the

---

* This passage stands indebted to the work of Charles Press, a retired Michigan State University professor who published an account of "Herlock Sholmes in *The Wipers Times*" in the Winter 2013 edition of the *Sherlock Holmes Journal.*

seed of Europe," in Wilfred Owen's phrase, and it destroyed the world of Conan Doyle's gaslit crime fantasias. When armistice came at the end of 1918, it declared peace in a world transformed. (Conan Doyle himself, in a sprightly moment, would say that London was never quite the same after wounded Australian soldiers first encountered the newly minted flapper girls who worked in the War Office.) As those roughly made soldiers' newspapers hinted, however, Sherlock Holmes would go on into the new world, our world — with or without Conan Doyle. There would never be a last bow.

8

BLACK MASK

ONE DAY IN the late 1990s, an English playwright named Lucinda Coxon sat aboard a train bound for south Wales. She'd written a play set there, about her father's family origins in the area, and she was headed to consult on a local company's production of the work.

Coxon idly browsed the nearest newspaper to hand. Deep in the back pages, she stumbled on a three-line item — a book review, she remembered years later — making passing mention of Sir Arthur Conan Doyle. "In the space of those three lines," she recalled, "the writer mentioned that Conan Doyle had traveled to south Wales. And he'd done so, the paper said, to pay a visit to a psychic medium." Conan Doyle. A psychic medium. South Wales. Wisps of suggestion floated through Coxon's dramatist mind: potentially a great story, most definitely a challenge. "I'd never attempted to write a character based on a historical figure, and here was this huge, iconic person, doing something that sounded very strange and vulnerable," she told me. "I thought I could use that scenario, this incredibly odd juxtaposition, to really dig under the skin of this legendary man.

"Then, when I did, he proved a real nightmare. There was just no getting rid of him."

· · ·

Conan Doyle's own picture appeared in the March 1919 issue of the *Strand*, Sherlock nowhere in sight. Instead, a grave portrait of the aging author ran atop a story by a journalist named Hayden Church: LIFE AF-TER DEATH: AN INTERVIEW WITH SIR ARTHUR CONAN DOYLE.

The previous October, Conan Doyle had given a remarkable speech to the London Spiritualist Society. For most of his adult life, he'd maintained a sideline interest in psychic phenomena: messages from the beyond, automatic writing, and the like. He'd kept vigils in haunted houses, hosted or attended many séances and medium demonstrations, and read deeply in the literature of the subject. Back in 1887, the year of *A Study in Scarlet*, he corresponded with the Spiritualist magazine *Light* regarding an uncanny message given him by an alleged medium. He had long been a member of the Society for Psychical Research, the movement's more or less respectable public face.

Spiritualism dated to a series of eerie 1840s events in upstate New York, and the loose-knit movement paralleled and shadowed mainstream culture. The Victorians' affinity for new technology and science echoed in spiritualistic attempts to "prove" life after death or photograph otherworldly "ectoplasm." This impulse to reconcile science and religion grew particularly strong after Darwin, and many eminent people joined the SPR, which aimed to conduct itself as an objective and rational body of inquiry. On the other hand, mediums and spirit communicators had a gaudy appeal in a society hooked on "sensation" and novelty. Many otherwise conventional people attended a séance or two.

By degrees, a faction of Spiritualism shaped itself into a nascent religion, acquiring that capital "S." Before the London assembly, Conan Doyle reiterated a proclamation he'd recently made public: he was himself a convert. (He had already revealed his stance in the pages of *Light*, in 1916, and spoken at a number of Spiritualist meetings around the country.) Spiritualism, he declared, had been proven, full stop. A sufficient number of séances and psychic connections demonstrated that the soul carried on after death, distinct and largely unchanged, in a world surprisingly similar to this one. Now he was ready to elaborate. This Spiritualist truth, "proved beyond question," as he would tell the *Strand*, could launch a new religious era. The established creeds would continue — you could still be a Buddhist or a Catholic — but accommodate themselves to the knowledge that not one of them held exclusive rights to the afterlife.

Conan Doyle quickly turned his speech into a slender book titled *The New Revelation,* published before the year was out, and began touring the country — he set a goal of delivering the New Revelation to every substantial town in Great Britain. Just two weeks after he spoke in London, as he prepared for a meeting in Nottingham, he was informed that Kingsley, his twenty-five-year-old son, lay dying. He had been wounded at the Somme, and contracted influenza and pneumonia during his recuperation. Conan Doyle carried on; he even spoke the night after Kingsley's death, before visiting his body in the mortuary. The young man was just the latest entry in an inventory of familial woe. As Conan Doyle soon wrote, "My wife's brother . . . my sister's husband, my wife's nephew, my sister's son, all dead." Then, in February 1919, Brigadier General Innes Conan Doyle, the kid brother for whom Arthur essentially served as a father figure all through life, caught pneumonia and died in Belgium.

In *The New Revelation,* Conan Doyle wrote:

In the presence of an agonized world, hearing every day of the deaths of the flower of our race in the first promise of their unfulfilled youth, seeing around one the wives and mothers who had no clear conception whither their loved ones had gone to, I seemed suddenly to see that this subject with which I had so long dallied was not merely a study of a force outside the rules of Science, but that it was really something tremendous, a breaking down of the walls between two worlds, a direct undeniable message from beyond, a call of hope and of guidance to the human race at the time of its deepest affliction.

Conan Doyle would devote the rest of his life to promoting Spiritualism. First he toured Britain, then the world: from North America to Australia and New Zealand to Europe to South Africa and back to Europe. In a little more than a decade, he wrote a shelf of books on the subject, and basically forced the *Strand* to print whatever he wanted it to print. He fired off innumerable letters to the press, battling his newfound legion of critics and skeptics.

Oy, the Spiritualism. Those of us sworn to the cult of Sherlock

Holmes, for the most part, would prefer to gloss over the whole thing. *Yes, the séances and whatnot. But Sherlock!* I once sat at lunch with a friend, babbling on about the Great Detective. He gave me a sidelong look and said, "But didn't Arthur Conan Doyle . . . go insane?" This sentiment is not entirely unknown. Over the years, some Sherlockians have dealt with late-period Conan Doyle rather as we might today regard a slightly batty uncle who bombards Facebook with shrill posts on the gold standard or fraudulent lunar landings. During one particularly florid passage of Conan Doyle's Spiritualist career — he was going around saying fairies could be photographed — an American newspaper pulled no punches: POOR SHERLOCK HOLMES — HOPELESSLY CRAZY.

The affair certainly has its pitiable aspects. Scammers duped Conan Doyle, most notably the young sisters who convinced him they'd taken those fairy photographs, some of the most pathetic fakes you've ever seen. Before her death, Touie, a quietly sensible Anglican, probably greeted her husband's spiritualistic pursuits with a that's-nice-dear hand pat. Jean, on the other hand, dove right in: conveniently enough, it turned out she was a medium herself! Who could have imagined? She used her "gifts" to influence Conan Doyle's travel decisions, among other crucial (to her) matters. Meanwhile, the couple sat their three young children — two boys and a girl — through encounters with various crackpot oracles and otherwise indoctrinated them. Jean always worked to marginalize Mary, Conan Doyle's surviving daughter by Touie, but they recruited her, too, as the manager of a Spiritualist bookshop her father founded and bank-rolled in London. He plowed a fortune into the endeavor.

It seems, in a word, strange. How could the creator of rationalism's great icon traipse after fairies and ectoplasm? I've often wanted to go back in time and grab him by the tweedy lapels. Believe what you will, man, but you're Sir Arthur Conan Doyle! What are you doing?

The wood-paneled chamber that serves as the nerve center for the Berg Collection of English and American Literature at the New York Public Library spins an atmosphere as ritualistic, hushed, and portentous as any séance. I had come to consult a century-old notebook, arrayed before me on a V-shaped tabletop cradle draped with a small felt blanket, roughly square with a blue, marble-patterned cover. Its pages bore the unmistakable handwriting of Arthur Conan Doyle — a stray scrap of his mind, un-dated, unedited. Most of the book's notes concerned his own researches on the career and writing of Emanuel Swedenborg, the eighteenth-century polymath who turned a brilliant mind to inquiries in the spiritual realm. "His spirit eyes were opened in 1743," Conan Doyle jotted, noting that the "Lord" visited Swedenborg at home to tell him he was eating too much. "An illuminated condition," Conan Doyle noted.

The notes-to-self ran through the pages, meticulous and cogent: long, verbatim transcriptions from relevant works, carefully annotated reflections. And after considering Swedenborg — who put together his own theology, like Conan Doyle's *New Revelation* on a grander scale — he moves on to his own conclusive epigrams:

> The man who sees ectoplasm but can see no spirit is like the man who can see photoplasm but sees no life.
>
> The lucidity of . . . seeresses appears to occur only because a spirit seems to intervene and reveal facts to them.

I could feel a shadowy consciousness roving and seeking on the far side of time's veil. (Maybe the hermetic quiet of the Berg was getting to me.) The piece of Conan Doyle preserved in that notebook represented an inquiring mind attacking difficult questions. What does happen after we die? Conan Doyle tried to find out, and here, in this New York archive, I could glimpse him at work, using the very method of discovery he had dramatized through Sherlock Holmes. He combed manuscripts, testimonies, and odd books for insight. He eagerly gathered physical evidence: unearthly photographs, his own eyewitness experiences, documents. He weighed the evidence as he believed he'd discovered it, and emphatically presented his conclusions — because to Arthur Conan Doyle, doing so was his duty.

People have been hard on Conan Doyle's Spiritualism. I would admit that it comes as a shock to the latter-day admirer of scintillating Sherlock Holmes and hardheaded John Watson to discover their creator humorlessly lecturing anyone and everyone on ectoplasm and automatic writing. But in the end I'm inclined to give him a pass. There's nothing malevolent in his *New Revelation* or his Spiritualist doctrine. If his actions reflected a certain misguided self-importance, his convictions reflected a basic kindness and liberal outlook. And almost none of the most vituperative comments over the years take into account the existence, then and now, of a small group of people for whom Spiritualism is a religion, not a curiosity. I think Conan Doyle was (and posthumously remains) entitled to freedom of conscience. The affair's most unsettling aspect, to me, lies in watching a person previously central to his place and time drift off down a side stream of history. Conan Doyle made a lot of mistakes — don't we all — but his big error perhaps consisted of misapplying the Sherlockian technique to matters singularly unsuited to that kind of analysis. Life after death? Holmes himself wouldn't have touched the case.

Fortunately, Conan Doyle's real magic power remains much stronger than his foibles. In the New York library, when I touched the handwork of a person dead forty-five years before I was born, I sensed the presence of a great intelligence. The same happens to people when they read "A Scandal in Bohemia" or watch an episode of *Sherlock*. Conan Doyle, long gone, is still doing his thing. Now that's a revelation — of a kind Conan Doyle, in his fervor, overlooked.

On a moonless night, Sherlock Holmes and Dr. Watson venture into the darkened, allegedly haunted crypt of an ancient noble family, a dreadful place strewn with shattered rock and stacked with coffins dating back a thousand years. By the solitary light of Holmes's lantern, they rummage amid the Saxon and Norman dead. Just then — the creak of a footstep above!

"The Adventure of Shoscombe Old Place": Conan Doyle dials up the Goth atmospherics, plucking those old chords he lifted from Edgar Allan Poe. It's the last Sherlock Holmes story. The detective's creator gives the great icon one final, fitting stage upon which to wield his powers and dramatic flair. As the crypt's owner — an indebted racehorse owner — blunders into the murky chamber, Holmes rips open a casket to reveal a freshly mummified corpse. "Who is this?" he demands. "And what is it doing here?"

The horseman stands agog — who does this intruder think he is?

"My name is Sherlock Holmes," the detective snaps back. "Possibly it is familiar to you."

Great moment. To be honest, though, it's not a great story. (It narrowly escaped being titled "The Adventure of the Black Spaniel," which perhaps indicates how it ranks alongside, say, *The Hound of the Baskervilles*.) Published in early 1927, "Shoscombe Old Place" catches Conan Doyle on the decline — as is the case with many of the stories anthologized as *The Casebook of Sherlock Holmes,* all published in the 1920s. Diehard Sherlockians have been heard to wish the *Casebook* didn't exist at all.* Conan Doyle wrote a few stories here, a few there, and the resulting bundle reflects wavering intensity and focus. The author himself always insisted these final rounds were as good as any, but even he felt the need for a unique, in his oeuvre, preface to the collection: "I fear that Mr. Sherlock Holmes may become one of those popular tenors who, having outlived their time, are still tempted to make repeated farewell bows to their indulgent public."

"The Adventure of the Mazarin Stone," told in the third person and notable only for a villain with the spectacular name Count Negretto Sylvius, simply recycled a play Conan Doyle had written, *The Crown Diamond: An Evening with Sherlock Holmes.* It's about half an act. "The Adventure of the Veiled Lodger" (spoiler: the lion did it) barely ranks as an anecdote. In two stories, "The Adventure of the Lion's Mane" (spoiler: a jellyfish did it) and "The Adventure of the Blanched Soldier" (it's . . . leprosy! But not . . . anyway), Conan Doyle deploys Holmes as narrator, with no Watson. He proves only that Watson was a very good idea.

Aside from literary flaws, the *Casebook* suffers from a problem Conan Doyle couldn't really help. All the stories take place before the Great War; they're out of their moment. The world, and the detective genre in particular, had moved on. In the United States, cheap pulp magazines like *Argosy* and *Black Mask* offered detectives that almost inverted Sherlock Holmes: the lone, cynical urban shamus in his trench coat (a fashion statement from the Western Front) roamed a flinty, dislocated modern world of speakeasies, criminal rackets, and fast cars, with no Watson and certainly no snug Baker Street. Dashiell Hammett's prototypical Continental Op didn't even have a name. Hammett, Raymond Chandler, James

---

* There is, however, an opposing minority view: the eminent Canadian Sherlockian Chris Redmond, for one, has championed the *Casebook* stories as some of the best of the Holmesian saga.

M. Cain, and other notable hardboiled practitioners served in the war in various capacities, and they channeled a hardened sensibility foreign to Conan Doyle's generation. Hammett wrote his first novel, *Red Harvest,* within about a year of "Shoscombe Old Place," but its ruthlessly bloody, street-Shakespearean tale of class and industrial warfare in a rotten Montana mining town (Poisonville, "an ugly city of forty thousand people, set in an ugly notch between two ugly mountains") comes from a dirtier, bloodier, sexier world.

Consider the opening of *The Maltese Falcon,* first published in serial installments by *Black Mask* in 1929–30:

> "There's a girl wants to see you. Her name's Wonderly."
> "A customer?"
> "I guess so. You'll want to see her anyway, she's a knockout."
> "Shoo her in, darling," said Spade. "Shoo her in."

Baker Street's cozy repartee and fireside welcome for every client are long gone.

"Hammett took murder out of the Venetian vase and dropped it into the alley," Chandler would write in his 1950 essay "The Simple Art of Murder." "He gave murder back to the kind of people that commit it for reasons, not just to provide a corpse; and with the means at hand, not with hand-wrought dueling pistols, curare, and tropical fish." Chandler's main complaint was with the Agatha Christie–inflected British writers of the interwar period. But he had grown up in England — gone to a good school, et cetera — at the height of the Holmesian era, so he spared a barb for the master as well: "Sherlock Holmes after all is mostly an attitude and a few dozen lines of unforgettable dialogue." The hardboiled writers looked to different inspirations: the Wild West gunslinger tales and a larger American tradition of placeless wanderers, the austere emotional and social landscape of an Edward Hopper painting.

The urge to write a new kind of crime fiction exerted itself on the other side of the Atlantic, too. "Since 1918 . . . a detective story not containing a murder has been a great rarity," George Orwell wrote in his 1944 essay "Raffles and Miss Blandish." (Orwell compared Raffles, the gentleman thief created by Conan Doyle's brother-in-law E. W. Hornung, as a tongue-in-cheek tribute to Holmes, with a violent piece of '30s British pulp fiction.) "The most disgusting details of dismemberment and exhumation are commonly exploited." Orwell found British crime fiction "written in the American language" particularly repellent. Elsewhere, he would lament that even crime itself wasn't what it used to be. "Our great period in murder . . . seems to have been between roughly 1850 and 1925," he complained in the aptly titled "The Decline of English Murder." That period's classic slayings, Orwell wrote, involved proper suburban poisonings. After the Great War, a different ethic (so to speak) took hold: "the anonymous life of the dance-halls and the false values of the American film." Modern British villains, he argued, aspired only to imitate Yankee gangsters.

Orwell was not alone in observing change. When I talked with Paul Collins, the Portland "literary detective," he noted that in the 1920s, when Conan Doyle wrote the *Casebook* stories, many old-time Scotland Yarders retired and produced memoirs. "Almost every one of them says that the biggest change in their profession was the automobile," he told me. "It made crime more anonymous and more mobile. Suddenly, if there's a murder, the scope of who might have done it widens out to include almost all of England. Where are the stolen goods? They could be in Leeds by now. You can't rely on the good old railway timetable anymore."

With the change in technology, Collins explained, "the notion that a guy sitting in a room in London, surrounded by his notebooks and newspaper clippings, can hear about a particular crime and say 'Aha! That sounds like the So-and-So Jewel Case of '81!' becomes less viable. A criminal could swoop in from anywhere, then disappear."

Meanwhile, the idea of an amateur detective who excels the official force had gone from pleasantly fantastical to implausible. "The old Scotland Yarders talked a lot about how police work had changed," Collins said. "Hans Gross published the first standard forensics text in 1893, and by the next decade police knew how to preserve crime scenes, maintain chains of evidence, proceed in an orderly and scientific way — all the staples of procedural detective stories now. They staffed cases in teams, with specialist bureaus taking on different aspects of investigations. It wasn't just Inspector Lestrade coming out to 'take the case in hand' anymore."

Plenty of readers still loved their Sherlock, of course — commerce-minded Conan Doyle wouldn't have worked without demand. But others began to find the Great Detective ridiculous. In a 1907 book celebrating the real-life *Revelations of Inspector Morgan,* an English journalist and diplomat named Oswald Crawfurd—hardly a Young Turk, born in 1834—opined: "The professional is a better man than the amateur detective ... To think otherwise is a pestilent heresy." Once the epitome of cutting-edge thought, by late in his run Sherlock Holmes could be made out as a faintly silly relic. His time had passed.

But wait.

The Casebook of Sherlock Holmes has a way of nagging at you. No, the stories do not capture High Holmes (no cocaine pun intended), first tuning up his violin and scribbling his now-ancient monographs on tobacco ash and "the influence of trade upon the form of the hand." At the same time, the stories strike notes heard nowhere else in the saga: weird resonances of the Jazz Age threaded into Conan Doyle's practiced Victorian airs. As he always had, from the classic *Adventures* on, the author reacted to and transposed news, fads, scandals, and criminal lore into his Baker Street fables. Sometimes the results are less than mixed: in "The Adventure of the Three Gables," Conan Doyle's attempt to portray Holmes amid two-fisted operators—Sam Spade in a dressing gown—takes hideous turns as a "huge negro" American boxer, given the head-slapping moniker "Steve Dixie," rumbles into Baker Street to threaten "Masser Holmes." (You read that right.) Sherlock plays it cool: "'Keep on talking,' said Holmes. 'It's fine.'" It gets much, much worse from there, in the one story that I, given the power, would vote off Baker Street Island.

Deep in his Spiritualist campaigns, Conan Doyle had undoubtedly lost the main thread of current affairs. His mother died in 1921, leaving him without the one person who would box his ears every now and again. His always mighty correspondence with the press came to revolve around Spiritualism, with occasional detours into the real world. (In September 1923, he sent a rambler to the *New York Times* regarding a purported spirit communication from his old dining companion Oscar Wilde. His verdict: absolutely genuine.) But sometimes, in the *Casebook,* Conan Doyle casts eerie or ironic sidelights on this new era. "The Adventure of the Sussex Vampire," for instance—a mother, accused of sucking her own baby's blood — only really works if one considers it as a parody of the vampire genre. Conan Doyle, a friendly professional acquaintance of Bram Stoker, loved *Dracula,* and would have watched with interest (perhaps amusement) as post–Great War culture gravitated back to those creatures of the night. In the very year he wrote "Sussex Vampire," the Stoker estate sued on copyright grounds to suppress the German cinematic classic *Nosferatu,* a film prompted by one of its creators' wartime contact with superstitious Balkan farmers. By the end of the 1920s, *Dracula* proper would be revived on the stage. Meanwhile, the decade's British press used "vampire" as a slangy synonym for "femme fatale." With his at first tantalizing, then practically goofy, story of a Latin beauty with an alleged taste for hemoglobin, Conan Doyle gave a puckish wink to both trends.

Then there is "The Adventure of the Creeping Man," which always leaves an impression — often, of bemusement. (Lyndsay Faye recently wrote, "Just go with God if you attempt to read 'The Creeping Man' without chemical assistance.") Holmes and Watson steam down to one of England's ancient university towns ("Camford") to investigate Professor Presbury, an eminent physiologist of mature years. Presbury has fallen in love with a woman four decades his junior. He has also begun receiving letters and packages from London, coded with a cross on the envelopes to designate them for his eyes only. This started shortly after a mysterious visit to Prague. (Bohemia!) And — not to bury the lead — he is acting like an ape.

Not metaphorically, either. About every nine days, Presbury sneaks — creeps, rather — out of his room by night, shuffling and springing along the ground, grunting in primal abandon, tormenting dogs and zipping up and down walls with the élan of a graceful macaque. He gave his daughter quite a start one evening when she glanced at her upper-story window and saw Daddy's face leering in. The atmosphere around the Presbury house has understandably begun to pall. Upon arrival, Holmes notices something else: the professor's knuckles have become "thick and horny in a way which is quite new in my experience."

Holmes dispatches an agent to investigate the London source of Presbury's secret letters, which originate with a "suave" Bohemian wheeler-dealer in the East End. Then, after ye olde Sherlockian night vigil, Holmes and Watson catch Presbury in the very act: "From branch to branch he sprang, sure of foot and firm of grasp, climbing apparently in mere joy at his own powers." The monkey-professor finally runs afoul of his own dog, which mauls him savagely. Watson manages to stanch the bleeding, then the duo invades Presbury's sanctum, where they find a hypodermic needle, some empty phials, and a letter from one Lowenstein, whose name rings a bell with Watson: "an obscure scientist who was striving in some unknown way for the secret of rejuvenescence and the elixir of life." Lowenstein's miracle cure, they discover, consists of serum derived from monkey testicles. Presbury's regular injections, undertaken to jump-start his sex appeal for his young girlfriend, transformed him into one lusty simian. Holmes shakes his head. "There is danger there ... Consider, Watson, that the material, the sensual, the worldly would all prolong their worthless lives ... What sort of cesspool may not our poor world become?"

What indeed? Monkey balls? A sex-crazed professor hybridized with a black-faced langur? Sherlock, sci-fi? One latter-day critic speaks for many in dismissing "The Creeping Man" as "risible." A brief survey of recent commentary—coming from Holmes fans, no less—points to a rough consensus that the story makes an unwelcome detour to the Island of Doctor Moreau. Can we get back to murder, please?

Poe, Wells, and Stevenson definitely do shadow Holmes and Watson's trip to Camford. I would argue that this is good company, actually, and that poor Presbury makes a fascinating villain/victim. Something disturbing palpably churns beneath this story's surface. In the *Times Literary Supplement* in 2010, writer Jonathan Barnes described "The Creeping Man" as "a sour parable about the endurance of lust"—sobering when one imagines Conan Doyle, in his sixties, burning himself out with ceaseless travel and argument in the Spiritualist cause, his own experience as an older man in love with a beautiful young woman rattling around the back of his mind. He knew something, perhaps, about virility's decline.

In the summer of 1923—the *Strand* published "The Creeping Man" that fall—the International Congress of Surgery met in London. Among its proceedings, it voted to praise and encourage the work of one Serge Voronoff, a Franco-Russian doctor and creator of a remarkable experimental technique. Voronoff took tiny shavings from monkey testicles and implanted them in human scrotums, a procedure he claimed would revitalize patients, retard or reverse aging, and ultimately yield prolonged life. Nor was Voronoff a reserved modern scientist, carefully subjecting guarded findings to peer review. In 1920, his wife and assistant, Evelyn — an American heiress, which came in handy — translated Voronoff's evangelistic book *Life: A Study of the Means of Restoring Vital Energy and Prolonging Life* into English. People should live to be 120 or 140, Voronoff argues, and only the scientific establishment's stubborn blindness holds us back, much to our cultural detriment. "The constant conflict between instinct to live and horror of dying has engendered that profound pessimism afflicting the greatest thinkers," he writes, "which mingles wormwood with all our joys." Voronoff believed he was on his way to curing the ultimate affliction. He did his first chimp-to-man testicular implant in the summer of that same year.

Conan Doyle followed medical developments. In Voronoff, he could have spied a strange reversal of his own persona: a driven man, expounding on arcane and almost forbidden knowledge, an enthusiast in controversial experimentation, aided and abetted by an adoring and talented wife. Conan Doyle championed spiritual immortality; Voronoff pursued physical immortality. They opposed and balanced each other, like Moriarty and Holmes, dark to light (as Conan Doyle would see it), noble to base. Throughout Conan Doyle's writing, the malevolent misuse of learning and accomplishment recurs: Moriarty, supreme mathematician turned supercriminal; Moran, army sharpshooter turned assassin; Grimesby Roylott, doctor and amateur zoologist turned murderous snake handler. In this case, he had to say something — Voronoff's work was gathering momentum. By decade's end, about five hundred men had undergone implantation, and by all appearances the procedure was headed for broad medical and popular acceptance.* Thus Conan Doyle found his "Lowenstein," complete with suitably oily Continental origins.

---

* Voronoff didn't suffer a serious reverse until 1927 — ironically, because Voronoff himself started to advocate for agricultural applications of the idea, and also because an international study of testes-grafted Algerian sheep discovered that . . . oh, hell, you get the idea. Still, as late as 1946, the Wolverhampton Wanderers football club became notorious for urging players to undergo treatments inspired by Voronoff. One of the players thus implanted scored four goals against Liverpool at Anfield, but I digress.

As for Professor Presbury — again, a man of learning and gravitas, self-mutated into something horrible — the author may have looked closer to home.

Charles Altamont Doyle had destroyed himself and his mercurial artistic talents with alcohol. Conan Doyle's mother wrote to doctors of Charles's dragging himself around the floor ape-like, unable to remember his own name, menacing his children, stealing shillings out of their money boxes. Conan Doyle may have had to restrain his father in his epileptic fits, exacerbated by drink; he had to sign papers committing Charles to a "convalescent home," as he euphemized in his memoirs. And yet he always kept his father's art on prominent display, and late in life arranged a London gallery show of Charles Altamont's work. Dark days in 1860s Edinburgh lived on in his mind, and so, too, did a squandered and forgotten talent, evidence of what can happen when a brilliant man goes bad.

A gifted artist ends his days locked up, jabbering at his attendants, calling them devils, claiming he receives messages from "an unseen world." An eminent professor surrenders to lust and willingly becomes less than human. Why do people do these things? What is choice, and what is fated by birth and inheritance? This question hangs over Conan Doyle's Sherlock Holmes stories. Moriarty, Holmes claimed, exhibited "hereditary criminal tendencies of the most diabolical kind." On the other hand, Conan Doyle made the detective, like himself, a descendant of painters, and has Sherlock tell Watson that "art in the blood takes the strangest forms." In an essay on his hero Sir Walter Scott, Conan Doyle misquoted a couplet from Dryden: "Great Genius is to madness close allied, / And thin partitions do those rooms divide." Why does the father end up in an asylum and the son become a world-conquering star of his own chosen art? The weird tales of *The Casebook of Sherlock Holmes* find Conan Doyle, after so many long years of investigation, still on the case — hunting, perhaps, for clues to a mystery that lurked at the center of his own life.

Any exploration of the world of Sherlock Holmes obviously requires a lot of time spent with Arthur Conan Doyle. And Conan Doyle makes a great subject — a storytelling genius, a colossal character, an epic adventurer. But, not to put too crude a point on it, he's also a pain in the ass.

He just did too much. One minute he's down in South Africa. Then he's launching some half-baked start-up company selling motors for bicycles (true story). Then he's running for Parliament, then he's in the Amateur Billiards Championship (got second, by the way), then he's investigating an unjust murder conviction, then he's fighting about Spiritualism with Harry Houdini. He exhausts you. There have been, as noted, many biographies of the man. Taken in mass quantities, they turn his life into a kind of Stations of the Cross: *Oh, here comes good old George Edalji.* I began to yearn for a different perspective.

There exists a parallel, unofficial tradition of portraying Conan Doyle as a fictional character in his own right. Several series of detective stories feature the author himself as investigator. Actors on screens large and small give the great man a go. I wondered if a practitioner of this craft might give me a fresh angle.

Lucinda Coxon, the British playwright who stumbled upon that three-line story about Conan Doyle visiting a medium in Wales, wrote a play titled *Nostalgia,* which debuted in 2001. The script puts Conan Doyle on a godforsaken farm; he's heard rumors that his son Kingsley is attempting to contact him via séances held by the indigenous rustics. The farmers prove a pretty grim gang of taciturn weirdos, including two lonely, drink-addled brothers and the mystical local part-time prostitute. In this company, Coxon's Conan Doyle blunders around, attempting to be his usual bluff, yarn-spinning self, telling everyone that voices from beyond mark a great moment in civilization. The Welshmen seem mulishly indifferent.

"I put him in the middle of nowhere, with nothing to do, and just let him unravel," Coxon told me when I asked her to remember, more than a decade later, how she created her own personal Conan Doyle. "When you think about the details of his life, it's very hard not to conclude that he was, somehow, in flight all the time—almost literally on the run. He was always pushing himself in the most extraordinary way. I wanted to show him stuck."

Many of Conan Doyle's biographers seem to start from their own love of Sherlock Holmes. This inevitably leaves them in a reverent state of mind. (I get it.) Coxon, on the other hand, approached her famous subject with marked skepticism. ("I mean, this business of an affair that's not really an affair," she said. "How long can you *not* have an affair if you're seeing a woman who is not your wife every chance you get?") And yet she gave her Conan Doyle a voice, for the most part his own, adapted from his memoirs. "I read a lot of biographies, of course," she recalled. "In an odd way they're all the same. Many of them start with some kind of bold proclamation that, at last, someone will solve the mystery — the 'enigma,' or however the writer puts it — of Arthur Conan Doyle. Then, about forty pages in, they all go belly-up. By the time they get to him cross-country skiing through Switzerland, or whatever, they just give in to the myth that Conan Doyle himself created. I decided that I might as well look to the man's own autobiography. He's not very truthful in that book, but he is quite revealing. A lot of it is about convincing everyone that he's absolutely, perfectly fine at all times. And, of course, he's not fine at all times."

Certainly not in her play, which leads to a harrowing dream sequence in which Conan Doyle finds himself manically tearing off his clothes, only to find another full suit underneath, again and again and again. Coxon's fictional Conan Doyle assumes a tragic, broken air, dimly aware of the depth of his own emotional oblivion, gamely struggling against the darkness. In this story, Conan Doyle's Spiritualism reads as the last attempt among many to rebuild the world the way Arthur Conan Doyle believed it should be, to create a realm of honor and logic and dignity, complete with happy ending.

"He was an enormous overgrown boy in many ways," Coxon told me. "You see a lot of wish fulfillment in his Spiritualism. His version of heaven — that you'd have whiskey and golf if you wanted, and all the dogs you'd ever owned would come back to you — is basically a kid's version of heaven. And after he'd tried to go to war several times, and not quite managed it, Spiritualism was his war, another way to prove himself.

"I do find it interesting that just about all the biographers are men," she added. "I began to wish that a woman would go after this guy, to bring a different sensibility to the mystique. For a straight white man, the problem with Conan Doyle is, look, he's more of a man than you'll ever be. He really cared about winning, all the time. And what's more, he cared about not seeming to care. That quality allowed him to dominate every man who crossed his path. He's still at it."

I must say, I know the feeling.

· · ·

In "The Adventure of the Three Garridebs"—an entertaining scam caper published in 1924, by which time, Conan Doyle evidently hoped, readers would have forgotten the basic plot of "The Red-Headed League"—Holmes and Watson capture "Killer" Evans, a Chicago criminal come to London. Everything seems to follow standard procedure, as Evans ruefully admits he's beaten. But then: "In an instant he had whisked out a revolver from his breast and had fired two shots," Watson recounts. "I felt a sudden hot sear as if a red-hot iron had been pressed to my thigh. There was a crash as Holmes's pistol came down on the man's head . . . Then my friend's wiry arms were around me and he was leading me to a chair."

Watson, shot! And Sherlock Holmes, after a mere four decades, drops the robot act and shows himself human after all.

"You're not hurt, Watson? For God's sake, say that you are not hurt!"

Watson reckons this well worth a minor bullet wound. Any reader who follows the one-sided emotional ordeal of the Great Relationship will agree. Watson at last gets to see the "loyalty and love" behind Holmes's adamantine demeanor. All that needling about Watson's writing, the indoor revolver practice, that one time when Sherlock pretended to be dead for three years—all expiated in a single moment of fierce tenderness. The golden thread that holds Sherlockiana together is friendship: sticking by someone you care about, even if he's on the difficult side. Even Sherlock Holmes, it turns out, has his way of expressing affection.

"If you had killed Watson," he tells the criminal, "you would not have got out of this room alive." Cue violin!

Conan Doyle scatters such highly satisfying moments throughout the *Casebook* stories. Today, we might call it fan service: in-jokes, jolts of familiar pleasure to loyalists. After so many years with Holmes and Watson, Conan Doyle—though somewhat immune to their charms himself—had at least some grasp on why readers stuck with them. I can imagine the old master at his desk, like a silver-tipped alpha grizzly, smiling faintly as he thinks, All right, they're going to *love* this bit.

And so "The Problem of Thor Bridge" begins with mention of a locked tin dispatch box, deep in the vaults of Cox and Company Bank, stuffed with Watson's unpublished case notes. The doctor rattles off a great mini-trilogy of tales for which the world is not yet prepared: *Mr. James Philli-*

more, who, stepping back into his own house to get his umbrella, was never more seen in this world . . . The cutter Alicia, *which sailed one spring morning into a small patch of mist from where she never again emerged . . . Isadora Persano, the well-known journalist and duelist, who was found stark staring mad with a match box in front of him which contained a remarkable worm said to be unknown to science . . .*

A remarkable worm unknown to science? That's the spirit. The tin dispatch box becomes a symbol of all those untold tales that lend the Sherlock Holmes stories their illusory infinity. When the *Casebook* appeared in book form in '27, Conan Doyle was finally finished — and what, after all, had he really made? Nine slim volumes of detective stories, which could just about vanish amid his huge body of work. There isn't much to Sherlock when you get right down to it. But Conan Doyle compacted an entire world into those adventures, with a vast array of alternative possibilities, yet-unexplored corners, and tantalizing personae only barely glimpsed.

In "The Adventure of the Illustrious Client," published in 1924 in the United States and as a two-parter in the *Strand* in 1925, Conan Doyle really opens the throttle. Fade in on Holmes and Watson savoring a smoke in a Turkish bath on Northumberland Avenue. As in "A Scandal in Bohemia," Sherlock holds a fancy letter. A high-society fixer named Sir James Damery proposes a problem: Violet de Merville, daughter of an eminent army general, is romantically obsessed with one Baron Gruner, a sensationally evil Austrian who killed his last wife, wriggled out of it, and now plans to marry besotted Violet. Damery — acting upon instructions from a client who must remain nameless for propriety's sake — wants Holmes to pry the lady off the foreigner.

The ensuing adventure achieves the panoramic feeling of a novel in miniature, while zinging along at Conan Doyle's signature ebullient pace. In other circumstances (and if Conan Doyle had thought of it), "The Illustrious Client" could have rebooted the saga, like the first episode of a midperiod *Sopranos* season in which three or four new mobsters suddenly get out of the joint to hatch fresh subplots. Besides Damery, a host of fascinating new characters bubbles up. Sherlock has cultivated an underworld operative named Shinwell Johnson, who trawls the London gutter for leverage against the nobleman. The Baron himself shortly makes a Moriarty-esque appearance, suave as can be: "My dear man," he tells Holmes, "you will only ruin your own well-deserved reputation . . . You will have barren work, to say nothing of incurring some danger. Let me strongly advise you to draw off at once." Shinwell Johnson surfaces with a "slim, flame-like" woman, tough-talking dame Kitty Winter, who bears an ancient grudge against Gruner and whom Conan Doyle actually makes fairly affecting as well as melodramatic. "I'm easy to find," she tells Holmes and Watson. "Hell, London, gets me every time." Violet de Merville proves a formidable ice princess who avidly insists on her love for the wicked Baron.

Conan Doyle puts this off-kilter troupe in motion by midstory, setting up one of the great Sherlockian scenes. Watson (who no longer lives at Baker Street, and thus ducks nimbly in and out of the tale — half the time, he hears what's going on from Sherlock over fancy dinners in the Strand) strolls outside Charing Cross station. He spots a well-known one-legged news vendor. (Nice touch.) And sees: "There, black upon yellow, was the terrible news-sheet: MURDEROUS ATTACK UPON SHERLOCK HOLMES."

The stunned Watson snatches a paper without paying for it and reads that thugs mauled Holmes at midnight outside the Café Royal. (This was an old Oscar Wilde hangout, a mere two hundred yards or so from the Criterion. Thus Conan Doyle bustles us through Piccadilly, where the saga began in *A Study in Scarlet*.) Watson finds a famous surgeon at Baker Street, and Holmes a bit rough around the edges. The detective does note with pride that he parried the Baron's assassins with his single-stick skills, adding to the combat *vita* that includes baritsu, boxing, and fencing. At his moment of maximum apparent weakness, of course, Holmes finds himself a wedge against Gruner: the filthy man keeps a book detailing his "romantic" conquests, hidden in his study. They need to get in there.

But how? Ah: the Baron also happens to love ancient Chinese pottery. Watson hustles down to the London Library and meets up with his librarian buddy Lomax — another tantalizing incidental character in a story stuffed with them — and crams as much Chinese pottery knowledge into his head as possible. Thus does Watson come to stand in Baron Gruner's study, under a fake name, bluffing his way through a hilarious conversation with the diabolically handsome Austrian regarding "Emperor Shomu"—who, not to be picky, was *Japanese*. But no one cares, because the ruse works. And then, instantly, comedy explodes into a violent climax: vengeance taken, a life shattered, burglary of Gruner's private papers accomplished.

"The Adventure of the Illustrious Client" unites much that is great in Sherlock Holmes. High-toned fun mixes with darkness, which needs only suggestion rather than graphic exposition. For glossy period detail, we get allusions to mesmerism, the Cunard liner *Ruritania,* and telephone messages left care of the Carlton Club. Conan Doyle switches with whiplash efficiency between arch comedy and ripping tragedy. Above all, we see the honor-bound alliance of Holmes and Watson, the singular force capable of bringing order to chaos. (Or, when necessary, chaos to order — ask Baron Gruner.) This grand finale is about doing things with the proper style. Learn some single-stick, treat yourself to a Turkish bath and dinner in the Strand when you can, and keep a handy reference librarian or a reformed underworld thug on call. Act boldly. Be discreet. Uphold standards. Watson himself slips, just slightly, at story's end. That titular client, you see, has remained anonymous throughout. The good doctor, stepping into Baker Street, sees a telltale coat of arms on a departing carriage and runs back up to reveal all.

"I have found out who our client is . . . Why, Holmes, it is —"

Sherlock stops him: "A loyal friend and a chivalrous gentleman . . . Let that now and forever be enough for us."

Good show, old boy.

I met Arthur Conan Doyle this morning. He emerged from the garden door of his fine country home, gave his Irish terrier Paddy a tousle, removed his hat, and sat down. "There are two things people always want to ask me," he said. "One of them is, how I ever came to write the Sherlock Holmes stories." (Yes!) "And the other is, how I came to have psychic experiences." (Mmm. Do they, really?) Conan Doyle spoke with a winsome, squinty half smile on his broad face. I noticed his hair had thinned out up top, which he compensated for with a precise wedge of thick, pewter mustache. He wore a dignified suit and held himself with mountainous serenity. His accent sounded clear and regulated, with just a faint, delicious Scottish thrum to words like *qwehshh-chun.*

The ten-minute film interview, shot in 1928, about two years before Conan Doyle died of heart failure, lives now on YouTube and elsewhere. This trivial clip, I feel, captures some essence of the man, who delivered a mellow, patient monologue on his Sherlockian oeuvre — no doubt as a pretext for talking about Spiritualism — illuminated by the wry irony he'd often flashed on the page. (In talking of Sherlock, he made straight-faced mention of "his rather stupid friend, Watson" — Conan Doyle's own avatar, of course.) He told the Joseph Bell origin story and how he conceived a detective who would be different, scientific, precise. "I thought of a hundred little dodges, as you may say, a hundred little touches by which he could build up his conclusions," he said. "Sherlock Holmes fairly took root" — fantastic pronunciation: *rrrr-hoot*. "I've written a good deal more about him than I ever intended to do, but my hand has been rather forced by kind friends who continually wanted to know more. And so it is that this monstrous growth has come out of what was really a comparatively small seed."

On the "psychic matter," Conan Doyle observed the curious fact that he first gravitated to Spiritualism at "just about the time when Sherlock Holmes was being built up in my mind. That would be about the year 1886 and 1887 . . . just forty-one years now." And it is curious: the two things for which he remains best known, usually portrayed as bizarrely paired opposites, evolved in tandem. To Conan Doyle, Sherlock's ratiocination and his own investigation of worlds beyond ours did not conflict, but rather entwined. "I suppose I've sat with more mediums — good, and bad, and indifferent — than perhaps any living being," he said. "Anyhow, a larger variety, because I've traveled so much." He had seen and observed. "I never risk hallucination."

He spoke on, emphatic but benign. He carried no great air of dark mystery or torment about him. I liked the guy. He really just wanted to help. "I'm quite sure I could fill a room of my house with the letters that I have received from people," he said, "how they have once more heard the sound of a vanished voice, and felt the touch of a vanished hand."

Then he stood, gathered his hat and his book, petted his dog, and bowed slightly, half amused and almost bashful. "Well," he said, "goodbye."

9

THE GREAT GAME

> "I don't think we're safe."
> "No one in the world is safe now, Watson. Least of all us."
>
> — NIGEL BRUCE AND BASIL RATHBONE IN
> *SHERLOCK HOLMES AND THE VOICE OF TERROR*

NIGEL BRUCE ("Willie" to his friends) was having a bad day. The veteran actor — ordinarily the most bon of bon vivants, much given to parties, cricket (despite his war wound; he'd taken eleven — yes, eleven — bullets in his leg at Cambrai), and high-spirited banter — was in New York, stuck in a Broadway disaster titled *The Knights of Song*, a biographical musical about Gilbert and Sullivan that somehow folded in the Prince of Wales, Oscar Wilde, and George Bernard Shaw. Oscar Hammerstein produced, Bruce played Gilbert, and people loved G & S, didn't they? Not always, apparently. The show opened on 17 October and no one came. Maybe autumn 1938 was the wrong time for musical comedy. Hitler had just marched into the Sudetenland. Orson Welles was about to spook the nation into believing Martians had invaded. Everyone was a trifle edgy.

A few days before Halloween, Hammerstein performed euthanasia on the show. Bruce moped after hearing the news. This role's demise meant another round of that delightful game beloved by jobbing actors: How Shall I Survive? He was a steady worker, with plenty of stage success and a solid record as one of Hollywood's useful gentlemen with all-purpose British accents. That very year, he popped up in the movies *Kidnapped* and *Suez,* a Tyrone Power vehicle. Secondary roles, of course. He could scrape something up. He always did.

Nigel Bruce felt, he would recall, like putting his head in a gas oven.

In the midst of the gloom, a telegram arrived from dear old Basil Rathbone, one of Nigel's chief chums in the British expatriate colony in Los Angeles. "Do come back to Hollywood, Willie dear boy," the message read, "and play Doctor Watson to my Sherlock Holmes. We'll have great fun together."

Basil and Nigel. Holmes and Watson. What a jolly good idea.

Dartmoor: huge, murky, strewn with freakish rocks and recessed with shadowy caves. A miasmic fog wrapped the landscape. Meandering streams laced the treacherous, mossy ground. Perfect. A hundred-man crew built the sixty-thousand-square-foot moor on Twentieth Century–Fox's "cyclorama" stage to complement an elaborate London and creepy Baskerville Hall, all backdrops for Sherlock Holmes's pursuit of that legendary hell-beast in *The Hound of the Baskervilles.*

Fox outdid itself for the most ambitious Sherlock Holmes movie yet, putting iron-handed director Sidney Lanfield in charge and going for full-dress period Victoriana — which is not to say the costumes and sets were historically accurate, nothing so time-consuming and dreary as that, but they evoked the proper atmosphere. (Holmes films, plentiful since 1900, had almost all been shot in contemporary dress.) Once, Richard Greene, the handsome newcomer cast as Sir Henry Baskerville, wandered into the "moor" between takes. He became hopelessly lost, calling for help with mounting desperation. It was almost Method acting.

Bruce would remember how he and his friend Basil charmed Lanfield, a known hothead. Every morning, the leading men would greet the director with warm embraces and kiss his forehead. After every take, Rathbone and Bruce would shake hands and "solemnly congratulate one another on our 'excellent performance.'" They were determined to make it fun, and while this deeply confused Lanfield, he ultimately gave in to the reigning bonhomie. And it worked. *The Hound of the Baskervilles* debuted in American cinemas at the end of March 1939, just five months after Rathbone sent Bruce that telegram: a sumptuous creation, from a swords 'n' tights film-within-a-film depicting wicked Sir Hugo Baskerville all the way to the gripping final confrontation on the moor. A skilled cast milked the novel's rural weirdos and schemers: Lionel Atwill goggled and palpitated as Dr. Mortimer; the twenty-one-year-old Greene defined big-chinned, witless charm as Sir Henry; John Carradine and Eily Malyon, as Baskerville Hall's creepy servants, competed to be more gaunt and spectral than the other.

There had been many cinematic Sherlocks by this time — twenty-two by one researcher's count, which may be conservative. From the moment pictures began to move, producers and directors gravitated to the Baker Street scene. *Sherlock Holmes Baffled* survives, but an entire corpus of silent Holmes films made throughout the world has mostly vanished. Americans adapted *The Sign of the Four* in 1905. An Italian company made *Un rivale di Sherlock Holmes* in 1907. French actor Georges Treville bequeathed to posterity a somewhat wan Holmes (with no Watson) in 1912 — on YouTube you can watch the creative team behind Treville's *The Copper Beeches* labor to relay Conan Doyle's intricately nested narrative without using words. William Gillette himself gave it a shot, in a 1916 film made in Chicago by the Essanay Studios — a work thought lost for nearly a century before its rediscovery in a French archive made worldwide headlines in 2014. When Gillette's *Sherlock Holmes* reemerged at film festivals in 2015, it proved a revelation: a riveting (if fleeting) glimpse of a galvanic actor's signature role. John Barrymore was languid but sharp-eyed in the role in 1922, but never tried again.

Eille Norwood, a British actor who starred in an extensive series from the Stoll studio starting in 1921, stands out as the truly great Holmes from these flickering, mute early days. Norwood strikes poses exactingly reproduced from Sidney Paget illustrations: Holmes curled in an armchair, knees hugged up; Holmes pensive in the corner of a crime scene, head bowed, rapt in thought. One handy thing about Sherlock Holmes is that in every guise — books, films, Minecraft — the character reveals how culture is produced at a particular moment. The leap in cinematic sophistication elevating Norwood's films above the clunky Treville version from less than a decade earlier is especially striking. Editing has been invented. Rather than the stage-play-like tableaux filmed in France, the Stoll crew builds scenes with rhythmical cuts between midrange and close-up shots. This allows Norwood to craft a reserved, nuanced performance — a scientific, unemotional Holmes who nonetheless projects great depth of soul with his eyes and worried brow. (The actor tackled the role with tremendous intensity, reading every scrap of the original and teaching himself some violin. During casting, the producers had their doubts about Norwood, who campaigned for the part. One day, or so the story goes, a strange, wizened old man appeared at the studio demanding to speak to those responsible. Reluctantly, they let him in — and Norwood plucked off his disguise and announced, in no uncertain terms, that *he was Sherlock Holmes*. Who would argue?) The filmmakers have also learned, even in silence, to approximate Conan Doyle's flashbacks and drum-tight stories-within-stories. Thus Norwood becomes a significant figure in Sherlock's evolution: the first great dramatic interpreter to leave behind a deep surviving cache of work that we can still watch.*

Sound, however, would make a tremendous difference. Starting with 1929's *The Return of Sherlock Holmes*, Clive Brook could convey verbal incision and debonair humor in two ominous Fox productions that, suddenly, behave like modern films. Arthur Wontner created a superb Holmes — ironic and bone dry but slyly affectionate and humorous with his Watsons — in features made through the '30s. A cinematic tradition had begun.

Philip St. John Basil Rathbone was born in South Africa in 1892,† though the family soon evacuated because the Boers suspected his father of being a British spy. (Basil never did figure out if that was true. He did hold that his father knew Conan Doyle in South Africa.) Raised in Liverpool, seat of the distinguished Rathbones since the seventeenth century, educated at a fine school, Basil took to the stage as a young man and established a

---

* Norwood found a fan in the elderly Conan Doyle, who praised his Holmes as "masterly."

† William Nigel Bruce, son of a British diplomat, was born in Mexico.

promising career as a touring Shakespearean with the great Frank Benson, his cousin. Then came the war. "In August of 1914 I would not have believed it possible that I could eventually become a competent and reasonably well-adjusted soldier," he wrote in his memoirs, decades later.

And yet he did, as a captain with the Liverpool Scottish Regiment, handling dangerous front-line recon. In late spring 1918, when British commanders suspected German forces might be crumbling, Rathbone volunteered for a two-man daylight scouting mission. He and a corporal hid in no-man's-land before dawn, waited while a German fighter squadron strafed British lines, then crept into the nearest German trench. They found it deserted, and proceeded to explore until they encountered a single infantryman, whom Rathbone promptly shot and killed. They ransacked the man's pockets — Rathbone claimed his diary and other documents verified a German retreat — and escaped under heavy machine-gun fire. Back in the British trench, Rathbone discovered that he'd stepped into a decomposing corpse during his flight. "With one shoe off and one shoe on," he wrote, "the reality and horror of war came rushing in on me."

Barbed wire scarred his legs as he scrambled out of that German trench. On another section of the front, his beloved brother John was killed. His mother died while he was deployed. But Rathbone carried on, as most survivors did, and after the war his success on the London stage eventually propelled him to Broadway. He was playing Romeo to Katharine Cornell's Juliet in 1935 when MGM offered him a contract. It was a good time to be a handsome Brit with glossy manners, Shakespearean range, and stage-fencing training in Hollywood. Rathbone frequently worked as a swank period villain; in 1938's *Adventures of Robin Hood,* his lush-locked Sir Guy of Guisbourne slashes and gibes with Errol Flynn through two minutes of scintillating blade-on-blade action, before finally tumbling dead (but still good-looking) off a high balcony.*

In *The Hound of the Baskervilles,* Rathbone's Holmes bursts to life fully formed, imbued with the supple steel of the front-line intelligence officer and the smoldering allure of the Hollywood star. The actor (on loan from

---

* Rathbone, who had been fencing since his teens, relished that the glamorous Flynn didn't really know how. He basically had to choreograph the swordplay for both of them.

MGM, per studio-system practice) appears first wearing the famed dressing gown like a second skin, his sleek raven hair lacquered into a tight helmet, his elegantly bony profile like an extract from Paget. He nails Sherlock's amusement at his own cleverness and avid attention to what must be seen, what must be done. An acting treatise could be written on Rathbone's use of his own eyebrows. Soon he and Bruce are dashing over the ersatz Dartmoor's fog-dampened fake rocks, Rathbone snug in his Inverness cape, to the deerstalker born. The poor dog doesn't stand a chance.

The *Hound* hit cinemas around the world in the politically grim spring of '39, and was a big enough hit that Fox ramped up a sequel. *The Adventures of Sherlock Holmes* turned out to be a bit too quick off the mark, in fact. Bruce rued its "rather rambling and complicated story which had no resemblance to any of the writings of Conan Doyle." Lanfield did not return as director, and the film — a cod-Victorian mash of Moriarty and this and that — lacked the *Hound*'s self-assurance. Timing didn't help: *The Adventures* debuted on 1 September 1939, the day the Wehrmacht invaded Poland. Distracted audiences yielded middling box office returns. Meanwhile, behind the scenes, Fox engaged in a maddening multi-threaded correspondence with various representatives of the Conan Doyle estate, by this time in the clutches of the late author's sons Denis and Adrian, a pair of work-shy playboys eager to milk the family franchise.

Given all this, Fox decided that two Sherlock Holmes films made a complete set. The Rathbone-Bruce alliance, however, proved too formidable to evict from Baker Street. By autumn — as Poland succumbed and France and Britain faced off with Germany in the so-called Phony War — the duo began a long run playing Holmes and Watson on NBC's Blue radio network. They beamed into millions of American homes every Monday night for half an hour, their smooth repartee coming courtesy of Bromo Quinine or Petri Wine. These radio plays were superintended by one of Conan Doyle's best translators, Edith Meiser. A self-confessed Holmes addict, Meiser was a veteran actress who developed the knack for radio writing early in this new medium's life. (By the time Rathbone and Bruce came on the scene, she'd already been writing Sherlockian radio plays for years, starting with a "Speckled Band" for Gillette himself.) Her scripts often launch with a device that now seems odd but suited radio at the time. After a plummy announcer delivers a few words from the benevolent sponsor, he pauses briefly, then proclaims: "And now here we are, seated once more in Dr. Watson's study. The good doctor is wandering aimlessly about the room . . ." (So begins Meiser's "Adventure of the Musgrave Ritual," broadcast 11 December 1939.) The announcer (sometimes, later, a characterization of Joseph Bell) then engages Watson in a dialogue. Watson, now apparently retired to California, starts telling a story. A quick hit of violin shifts the setting from the contemporary United States to Victorian England. Enter Rathbone, his incisive voice glinting amid the ambient fog, and Meiser lets Conan Doyle's natural storytelling momentum take over. People would turn the lights off to listen.

Within two years, Universal Pictures signed Rathbone and Bruce to revive the film series, which was just too promising to let die. The rapier cunning (that was Basil), the fuzzy-brained buffoonery (Nigel), the thrill of the chase: these two were perfect for each other.

Like Conan Doyle before them, Basil Rathbone and Nigel Bruce stumbled upon the secret power of Sherlock Holmes, as palpable in the 1940s as in the 1890s, or, for that matter, today. People can't get enough. In apparent defiance of all known economic laws, demand almost always outstrips supply. One might think that by the time Conan Doyle took his last bow in 1930, the world would have looked upon the Canon — oh yes, that's what the most reverent fans call original-article Holmes — and said, That is it, and it is good. No. Those whom Holmes beguiles want more. They wanted more from Conan Doyle, and would want more from Rathbone and Bruce.

Not only that, but from almost the very beginning, Holmes and Watson inspired an apparently irresistible desire to climb into their world and play around. It's as if Conan Doyle laid down a colossal creative dare — or, maybe, crafted the ultimate Lego set for imaginative minds. The two actors would become enmeshed in a much larger, more elaborate diversion: the impulse to re-create, remix, remodel, celebrate, subvert, and generally tinker with Sherlock Holmes. This pursuit, driven by a potent mix of love and money, would only become more complex and diffuse and, honestly, odd as the twentieth century ran its course. The game was on.

• • •

In 1920, Vincent Starrett, the Chicago journalist who would become the chief sage of Sherlockiana in his time, published "The Unique Hamlet: A Hitherto Unchronicled Adventure of Mr. Sherlock Holmes" in a lavish private edition. He sent a copy to Conan Doyle, expressing hope that the tribute didn't add "insult to injury." Many others had tried their hands. In 1893, a Midlands newspaper called the *Burnley Express* published a story, "The Man Who Bested Sherlock Holmes," about a detective who strives to outdo Sherlock, who in this story is very real.* In 1897, with Holmes officially dead, novelist John Kendrick Bangs put the detective in charge of an afterworld investigation in *The Pursuit of the House-Boat.* Early in the twentieth century, English-speaking visitors to the Continent often noted remarkable Sherlockian libraries, full of titles completely un-known to Conan Doyle, viz., *From the Secret Files of the World-Detective,* a pulpy German series featuring lurid covers—Holmes in a dungeon full of hanged women, that sort of thing. (Germans!) The first Greek de-tective novel was a Sherlock Holmes knock-off. Starrett's effort, though, signaled a new tradition: pastiche, the effort to "do" Conan Doyle and the Baker Street scene in loving tribute rather than wholesale theft. The impulse emanates from all those untold adventures Watson, incorrigible tease, mentions but never explains. If Conan Doyle refused to reveal the Giant Rat of Sumatra or the Paradol Chamber or the Amateur Mendicant Society, why not take a shot?

In 1928, August Derleth, an enterprising Wisconsin lad, wrote Conan Doyle a fan letter, asking if he planned to write any more Holmes sto-ries. Conan Doyle, who probably received a half-dozen such things a day, scrawled a curt demurral straight onto Derleth's own letter and pitched it back across the Atlantic. Not one to sit idle—he later estimated, at one point, that he'd published 3,000 pieces in 350 magazines—Der-leth cranked out "The Adventure of the Black Narcissus," a story of a 1920s detective named Solar Pons, who lives in London's Praed Street, maintains a friendship with a doctor-writer named Parker, and runs a street-youth operation called the Praed Street Irregulars. After the pulp magazine *Dragnet* published the tale, Pons would become the mightiest

---

* This story's original publication was tracked down by none other than my old Swedish comrade from the Street Arabs, Mattias Boström.

pastiche franchise, pursuing scores of adventures — more than Holmes, in fact — for decades, inspiring a miniature fan subculture of his own.*

Today, my local bookstore, Powell's, packs whole shelves with Sherlockian imitations and tributes and spin-offs and crossovers. Several publishing houses, like MX in Britain and Titan in the States, produce lists full of neo-Sherlockian adventures. (Titan publishes a rambunctiously gonzo series, The Further Adventures of Sherlock Holmes, including *Dr. Jekyll and Mr. Holmes* and *The Ectoplasmic Man,* in which — according to the jacket copy; life is short — Sherlock teams up with Harry Houdini.) Writers make whole careers and subcareers of this game: Donald Thomas, whose nonfiction book *The Victorian Underworld* served as my Rough Guide to wicked nineteenth-century Britain, coined the attractive idea of "Sherlock Holmes on Her Majesty's Secret Service" and has written multiple volumes on the theme. Full-fledged series feature, as their main detective characters, Lestrade, Mycroft Holmes, Irene Adler, Mrs. Hudson, and on and on.

Pastiche makes an unwieldy subject, with the word itself hardly stretching to contain the most rococo variations. Is Neil Gaiman's "A Study in Emerald," which remixes Holmes and H. P. Lovecraft to memorable effect, a pastiche? What about Michael Chabon's *The Final Solution,* a crushing little novel in which an elderly detective, retired to keep bees, encounters a young World War II refugee with an inexplicable parrot that rattles off numbers in German, and struggles to figure out what it might mean? (Mitch Cullin's *A Slight Trick of the Mind* also considers an aged Holmes, slipping into dementia, memorably incarnated by Ian McKellen in the 2015 film *Mr. Holmes.*) What about Emma Jane Holloway's steampunk-sorcery fantasies featuring Evelina Cooper, Sherlock Holmes's magical niece?

What should we make of this unending hive-mind reinvention of Sherlock? I admit that pastiche and the related quasi-Doylean corpus inspires

---

* To my taste, the best thing about the Solar Pons stories — written with charming, if workmanlike, ardor but lacking (again, for me) the true Sherlockian sizzle — is Derleth's fantastic way with a title. A sampling: "The Adventure of the Frightened Baronet," "The Adventure of the Three Red Dwarfs," "The Adventure of the Man with the Broken Face," "The Adventure of the Tottenham Werewolf" (!), "The Adventure of the Little Hangman."

in me the vague dread of an all-you-can-eat buffet. Bits and pieces look okay — not lethal, at any rate — but the sheer volume threatens my frail constitution. On my bedside table sits *The Mandala of Sherlock Holmes,* Tibetan novelist Jamyang Norbu's deft interweaving of dialogue from the Canon and the political and spiritual worlds of India and the Himalayas. On a shelf upstairs somewhere, I have a book of Sherlockian adventures set in Montana. ("Sherlock Holmes goes to _____" is a reliable formula.) Craning my neck, I spy a battered paperback of *The Exploits of Sherlock Holmes,* one of Adrian Conan Doyle's many attempts to cash in on Daddy. (Accomplished mystery novelist John Dickson Carr served as Adrian's coauthor for half the stories — until Adrian became truly intolerable — so it's not *awful.*) And right here: a list of a score of stories by different authors that feature Sherlock Holmes versus vampires. I'm tempted to drape it in garlic just to be safe.

The problem is that approximately 98 percent of pastiche, especially in its purely imitative form, is bad. Very. When another writer tries to warm up the magic lantern of 221B, the results usually flicker at best. Dialogue clunks with faux Victorianisms and leaden exposition. Artificial Holmeses and zombie Watsons creak about like creepy broken wind-up toys. Conan Doyle's familiar arsenal of world-weaving tools gets thrown around with artless abandon: the pasticheur name-drops a dozen or so "untold tales" while Sherlock Holmes shoots coke, Watson cleans his revolver, Mrs. Hudson fumbles with the gasogene, and Inspector Lestrade faints on the rug. The Watsonian narrative voice defies reproduction. I sympathize. I've tried it myself. The results, so far, have been carefully destroyed.

Sometimes someone gets it mostly right. Donald Thomas's spy intrigues and Sherlockizations of true Victorian crimes rollick along quite nicely. Jamyang Norbu's subcontinental oddity (with a character from Kipling in the Watson role) lends the Great Detective cross-cultural dimensions. And in her novel *Dust and Shadow,* Lyndsay Faye (of the Baker Street Babes, recall) sends Holmes and Watson against Jack the Ripper — an irresistible pastiche concept — with an uncommon fealty to the voice and texture of the originals and a modern sensitivity to social conditions.

As a public service to future authors and readers, I asked Faye how the pastiche game, at its best, is played — for a Pasticheur's Prime Directive. "You have to love the characters first," she replied. "Passionately. You need, as well, an eye for detail. A dogcart is not a hansom, and a gasogene is not a tantalus. Next, you need to understand that John Watson is the most important character in those stories, period, full stop.

"You cannot listen to a word Watson and Sherlock Holmes say when describing themselves or you will run into trouble. Pay attention to how they act. People screw up pastiches constantly by making Holmes a misogynist, when he is actually very kind to women and quite chivalrous to them. They screw up pastiches by making Holmes constantly angry and brooding, forgetting that the man plays pranks for the sheer joy of surprising people and is more a showman than an iconoclast. But that harks back to my initial advice: love the characters and read the stories often enough, and you will already know that."

Over the course of a century, thousands of writers from around the world have gang-tackled these characters and the mythos that surrounds them. It must be a clue. What, exactly, has impelled this monstrous growth from a comparatively small seed? I could have called many people to find out, but I called Laurie R. King. King was born in Oakland and still lives in California — a cosmos removed, geopsychologically, from Sherlockian London. For twenty years, however, the mystery author has written novels about Sherlock Holmes. Or, I should say, about his wife.

Yes, King boldly outfitted Holmes — in her fictional world, the aging beekeeper of 1915 onward — with a female apprentice turned soul mate, bright young Mary Russell, who becomes his wife and Watsonian investigative partner. In more than a dozen novels, Holmes and Russell venture through the Great War and its aftermath, from Hollywood to India. They are, in their own dry and intellectual fashion, in love. Physically, even. This strikes ye olde Sherlockian (me) as a somewhat heretical prospect, but it does serve to generate a whole new cycle of adventures for the old boy, and to tilt an authentic feminine eye at a fictional world heretofore depicted almost exclusively with a male sensibility. It certainly works commercially. King's Russell series (yes, Mary gets top billing) regularly makes bestseller charts, and runs deep enough as a fictional world to justify its own annotative *Companion*, published in 2014.

I asked King what in Conan Doyle made her work, and the other literary adaptations of Holmes, possible. "Arthur Conan Doyle opens many doors that he never explored himself," she said. "One of the more interesting, to me, is that Sherlock Holmes is a misanthrope who somehow dedicated his life to serving people. He's a man standing on both sides of a chasm. So what is he like? Would you want to be his roommate? Would you want to be his wife?"

Here we have the Canon's odd "unfinished" quality — the sense that, hold on, there must be more to it. This apparent flaw in Conan Doyle's work has become a major factor in Sherlock Holmes's success and endless reinvention. What was Holmes like when he was young? When he grew old? What was he doing in Tibet, or Odessa? When did Watson go to Australia? Laurie King, very cleverly, found a seam of untapped Sherlockian possibilities and mined it.

"Conan Doyle could not envision Sherlock Holmes after the war," she told me. "As far as he was concerned, the world had no place for that kind of mind any longer. Mary Russell is the young, female, early-twentieth-century-feminist version of Sherlock Holmes's mind, and to begin with, I was primarily interested in her. I could have put her in San Francisco, or done many different things with her. But once I paired Russell with Holmes, I began to see his possibilities. I realized that I was selling Holmes short, just as Conan Doyle sold him short. Holmes was vigorous, flexible. He could change. And because I started in 1915, I could do whatever I wanted with him, because at that point Conan Doyle is done with him."

In a way, King and the others who write in either imitation or interpretation of the original Sherlock Holmes only follow the lead of an author who used those two primary characters as a vehicle for storytelling of all kinds. Conan Doyle built limitless narrative possibility into his Holmes stories, and a new iteration like King's takes advantage of that quality. "You can do anything you want with the Giant Rat of Sumatra," she said. "You can take Sherlock Holmes to India, and he allows you to ask, well, what else was going on in India right then?"

An odd thing — alarming, from a staunch traditionalist point of view — is that there must be many readers for whom King's elderly married man *is* Sherlock Holmes. "I do weave glancing references to the Canon into every one of my novels," said the woman who married off

Sherlock (of course, William Gillette did the same). "It's like a nudge of the elbow, and for many readers, that's one of the pleasures. But that's just one game. Many people who read my novels have never read Conan Doyle — strange as that is — and they must derive pleasure from seeing Sherlock Holmes in the way I portray him."

It is true: many people — the majority, actually — who enjoy Sherlock Holmes will never crack a Conan Doyle volume. That dates straight back to the 1890s, when someone might have encountered (even loved) the detective as a music-hall parody or a newspaper knock-off. For millions, Gillette was Sherlock Holmes, as was Eille Norwood. In pastiche and its many mutations, every author creates his or her own Holmes. No matter how far removed from Conan Doyle, each depends on a singular characteristic of the original: you can take Sherlock Holmes anywhere, and make him do almost anything. Somehow, he's always Sherlock Holmes.

"This is the Voice of Terror! This is the Voice of Terror!"

The time: some perilous early moment in World War II. The place: London. Poland lies in ruins. The Nazis rule Norway. France has collapsed. The Americans are playing baseball, or whatever. Britain stands alone as the Germans bomb it to splinters. To make a fevered atmosphere even more intense (at least in *Sherlock Holmes and the Voice of Terror,* released by Universal on 18 September 1942), an anonymous propaganda broadcast breaks into British airwaves with eerily prescient harangues about violence to come. Troop trains sabotaged. Docklands incinerated. Dams obliterated. Who's behind it? Can it be stopped? The ministers of the government's "Inner Council" scramble to stem the damage. "In this emergency," one official says, "we must take advantage of everyone's peculiar talents." They call in Sherlock Holmes.*

---

* Holmes had a good war. Soviet troops toted "The Man with the Twisted Lip" as part of the Little Library of the Journal of the Red Army Soldier. Britain's Ministry of Information produced a minute-long instructional clip, "The Sacred Flame Coal Fire," in which Holmes and Watson explain heating-fuel conservation. ("Deduction, my dear Holmes?" "No, *reduction,* my dear public.") The Special Operations Executive, a gung-ho British espionage and sabotage outfit, operated out of Baker Street and inevitably became known to insiders as the Baker Street Irregulars. And the 1937 German

Basil Rathbone and Nigel Bruce take charge of the matter with an aplomb honed by scores of radio performances, Rathbone sporting a floppy Wildean haircut, Bruce fulminating like a champ. Baker Street's reigning tandem returns with new paymasters, a new mission, and a new chronology: Holmes and Watson now operate in the 1940s. (What of the same actors, playing the same characters, in an 1880s and 1890s setting, just three years before? Hollywood!)

Universal gave the series a creative and infrastructural overhaul. Whereas Fox produced the *Hound* and the *Adventures* as pricy A pictures, Universal deployed its B unit, a high-speed, tight-budget craft outfit that could hammer together a theatrical feature in a matter of weeks, then turn around and do it again. Meanwhile, the studio made Holmes and Watson leap — as promotional materials put it — into "the front-page headlines and excitement of today."* Despite the contemporary setting, Universal's producers explicitly planned to seal the duo inside a magical time bubble. While characters they encountered lived (and dressed themselves) in the 1940s, Holmes and Watson would carry themselves as Victorians. (Nigel Bruce simply wore his own clothes.) Their 221B would function as a temporal safe house bearing relics of 1895. They would be men out of time.

The conceit allowed for certain hijinks. In *Voice of Terror*, as Rathbone prepares to dash out of Baker Street in pursuit of Nazi evildoers, he grabs a deerstalker. "No, no, no," Bruce protests. "Holmes, you promised." Sherlock ruefully puts on a fedora. But there was a larger point. By preserving the character's Victorian essence and transporting it into the modern world, the films issue an unsubtle manifesto on Anglophonic endurance. Up against totalitarian modernism, a pair of tweedy English gentlemen — in a dingy flat, armed with Webley single-action revolv-

---

production of *The Hound of the Baskervilles* was allegedly one of two films found in Hitler's Berlin bunker.

* My description of Universal's creative process owes much to *England's Secret Weapon* by Amanda J. Field. Field uses a considerable volume of archival material — production notes, studio memos, budget records, correspondence between the movie studios and the Conan Doyle estate's representatives, and the like — to create a compelling analysis of the decisions and strategies that shaped the Rathbone-Bruce series.

ers and their wits—will never surrender. In a scene in 1943's *Sherlock Holmes and the Secret Weapon*, Rathbone strides through the rubble-strewn streets of Blitz London with flinty nonchalance. In the same film, as a military scientist Holmes has sprung from Switzerland glances nervously out of an RAF plane at rows of naval ships defending the Channel, Sherlock dozes next to him, serene in his trusty elderly-bookseller disguise. Sherlock Holmes will prevail. We will win.

Secret Weapon—the second Universal film, one of three made in quick succession with wartime, Nazi-hunting plots—introduced a secret weapon of its own: director Roy William Neill. Neill, who helmed the series from then on, was one of those forgotten culture-industry heroes, a commercial workhorse who'd learned his trade back in the silent era and could whip off a Sherlock Holmes feature in three weeks. Nigel Bruce would remember him as a fastidiously dressed little pipe smoker (nickname: Mousie) with a master craftsman's repertoire. He forged a smooth collaboration with Rathbone and Bruce, effectively a troika that handled day-to-day operations, viewing daily rushes together and smoothing out any shift in shooting schedule through the actors' stage-style command of the scripts.

Through the rest of the series—fourteen films all told, counting the Fox duo—Neill's lighting and camera work build a dense Sherlockian palette of murk and shadow, from obsidian blacks to flaring, blown-out whites. He lingers on expressive faces—the secondary characters are perpetually terrified—and stalks ominous interiors and darkened landscapes. You can smell the dust and cordite. The director's signature look saturated this vision of Sherlock Holmes with '40s glamour—it was Neill who made the Great Detective modern. (His formidable skills also helped sell some bizarre conceits: 1944's *The Spider Woman* features a killer tarantula, a pygmy in a suitcase, and Holmes disguised as a turban-wearing Indian. Neill makes it work.) The director would die prematurely, in '46—he dropped dead of a heart attack in the Strand—but is regarded as an undersung progenitor of the classic film noir era.

The films' sets must have felt like a secret society clubhouse involving half the middle-aged male Britons on the Pacific Slope—notably Dennis Hoey as a meaty Inspector Lestrade and Henry Daniell, a serpentine Moriarty. Rathbone, though, is the revelation, wielding his monumental profile like a rapier. He makes his Sherlock brisk and prickly, with a carefully honed edge of rudeness and diction crackling with urgency. With Rathbone at the helm, the nine syllables of "Elementary, my dear Watson" become a steam-driven express. The actor realizes some of Sir Arthur Conan Doyle's anthropomorphic leanings, roving like an elegant bird of prey or keeping a panther's watch over his natural habitat of fog, shadow, and high-collared tweed. A cool customer, the Rathbone Holmes: "Yes, horrible," he tells a distraught Inspector Gregson over a girl's corpse in *The Woman in Green*, "let's go get a drink." If anything, Rathbone misses some of the character's bohemian humor and gentleness. You can't really imagine Rathbone's Holmes playing Watson to sleep with a sweet violin lullaby. All business, our Basil.

Rathbone's relentless precision serves him well, but he would be intolerable without Nigel Bruce. Much misguided commentary has targeted Bruce's Watson, who blithers through the fourteen films with wide-eyed joy. Some object that his approach fails to recall Conan Doyle's muscular man of action; these critics are both correct and completely missing the point. Bruce's Watson, ostensible second banana to Captain Super Sleuth, never meets a scene he can't walk away with in his lint-strewn pockets. That raspy *harrumph*, clueless dignity, sloe-eyed gaze, and shambling physicality — all apparently artless, all requiring attentive craft. The duo exudes tremendous chemistry; off-screen, they were mischievous drinking buddies and frequently got the wives together for cocktails. (Bunny Bruce couldn't stand Ouida Rathbone, but one imagines she kept up appearances.) While Rathbone's Holmes is all ego, Bruce delivers a generous, almost self-sacrificial performance of comic genius. He gives sinewy Holmes a necessary cushion, and gives these films a wit and a soul. His Watson deserves at least half the credit for their long life.[*]

They made the things at startling speed: a dozen releases between autumn 1942 and spring 1946 — not perfect, but well crafted and fun, which is what people wanted as the world buckled around them. (Interestingly, by as early as 1943 Universal decided that the American public was tiring of all this war business, at least when it came to entertainment.

---

[*] When I was a kid, the films were a staple of daytime cable TV. Today, they're all available in their entirety on YouTube. And they say there's no such thing as progress.

After the trilogy of geopolitical adventures, the series veers off toward Gothic horror, under exquisite titles like *The Scarlet Claw* and *The Pearl of Death*.) The films made stars of Rathbone and Bruce — to his supreme annoyance, Rathbone couldn't go anywhere without some rube yelling "Elementary!" — and engraved Holmes and Watson into the public consciousness all over again.

The Universal films in particular reveal what Sherlock Holmes would become in the twentieth century: a flexible time traveler, ready-made for any future generation or medium. While earlier films had shown Holmes in contemporary dress, Universal made the first true strategic chronological redeployment. On a grand scale, Neill and Rathbone and Bruce did what August Derleth had and what Laurie King and so many others would, summoning up the Baker Street aura to illuminate both what had changed and what would never change. True to Conan Doyle, they offered humor and style and thrill — and a message tailored to the moment. A culture capable of fun this refined could never lose to some humorless Austro-Bavarian corporal.

In December 1944, Edgar W. Smith, the General Motors executive who had launched the *Baker Street Journal* and by then ran the Irregulars, received a notable letter. (Christopher Morley, the BSI's founder, liked starting clubs but not operating them.) Smith's correspondent propounded a radical theory: Sherlock Holmes was an American. "He was brought up by a father or a foster father in the underground world, thus learning all the tricks of the trade in the highly developed American art of crime," the gentleman wrote. "His attributes were primarily American, not English."

The correspondent: Franklin Delano Roosevelt, commander in chief and secret member of the Baker Street Irregulars. Roosevelt wrote a series of jaunty letters to the BSI throughout the war, reporting, among other things, that the Secret Service cabins at what would become Camp David were informally known as Baker Street. Smith arranged the President's honorary membership, to be kept quiet until Victory Day. (Harry Truman would become a member, too.) And Roosevelt's Holmes-as-American theory — for which he offered little evidence except presidential prerogative — exemplified the central pursuit of the Sherlockian subculture he had surreptitiously joined: the Great Game.

The Great Game began early, probably when Frank Sidgwick wrote open letters to Dr. Watson, questioning the internal consistency of *The Hound of the Baskervilles* with the novel's serial publication still in progress. In 1904, a Russian psychologist named Michael Mayevsky published a monograph analyzing Holmes's investigative methods. In 1911, at the Gryphon Club, an Anglican priest named Ronald Knox presented "Studies in the Literature of Sherlock Holmes," a slyly mind-boggling satire that applied the techniques of German biblical critics (the "higher criticism") to the Holmesian Canon.

In surveying these formative works, one notices one name by its absence: Arthur Conan Doyle. The Great Game often involves the pretense that Sherlock Holmes and John Watson (and their retinue, right down to Billy the Page) were real; that their adventures really happened; that Watson really chronicled them; and that Conan Doyle, at best, served as Watson's "literary agent." From there, the Game goes just about anywhere. (Sometimes you even find work that acknowledges Conan Doyle as creator, and comes close to conventional literary criticism.) The Game's most basic form examines the "real" chronology of the sixty stories — Watson's dates, of course, make no sense whatsoever, but there are phases of the moon, weather reports, oblique references to political events, allusions to newspaper articles, and elaborate chains of interdependent references to reconstruct. That will keep you busy for a while. (Or just dig up a copy of Gavin Brend's well-wrought 1951 book *My Dear Holmes* for a serviceable, if by no means universally accepted, example.) Watsonian chronology is merely a gateway drug: this elaborate quasi-scholarship has examined the imaginable (where did Holmes attend university?) and the unimaginable (was Watson a woman?) with varying levels of irony, and sometimes none at all. The English essayist and mystery novelist Dorothy L. Sayers — whose acerbic 1946 collection *Unpopular Opinions* theorizes on Watson's middle name ("Hamish," a position that has become almost canonical) among other things — laid down the most important dictate: the Great Game "must be played as solemnly as a county cricket match at Lord's; the slightest touch of extravagance or burlesque ruins the atmosphere."

The result is a micro-literature so focused it attains the approximate density of Jupiter's core. The Great Game, properly speaking, doesn't even deal with the entire Sherlock Holmes phenomenon. Despite the frequent conceit that Conan Doyle had nothing to do with it, the Game concerns itself only with the Canon. This "in-world" Sherlockian tradition was once aptly described as (to paraphrase slightly) the most ever written by so many for so few.

I have before me a run of the *Sherlock Holmes Journal*, flagship publication of the Sherlock Holmes Society of London, dating back to the mid-1980s but representing only a fragment of the *Journal*'s long existence. It is a modestly beautiful example of semiprofessional publishing, its texts set in stately twin columns beneath bold headlines, its cover design essentially unchanged for decades. (As illustration, always, readers greet artist Howard Elcock's portrayal of the one-legged news vendor from "The Adventure of the Illustrious Client.") This stack brims with exacting investigations into events that never happened and people who never existed. Open on my desk, from the winter of 2002: a street-savvy analysis of the location of Jabez Wilson's pawnshop in "The Adventure of the Red-Headed League." Flip back to summer 1986: we find the subject of Watson's war wound, which notoriously migrated between his shoulder and his leg. In 1999, a writer surveys the current events of 1899, her date for "The Adventure of Charles Augustus Milverton."

And so on. The *SHJ* is one of several major organs of Sherlockian scholarship. The *Baker Street Journal*, founded by Edgar Smith immediately after World War II as the BSI's house magazine and going strong, after the odd start and stop, publishes work in much the same vein, as do *Canadian Holmes*, journal of the Bootmakers of Toronto, and Australia's *Passengers' Log*, and many even smaller concerns. The striking characteristic, on first examination, of all this Sherlockiana is its apparent changelessness. Great Game scholarship published in 2014 often seems as if it could have appeared in *Profile by Gaslight*, an "Irregular reader" edited by Smith and printed on grainy, war-rationed paper in 1944. (That anthology includes an analysis of Holmes's home library and such inquiries as "Was Sherlock Holmes a Drug Addict?" and "Was the Later Holmes an Imposter?") The Canon, after all, is fixed.*

---

* Which is not to say the field lacks its own revisionist tendencies. In 1976, in the now-defunct *Baker Street Miscellanea*, a certain Vivian Darkbloom published a piece argu-

Not to strike the note of a jaded rock-and-roll fan, but I tend to like that "early stuff": the gorgeous and ironical writing compiled by Smith in *Profile* and the 1946–49 Original Series of the *Baker Street Journal*. The latter's lovingly made artifacts, replete with Victorian typography and whimsical illustrations, offer a fragmentary glimpse of the time when the hardcore Sherlockian fan culture really found its enduring form.

The small circle of people singularly devoted to the original-article Holmes included some great characters. (The masses could keep *The Scarlet Claw* et al.; the Rathbone-Bruce films, radio serials, comic books, and other popular manifestations barely rate a mention in the early *BSJ*.) The Sherlockians helped each other shake the gloom of the war, smooth out the modern age's sharper edges, and mix drinks. (I am acquainted with a few of these folk indirectly, through living people who knew them firsthand. I'm also extrapolating from photos of 1946 BSI meetings included in the *Journal*, which show exactly the kinds of bleary-eyed gatherings that once had a soused Vincent Starrett on hands and knees, baying like the Hound. I mean, allegedly.) A fellow named Clifton R. Andrew somehow induced a small-town newspaper in Freeport, Ohio, to publish a two-part Sherlock Holmes pastiche of his devising. On 1 February 1946, as Andrew presided over the first meeting of the Scandalous Bohemians of Akron, a "percentage [of members] held out for 'Stingers' concocted of apricot brandy and crème de menthe." (Andrew and his wife, Lisa, I have on good authority, rode the Greyhound to New York City from Chicago, where they lived in the 1960s, every January for the Irregulars' gathering — a long, cold trip, one imagines, warmed only by love, and possibly Stingers.) A few years later, the Marquess of Donegall, a sauntering journalist and international sportsman, took the editorship of the *Sherlock Holmes Journal* and conducted a freewheeling correspondence with Sherlockians of all stripes. "Don" once wrote a friend that he was having the damnedest time completing a letter, because the bucking of his yacht kept tipping the typewriter onto the deck.

---

ing that Sherlock Holmes had actually contrived to murder the villainous Grimesby Roylott in "The Adventure of the Speckled Band"— with the motive of seducing Roylott's stepdaughter and putative victim, Helen Stoner. "Vivian Darkbloom" is an anagram for "Vladimir Nabokov."

Each thick 1940s issue of the *BSJ* begins with an elegy from beneath "The Editor's Gas Lamp." "It has been given to us, in this fifth decade of the Twentieth Century, to be present at the ending of an age. Our eyes are witness to the crumbling in the dust of the elemental matter from which the fabric of our civilization has been wrought." Such somewhat melancholy notes put the mock-serious jollity of the pursuit in context. Amid postwar atomic uncertainty, the *BSJ* allowed a tiny fraction of the intelligentsia to have some fun. Style, with a wink and a rueful grin (and perhaps a shot of rye): the *Baker Street Journal* distilled the ethos of mid-century Sherlockiana into print.

One might be tempted to think they said it all back then. But no. One current editor of a Sherlockian specialty journal told me his only real concern is the vast backlog of material awaiting publication. Leslie Klinger, a Los Angeles lawyer and litterateur, edited 2004's monumental *New Annotated Sherlock Holmes,* a lavish three-volume set that pairs each of the sixty canonical stories with copious notes drawn from Great Game scholarship. When we first spoke, Klinger told me that while the tradition may seem monolithic, the Game is actually evolving rapidly. "This is a golden age," he said, "because of the research power of the Internet. Google and others scan in an incredible amount of Victorian material every day, and all the major sources of published Sherlockian scholarship are searchable online.

"The strange and perhaps funny thing is that we're in no danger of running out of things to write about. For all the thousands of essays that have been written, there is enough stuff in Sherlock Holmes to keep us all busy for another hundred years. I constantly receive emails: can you think of someone who has written about this, or that, or made this argument, or looked into a particular question? And the answer, many times, is no. No one has thought of a certain approach or theory before. You still get these eureka-moment essays. For years, Sherlockians speculated about a passing mention of a cave on Long Island. Finally, a Sherlockian named Steve Doyle actually went out to Long Island and found a cave. This must be it! You can buy it or not, but it keeps us going." Klinger noted the work of Leslie Katz, a retired Australian judge of Canadian extraction. "He comes out of nowhere," Klinger told me. "He's not part of any Sherlock Holmes society. He's not publishing in any of the established journals.

And his stuff, I must say, is fascinating." Katz, I would discover, uploads (then endlessly revises) monographs to something called the Social Science Research Network, an anarchic wilderness of unmediated scholarship. Like Sherlock himself, he pursues trifles. For example, Katz latches on to a brand name that appears etched on trouser buttons at a crime scene in "The Adventure of the Norwood Builder." He establishes that this company really existed, tracing its tangled corporate history through Victorian newspaper archives and 112-year-old issues of the *Economist*. He then proves that the company, Hyam, did indeed put its name on its buttons — in part by citing testimony in an 1869 theft case in which its stolen goods were identified by that mark. (The thief got ten years.)

The Canon is full of such trivia for the curious reader to pick at: confused dates, veiled characters, stray bits of Victoriana that Conan Doyle's original readers blazed right through but which now shed light on the creation of Sherlock Holmes. In the irony of ironies, many of the "problems" investigated in this refined and deliberative genre of metafiction exist only because Conan Doyle wrote so hastily. He didn't really care — certainly not about dates, or minor matters like where Watson took his Afghan bullet. To him, the Holmes stories were fairy tales and formula moneymakers. It takes a cheeky, intentional misreading to transform them into a "canon" for study, even a kind of factual report from a parallel universe. This would drive Conan Doyle mad, but it turns out to be fun. Thus does the Great Game go on.

Catherine Cooke pulled open a gunmetal-gray filing cabinet. "Here they all are," she said. "All the little journals we've received."

Cooke, a well-known Sherlockian, works as a librarian for the Borough of Marylebone, the London district that encompasses Baker Street. As part of her duties, she oversees a notable collection of Holmes-related books, manuscripts, magazines, and ephemera. When I visited, this all was crammed into a pair of dusty back rooms, a veritable Lost Ark of Sherlockiana. (The library was in the throes of some bureaucratically nightmarish relocation.) There, under Cooke's tutelage, I beheld some remarkable things: gorgeous editions of the saga in Gaelic, Thai, and Latin; Turkish pastiche from the 1930s; the *Strand* from its foundation in 1891 until the sad moment in 1950 when the old thing merged with a lad-mag called *Men Only,* which soon ran a droopy cartoon of Holmes on its cover to celebrate.

A pair of filing cabinets contained hand-stapled magazines and mimeographed journals going back decades. As we pawed through these micro-published efforts — most much like the Kinko's-made punk zines I loved in my teenage and college years — Cooke exhibited touches of nostalgia. "Oh, that was a good one," she would say. "Haven't seen a new issue in quite a while." Or, "They come and go, you know. And now, with the Internet . . ." The tradition of physical publication was slowly drying up. Most of these journals, she explained, depend upon the enthusiasm and pocketbook of a single person. When that person dies, loses interest, or decides that a free blog would suffice, the title fades out. The clubs themselves, she noted, are fragile things; apart from the BSI, the Sherlock Holmes Society of London, and a few other large national societies, they usually amount to a few enthusiasts who gather for a drink once every few months. That kind of ritual can drop off without anyone really noticing, until it's too late. The Marylebone Library's collection of Sherlockian journals serves as an unintentional register of subcultural mortality.

I shivered inwardly, for I, too, had let a Sherlock Holmes club die. A few short years after my brother and I labored so long and hard to assemble the Street Arabs — after all those letters to Sweden and Scotland and Japan — adolescence took me in its grip. Slowly, then all at once, I wanted quit of Sherlock Holmes and the version of me who, of all things, ran a Sherlock Holmes club. (A fifteen-year-old finds no one more tiresome than his twelve-year-old self.) I wanted to play in deafening bands and impress girls, not — just for instance — continue my awkward meetings over shopping mall pizza with an old dear from an East Coast Sherlock society, who would come calling during her annual trips west. (The last time this poor woman telephoned me, I was nineteen and ensconced in virtual seclusion at my girlfriend's house. I pointedly, if passive-aggressively, never returned the call. I've never entirely forgiven myself.) I wanted to end the painstaking production of *Wiggins's Report,* the official Street Arabs' journal (it was pretty good!), and refashion my writing career on the Hunter S. Thompson model. We're young. We make mistakes.

And I think I perceived something just slightly . . . off — a unwholesomeness in all those magazines read by nobody, really (thought teenage me), and in people spending thousands of hours obsessing over a fictional cocaine enthusiast. (Of course, my high school interests inclined toward equally obscure publications, not to mention very real cocaine enthusiasts.) And Arthur Conan Doyle? *Seriously?* With his mustache and cricket bat and séances?

Yes, standard-issue angst, probably somewhat Oedipal. It can become a bit overwhelming, though. After all these decades of pastiche and parodies and movies and the Great Game, there is just *so much* Sherlock Holmes. You could spend your life reading pseudo-Sherlockian stories, or essays attempting to establish how many times Watson got married, or, for that matter, watching Holmesian clips on YouTube. If you love Sherlock Holmes, the rabbit hole beckons, always. Others have noticed the danger — or fallen into it. Toward the end of his life, the renowned Sherlockian scholar Richard Lancelyn Green could become distraught, telling friends he had wasted his life on a "second-rate" writer.[*] In a candid exchange of emails with me, one veteran Sherlockian mused, "When does a hobby become a mania?"

Of course, this is all merely a variation on Conan Doyle's own dilemma: how much Sherlock is too much? And then there is the related problem of the author himself. As I looked through the Marylebone cabinets, Cooke and I chatted about the Great Game. "I wonder if the whole thing started because the Sherlockians were a bit embarrassed by Conan Doyle," she said. "He died at the height of his infamy over Spiritualism, in some ways, and the tradition of the scholarship formed in the shadow of that. Perhaps it seemed more respectable, somehow, to pretend that this Spiritualist fellow really didn't have anything to do with Holmes and Watson."

As a teenager, I recognized a vampiric quality shared by Holmes and Conan Doyle. Between the two of them, they can take over your life, if you let them. Being a teenager, I chose the most inelegant way out: I ignored the Street Arabs to death. I stopped returning letters. I stopped creating *Wiggins's Report*. I let my subscription to the *Baker Street Journal* — the first forum in which I ever published a piece of writing — lapse. I stuffed

---

[*] Green died under tragic and murky circumstances, an affair outside the scope of this book. This allusion is drawn from a 2004 *New Yorker* article by David Grann, anthologized in his collection *The Devil and Sherlock Holmes* (Vintage, 2010).

almost all my Sherlockian papers into storage and basically suppressed the fact that I'd ever been involved in this obscure pastime. Sayonara, Baker Street! I was into Kerouac now.

I closed the filing cabinet with a private regret that it contained no trace of the Street Arabs. Maybe I could dig up a few copies of *Wiggins's Report* and send them to Marylebone, where judicious Catherine Cooke would take much better care of them than I ever would. I looked around the back-hallway rooms, stuffed to overflowing with the physical evidence of the world's Sherlockian passion. Baker Street was just steps away. I now suspect that for me, as for so many others, it always will be.

"Yes! It's Elementary . . . Always Buy Chesterfield."

— CIGARETTE AD FEATURING BASIL RATHBONE,
AMERICAN MERCURY, 26 OCTOBER 1946

Basil Rathbone's friends thought he'd gone mad. His agents considered him (he would recall) "sick-sick-sick." Nigel Bruce was furious. Rathbone sat in New York, drinking gin and tonics, and calmly told them all where to go. He quit.

Sherlock Holmes was ruining his career, almost his life. The incessant film and radio production schedules left no time for anything else. Worse, the idiot public now seemed to think he *was* Sherlock Holmes. His other work — Shakespearean stage career, two Academy Award nominations, everything — was vanishing into a haze of meerschaum smoke. In the age of typecasting, Rathbone feared he would be "more completely 'typed' than any other classic actor has ever been or ever will be again." (So he wrote in his 1962 memoir, *In and Out of Character*. He could be a bit of a drama queen.) As an artist, he felt he had done his best Holmesian work in the *Hound* and that each subsequent performance was really just a carbon copy. Above all, he had come to dislike Sherlock Holmes on an almost personal level. "There was nothing lovable about Holmes," he would write. "It would be impossible for such a man to know loneliness or love or sorrow because he was completely sufficient unto himself."

So in 1946, Rathbone decamped to Broadway. He abandoned the radio series as well, leaving Nigel Bruce to carry on with a replacement and stew about paychecks lost as the film series evaporated. (Bruce was more financially aware than Rathbone. In his own memoir, only ever published in short excerpts, Bruce tracks how much he received for each installment of his Watsonian adventure.) Rathbone now considered the series misbegotten. "Our *timing* was bad," he wrote in *In and Out of Character*. "'Dated,' that's the word. The Sherlock Holmes stories are dated and their pattern and style . . . unacceptable to an age where science has proven that science fiction is another outdated joke . . . The only possible medium still available to an acceptable presentation of Sir Arthur Conan Doyle's stories would be a full-length Disney cartoon."

How could he be so wrong? As a matter of fact, at the very moment Rathbone wrote, a hugely successful BBC radio series of all sixty original stories, starring Carleton Hobbs, was under way. In 1959, the first color Holmes film had been made. The Conan Doyle stories were never out of print — the very bookstores that carried Rathbone's memoir shelved the Holmes stories a few feet away. He had developed, let us say, a skewed perspective.

Perhaps Rathbone had glimpsed Sherlock Holmes's strange infinitude — and though he didn't accurately recognize it, he knew he did not like what he saw. As it turned out, this great actor (with his great foil, Bruce, and the neglected master craftsman Roy William Neill) found himself aboard the Holmesian starship not as it was cruising back to base but just when it was revving up to warp speed. The decades to come would bring movies, TV shows, radio serials, comic books, scholarly papers, pseudoscholarly papers, pastiches and parodies, the musical, the ballet, video games, and *Sesame Street* skits. Without meaning to (shades of Conan Doyle), Rathbone's work provided the best demonstration yet of the Sherlockian trick: get the right detective and the right doctor, and you can send them anywhere.

I know one person briefly acquainted with Rathbone late in his career. This source relays that he was, even in a casual encounter, a most attentive and sensitive listener, a person who drank in his interlocutor, who heard everything said and everything not said. Basil Rathbone, the midcentury incarnation of Sherlock Holmes, both heard and observed.

In the early '50s, Rathbone decided to give Holmes another try. (Like

Conan Doyle, he found the financial prospects too good to resist.) He asked his wife, Ouida — let's just say Bunny Bruce wasn't the only person who found her irritating — to write the theatrical script. Many people told them it was no good, but they forged ahead, scraping together a production. The Boston tryouts were a moderate disaster. In New York, the show suffered near-instantaneous death via critical antipathy and public apathy, but not before the cast had to play one scene in total darkness thanks to a mysterious lighting failure. Rathbone blamed television; he blamed the uncultured and barbaric Youth; he blamed the ghost of Edgar Allan Poe. And, of course, he concluded that he'd been right all along: Sherlock Holmes was irrelevant and obsolete. He wanted nothing more to do with him. By the time my informant encountered him, Rathbone would recoil at any mention of the detective's name.

One might say that he didn't quite appreciate the real situation. The world wasn't done with Sherlock Holmes; Sherlock Holmes was done with Basil Rathbone. The last time the teller of this tale saw Rathbone, the actor was touring a lovely one-man show, enjoying his celebrity, which owed in part to his Holmes, of course. The two of them strolled through the night on a small midwestern college campus. When the time came to part, Rathbone said goodnight, turned, and vanished into the fog.

10

THE RETURN(S) OF SHERLOCK HOLMES

FOR A MAD second, I thought the mob would tear Benedict Cumberbatch to pieces. Bodies surged forward with the tidal force of a marathon start while the actor sat on a low stage with a paralytic look about him. The swarm reached Cumberbatch and . . . right, they were entertainment journalists, not godless cannibals. There is a difference, despite what everyone says. They carried digital recorders, not machetes.

I circled the edge of the chaos. I tend to go as bashful as a seventh-grade boy at his first dance in the presence of truly "mass" media, an unhelpful trait in a reporter. A formal press conference had just ended. Now my colleagues rushed to approach Cumberbatch's cheekbones of legend, his sculptured hair, his penetrating gaze — the attributes that helped make this thirty-eight-year-old actor, at that moment in early 2014, one of our leading cinematic stars and certainly, it seemed, the busiest. Cumberbatch had recently played major roles as the *Star Trek* villain Khan, Julian Assange, Tolkien's dragon Smaug, a slaveowner, and a dysfunctional Oklahoman. Not long before, he'd played both Frankenstein and the Monster on stage, on alternate nights. The press, however, did not much care about any of that just then. They cared about Sherlock Holmes.

I had flown to Los Angeles for the Television Critics of America media conference, a semiannual two-week luxury prison camp for TV stars, producers, and my fellow hacks. The Langham Hotel in Pasadena, a faux-historical cupcake of chandeliers and oil paintings, crawled with television writers and shell-shocked actors. The scene made me glad to be a dilettante. Some poor souls had been interned at the Langham for days and days, but I just skipped out on January in Portland to wander around 80-degree LA in shades and shirtsleeves and feel, I must say, pretty damned pleased with myself.

During the TCA gathering, every network frog-marches the creators of its forthcoming season through press conferences and interviews. This day belonged to the Public Broadcasting System — a schedule slot that, all due respect to Big Bird, may have lacked a certain glitz in prior years. Not this time. Outside, dozens of fans huddled in an improvised compound bounded by velvet ropes, holding signs that proclaimed themselves the CUMBER COLLECTIVE. The network's prime-time flagship, *Masterpiece*, was unveiling its latest round of imported British dramas, with the third season of *Sherlock* (a BBC and WGBH-Boston coproduction) twinned with *Downton Abbey* as the double centerpiece. *Sherlock* was hotly anticipated. Two years had passed since Cumberbatch's Holmes plummeted from the roof of St. Bartholomew's Hospital to his apparent death before the eyes of Martin Freeman's devoted Watson.

Spoiler alert (not really): Sherlock Holmes was not dead. But Mark Gatiss and Steven Moffat — the Holmes enthusiasts who devised *Sherlock*'s twenty-first-century update to the Baker Street scene — had gone Sir Arthur one better. "The Reichenbach Fall" gave Watson a brief, chaotic glimpse of (what seemed to be) Sherlock's corpse, shattered by his plunge from the roof of the same institution where the two characters first met, in both *Sherlock*'s 2010 premiere and *Beeton's Christmas Annual* in 1887. The spectacular death scene and subsequent two-year lag provoked a flood of Internet speculation: How did Sherlock do it? Why did he do it? *How* could he do that to poor John Watson? The worldwide fan freak-out over the cliffhanger chimed eerily with the aftermath of the *Strand*'s December 1893 issue. Time's arrow reversed its flight.

This was *Sherlock*: a stylish flip on Conan Doyle, delivered in addictive three-episode bursts sometimes separated by years, owing much of its popularity to the Internet, densely woven with Sherlockiana. (In this version, when John Watson's blog malfunctions, the visitor counter sticks at 1895, a tribute to Vincent Starrett's poem.) Still, Cumberbatch and Freeman — who combines military ferocity with Nigel Bruce–caliber comedic timing — give the enterprise its heart. In January 2014, the same month as the TCA dog and pony show, *Sherlock* played to a US audience of about four million viewers. In Britain, nearly nine million watched the season's finale, one-third of the nation's total television audience. A *Sherlock*-themed coffee shop opened in Shanghai in 2013.

Cumberbatch and Freeman had become the Rathbone and Bruce of our day — the latest embodiment of Holmes and Watson. In Pasadena, poor Benedict was experiencing one aspect of just what that meant.

Holmes and Watson have taken a long, strange hansom cab ride through modern times. Every decade reinvents them, and the variations can become a bit . . . elaborate. In 1959, thirteen years after Rathbone walked out on Baker Street, the legendary British horror studio Hammer Films made the first color Sherlockian film, a full-throttle-Gothic *Hound of the Baskervilles* ("Terror Stalks the Moors! Horror Fills the Night!") with Peter Cushing as a wigged-out Holmes. The creators managed to work in ritual sacrifice, a tarantula, and a collapsing mine shaft. That strangeness is as nothing, however, to *Sherlock Holmes in the 22nd Century,* a 1999 Scottish animated series in which Holmes — his corpse helpfully preserved in a honey-filled coffin in Scotland Yard's vaults — is reanimated in a "New London" featuring flying cars, gigantic *Blade Runner* video screens, and a crack detective named Beth Lestrade, with whom he battles a Moriarty (also alive, again) with an excellent werewolf pompadour.

Someone always wants another shot at Holmes. Thus we have the black-and-white comic book *Sherlock Ninja* (Sherlock is — wait for it — a ninja; Watson, a young woman named Watsu). And we have *221B*, a rather cute Canadian-made series of short films, accessible on the video-sharing website Vimeo, in which Sherlock is a pixie-coiffed twenty-something woman with a bemused, middle-aged male roommate. And we have uncountable thousands of stories published in recesses of the Internet which depict the Cumberbatchian Holmes and Freemanite Watson deeply and lustfully in love.

Meanwhile, global audiences are gobbling up a blockbuster feature-film series, with Robert Downey Jr.'s ultrabohemian Holmes and Jude

Law as studly Watson incarnate; the literally phenomenal *Sherlock;* and *Elementary,* American TV's twist on modern Holmes, with Jonny Lee Miller as a tattooed detective and Lucy Liu as a notably un–Nigel Bruce–like Watson. These successes have spurred yet more speculative forays down Baker Street, some of which will happen, others of which will ever remain show business rumor.

It's tempting to dwell on this boom time as the end point of Sherlock's saga. Someday, however, today's efforts will fade away — only to be replaced, if history is any guide, by new versions of Sherlock Holmes. (In the late 1980s, Jeremy Brett's portrayal of Holmes as a period-costumed neurotic with an advanced coke problem was judged as definitive as Cumberbatch's steely, tech-savvy clotheshorse savant is now.) Our current Sherlockian gold rush illuminates something more: how we seize on characters and ideas and transform them from private creations into mass-made mythologies that can suit any cultural moment. This happens to almost every big character now. How many times has Spider-Man been rebooted, or James Bond, or Captain Kirk? It has been happening to Sherlock Holmes and John Watson for almost 130 years. Their many incarnations reveal the craft and commercial impetus of mass-media creativity: the whole art of adaptation.

"To be perfectly honest, it was New Year's Eve and we were drinking," Brandon Perlow told me. We sat in one of Manhattan's generic pay-by-weight buffet lunch spots. "We were talking about what we could do, what hadn't been done, what was out there. And we started talking about Sherlock Holmes — a *modern* Sherlock Holmes. About how we would reinterpret Moriarty, and Irene Adler. It was one of those conversations you actually remember the next day."

Perlow, a cue-ball-headed Caucasian gent wearing, at that moment, a ratty New York Giants T-shirt, is the cofounder of New Paradigm Studios, an independent comics publisher. (He started the company after quitting the film business: "Good ideas sit for years, or just die. I wanted to tell stories, produce a lot of projects, get them out there, and see what works. You can do that in comics.") One night's boozy inspiration spawned *Watson and Holmes,* a pen-and-ink reimagining of Baker Street as a gritty present-day New York. Two things: the series focuses on John Watson (hence the title), and Holmes and Watson are black. "My cofounder and I could just feel this was the right idea," Perlow said. "We also knew we couldn't write it. We could come up with general story arcs, but we would miss the nuance and authenticity. Someone said, 'Karl Bollers — he could nail this.'"

Bollers soon joined us at the table, a lithe, bespectacled African-American man in a natty knit cap. A veteran comics writer — he had worked his way up from a Marvel internship, steered the *Sonic the Hedgehog* franchise for a while, and at one point scripted Emma Frost, a "mutant telepath" — Bollers saw what Perlow needed. "I was familiar with Sherlock Holmes, of course," he said. "I recognized that there are certain characteristics that make Sherlock Holmes, and you don't mess with them. When you work with African-American characters, you face knee-jerk expectations, and we also had to avoid those. I didn't want a Samuel L. Jackson Sherlock Holmes. I don't want Holmes running around calling people 'motherfucker.' I tried to create a cool, erudite, very learned guy who has stumbled upon this almost superhuman observational ability. He's not some blaxploitation dude who happens to be named Sherlock Holmes. He's *Sherlock Holmes.*"

At first I thought *Watson and Holmes* faced a lethal triad of adaptive challenges, risking the opprobrium of comic book fans, Sherlockians, and, well, black people in general. But by the time I sat down with Perlow and Bollers, their work had vindicated them. It was good stuff, with a burly Watson, just back from a paratroop tour in Afghanistan and employed at a Harlem hospital, and a laconic Holmes with dreadlocks, a fedora, and pickpocket ("stealth procurer") skills. Bollers had translated the Sherlockian milieu for streets Conan Doyle would not recognize. Of course, in comic books — a genre of multiverses and reboots and decades-old continuities — translation is often the writer's primary task.

"I did it many times at Marvel," Bollers said. "I'd work with characters that in some cases I'd been reading about since I was a kid. The main thing is, you've got to be humble. These characters are not your characters. You make them your own for a while, but others have done and will do the same. This is not your show. But you add what you can to express elements of the characters that are authentic, but have been underplayed or can be interpreted in a new way. You look around at what's already there, and you have to be very respectful, but still confident enough to use it.

"At first, for example, we weren't going to have Mycroft in our story. But I realized, no, Mycroft's important. Mrs. Hudson is important. The characters on the fringes of Doyle's world are part of what makes Holmes who he is. So I found a way to get 'Mike' in. I mean, he's Mycroft, but he prefers Mike."

"And our Holmes doesn't like being called Sherlock," Perlow interjected. "Not at all."

"No, it was probably a real sticking point for him, growing up in the 'hood," Bollers said. "The name drives him crazy. In fact, not to give too much away, but when we bring in our Moriarty, *he* gets to say the immortal line 'No shit, Sherlock.' I'm saving that for him."

The two of them went on to discuss black characters in comics and their flaws, a conversation which, I confess, flew some distance over my head. (It involved a lengthy dissection of a character called War Machine, apparently "the black Iron Man." I would have been on safer ground with Black Lightning, a late-'70s creation I remembered sporting the lonely Afro amid the masks and capes of my childhood.) "Writers get caught up in the blackness of it all," Bollers said. "They forget to create full characters. They forget that for an individual person, blackness might be a secondary or tertiary issue at a given moment. With Holmes, we have an opportunity to work with a character who is already well established — maybe the best established, right? — and make blackness a part of that, rather than the main subject."

Bollers was on his way to the first-ever Black Comics Festival with a bundle of *Watson and Holmes* in his satchel. I observed that this marked a new adventure indeed for two characters who started out as — I thought we could all agree — pretty damn white. Bollers laughed. "Well, for whatever reason, these days the names Holmes and Watson kind of *sound* black somehow," he said. "And — again, for whatever reason — African Americans really seem to dig Sherlock Holmes. We were at New York Comic Con, and when black folks would walk by our table, we'd be like, 'You like Sherlock Holmes?' And they'd by and large say yeah. And then we'd be like, 'What about a *black* Sherlock Holmes?' And they'd stop dead in their tracks."

Perlow and Bollers had found yet another seam of possibility in the Baker Street world. I asked how the serious devotees were taking it. "Oh, the Sherlockian groups?" Perlow said. "They've been great — absolutely open and supportive, and I really didn't think they would be."

"The more I get to know those folks," Bollers said, "it seems like they just want *more*. And, of course, we've got a lot more to work with, stuff we haven't even touched."

Perlow perked up. "Ooooh, that reminds me. I just had a great Baskervilles idea."

Bollers smiled. "No kidding? I did too. Super-modern. Super-gritty."

The Langham Hotel's bar was — fittingly, I guess — a pastiche-Victorian atrocity of black-stained wood complete with climatically inappropriate roaring gas fire. I considered the temps in the 80s and opted for the outside patio. As for the larger irony, it's possible that Steven Moffat and I were the only ones who appreciated it: at the real Langham, in London, young Arthur Conan Doyle dined with Oscar Wilde and began hatching *The Sign of the Four,* arguably the first Sherlock Holmes relaunch. Now the cocreator of *Sherlock* and I sat in the blazing Pasadena sun, a pair of genetic Celts ill suited to such climes. The fifty-two-year-old Scotsman and I were joined by his wife, Sue Vertue, *Sherlock*'s producer, who struck me as a steely and watchful presence. We talked *Sherlock* and Sherlock, and why this character lends itself to endless reinvention.

"I think it's simple, really," Moffat began. "It's the quality of the storytelling. Arthur Conan Doyle is as good as that. Those stories are works of genius — they'll never be regarded as literature because people are snobs. But of their kind, they have never been surpassed."

The story goes that Moffat's work on *Dr. Who,* another cult character he reinvigorated, required long train rides from London to Cardiff with Mark Gatiss, the English comedian and actor who collaborated with him on *Who.* Gatiss, Holmesian since boyhood, once constructed a Victorian chemical laboratory in his own home. ("They spark each other off," Vertue quietly noted.) The idea for a small vanity project took root. "Holmes has become layered over with nostalgia and Victoriana, with the post–*Brideshead Revisited* idealization of the past," Moffat said. "Our idea was re-create the impression you would have had if you'd just read Sherlock

Holmes in the *Strand* for the first time: he lives in your world, and you can meet him, and he's real. He's not your dad's hero. He's your hero."

In 2010, they recruited Cumberbatch — at the time, a talent rising from a solid stage career and a journeyman film résumé — and Freeman based on casting session chemistry. After a never-aired pilot, the BBC commissioned a miniature season of three ninety-minute episodes, setting the *Sherlock* template. "A Study in Pink" began with John Watson's return from Afghanistan, his London aimlessness, a random encounter with his old friend Stamford, who mentioned another chap seeking affordable rooms, one Sherlock Holmes. Off the two went to St. Barts Hospital. Moffat and Gatiss were on to something. Their material was sitting there, ready for them.

"It's curious, isn't it, that because we all fall into this fantasy that Sherlock Holmes was real, we forget that someone *invented* all this stuff," Moffat said. "There's so much stuff — stuff that people don't even know about Sherlock Holmes, brilliant pieces of dialogue hardly ever used on-screen. Holmes's observation that 'oscillation on the pavement' always indicates an affair of the heart — it's a beautiful thing. 'The curious incident of the dog in the night-time'— an amazing piece of writing, and it goes by in twenty seconds. Mark and I rely most on the original stories and their glorious little details."

Sherlock — which, as of 2015, consisted of ten episodes released over four years — contains the essence of such Conan Doylean details, remixing them with modern techno-thriller plotting and mesmeric film techniques. Electronic dialogue floats into the air from characters' mobile phones. Cumberbatch occasionally spins off into surrealistic interludes of flashback and fantasy that dramatize Holmes's interior thoughts. Good stuff all, but it merely dresses out a robust framework hewn from Conan Doyle by Gatiss and Moffat, and Cumberbatch and Freeman locked into the Baker Street relationship like a pair of perfectly meshed gears. The filmmaking and storytelling are quite clever. The actors made the show a hit.

Cumberbatch plays Holmes — Sherlock, since we're all on a twenty-first-century first-name basis now — as a well-marshaled sociopath, so dedicated to his extraordinary faculties (and his Belstaff coats) that he can scarcely bother to act like a human being. Freeman takes care of that, with a Watson (John!) who simultaneously worships Sherlock as a genius, loves him as a brother, and finds him the biggest idiot on earth. Freeman's weathered, lovable face is one of current drama's more sensitive instruments, flickering from annoyance to affection with the slightest adjustment of his rumpled squint. As Watson always must be, he is the show's heart.

Sherlock seems a real family affair. Its principals have been known to refer to the productions as a "hobby." Cumberbatch's parents play Sherlock's parents; Amanda Abbington, Freeman's real-life partner, plays John's wife, Mary. This cozy team makes new episodes whenever it gets around to it, and the two networks involved, the BBC and Public Broadcasting, seem content to let the friends proceed at their own pace. The show is thus an odd combination of cottage industry and global media sensation. It does not seem to obey the usual dictates of the entertainment economy, yet it has inspired tribute tea sets, Finnish flash mobs, and tweets and Tumblr posts in Alexandrine quantities. "You're speaking to a more informed conversation these days," Vertue observed. "And it's a worldwide conversation — you're instantly hearing from fans in China, in Scandinavia."

"It does feel like right now is the exact time to bring it back," Moffat said. "Our Watson can write a blog, and we have our own version of the *Strand Magazine* — that's an overlooked but important factor in the original stories, that everyone is aware that Watson is chronicling these tales in public. For many years, people didn't keep diaries. Now they do again. Sherlock Holmes always preferred to send a wire. Now we do that again, with texts. Two young men sharing a flat because they don't have enough money — you get that. We didn't even have to restage a war in Afghanistan. It's all right here."

The televisual Sherlock, not surprisingly, goes way back. Conan Doyle's stories themselves suggest TV episodes, with their recurring setting, guest-starring characters like Lestrade and Mrs. Hudson, and tightly packaged plots. The elevator pitch writes itself.

Even so, consistency has proven elusive. In 1937, Louis Hector, a veteran radio Holmes, starred in "The Three Garridebs," broadcast from Radio

City Music Hall as an experimental test of the new medium. In '49, Alan Napier—Alfred the Butler in the 1960s *Batman* series—loomed large in a mostly faithful one-off "Speckled Band," brought to you by Lucky Strike and a professorial narrator chain-smoking in a book-lined study. (Napier makes a solid Holmes, while the production—readily available on the Internet—is notable for a pipe of truly staggering size, a Watson whom Nigel Bruce could sue for plagiarism, and a half-decent mechanical snake.) John Longden's portrayal of the detective in a 1951 adaptation of "The Man with the Twisted Lip" features well-wrought intrigue down by the murky Thames, but the stately star is far too elderly and creaky; the pilot never became a series. (The BBC made its first foray with a six-episode series that same year, none of which survives.) Basil Rathbone himself gave it a shot, in a single 1953 production of an *Adrian* Conan Doyle story. Everyone seems quite relieved that it is lost to history.

The sterling early success came in 1954, when for one season producer Sheldon Reynolds created a jaunty Baker Street, shot in Paris. This series' thirty-nine gems of vintage American television stand as an underappreciated midcentury Sherlockian triumph, with an authentically unkempt 221B, a score of bloodcurdling violins, and plots—while mostly extracanonical—tailored to the Conan Doyle model. Reynolds reacted against the modernized Rathbone-Bruce series, using Paris to create a credible Victorian setting, and broke the oddly persistent tradition of casting wizened codgers as principals, instead opting for two younger actors. Ronald Howard plays Holmes with a laconic but amiable twinkle—a bright-eyed, ambitious man who happens to keep his tea next to his snake poison. H. Marion Crawford gives us a bumptious Watson for the ages, all thick-muscled physicality and popeyed outrage at Sherlock's eccentricity. In many episodes, Archie Duncan imposes his joyously boneheaded Inspector Lestrade as scene-stealing third wheel. These half-hour shows, made quickly over a single year, evoke Conan Doyle at his bubbliest: romantic, funny, thrilling, delivered with proper dash. As history proves, the formula remains elusive. The Reynolds productions, which must have glistened indeed in the feral wastes of early-'50s television, would be the only extended American Sherlock Holmes TV series for almost sixty years. Go ye forth and discover them.

In the late '60s, the BBC produced a haphazard run, for which it eventually dragooned Peter Cushing back into the role* he first assayed in the 1959 Hammer *Hound*. Even at the time, this series, popular though it was, was notorious for sloppy production, which maddened the actors involved but lends its episodes a certain whacky retrospective charm. It's like watching an exceptionally talented high school drama corps give it their all in faux-Victorian costumes and undead "living color," with Cushing the single long-suffering adult. (I do commend the full-scale adaptation of *A Study in Scarlet*, relatively neglected as that novel is. Plus, there's an amazing, long scene in which Cushing and his Watson, Nigel Stock, struggle desperately and visibly to remember their lines.) Then there was the time, in 1976, when a shaggy Roger Moore tried his luck in the made-for-TV *Sherlock Holmes in New York*, an affair cheerfully summarized in a recent British newspaper account as "a total disaster" and "the worst Sherlock Holmes movie of all time." In very recent memory, Rupert Everett investigated something called *Sherlock Holmes and the Case of the Silk Stocking*, looking wan, heavily made-up, and distinctly like he'd rather be somewhere — anywhere — else.

Many dare. Few succeed. In fact, in the Great Detective's Americo-British television odyssey between Sheldon Reynolds and *Sherlock*, one name, and one name alone, stands out among the half-baked, half-cocked, and half-amusing: Brett.

My brother and I would ensconce ourselves on the sofa once a week, awaiting the theatrical harpsichord and charming creep of animated Edward Gorey figures, depicted at one of the artist's lethal Edwardian garden parties. (As a well-shod assembly sipped tea, some poor guy slipped head-first into a nearby pond.) The title sequence for public television's *Mystery!* evoked morbid Anglophile gentility for an American viewership. I was on board.

---

* Douglas Wilmer was the original '60s BBC Holmes: a good, prickly one, if a little physically off-kilter — enormous chin, for example. Wilmer retains a cult following among Sherlockians; Moffat and Gatiss brought him in, at the age of ninety-two, for a cameo in an episode of *Sherlock*.

In 1982, the Manchester-based television network Granada con-cocted ambitious plans for Holmes, with John Hawkesworth, writer of *Upstairs, Downstairs,* leading the effort. The network aimed to make the most rigorously Victorian Holmes ever. No pseudo–Conan Doyle plots; no Rathbonian modernization; no screwball Peter Cushing costumes. Scripts would come straight out of the Canon. Sets would capture Victo-rian London in its squalor, smoke, and elegance, with Sherlockian streets thickly populated by period-costumed extras. At its production facility in Salford, Granada constructed a lavish miniature Marylebone, lit by gas lamps made by the Birmingham firm that still supplied Buckingham Pal-ace, and in a cavernous warehouse, craftsmen regenerated the 221B living quarters down to the mantelpiece jackknife.

Into this palatial confection dropped Jeremy Brett. Then entering his early fifties, the English actor had been one of British theater's beautiful young things, a protégé of Laurence Olivier and a well-traveled Shake-spearean. His screen résumé included a turn opposite Audrey Hepburn in *My Fair Lady,* but Brett had never broken through as a leading man. He invariably found himself in throwback costume, in supporting roles. (He'd played Watson on stage, opposite, of all people, Charlton Heston.) He did worry that Sherlock Holmes would typecast him forever, but the gig represented his last, best chance for top billing.

Brett tore into the role, filling a notebook with Sherlockian aphorisms, mannerisms, trivia, plot points. The Granada scripts hewed with unusual fidelity to Conan Doyle; the first season even began with "A Scandal in Bohemia," just as God and the *Strand* decreed. In a near-verbatim ren-dition of that story's opening scene, Brett's Holmes gleefully tortures a mustachioed King of Bohemia for nearly twenty minutes, with few cor-ners cut for the sake of an impatient '80s audience. Even so, Brett became notorious on set for battles over dialogue and plot. His commitment to canonical accuracy soon forced Granada to build an extra week into each episode's shooting schedule.

To watch Brett in his early pomp, though, is to concede that he earned a few prima donna moments. Hawkish and lean in funereal black suits, the actor blazes with mercurial expressions and bristling diction. He's the rare screen Sherlock to heed Conan Doyle's frequent descriptions of

Holmes's laziness: he subjects his Watsons* to diva-ish bohemian lassitude as well as amped-up intensity. When, in "The Speckled Band," he tells the afflicted Helen Stoner, "Pray—be precise as to details," he folds cold command into sympathetic charm, then kicks back as if for a catnap. At key investigative moments, Brett's eyes sizzle with Holmesian fervor: seeing, observing, dissecting. The actor stokes the secret fire of Sherlock's emotions, which on occasion ignite into wiry action. As Moriarty's henchmen pursue him in "The Final Problem," Brett uses a drainpipe for leverage to propel a kick into a baddie's face.

I discovered this phenom a couple of years after his debut in the role, and thought he was the greatest thing I'd ever seen. In retrospect, though, the Granada production can now seem a bit overegged. (Mid-Thatcherite versions of Victorian facial hair can be particularly unfortunate.) But Brett lent the character a nervy charisma that, for all the period trappings, echoed the '80s perfectly. (Perhaps not surprisingly, the series spent a lot of time on the cocaine needle.) Three decades later, Brett remains the definitive screen Holmes for a clique of "Brettheads." His performance—florid, glittering, at its best a masterpiece of control and bravado—deserves that following, all these years later.

I did not realize, as I sat enraptured in Montana, that Sherlock Holmes was crushing Jeremy Brett. From the beginning, he called the role his most demanding, Hamlet included. Granada's workdays began at 3 a.m. and ran late; Brett lost about fifteen pounds during the first season's production. And after that run ended with "The Final Problem," the British and American publics demanded more. (More Holmes! Always. Conan Doyle and Basil Rathbone could have warned him.) Over a decade, Brett played the role in forty-one distinct productions—possibly more than any other screen actor except Eille Norwood in the 1920s. He became more exhausted and fragile and obsessive. By some accounts, he began referring to Holmes as "You Know Who" and "Him." To a friend, he compared playing Holmes to inhabiting the dark side of the moon.

Brett suffered from bipolar disorder—champagne for everyone when

---

* Brett played opposite two very good Doctors: David Burke, who imbued the role with gumption and enthusiasm, and the fantastic, subtle Edward Hardwicke, who one could believe was the actual author of immortal adventure stories.

he was up, goodbye universe when down — and the lithium prescribed as treatment bloated his body. As the Granada productions wore on, he suffered harrowing breakdowns and institutionalizations. He arrived on set for the final production cycle in a wheelchair, sucking at an oxygen mask. In 1994's "The Cardboard Box," the last episode broadcast, Brett's performance devolves into a self-parodying haze, his physical bulk now a dead weight at the center of the production. He died of heart failure, age sixty-one, the following year, defined by Holmes, and maybe, in part, killed by Holmes.

Still, not even Brett could quite bear to leave Baker Street. At a memorial luncheon, a tape recording made not long before his death played. "If you see *him,* whisking around the corner . . . then wait, because that's all you'll see of him. Bless his darling heart, isn't he wonderful? Streets ahead of us, still."

Up against the assembled Television Critics of America, I asked a single question of Benedict Timothy Carlton Cumberbatch. My fellow journalists had already quizzed him on the Internet popularity of a clip in which he and Andrew Scott, *Sherlock*'s high-camp Moriarty, lean into each other as if for a kiss. (A: "We never actually made contact, you know.") And they'd asked him about the series' fanatical fandom. (A: "They're by and large lovely, and some of them normal. Seriously, I love that people sit around and watch this *en famille,* and debate it, perhaps across generations. 'Mmm, I preferred Brett.' 'No, he's cool — he's Khan.'")

I found Cumberbatch charmingly nervous (couldn't blame him) and self-deprecating (I'd struggle, with that visage) in this insane setting. I wondered how it all might wear. Just a few years before, he'd been an almost normal person himself. Now he was a major-magazine cover boy. He received weird letters from Julian Assange. Many, many fan-built websites made him their subject, or perhaps object; one notable example, Imagine Benedict Cumberbatch, renders celebrity obsession as Zen koans. ("Imagine Benedict Cumberbatch trying to dye his hair, but something goes terribly wrong and he gets really self-conscious about his discolored hair.") When his Sherlock goes into deductive hyperdrive, the viewer fears that Cumberbatch, reeling off hundreds of words at a frenzied clip, might combust from sheer synaptic heat. (In one scene, as

Sherlock delivers a rapid-fire biography of a "sentimental widow and her son, the unemployed fisherman," to whom he ascribes a terrier named Whisky and a financially fraught relationship, a sheen of sweat gathers along his windpipe.) And *Sherlock* is not merely verbal in its demands. Cumberbatch finished the previous season, after all, plummeting from a sizable building.

So when the chance presented itself, I asked him whether he feared the fates of Rathbone and Brett. In different ways, both took it too far. Could he avoid the curse of Sherlock Holmes?

Cumberbatch paused. "Well," he began, "I'm younger than either of them were when they started in the role. And both of them had a much bigger volume of the thing to deal with than I do. I simply have a better schedule with it — we make three of these films every once in a while, when we can all manage it. Jeremy had his own demons, of course, which became mentally linked to the role itself somehow. It makes his work almost painful to watch at times." He ruminated a moment more. "You could do a chart, I suppose. Where does the dementia set in? I guess I do that already. I mean, I love it. I find it invigorating. But I do remember a conversation with my mother"— Wanda Ventham, a longtime professional actress —"when she looked at me quietly and said, 'Be careful, darling. Be careful.'" Someone else wanted to know, did Sherlock always stay with him? A: "One way to stay sane in this job is to know when and where to shed the role and start being yourself. But I do miss him at the end of each run. I get oddly sentimental about him."

I wondered if Cumberbatch had, indeed, stumbled into the role at the most fortuitous possible moment. He's not under some feudal bond to a studio like MGM, which lent Rathbone to Universal as if he were an interesting paperback. Typecasting is now a far less stultifying force, in part, I think, because today's audiences are in on the game to a degree those of the past were not. In the 2010s, we know that cleverly stage-managed reinvention of classic characters is pop culture's lifeblood. We take pleasure in watching talented people manipulate well-worn plot points and hoary characters. Robert Downey Jr. can be Sherlock Holmes, and he can be Iron Man. Audiences enjoy seeing *Star Trek* pull a continuity sleight of hand to give Kirk and Spock an alternate timeline. They like seeing the new Batman, whoever it may be. Imagine — we're not DC Comics' trademark attorneys, so we can — if there could be two Batmen at once, or even three.

So it is that huge audiences can embrace Robert Downey and Cumberbatch and Jonny Lee Miller, all at the same time, as radically different Great Detectives. The Sherlock Holmeses of the moment reveal what the culture is after: just as Rathbone's suave Nazi hunter spoke to the 1940s, each present adaptation trades on the current entertainment-industrial complex. Guy Ritchie, Downey, and Jude Law* give us Holmes and Watson as action heroes in bombastic, billion-dollar productions full of fireballs, fight scenes, and cocky one-liners. Cumberbatch channels our obsession with communications technology and the cult of the hyperverbal innovative thinker — his Sherlock could throw down an incendiary TED Talk. *Elementary,* a suspiciously coincidental modernization conceived shortly after *Sherlock* came along, churns out formula police procedurals set in New York, highlighting that 90 percent of American TV programming seems to consist of formula police procedurals set in New York.

(I resisted *Elementary,* with its Lucy Liu stunt-casting and its amendment of Holmes's character to include a rather alarming heteronormative sex drive. I was not alone. The hardcore Sherlockian world greeted the series with a sneer; one American Sherlockian, Brad Keefauver, continues, as of this writing, to keep a weekly aesthetic deathwatch over *Elementary* on his blog: "Sad and lazy. It must be Thursday," and so forth. And it's certainly no Moffat-Gatiss-style labor of love. The script's Conan Doyle references are occasional and often pro forma. But, you know, I've come to like the thing, chiefly for Jonny Lee Miller's supple interpretation of Sherlock Holmes as a top-button-buttoned emotional disaster embroiled in twelve-step recovery. Miller and Liu inhabit an enviably shabby-chic New York brownstone in place of 221B, and the creators get up to some entertaining mischief: Mrs. Hudson as a towering transsexual, Sebastian Moran as a shaven-skulled Arsenal hooligan, et cetera. To discuss

---

* Law makes a terrific Watson, whatever one thinks of the movies. (I enjoy them in the same way I enjoy cotton candy, roller derby, and dubious pop music.) In an instance of Sherlockian kismet, the actor's pretty young face can be spotted in a minor role in one of Jeremy Brett's Granada productions, "Shoscombe Old Place."

what they do with Moriarty and Irene Adler would constitute the greatest spoiler of all time. It's not genius, but it's fun.)

Sherlock, in particular, belongs to an ascendant class of upscale television, driven less by the traditional networks and more by an engaged, social-media-wired audience. *Masterpiece*, the show's American presenter, happily takes three episodes every two years to reap a bumper crop of tweets and a demographic fillip. In an interview along the TCA sidelines, Rebecca Eaton, the *Masterpiece* franchise's veteran executive producer, told me that *Sherlock* helped the venerable costume-drama showcase reinvent itself after several shaky years. "The first season, in 2010, was the first sign that *Masterpiece* was coming back," she said. "It was the November before *Downton Abbey* premiered, and for the first time in a long time we had a breakout hit. The reviews were, without exception, positive." Eaton's main concern, in fact, is that so many *Sherlock* fans watch the show on the digital black market. But she also noted that *Masterpiece*'s underwriting slots — public TV's genteel substitute for commercials — were sold out for the foreseeable future, to luxury brands like Ralph Lauren and Viking River Cruises. Eat your heart out, Bromo Quinine.

"It feeds our brand and our audience — and the best thing is that it's a complete fluke," Eaton told me. "When they first pitched it to me, I didn't get it. And now *Sherlock* is a shooting star. It comes along every once in a while, but it helps define what *Masterpiece* has become for a new era. We can be historical, but we can be completely hip. *Sherlock* gives us that."

As the experiences of Brett and Rathbone show, the detective can give and he can take away. But that need not be the ironclad rule. Even for a great Sherlock Holmes, life can go on after Baker Street.

I rounded the corner toward the Langham's gentlemen's accommodation. A familiar figure swooped through the door in front of me. I recognized the actor Christopher Plummer, trim and stylish in a dark suit. And in a confused flash of connection to which I have grown accustomed while working on this book — every trail *must* lead back to 221B! — I recalled that he, too, played Sherlock Holmes. Twice!: in 1979's *Murder by Decree*, with tongue entombed in cheek, and two years earlier, in a wonderfully literal *Silver Blaze* for British and Canadian TV. He was as good as one would expect. And then he moved on. The trick may be to define the Great Detective, for the fleeting moment when he's yours, and then let him go. As Brett noted, he'll always be streets ahead of you anyway.

A very confused version of these thoughts tumbled through my brain, then Plummer and I both pulled up short in a sort of marbled antechamber. The Langham had attained such palatial splendor, its men's room featured branching corridors. Plummer peered around. Fortunately, I'd been there before. "To your right, sir," I said. And so it was that, for the first and, I expect, last time, I solved a mystery for Sherlock Holmes.

Not long ago, I had a peculiar week. The Week of the Multiplying Milvertons.

Charles Augustus Milverton may be Conan Doyle's juiciest one-off villain: an oleaginous blackmailer clad in astrakhan (what else?), as fussy-mannered as he is ruthless, enthroned in a vulgar suburban mansion stuffed with incriminating documents. Holmes and Watson wage memorable war against Milverton in a short story published in the *Strand* in 1904. While it's often possible to trace Conan Doyle's inspirations, his blackmailer offers a rare transparency. Charles Augustus *Howell*, an art dealer (among other things — supposedly he briefly supported himself by diving for sunken treasure, and once conspired to assassinate Napoleon III), died fourteen years before the story's publication, found outside a Chelsea pub with his throat slit and a coin stuffed in his mouth. He did have his detractors. Ford Madox Ford recalled him as a sometime forger of masterpieces. At one point, Howell inveigled Dante Gabriel Rossetti, for whom he served as "agent," into arranging the exhumation of his late wife, Elizabeth Siddal, to retrieve poems interred with her. Charles Augustus had his ways. After his death, thick files of eye-opening correspondence were found at his home.

Howell lives on through Milverton. One quiet evening not long ago, I sat down to "Korol Shantazha (King of Blackmail)," an episode of the 1979–84 Soviet television series made by Lenfilm and shot in Riga, Latvia. This run ranks alongside the best English-language Holmesian productions, largely thanks to Vasily Livanov's Holmes and Vitaly Solomin's Watson. Livanov — both an anti-Brett and anti-Cumberbatch — plays Sherlock as a contained, ironical, middle-aged man of frayed elegance, gentle yet iron in his determination. Solomin creates one of the most appealing Watsons: handsome as Hades, intrepid as he scouts out the infamous blackmailer's manse, and touchingly hurt when he discovers that Holmes has been doing the same thing, at the same time, in disguise. ("Well, I'll be damned, Holmes," he pouts after a few seconds of stunned-kitten silence. Then he stomps off to his room.)

Livanov and Solomin pursue Milverton — Boris Ryzhukin, playing with deliciously revolting élan — in a script largely faithful to Conan Doyle, though somehow Mycroft and Moriarty get mixed into the plot. The disguised Holmes seduces the blackmailer's housemaid to obtain access to his compound. The detective and doctor invade the place by night, intent on retrieving a client's indiscreet letters. Matters take an unexpected turn that we need not discuss, but most everyone (except Milverton, and maybe the maid) lives happily ever after, in both the *Strand* and the Soviet Union.

I was, meanwhile, also engaged in my survey of the Jeremy Brett era. A sizable stack of borrowed DVDs of Granada productions had long languished, mixed in with some Thomas the Tank Engine videos, and the time came to sort them out. At the top of the pile: *The Master Blackmailer,* a feature-length production based on Milverton. It's late-period, unfortunately, with a lumbering, padded plot — secret gay affairs, tearful slaps in the back garden, suicide at regimental HQ, all sorts of business — with Brett sinking into his waxen terminal mode. I gave up at about minute 60 of 100, and resorted to American network TV. Strange but true, I stumbled straight into *Elementary,* to find Jonny Lee Miller and Lucy Liu pursuing a certain Charles Augustus Milverton, a flyblown creep who extorts money from rape victims. (They were midepisode, but *Elementary* always provides a big chunk of expository dialogue about halfway through, recapping the plot so far.) This is about as close to the Canon as *Elementary* ever strays, so I enjoyed every last forensic action-buddy second.

A few days later, news emerged from the *Sherlock* camp, at the time strategically doling out updates on its forthcoming third series. The prime villain would be a certain Charles Augustus *Magnusson.* In the event, Danish actor Lars Mikkelson turned in a memorably evil performance as the blackmailer, reimagined as a modern newspaper mogul with a taste for freaky power dynamics. As my week of Milvertons concluded, I could sense Conan Doyle's arch-manipulator trying to drive *me* insane, through persistence of the most unkillable kind.

The Sherlockian saga's evolution thus gives us a laboratory-like view of history's real people — Charles Augustus Howell, in this case, or Joseph Bell, or supercriminal Adam Worth — transforming first into fiction, then folklore, then myth. (Give it a millennium: Charles Augustus Milverton could be a minor demon in some neo-pagan cult yet undreamt.) A few stray bursts of Arthur Conan Doyle's creative energy have become perpetual-motion storytelling fuel. Vladimir Nabokov, who absorbed his Sherlock in English and in Russian pulp-fiction knock-offs, weaves "The Empty House" and a *Hound of the Baskervilles* allusion into *Pale Fire.*[*] (Academic listserve archives examine Nabokov's Sherlockianisms, including at least one alarming discussion of a Humbert/Holmes nexus.) Umberto Eco — who, as the world's most (only?) famous semiotician, owes much to Holmes's ability to read the world's telltale clues — grafts Holmes and Watson onto medieval Europe to create *The Name of the Rose.* Eve Titus gives children *Basil of Baker Street,* a mouse detective in the basement of 221B, and Nicholas Meyer gives adults *The Seven-Per-Cent Solution,* in which Holmes ends up on Sigmund Freud's couch. As a kid — though it seems very odd to think of him as a kid — Jorge Luis Borges read the Holmes stories in a Spanish-language magazine called *Sun.* In "Death and the Compass," Borges creates perhaps the eeriest example of the parody/pastiche/tribute tradition, channeling the style and structure Conan Doyle uses to begin many of his stories into baroque terror: "Of the many problems which exercised the reckless discernment of Lönnrot, none was so strange — so rigorously strange, shall we say — as the periodic series of bloody events which culminated at the villa of Triste-le-Roy, amid the ceaseless aroma of the eucalypti."[†]

---

[*] If you wanted to be really fancy, you could propose *Pale Fire*'s radically unreliable narrator Kinbote and hyper-perceptive poet Shade as one of the more perverse Watson-Holmes pairings.

[†] Borges also translated "The Adventure of the Red-Headed League" — the only one of 'em he thought had a decent plot, per se — into Spanish for a 1943 crime-fiction anthology.

Holmes can turn into Loennrot, or Eco's William of (naturally) Basker-ville, or he can sell Chesterfield cigarettes in one decade and *Masterpiece Theatre* in another. Long after Conan Doyle died, Sherlock Holmes shows how one man's invention can become everyone's imaginative property. Exactly why this has happened may have something to do with Holmes and Watson and Conan Doyle, but more to do with the human mind and what it craves: heroes and villains, gods and monsters, stories and worlds. In the 1990s, Alan Moore, sometimes called the greatest living comic book writer (also a wizard—long story), collaborated with artist Kevin O'Neill on *The League of Extraordinary Gentlemen*, featuring Captain Nemo, *Dracula*'s Mina, Jekyll/Hyde, the Invisible Man, and others on violent adventures in an alternate Victoriana. Airships battle in the skies over Limehouse. Nemo's *Nautilus* surges out of the Thames. Moore makes Mycroft Holmes his plot's chief orchestrator, while Sherlock lingers in the distance. In an interview with a comics website, Moore offered this: "The planet of the imagination is as old as we are. It has been humanity's constant companion with all of its fictional locations, like Mount Olympus and the gods, and since we first came down from the trees . . . A lot of the dreams that shape us . . . are fictions."

"Holmes knows that where storytelling is concerned, I am a rampant liar."

This line comes from a tale titled "The Presbury Letters," by a writer named Katie Forsythe (most of the time). The story is structured around an exchange of letters between Watson and Holmes in 1916, with Watson writing from a medical station on the Western Front and Holmes chipping in from Whitehall, where he's working alongside Mycroft on intelligence matters. The piece weaves an inventive backstory for the composition of "The Adventure of the Creeping Man," that weird confection of monkey glands and the neo-simian professor. Outside plot and its sensitive, period-authentic prose, a couple of characteristics mark this story. First, it can be found on a website called Liquidfic, one of several online outlets for Katie Forsythe, known as one of the most skilled and prolific practitioners of fanfiction ("fic" for short). Her writing can be found elsewhere online, but here she archives some two dozen stories about Holmes and Watson, a few of novel length. (Under the name wordstrings, she also writes stories in which the Cumberbatchian Holmes experiences vivid synesthesia and other intense internal effects, some obviously due to diagnosable psychiatric disorders.)

Second, in "The Presbury Letters" and all of Forsythe's work, Holmes and Watson are deeply, torridly, physically in love.

This latter is true in much, if not most, of the staggeringly vast body of Sherlockian fanfiction, which lives almost entirely online in posts to LiveJournal and other blogging platforms or within specialized forums like Archive of Our Own, a nonprofit site founded in 2007 to give "fic" a dedicated home. If I convey the impression that fanfiction is, as a phenomenon, big, that's incorrect. Fanfiction — workably but imprecisely, stories written by amateurs about fictional (usually) characters and worlds they did not originally create — defies puny adjectives of scale. Archive of Our Own contains 1.08 million distinct works as of this writing, produced by more than 300,000 registered creators. That's just one site. Those stories involve characters from every television show, major author, movie, manga series, cartoon, video game, real-life rock band, and sports team you might imagine, and many you would not. (Archive of Our Own features at least three stories set within the *Baywatch* "universe," if there can be such a thing.)

Appropriation of others' characters is, of course, not new. In the eighteenth century, dissatisfied fans of Samuel Richardson's novel *Pamela* rewrote the ending, or gave the characters new adventures, often bawdy.* This book has tracked the Sherlockian explosion of unauthorized music-hall performances, newspaper parodies, pastiche stories, pulp-fiction rip-offs, quasi-scholarly essays, allusive literary novels, all of it, dating back to the 1890s. Fans of *Star Trek* generally lay claim to creating modern fic in mimeographed zines which, by the mid-'70s, broached the possibility that Kirk and Spock might be more than just Federation shipmates.

Current fic, however, does stand apart, most notably by means of production: a boundless scrum of stories churned out by and for members of intricately interconnected and ceaselessly chatty online communities. With no central publisher or editorial authority, the form emerges from

---

* This insight, and most others here put forth regarding fanfiction's history, structure, and function, rely on the excellent book *Fic: Why Fanfiction Is Taking Over the World* by Anne Jameson (SmartPop, 2013).

feedback, volunteer "beta readers," comments, team writing ("I have no idea how I'd continue this, but you're welcome to"), peer recommendations, and debate — lots of debate — in a shared, sometimes impenetrable argot. An outsider faces some heavy-duty nomenclature here, from the "citrus scale" (it somehow indicates the relative erotic intensity of a given story) to AU (alternative universe) to darkfic (it's dark). Also, because fic writers often* portray characters and situations that cross — or detonate into sharp-edged smithereens — gender roles, sexual identities, power dynamics, social categories, body images, species boundaries, et cetera, et cetera, one must gird for politics so layered with nuance they could keep an enterprising anthropologist busy for quite some time. The positive side of this tendency is a radically inclusive culture, which the writer Laurie Penny described in the *New Statesman* as welcoming "women, people of colour, queer kids, horny teenagers, people who are not professional writers, [and] people who actually care about continuity (sorry)."

Sheer volume, too, distinguishes the medium. Fic takes on everything, but to focus on Sherlock Holmes: the web holds more Holmes fic than anyone could consume. There's "canonfic," which uses the characters more or less as Conan Doyle created them — undoubtedly the minority. One finds fic set in the Basil Rathbone Sherlock Holmes universe, Robert Downey fic, *Elementary* fic, *Great Mouse Detective* fic, Vasily Livanov fic. (There doesn't seem to be any Eille Norwood fic. Someone should get on that.) But Cumberbatch and Freeman caused a great catalytic reaction in the fanfiction world, and *Sherlock* now dominates the Holmesian fic scene. As the writer Wendy C. Fries puts it in an essay, "The actors and writers give us so much to work with. Have you seen Benedict Cumberbatch?"

Which brings us to the sex. I'll stipulate that plenty of fic does not involve sex, but seriously: the sex. Characters in fic get it on in every way, in every combination, in satiation of every kink. There's just lots and lots of sex. As has been noted by many commentators, women predominate in the fic world; many of these women, whatever their personal real-life leanings, like to write about sex between men. (Not exclusively, of course.

---

* Any generalization about fanfiction and the communities that support it is false. I need to make some anyway.

We all know by now that *Fifty Shades of Grey* began life as grimly hetero *Twilight* fanfiction.) In Sherlockian fic, this generally means Holmes and Watson—though a huge body of work, known collectively as Mystrade, centers on Mycroft and Inspector Lestrade deep in lust, and, trust me, every character gets his or her share. Even Mrs. Hudson. (Writing a book about Sherlock Holmes is all fun and games before you have to read about Mrs. Hudson's underwear at 5:30 a.m.)

Sherlockian fic takes maximum advantage of that canonical quirk Katie Forsythe calls out: Conan Doyle's Watson is an unreliable narrator at best. His dates are wrong. His snakes drink milk. What if he was telling less than the truth about, you know, *that?* Sherlock never did have much time for women, did he, apart from Irene Adler? (A Google search for "sherlock/irene" spades up some very polymorphous fic indeed.) The notion of Holmes and Watson as lovers would kill poor Arthur Conan Doyle a second time, but fic writers are not the first to play with the idea. They *are* using the wildest possible arsenal of toys. I just read a story in which a Nigel Bruce Watson goes after a Basil Rathbone Holmes because Moriarty has laced Watson's jam with an aphrodisiac. For example.

I consider myself generally open-minded on such matters. I must say, however, that I have as much interest in Baker Street sex scenes as in hardcore porn starring my grandparents. Not my area. Then there is the sheer techno-exploded scale: Archive of Our Own, LiveJournal, Tumblr, and all of fic's interlocking forums and blog posts make me feel that I face something less cultural than *biological,* a mutating ecosystem that constantly throws unheard-of creatures in my path. (In one micro-genre, Watson is a dog.) In need of a guide, I called on Elinor Gray. A charming twenty-four-year-old from Baltimore, Gray writes fic—she's got a nice hand for Victorian canonfic, though even her stories involve erotic acts that might conceivably startle Oscar Wilde—under the screen name mistyzeo. She has also come to serve as a sort of ambassadress between fanfiction and the traditional Sherlockian world. Gray compiled a useful cross-section of representative fic stories for Sherlockian.net, a website central to the old-guard world of scion societies and scholarly journals. (Her list pointed me to Katie Forsythe.) I felt that she might speak my language. And I had questions.

For instance, why the distinction between fic and pastiche? "The basic working definition is that pastiche is done for money, and fanfiction is available for free," she told me. "Another level goes to tone and intent: the difference between writing in Watson's voice and re-creating Conan Doyle, and using the characters and world to explore completely different possibilities." Gray loved the sixty stories as a kid. As a young adult, she discovered surprising new ways to express that love. "You're playing in the sandbox," she explained. "It's all predicated on the question of 'what if?' When it comes to canonfic, you're often taking advantage of Conan Doyle's many gaps and lapses. What *were* Holmes and Watson doing in 1897? Traditional Sherlock Holmes scholars play that game one way. Fanfiction plays it another: *what if* they were off having a torrid affair?"

Which prompted me to ask, trying not to sound terminally unhip or beholden to any latent phobia, if all that . . . you know . . . was really necessary. "A lot of fic, maybe most of it, is written by women," Gray told me patiently. "I think a major motivation for writing it is being allowed to play: to play with sexuality, with relationship dynamics. And, basically, sex is fun to write about, and fun to read about.

"For me, it's the relationship. That's why I write my stories, and that's what I look for as a reader. Even if the mysteries are terrible — and in fic, there often isn't even a mystery — the stories are often great in other ways. The two of them, Holmes and Watson, make it all work."

I wondered how she'd been received among old-school Holmesians. "I needed a community," she said. "I was pleasantly surprised to find more young women than I expected, and that everyone has been lovely. At first, I was a bit shy about explaining what, exactly, I do that has to do with Sherlock Holmes. 'Hi, I write gay porn!' But eventually I realized, yes, this is what I contribute, and I'm great at it."

In a few short years, online fan creativity — spurred by Cumberbatch, yes, but also drawing on Conan Doyle and the history of Sherlock Holmes — has taken the old icon to weird and occasionally wonderful places. (There is, for example, an enormous genre of fan-made visual art depicting Sherlock Holmes as an anthropomorphic tuna: collectively, Tunalock. It would confuse Sidney Paget, but I find it hilarious and rejoice in its existence.) Sex aside, fic provides yet another glimpse of a new way of making culture as it takes on (takes over?) Sherlock Holmes. "It's large — vast — but paradoxically close-knit," Gray said. "There's a huge exchange of media. We're all sharing what we do all the time, with everyone. There's no power, and no control. There's only finding more of what you love."

Here I glimpsed a new Sherlockian subspecies, equally adept at and at home with enthusiasms old and new. And in fanfiction, I could recognize a potentially disruptive force in the evolution of Sherlock Holmes. Giant bodies of Sherlockian fanfiction are growing, like coral reefs of collective consciousness, in Chinese, Japanese, Russian. Who can say where they will lead, or what future Sherlocks they foretell? Their development does reveal a surprising truth: after 130 years, Sherlock Holmes is still under construction, still up for grabs — still, you might say, young.

One might think, given all this, that Holmes and Watson would long since be as free for the imaginative taking as Romeo and Juliet. (Fanfiction writers, you're welcome.) But at the very crest of the Great Detective's early-twenty-first-century popularity, a nasty fight broke out over a surprising question: who owns Sherlock Holmes?

After Arthur Conan Doyle died, the intellectual-property history of his most famous creation became convoluted. (Suffice to say that at one point, the Royal Bank of Scotland owned the copyright to the Canon. At another, the whole thing devolved unto the Royal National Institute of Blind People.) By the early 2010s, the works had entered the public domain, as a layman's naïve mind might expect — except for the final ten stories, published in the 1920s and collected in the *Casebook*. Per the infinite wisdom of Congress, these remain under copyright, in the United States only, until 31 December 2022, more than 160 years after Arthur Conan Doyle's birth, almost a century after he died.

That copyright now resides with the Arthur Conan Doyle Estate, Limited, a British company whose owners include descendants of Conan Doyle's brother Innes.* (None of Sir Arthur's five children had children of their own.) This company seeks to make the most of its asset's waning

---

* A fact symptomatic of the rights' complex history: there is a rival claimant, which calls itself the Sir Arthur Conan Doyle Literary Estate. Its involvement in the matters under discussion here, and arguably its very existence, could be characterized as marginal at best.

days, and for many years obtained licensing fees from, for example, major screen adaptations. In recent years, however, the estate encountered a formidable opponent, in the form of Leslie Klinger, the lawyer and Baker Street Irregular who created *The New Annotated Sherlock Holmes.* In 2011, Klinger and Laurie R. King, author of the novels featuring Mary Russell as Sherlock Holmes's latter-day wife, planned to edit an anthology of Sherlockian stories commissioned from authors not normally associated with the character.

"We had a contract with Random House," Klinger recalled in conversation with me. "One day Random House receives a letter from the Arthur Conan Doyle Estate saying, Cease and desist unless you pay us. We say, Don't, they're wrong. Random House says, Forget it — we're going to give them five thousand dollars to make them go away; it costs more than that for us to open a file with our lawyers. So Random pays the money — their money, not our money — and the book is published." (The book: *A Study in Sherlock: Stories Inspired by the Holmes Canon,* 2011.)

"Fast-forward to 2012, and we're doing another book with a different publisher, Pegasus. And the estate comes to them and says, You need a license or we'll block distribution — we'll work with Amazon and Barnes and Noble and others to make sure your book doesn't get sold. The publisher freaked out, and we decided to take action."

The resulting case, *Klinger v. Conan Doyle Estate Ltd.,* roiled the small Sherlockian world — the estate's longtime US representative, Jon Lellenberg, is also a prominent Baker Street Irregular — with a notable number of prominent Sherlockians coming out resoundingly in favor of Klinger. Many partisans used the Twitter hashtag #freesherlock to show support for the plaintiff's philosophical declaration that "Sherlock Holmes belongs to the world." Given that it touched on control of characters worth — as everyone suddenly remembered, in the wake of Downey, Cumberbatch, et al. — billions, the suit also garnered plenty of mainstream media coverage. "If this case was being tried in the press," Klinger noted when we discussed the matter early in its legal evolution, "we already won."

As the core of its case, the estate contended that its copyright to those final ten stories gives it a broader right to Holmes and Watson in the United States. "Is there any way to protect an author's final development of a complex literary character in copyrighted stories other than to protect the character in its entirety?" the estate asked in one filing. The estate cited various developments in those ten stories, many relating to subtleties that emerge in Holmes and Watson — the depth of their friendship and the ultimate mellowing of Sherlock's spiky personality, for example. Essentially, it argued that those developments now inform the entire conception of the characters, therefore placing them, as complete imaginary entities, under that still-running copyright. If you create a new work depicting the 1880s Holmes of *A Study in Scarlet,* the argument implies, you're inevitably drawing upon conceptual material from, say, "The Adventure of Shoscombe Old Place."

To me, it gets a little theological. Klinger had other words for it. "It's novel," he told me. "We never argued that the last ten stories are in the public domain. We say very clearly that they're not. However, you can't say that because those ten stories are under copyright, the whole character of Sherlock Holmes is under copyright. That doesn't wash." Klinger added that, in his view, not even the extant copyright gives the Conan Doyle Estate absolute say-so over every aspect of those ten stories. "Say you want to write a short story about Watson playing rugby for Blackheath," he said. "That's a minor fact, mentioned in one story. There is such a thing as fair use, and you're not damaging the commercial prospects of the original work. No one reads 'The Adventure of the Sussex Vampire' to find out where Watson played rugby."

A federal district court judge ruled just about entirely in Klinger's favor, which triggered a rush of headlines proclaiming that *Sherlock Holmes is public domain!,* but the estate appealed, with oral arguments before the Seventh Circuit Court of Appeals on 23 May 2014, the day after Arthur Conan Doyle's 155th birthday. Judge Richard Posner — well known for his own literary work and his vigorous way with an opinion — ruled in Klinger's favor. And after Klinger sought an injunction to force the estate to pay the case's legal fees, Posner went further. "There is no ground known to American law for extending copyright protection beyond the limits fixed by Congress," he wrote in an order. "The estate's appeal bordered on the quixotic." As he ordered the estate to pay about $30,000 of Klinger's fees, Posner did not restrain his views regarding the recent use of Conan Doyle's lingering copyright. "The . . . business strategy is plain: charge a modest license fee for which there is no legal basis, in the hope that the 'rational' writer or publisher . . . will pay it rather than incur a greater cost, in legal fees," Posner wrote. He then characterized this practice as "a form of extortion," lauded Klinger as "a private attorney general," and darkly warned that the estate was "playing with fire," antitrust-wise, in its threats to dissuade Amazon and other retailers from selling Klinger's works. At the conclusion of these strong remarks from the bench, Posner advised the estate to find another business model. The estate tried to fight on, but by November 2014 the Supreme Court had rejected its attempts to stay and appeal Posner's ruling.

Meanwhile, Klinger — to whom I spoke before oral arguments in the appeal — offered some wry insight into the dynamics of the entertainment industry the case had revealed to him. "One thing I found interesting at first," he said, "is that we got no support from Warner Bros. or CBS, and I thought we would. Then I realized that it makes perfect sense. They have characters that they'd like to tie up forever, too, and they don't want this ruling. They'd all like to have what Disney has, which is basically a permanent copyright on their most lucrative characters."

I wondered aloud, what would happen to Sherlock Holmes next?

"Nothing," Klinger said. "Nothing that hasn't happened so far. We will continue to see good and bad pastiche. We will continue to see movies and TV shows, good and bad. That's been happening for a long time, and sometimes the estate goes after people and demands a licensing fee, and sometimes they don't. Laurie King's entire series of novels about Mary Russell and the older, post–World War I Sherlock Holmes has never had a license. It's been very inconsistent. The only thing that will change is that the estate won't be able to selectively pursue people anymore."

Philosophically and conceptually, I look to Arthur Conan Doyle for guidance on the matter: he, of course, told William Gillette he could marry, murder, or do what he liked with Sherlock Holmes. At this late date, Holmes is more idea than image — more Hamlet than Mickey Mouse. He can be conjured with a deerstalker hat, or a few strains of improvisational violin music, or a snap of dialogue about a dog that did nothing in the nighttime, or something else. Eille Norwood and Benedict Cumberbatch are nothing alike, but both are Sherlock Holmes. Vitaly Solomin and Lucy Liu can both achieve Watsonhood. Sherlock Holmes resides in an increasingly universal Baker Street, where it may or may not be 1895. Under US copyright law, the last vestige of Arthur Conan Doyle's proprietary rights to his characters — created in 1886! — will vanish soon enough. (That those rights can be at issue in a twenty-first-century court case only testifies to the author's genius. But, really, it's been a good run.) The viability of a given Sherlock will depend solely on the skill of its makers and the public taste. I have a feeling that even then, as now, the Great Detective will be worth fighting for.

"Have you seen *The Private Life of Sherlock Holmes*?" Steven Moffat asked me. "What do you think of it? It's a bit of a touchstone film for Mark and me."

This remark ultimately cued my plunge into the quirky but potent Sherlockian wavelet of the late '60s and early '70s. The Broadway musical *Baker Street* and the goofy-gory film *A Study in Terror* (knives through necks, to start with) stoked things up in '65. For about a decade, big-league entertainment toyed with and examined Holmes in a very Age of Aquarius way, all sex-and-drugs psychology and subversive satire. Notable artifacts include Samuel Rosenberg's kooky literary analysis of the Canon and Conan Doyle's psyche, *Naked Is the Best Disguise;* the book and film versions of *The Seven-Per-Cent Solution* (here's some casting: Alan Arkin's Sigmund Freud and Robert Duvall's Watson trying to get Nicol Williamson's frenetic Holmes off coke); and Gene Wilder's *The Adventure of Sherlock Holmes's Smarter Brother,* featuring the jealous Sigi Holmes. (This is well worth tracking down for Marty Feldman's amazing face in the Watson-ish role, and Leo McKern as the only vaguely lovable Moriarty.) Taken together, these books and films show a generation going back and discovering that Sherlock Holmes and his milieu contain oddities and depths worth plumbing. *The Private Life of Sherlock Holmes* — made by the brilliant director Billy Wilder, with Robert Stephens as a moody, queenly Sherlock, Colin Blakely as an emphatic man's-man Watson, and all the retrospective ambiguities of the Great Relationship as its subject — was the most audacious project of this little era.

Or it would have been, but the studio made Wilder cut its three-plus hours in half. In the event, the film became a miserable experience for all concerned — Wilder and his cowriter didn't speak for years — and a box office failure. Its afterlife, however, proved more interesting. "It's not often someone as good as Billy Wilder gets a hold of Sherlock Holmes," Moffat continued. "There are things in that film that are better than Conan Doyle. We stole Wilder's version of Mycroft, for example." Christopher Lee's Mycroft haunts *Private Life*, commanding British secret services and trying to control Sherlock from the Diogenes Club. Mark Gatiss himself repeats the trick in *Sherlock* with a Mycroft repressed and peremptory, stationed at the center of the UK security apparatus. "The spikier relationship," Moffat observed. "The massive power. It's just better."

Indeed, *Sherlock* treats the entire history of Sherlock Holmes, inside and outside of Conan Doyle, as a toy box to plunder. While the Cumberbatchian Holmes is off playing dead, for instance, a group of obsessed conspiracy theorists meets to argue his fate, all wearing deerstalkers, calling themselves the Empty Hearse: a spot-on parody of any Baker Street Irregulars spin-off society. "Mark and I have a saying," Moffat said. "Everything is canonical. Everything to do with Sherlock Holmes is fair game. In our series, when Moriarty comes to Baker Street, he's walking up the stairs and hears Sherlock playing the violin. Then it stops. Then it starts again. Sherlock knows he's coming, but doesn't care. Well, that scene is lifted entirely from the Basil Rathbone film *Woman in Green*. We just restaged the whole thing. All the things that surround the character, we can make use of. Sherlock has to put on a deerstalker cap at some point. Watson has to have a mustache at some point. These things have to happen."

Sherlock thus avails itself of one of the culture's more formidable storytelling toolkits: a dash of Sidney Paget, a little Basil Rathbone, knowing nods to the show's own Twitter-happy fan base, everything. Even so, Moffat and Gatiss rely most on that old, dead Scottish author. "Everyone knows Irene Adler and the Hound and Moriarty," Moffat said. "But Charles Augustus Milverton — what a character! 'Black Peter,' when Holmes shows up back at Baker Street carrying a harpoon. So many times, when we're stuck, we just go back to the originals. Now, most of them are not fully adaptable as plots. This is a world in which a credible murder method is releasing a dog at night on Dartmoor. And those stories tend to carry about twenty minutes of action.

"In any case, plot is not what's great about them. What's great about them are character moments and incidents, bits of dialogue. 'The Speckled Band' is a treasure trove. When I read that when I was twelve, I thought, Well, that just about wraps it up for fiction as far as I'm concerned. Nothing can top this, ever. It took me years to realize that it's a story about a man who tries to murder someone by training a snake to go down a bell rope and lure it back with a whistle and a saucer of milk. It's absolutely ridiculous. But it doesn't matter, because the villain bends an iron poker — then Holmes bends it back. Those stories are really all about these great little bursts of inspiration, these vivid moments you remember long after you forget the plot."

Weaving those golden moments into viable twenty-first-century television does require some retrofitting. *Sherlock*'s Irene Adler, played by Lara Pulver, is a high-class dominatrix with a mobile phone loaded with sensitive secrets. Andrew Scott portrays Moriarty as a live-wire psychopath. "You have to do that sometimes," Moffat explained. "With Moriarty, the original, Conan Doyle — in another moment of genius — invents how to write every single supervillain from then on. If we did that all over again, our Moriarty would just sound like Goldfinger, with his suave exchange of villainies. He would seem like a rip-off. Today, what we're scared of is the madness of the suicide bomber. Irene Adler — there's so little to the story. And yet you want to know more. What kind of person has Sherlock Holmes talking like that? You have to give her more to do than Conan Doyle does.

"Sherlock, I think, retains the same fascination he's always exerted on people. He's called this cold, calculating machine, but the fact is, he's not. He's full of emotion and passion. You're always staring at the most formidable armor of all time, so it's a thrill when you see a chink in that — when you catch a glimpse of the real Sherlock Holmes. We haven't added that. That's in the stories: 'the flash of lightning on the darkened plain,' as Watson calls it. We love the idea of the supreme rationalist, the man who has perfected the only superpower we human beings have — this rather feeble animal with a big brain. We're flattered by the idea that the mighty brain can be perfected. He wasn't born with superdetective powers. He learned it."

Some critics find *Sherlock* too clever by half — its Sherlockian Easter eggs too abundant, the clubby feeling of a production conducted by a gang of friends a bit too evident. I raised these issues. Moffat laughed. "I read something that suggested that *Sherlock* had 'alienated the casual viewer,'" he said. "This, about the number-one hit in the United Kingdom. So either we are not alienating the casual viewer or, alternatively, there are sixteen million hardcore Sherlock Holmes fans in Britain. I can live with either.

"Look, with Sherlock Holmes you're dealing with the biggest hit in fiction. So if you get it wrong, that's your problem. If you do it really well, and properly — you're not just borrowing the name — you're going to have an audience. And in our case, by updating the stories, we removed the distance between the audience and the character. Doyle never intended distance, at least at the beginning. So if you do that, you have a chance of re-creating the fuss that was made the first time. And I think we've come close. It's a big hit in Russia — *again*. When we killed Sherlock Holmes, there was a huge outcry — *again*. Sherlock Holmes is sexy — *again*. Part of that, of course, is down to your Sherlock Holmes. For as many actors who take on that role, you realize how few cut through. In the modern era, it's Rathbone, Brett, and — I think, now — Cumberbatch."

I complimented the German girl, who waited outside the Langham with her fellow self-proclaimed members of the Cumber Collective, on her deerstalker. "Yes," she said, "it is authentic, not costume. I also have a Sherlock coat. So, dedication."

Quite right.

I was, at that moment, one of three males in the crowded containment area the hotel had established for fans, who'd waited patiently all day, contenting themselves with making hand-lettered signs and staring into mobile phones at the hashtag #cumberbatchday. "You'll get sucked into a vortex if you hang out with us," one young woman had merrily warned me when I showed up. (Inside, I heard Nigel Bruce's voice speaking as my own: "Hmmph. Vortices. I could tell her a thing or two.") At last, late in the afternoon, Benedict Cumberbatch emerged. He walked down one side of the velvet rope. The Cumber Collective burbled on the other, with things to sign and handshakes and hugs to request. "Lovely crowd," Cumberbatch's British PR handler observed, hopefully, soothingly, coaxingly, as one might address a skittish colt. "Intelligent crowd. Everyone so very polite."

And it was true. Cumberbatch gave the fans his time and attention, and they gave him just enough distance to stay human — or, as the case may be, superhuman. Seeing someone like Cumberbatch in a group of civilians is like finding a baby black panther at your local humane society. The trained purr of his conversational voice cut through all the clamor and set my breastbone vibrating at five yards. He radiated a certain essence of self-assurance and sharpness, style and acuity, intelligence and spirited fun. The people around him looked at him with the wary affection with which a slightly star-struck companion might regard his scintillating, maddening, emotionally elusive best friend. The man was not like us, but he made exciting company. And that only followed: he — like so many before him and untold others yet to come — is Sherlock Holmes.

CASEBOOK

AFTER A WINDING drive through Portland's lush and confusing suburbs, I pulled up before a nondescript '70s-modern house. I knocked on the door, and Jerry Margolin let me into a fantasy clubhouse of Sherlockian treasures and oddities.

Margolin was initiated into Holmes by his brother, who gave him the Doubleday *Complete* when he was ten years old. (Art in the blood: that brother became a renowned mystery writer.) He received the coveted summons to the Baker Street Irregulars in 1977. But his distinction in the Sherlockian world, he said, owed to a quality innate. "You can't be made a collector," he told me. "You're born a collector."

Margolin is known as one of the great amassers of original Sherlockian artwork, and his house induced a disorienting giddiness in me. Every surface bore the image of the Great Detective in some form or another — cartoons, portraits, posters, paintings, doodles, deerstalkers, and pipes everywhere, all presided over by a cat named Paget (successor, I learned, to Sumatra). Margolin had purchased, or, in many cases, solicited or commissioned, works on Sherlockian themes by a roster of art titans, a collection built on relentlessness ("I'm always on eBay") and chutzpah. "I'm never afraid to call anyone up and ask," he said. "Sometimes they say yes, sometimes they say no. Charles Addams turned me down. Al Hirschfeld, I talked to for half an hour. He was ninety-six but said he'd love to do it. Maurice Sendak always said he would, but never did. Leroy Neiman was all 'How'd you get this number?' Chagall, I just called information in Paris."

The result is one of the great real-world Sherlockian rabbit holes. You could spend a minor eternity in the Margolin Museum, because everywhere you look there's something curious or wonderful, Sherlock Holmes in so many guises as to produce a pop-cultural hall of mirrors. Alfred E. Neuman of *Mad* magazine in a deerstalker. Spider-Man in a deerstalker (drawn by a cocreator of the character). Jimmy Stewart's sketch of Harvey the Rabbit in a Holmesian hat. Sherlock Holmes interpreted by Ralph Steadman: "It took me thirty years to track Steadman down," Margolin said, "and I finally found him through a guy in Kentucky, I think."

I was particularly beguiled by a long, tall pen-and-ink drawing of Pete Townshend, the legendary guitarist, in full Sherlock regalia, holding a shattered violin. My host explained that the piece's creator was John Entwistle, bass player for the Who. Margolin displayed fantastically lurid Brazilian comic book covers: he had Sherlocko the Monk from 1912, he had both Batman and the Joker as Sherlock Holmes, he had Dr. Seuss's version of the Baker Street icon. (This artistic profusion, I might note, was what remained *after* Margolin liquidated his ten-thousand-volume Sherlock Holmes library. "I had eighty-eight cartons to ship, and it took me two weeks to pack it all," he recalled. "It didn't hit me until the truck pulled away.") He kept the real trophies upstairs, including an original Charles Altamont Doyle — a man asleep in a chair surrounded by fairies — and a letter from Frederic Dorr Steele to Vincent Starrett. Basil Rathbone, no doubt in one of his weaker moments, had doodled a Sherlockian drawing, which Margolin now owned.

The greatest thing, of course, was the original Paget: an illustration from "The Adventure of the Resident Patient," created for the *Strand* in 1893. "I followed that drawing for twenty-two years," Margolin said. I barely heard him. Out from under protective glass, Sidney Paget's ink wash glowed like the Black Pearl of the Borgias, with an angularity and precision to its lines and a textured density to its gradations of gray. As I looked into the drawing's smoky depths, it happened all over again: I slipped for a moment into that realm of melancholy glamour in which one investigator's mind holds sway over a panorama of gaslight and fog. I was in Jerry Margolin's treasure-decked house; I was in the world of Sherlock Holmes — and the intersection point, the imaginative craft of a young artist working to manifest a young writer's vision, sat on the table before me, drawing me deeper.

One afternoon, I trudged down Gower Street, which seemed the longest and most pub-deprived street in London. Georgian houses stood in well-tailored rows opposite the domain of University College London and University College Hospital, institutions a young John Watson would have known in his student days — had he actually existed, of course. Fictional John Watson knows this quarter today, as a matter of fact, via his incarnation as Martin Freeman in *Sherlock*, which uses Gower Street as its Baker Street. Yes, it gets a bit confusing.

At 187 North Gower Street, I found a blue historical plaque — the Italian patriot Giuseppe Mazzini once lived there — and a café named Speedy's. I had just missed closing time, which I regretted because Speedy's has become a latter-day Sherlockian pilgrimage site, a displaced fragment of the Baker Street scene, thanks to the notional residence of a certain handsome detective and his devoted chronicler in the flat upstairs. (In reality — whatever that is — *Sherlock* shoots its moody interiors in Cardiff. But there's enough Baker Street to go around these days.) I had to stand on the pavement, trying to conjure that ineffable Sherlockian vibe.

Then I spied a Chinese woman, maybe twenty, across the street, snapping pictures of that well-remembered (or, at least, frequently imagined) domicile. I crossed to say hello. I learned she was from Hong Kong, but not much else. We did not share a language. Or much of one, at any rate.

"Do you love Sherlock?" she asked. "I love Sherlock."

"Sherlock Holmes saved me from a dangerous and illogical world."

Joe Riggs, a professional "mentalist" and "psychological entertainer," was explaining how he came to identify with the Great Detective so thoroughly that he is known at times as "the Real Sherlock Holmes." Riggs has developed a traveling stage show that revolves around observational and deductive feats that startle his audiences — he adapts the old Method of Joseph Bell into an act. "On stage, sometimes I just figure out a little about a person, and sometimes I scare myself," the Florida-based performer told me. "I've told people where they last went on vacation. I've described their personality traits and watched their jaws just drop. And I do it entirely by using what I've learned from Arthur Conan Doyle and Sherlock Holmes. The theatrics of what I do relies on Holmes — I constantly recite quotes from the stories on stage, and I basically copy his whole style of surprising Watson with a sudden deduction. I'm trying to get as close to Sherlock Holmes as possible, in fact, except I don't study crime. I study the reading of people. I'm one hundred percent focused on discovering information about people I'm not supposed to know."

Even in the circles I traveled in researching this book, Riggs had perhaps the most intense relationship with Sherlock Holmes. (He also has a telephone number featuring the talismanic digits 1895, for which I salute him.) He credited the detective with rescuing his sanity. "I was raised by professional psychics," he said. "Hustlers. Charlatans. The best of the best. I was taught from an early age how to read people and pull off elaborate linguistic scams. We went to a metaphysical church, but really it was a huge moneymaking operation. Today, I expose fraudulent psychic mediums — it's part of what I do. I reveal the tricks used to prey on people.

"My mom was trying to instill one set of values in me, but as a kid I got obsessed with Encyclopedia Brown," he continued. (Children's writer Donald J. Sobol launched this most excellent boy detective in 1963, and a very good time can still be had with his adventures — clue-laden narratives that end in mysteries, with the solutions in the back of the book.) "I loved Encyclopedia Brown. And when I learned he was based on Sherlock Holmes, I had to check out Sherlock Holmes. As a kid, when you're into Superman, you try to jump off the roof, right? As a kid who identified with Sherlock Holmes, I applied his methods of logic to the beliefs I was slammed with by my elders. Holmes put no stock in any of that. I still study nonverbal behavior, just as I was raised to do, but now I present my deductions as the product of observation, not psychic powers, as my family did.

"It's awkward at holidays."

I asked Riggs to give me an example — a trick of his trade that illustrated his application of the Holmesian dictum that in observation, nothing can be so important as trifles. "Even experts in nonverbal communication overrate the importance of facial expressions," he replied. "Actually, the face is something a person can consciously control. It's one of our more dishonest features. I look at someone's feet — the most honest part of the body. You can modulate your facial expressions, but it's much harder to suppress the fight-or-flight response. If you're trying to pick someone up at a bar and you're not sure if they're interested, look at their feet. Are they pointed at you or at the nearest exit?

"A lot of my show has to do with distracting the audience and people I'm making deductions about. I get a person to tell me about their afternoon, so I have time to look at their shoelaces. How old are those shoelaces? What kind of shoes did they choose to wear to this event? In that situation, I have the advantage, and it's all because of Sherlock Holmes. The problem, of course, is that once you learn to see things his way, you can't really shut it off. I look at the world through a very strange lens these days. If only the girl in the Walmart aisle knew what I know about her, right?"

The professional mentalist; the Chinese *Sherlock* tourist in Gower Street; the relentless collector in the Portland suburbs — I don't have much in common with any of them, really, but we are united by the Great Detective. I embarked on this book, in part, to figure out how that bond came to be, and what it means.

I began, as the patient reader may recall, with a few questions. Why has Sherlock Holmes not only survived 130 years of vigorous pop-cultural life, but thrived? How did his global rise and endless mutation into new (but always recognizable) forms come to pass? And — implicit in those points of inquiry — what is Sherlock Holmes anyway, and why does he continue to matter?

Sit with me by the coal fire and we will discuss my conclusions, as the equinoctial gales sob like a child in the chimney. The gasogene and tantalus are over there, fully loaded. Leave the needle in the morocco case, please. It's not that kind of party.

I think Sherlock Holmes's enduring appeal, like a few other conceptual constructs we won't get into here, rests upon a metaphorical three-legged stool.

First (here's a brilliant deduction for you), there's Sherlock Holmes himself. He is, we can safely conclude, quite a guy. We'll never really get to know him, as he retreats into his psychic and residential Baker Street lair, surrounded by his horrifying books and deadly chemicals, snug as a lobster in its carapace. As some real-life humans know all too well, such behavior can provoke abiding fascination. Sherlock Holmes, gray-eyed and lean, masters the science of seduction.

He also embodies the spirit of an age, an age still very much with us even as many of its essentials have vanished. The historian A. N. Wilson once called Holmes "by far the greatest Victorian of the later part of the Queen's reign," and to me this assertion implies no disrespect to those great Victorians who were, technically speaking, real. In his deductive method, adapted by Conan Doyle (actual great Victorian) from Joseph Bell (actual great Victorian), Holmes distills and symbolizes the best of the period's commitment to rationality and progressive thought. This ethic has its roots in earlier times and the rise of the scientific method, of "natural philosophy" and empiricism. Wordsworth supplies a pre-Holmesian manifesto:

> . . . with an eye made quiet by the power
> Of harmony, and the deep power of joy,
> We see into the life of things.

As Sherlock Holmes works his cases, he channels Darwin in the Galápagos, Edison in his lab. He brings the Victorian impulse to explore and discover to the proximate frontiers of his city and its information — its wilderness of data, constantly expanding, which the Great Detective tames in his indices of newspaper cuttings, his "exact knowledge" of London's streets, and his monographs on the ways modern life expresses itself in the physical world. Sherlock's power to turn knowledge into both a tool and a vehicle for adventure are two of the characteristics that allow him to transcend his time. He can work in any Information Age, even ours.

Yet he's no mere calculating machine. He hides a crucial secret treaty in the breakfast dish, just to be cheeky. He pops in and out of hidden lairs in ridiculous disguises. He plays late-night, one-man violin jam sessions, does a bit of amateur boxing on the side, studies bees, stuffs his cigars into the coal scuttle, kicks back in the Turkish bath. Behold, a man who lives on his own terms. And even though full adoption of a Sherlockian lifestyle would probably kill a person — and would certainly lead to evictions, rehab, various forms of protective custody, and a terrifying tobacconist's bill — reading about it can provide a temporary liberation. If you're a nineteenth-century clerk or homemaker, a Soviet soldier on the Eastern Front, a retired 1940s corporate executive looking for something to do, a twenty-first-century Portland journalist hunting a good story, a young woman with a Tumblr page and nothing to put on it yet — anyone, really — Sherlock Holmes offers a bracing glimpse of a wicked-fun way of life. His inimitable style can encompass pithy quotations from Goethe and sensational outerwear from Belstaff. It's not real, but still.

Second: the Great Relationship. Without John H. Watson, Sherlock Holmes does not work. Full stop. (We know this, because it has been tried.) Conan Doyle's smartest move of all was taking the nameless and personality-deficient sidekick from Edgar Allan Poe's 1840s mystery stories and imbuing him with life — a somewhat tortured life at that, full of loss and hardship, all borne with rock-ribbed dignity. That existence finds its purpose in the meteoric career of the Great Detective, and in the process Watson makes that career possible. In the Sherlockian saga's most elaborate irony, for all the talk of Holmes's all-seeing observational powers, Watson is the one who does the observing as our narrator. The doctor notices and explains and translates everything into drama, with his fine eye for color, his sensitive appreciation of the thousand gradients of Sherlock's mood, his skill at making the weather sound interesting, his ability to capture a walk-on character in a few bright sentences of reportage. Who's the real Great Detective? Sherlock Holmes may be the phenomenon we admire, but John Watson is the human we can love. And as he wrote sixty stories about those two, a labor that touched five decades and often progressed under protest, Arthur Conan Doyle created one of literature's finest portraits of friendship.

But even brotherly love can get boring if there's nothing to do but sit around Baker Street eating Mrs. Hudson's curry. The third essential ingredient in the Holmesian mythos lies in the wider world the author portrays, and in how he portrays it. Conan Doyle creates a folkloric cycle set in the sprightly formative years of modern popular culture: spy stories and Westerns, sporting adventures and horror novels, urban noir and Imperial Gothic, even a heartwarming Christmas number. No wonder people keep going back and "borrowing" this and that — the Sherlock Holmes Canon is a *Whole Earth Catalog* of storytelling strategies. The adventures zip and fizz at such pace and with such style, one hardly notices their complete improbability. (I know it seems sort of square and conventional to consider authorial intent these days, but something I keep reminding myself: Arthur Conan Doyle did not regard his Sherlock Holmes stories as realist narratives. He saw them as fairy tales.) You're deep in a Thames-side opium den, or you're on the train to a rural murder scene, or you're scampering across London in search of some lunatic who's smashing busts of Napoleon all across town. You're too busy to check Watson's dates. The Sherlock Holmes stories realize a literary ideal of all action, all the time — the ultimate antidote to boredom and, to give them their artistic due, a paean to life's dynamism.

They also teem with small wonders and exquisite fascinations, which is why certain people (ahem) keep going back, tumbling repeatedly into their richly imagined gaslit world. Sonia Fetherston, a Baker Street Irregular who lives down the road from me in Oregon, summed up this quality when we exchanged notes about the Great Detective. "There's a marvelous line in *The Valley of Fear*," she wrote: "'The interplay of ideas and the oblique uses of knowledge are often of extraordinary interest.' And so a Sherlockian is the one person at the cocktail party able to speak knowledgeably about submarines, bootlaces, beekeeping, the motets of Lassus, vitriolic acid, and the fifth proposition of Euclid — and tie them all together."

As to the matter of *how* Sherlock Holmes keeps living this extraordinary immortal life, we could get metaphysical. But a nine-volume collection of short stories and compact novels is not, in and of itself, sentient. (Right?) Sherlock needs our help. Real people — actors, artists, novelists, radio scenarists, filmmakers, comic book illustrators, fanfiction writers — have propagated and revived (and re-revived) the character, decade after decade. Why? Of course, the stories do have their archetypal appeal: the original superhero in Holmes, the original supervillain in Moriarty, a battle to control London (and, by implication, the world) between them. But I think the saga's real advantage goes a bit deeper. It is, if you'll bear with me, structural.

Conan Doyle wrote *A Study in Scarlet* as a one-off. Then, when an American editor took him out for a fancy dinner and asked for a short novel on the quick, he wrote *The Sign of the Four*, which connects to the earlier narrative by a pretty frail thread of continuity. Then he had a thought. Really, he exhumed another Poe insight: you can send a detective on one adventure after another; each can function as a self-contained unit (problem → investigation → wine and sandwiches → solution). With the *Strand* and the time-crunched urban reader (some things never change) in mind, Conan Doyle wrote the rest of the stories as semidetached episodes. With minor exceptions — notably "The Final Problem" and "The Adventure of the Empty House" — you can read them in pretty much any order (although don't start with "The Mazarin Stone"). And then Conan Doyle has Watson making all those references to *other* episodes, the ones he can't (or just won't, the flirt) reveal. The Giant Rat of Sumatra. The Remarkable Worm Unknown to Science. The Dundas Separation Case (a personal favorite). The Colossal Scheme of Baron Maupertius. The Paradol Chamber. The Politician, the Lighthouse, and the Trained Cormorant (?!). Our beloved but unreliable narrator constantly provokes us with these feints.

Conan Doyle didn't mean to, but he salted his Sherlockian work with storytelling prompts. Watson repeatedly whispers "Go" into the imaginative reader's ear. And so, from almost the very beginning, other people have felt compelled to make up their own Sherlock Holmes stories. (And it is a compulsion. Just about everyone who develops any affection for the character does it. The newspaper hacks of 1892 did it. Warner Bros. does it. My first-grader does it.) First, people created their own Sherlocks on music-hall stages, in parody magazines, in newspaper columns. Then they wrote full plays about Sherlock Holmes. Conan Doyle saw the potential, and he invited first William Gillette, then other cocreators, to step in and remodel his world for media old and new. He had created the basic Sherlockian scheme, but anyone could work within that scheme. The show even proved transportable in time — Basil Rathbone and Nigel Bruce could simultaneously play Holmes and Watson as Victorians somehow shuttled to the 1940s in Roy William Neill's films and as plain-Victorian characters in the radio dramas scripted by Edith Meiser. No one saw any contradiction. Get a few things right, and you can get everything else wrong: Jonny Lee Miller's *Elementary* character lives in twenty-first-century New York with a female partner and no deerstalker in sight, but somehow he's still Sherlock Holmes. Benedict Cumberbatch and the hive-like collaborators of fanfiction both take advantage of the same truth about Holmes: you can marry or murder or do what you like with him. (Well, not murder — Conan Doyle tried that. The move proved financially ill advised.)

It works only because Conan Doyle did it all first, collaging the disguised 1914 spy of "His Last Bow" with the eccentric freelance medical student of *A Study in Scarlet,* set in 1881. Because Conan Doyle's Holmes and Watson have already done just about everything we can imagine (or so Watson constantly implies), we are free to make them do anything. Thus we have this curious construct: Sherlock Holmes, work of many hands, yet still the invention of one person; constantly mutating, yet always staying exactly the same.

And this brings me back to the question I found most puzzling at the outset of my adventure. *What* is Sherlock Holmes?

He is not a real person. (I know, I know, *I know.*) But he and Watson have become real personalities, ones that exist in an intriguing distributed form: lacking mortal bodies, they live via millions, maybe billions, of minds. The traditionalist Sherlockian discussing "The Boscombe Valley Mystery" over brandy and the anonymous woman in Harbin or Chongqing writing sexually explicit Benedict Cumberbatch fanfiction may harbor radically different notions of what these characters are all about; likewise the Hollywood executive devising a blockbuster franchise and the twelve-year-old kid in Montana obsessing over antique fiction. Yet we all make our fragmentary contributions to the modern-day Baker Street scene, which has become a great borderless and ongoing collaborative project. Arthur Conan Doyle hasn't been around for many decades. It's up to us to keep the Great Detective going. In an economic regime in which ideas are increasingly branded and restricted and "proprietary," here is a form of intellectual property we can all believe in. What is Sherlock Holmes? At this point, he is what democracy looks like.

It all must be a clue.

Why do we keep coming back to 221B? I observe that different aspects of the Sherlockian world seem more salient in our world at different times. In the trenches of the Western Front, Sherlock could serve as both a symbol of home and a satirical device for highlighting just how absurd the situation had become. At the end of Prohibition, the original Baker Street Irregulars used Sherlock Holmes as an excuse for raucous cocktail parties. Rathbone and Bruce made Holmes and Watson symbols of Allied pluck. Just after World War II, with Europe and Asia in ruins and the atom freshly split, writers for the *Baker Street Journal* looked to Baker Street as a lost Eden of civilized behavior and gentler interior lighting. In the '60s and '70s, people used Sherlock as a psychosexual case study with subversive comedic potential.

Today, the fashionable thing is to see Sherlock Holmes and John Watson as our peers — modern figures, at home in our time. I think I know why. As one reads Conan Doyle (or, for that matter, watches Basil Rathbone), it's possible to deduce a certain ethic, a set of Sherlockian values implicit in how Holmes and Watson handle their adventures. Comradeship, bravery, loyalty — of course, of course, the Baker Street duo embodies all of these qualities. But those traits serve a particular system of principles, too, which meets a contemporary demand.

First and foremost, Sherlock Holmes practices rigorous commitment to the facts. *Data, data, data* — concrete, observable, discoverable reality provides the raw material from which the Great Detective carves his career. He refuses to theorize without data, because — as Holmes himself puts it in "A Scandal in Bohemia" — "insensibly one begins to twist facts to suit theories, rather than theories to suit facts." Sherlock's mind remains open to every possibility. As he observes the scene of the crime and — most important, in Conan Doyle's talky universe — speaks to the players of the drama, he eliminates the impossible. Whatever remains, however improbable, must be the truth, as proclaimed in *The Sign of the Four*. This empirical discipline allows Sherlock Holmes to keep his head when everyone else is losing theirs, as in *The Hound of the Baskervilles,* when the cast of characters goes half loopy imagining unseen killer dogs and Holmes stays in the background, combing public documents. The Zen-like detachment of the trained observer also helps Holmes manipulate all the normal humans around him like a chess master. He sends Watson off on crazy missions — go to Dartmoor; go learn all you can about Chinese pottery; here, throw this incendiary device through Irene Adler's window — precisely so he can sit back and watch what happens.

And that's just it: Sherlock Holmes watches *what actually happens.* He will do anything to get the facts — dress in a funny outfit, sleep in a prehistoric stone hut, go undercover as an Irish revolutionary for two years. But until he has the facts, he reaches no foregone conclusions. He safeguards his analysis from ideology and prejudice, unlike, say, the saga's average Scotland Yard inspector, generally happy to arrest the first dodgy-looking character he comes across. (An early comic epiphany comes at the climax of *A Study in Scarlet,* when Inspectors Gregson and Lestrade learn simultaneously that they've been pursuing separate, equally useless leads, only to have Holmes reveal the murderer with a self-satisfied flourish.) Meanwhile, in his own very different way, Watson does the same. In his guise as a prickly metaliterary commentator, Holmes often criticizes Watson's accounts of their shared adventures, basically for being too interesting. Too much romance, not enough scientific deduction, Holmes repeatedly says. (To which the reader is tempted to respond that it's *induction* anyway, you idiot.) Watson rebuts this critique by saying that he's just reporting facts, an argument Holmes finds annoying but impossible to refute.

All this may sound obvious. What else would a detective do? But consider how desperately we need this discipline right now. For a supposed Information Age, we drown in fact-twisting theory, misbegotten conclusions, and self-serving "analysis." Spend five minutes on any newspaper's online comment section and you will find a sterling example of anti-Sherlockian thinking. Whenever an eminent figure denies that carbon dioxide emissions disrupt the atmosphere; whenever someone says biological evolution is "just a theory"; whenever an all-caps email foists elaborate conspiracies orchestrated by mundane federal government departments — such assertions constitute metaphorical slaps to the face of Sherlock Holmes. Fortunately, Holmes, expert in the Japanese system of wrestling, stands prepared to defend himself. What about the rest of us? Time and again, we twenty-first-century citizens encounter rhetorical equivalents of a glow-in-the-dark dog, unleashed to make us scurry about without a clue. We need to remember our eyes, ears, and all life's opportunities to sit on an Eastern divan fashioned from five cushions, thinking over the facts — shag tobacco optional and, these days, discouraged. In a willfully confusing world, the Great Detective reminds us of our duty to both see and observe.

He also reminds us that the facts alone are not enough. It's one thing to come up with an answer. Sherlock Holmes always seeks a *solution:* the right action, based on his discoveries. Sometimes that requires his puckish flair for the dramatic — smashing a bust of Napoleon to reveal the Black Pearl of the Borgias (Watson and Lestrade burst into applause after that one), or pretending that he's close to death to con a would-be murderer into confessing while Watson hides behind the bedstead. But at other times a Sherlockian solution involves choosing which facts need to be discreetly forgotten. In "The Adventure of the Blue Carbuncle," he and Watson corner a weasely thief who has tried to frame another man for the titular jewel heist. Holmes extracts a confession, then lets the malefactor go. "I am not retained by the police to supply their deficiencies," he remarks. "I suppose that I am commuting a felony, but it is just possible that I am saving a soul." In "A Case of Identity," Holmes chooses not to reveal the mystery's solution to his own client because it would break her heart. In "The Adventure of the Second Stain," Holmes covers up a crime that almost precipitates a Europe-wide war because its revelation would ruin a marriage.

In Holmes's practice, facts may rule, but they must be filtered through art and mercy. He solves mysteries with a science of his own devising, but he also infuses science with soul and conscience. And that, more than anything, marks the Great Detective as a man for our times. We need Sherlock Holmes. Fortunately, the door at the top of the seventeen steps is always open.

Over pints of Sherlock Holmes Ale at the Sherlock Holmes Pub, Roger Johnson, Jean Upton, and I talked about — well, what do you think? Johnson, a robustly betweeded and bewhiskered embodiment of Englishness, edits the *Sherlock Holmes Journal* of the Sherlock Holmes Society of London. Together, he and Jean recently produced *The Sherlock Holmes Miscellany,* a book that could serve the curious literary wayfarer as an introduction to the phenomenon. Their very marriage, in fact, owes to the Baker Street scene: Roger met Jean, an American, at a Sherlockian society meeting. This day, they had come down to London after a trip to Cardiff, where they'd visited the elaborate interior set of *Sherlock.*

"I love how they've done the Baker Street rooms, of course," Johnson remarked with a slightly dreamy expression. "There's a great texture and reality to it all. I told Jean, You know, I could live in those rooms."

"And I told him," Upton interjected, "that he basically already does."

This pair reminded me of all the ways, gentle and profound, that a love for Sherlock Holmes shapes sensibilities so far removed from the character's creation. "The stories are just the most wonderful windows into social history," Upton said. "Really, they show you the whole beginning of our modern world." We talked about how Sherlock's adventures inadvertently reveal the nature of Victorian women's lives and the technology of that formative societal moment. But the conversation soon moved on to life today, and friendships formed through the worldwide Sherlockian subculture. We knew, it proved, quite a few people in common. Our table in a pub — named for the character in 1957, by the way, and a de facto clubhouse for the Great Detective's devotees in London — served as a temporary nexus for a real-world network of creativity, frivolity, and devotion.

How improbable: a series of stories replete with skullduggery, violence, and legerdemain has created a global community of friendship and play.

"It is curious, the degree to which Arthur Conan Doyle has influenced our lives," Johnson said. Without him, we three would certainly not be met in a graceful Victorian dining room decorated with Sidney Paget drawings and an oil portrait of a certain mustachioed Scottish doctor. Reality — Victorian crime, the discipline of medical observation, a host of Conan Doyle's private fascinations — shaped the fantasy of Sherlock Holmes. Now the Sherlockian saga demonstrates the power fantasy can wield in reality: a mostly benign example, it must be said, of real-world dedication to people, events, and places that never existed.

Or, at least, did not originally exist. For while Holmes and Watson themselves may remain elusive in the flesh, the world Arthur Conan Doyle began and so many others helped build is remarkably tangible. Roger Johnson reported the Sherlock Holmes Society of London's membership at an all-time high, his editorial files stuffed beyond capacity with submissions to the *Journal*. And, of course, the phenomenon manifests itself in so many other ways. Any of us could have taken a dive into our mobile phones and down a warren of tweets and videos and essays and stories. (Though to forsake ale and good conversation to check one's phone would, needless to say, be highly un-Sherlockian.)

When the time came to leave, we peered around a corner of the pub, into a small, cordoned-off room. Or maybe I should say the Room: yet another re-creation of 221B, this one perhaps the most distinguished of them all. First assembled as the Borough of Marylebone's contribution to the 1951 Festival of Britain, this version of the well-remembered chamber has been maintained at the pub since its opening. We gazed in. There stood the wax bust used as a decoy for air-gun bullets. There, the violin. The chemical laboratory. The Persian slipper, handy for tobacco storage. The jackknife, doing its duty in securing unanswered letters to the mantel. And beyond any detail: faded but alluring Victorian rococo layered over Georgian elegance, every object suggesting an adventure suffused with fog and gaslight.

"Quite something, eh?" Roger Johnson said.

Yes. I imagined a voice, sharp and precise, reflecting upon the sheer improbability of it all—this never-finished communal project to make and remake Sherlock Holmes and John Watson and their milieu. "If we could fly out of that window hand in hand," Holmes once told his tireless, deathless friend and chronicler, "hover over this great city, gently remove the roofs, and peep in at the queer things which are going on, the strange coincidences, the plannings, the cross-purposes . . . working through generations, and leading to the most outré results, it would make all fiction with its conventionalities and foreseen conclusions most stale and unprofitable."

As I descended the steps to the London streets, I felt—as I have many times since I first pulled a battered volume of old detective stories from a library shelf—at home in two realms united: our world and the Great Detective's world, a singular global country of the mind.

ACKNOWLEDGMENTS

Like the larger and grander Sherlockian phenomenon, this book is the work of many hands. My deepest thanks go to all the friends, family, colleagues, scholars, and fellow Sherlockians who assisted me along the way. In particular:

Melissa Flashman, my sagacious agent,
and her comrades at Trident Media

Ben Hyman, the best of editors, who took a chance on this book and then did so much to help create it (and talk its author off various Reichenbachian ledges)

The good people at Houghton Mifflin Harcourt, especially Larry Cooper, Hannah Harlow, Michelle Bonanno, and Giuliana Fritz

Patrick Barry, for the great cover,
and Chrissy Kurpeski, for the lovely text

The wonderful staff at the Multnomah County Library,
especially Ruth Allen

The amazing Interlibrary Loan Program, wonder of civilization

The British Newspaper Archive

The staff at the Berg Collection of English and American
Literature at the New York Public Library

Lyndsay Faye, who provided early guidance and connections and
answered many questions about many things

Leslie Klinger, likewise, particularly for his insights on the
current state of the Great Game and the Free Sherlock initiative

Miles Patrick Bryan, ace researcher

The staff at the Oregon Museum of Science and Industry and the
curators and creators of the International Exhibition of Sherlock Holmes

Artists Repertory Theatre

Paul Collins, the Literary Detective

Judith Flanders, author of *The Invention of Murder*

Simon Blundell at the Reform Club

The Baker Street Babes, in particular Kristina Manente,
Ardy, and Kafers

Matt Marden and Bobby Graham, for the Hell's Kitchen crashpad

Mattias Boström, BSI, Street Arabs (ret.)

The Noble and Most Singular Order of the Blue Carbuncle,
for the hospitality

Amy Sturgis, for insight on the history of fandom

Michael Saler, for his time and expertise

The far-flung erstwhile members of the Street Arabs, with apologies

Joe Frey, Ashley Polasek, and my other tablemates at the 2013 BSI
Weekend finale

Tom Soby, *the* man for the moors

Lucinda Coxon, for explaining the creation of her Conan Doyle

Laurie R. King, for insight on the craft of pastiche (and nonpastiche)

Leslie Katz, for discussing his version of the Great Game

Catherine Cooke, of the Sherlock Holmes Collection
at Marylebone Library

Brandon Perlow and Karl Bollers of *Watson and Holmes*

Dave McCoy and Jaime Natoli, for hospitality in Los Angeles

Ellen Dockser at WGBH, for making the arrangements at the Langham

Steven Moffat and Sue Vertue, for a quiet talk on the terrace

Rebecca Eaton, re: the dynamics of a shooting star

Benedict Cumberbatch — hey, I stood *near* him

Elinor Gray, for patiently explaining the world of fanfiction

Jerry Margolin, amasser and steward of Holmesiana

Joe Riggs, the Real Sherlock Holmes

Roger Johnson and Jean Upton, for the pint of Sherlock Holmes

Aaron Katz, who brought Holmes to twenty-first-century Portland

A special thanks goes to my colleagues at *Portland Monthly,* who both
tolerated and supported me through the writing of this book: Rachel
Ritchie, Randy Gragg, Mike Novak, Kate Madden, Marty Patail, Nicole
Vogel, Bill Hutfilz, Carrie Hinton, and the editorial, sales, and production
staffs, 2012–present.

My own personal Baker Street Division of the Detective Police Force:
Peggy Maclay Gadbow (1924–2013)

Mom and Tim

Dad and Mary Anne

George, *il Padrino*

My brother Chad, first enlistee in the Street Arabs, and Courtney and
Beatrice and the new kid

Grady and Ali, long-suffering cousins, and Jessa and Jason, their awesome consorts, and Wells, the other new kid

Crucial aunts and uncles: Katie, Daryl, Harry, Vicki, Suzanne

Don and Gretchen

Susan

Lisa

Heather

Helen

Friends and comrades, blessedly too numerous to mention, in Portland, Montana, New Hampshire and New England, and beyond

Watson the Cat (2000–2013)

I could not have written this book without Christina, Cash, and Tabitha.

Finally, I am so very grateful to Arthur Conan Doyle for the invention of Sherlock Holmes and John Watson, and to all who've made their world come alive. Carry on.

NOTES & COMMENTS

The most important source material for this book is, of course, the sixty-story Sherlock Holmes saga created by Arthur Conan Doyle. You've read it all, of course. Yes? If not, avail yourself of any of the many editions, ranging from free-to-download to expensively bound. For a deeper exploration of the many byways of Baker Street, see Leslie Klinger's *New Annotated Sherlock Holmes,* a monumental dissection of Conan Doyle's text and Sherlockian issues great and small, drawing primarily upon Great Game–style analysis published over the decades in the *Baker Street Journal,* the *Sherlock Holmes Journal,* and other organs of the traditional Sherlockian subculture. (Scholarship and quasi-scholarship aside, Klinger's volumes include a terrific range of illustrations of the Holmes stories and the Victorian era, many quite obscure.)

For those who seek a distilled reading experience, I humbly offer my own selection of:

THE TWENTY ESSENTIAL SHERLOCK HOLMES STORIES
(IN ORDER OF PUBLICATION)

A Study in Scarlet

The Sign of the Four

"A Scandal in Bohemia"

"The Adventure of the Red-Headed League"

"The Man with the Twisted Lip"

"The Adventure of the Blue Carbuncle"

"The Adventure of the Speckled Band"

"The Adventure of the Noble Bachelor"

"Silver Blaze"

"The Adventure of the Musgrave Ritual"

"The Adventure of the Cardboard Box"

"The Final Problem"

The Hound of the Baskervilles

"The Adventure of the Empty House"

"The Adventure of Charles Augustus Milverton"

"The Adventure of the Six Napoleons"

"The Adventure of the Second Stain"

"The Adventure of the Bruce-Partington Plans"

"His Last Bow"

"The Adventure of the Illustrious Client"

An alternative approach to familiarizing yourself with at least one dimension of Conan Doyle's storytelling brilliance: (re)read the first few paragraphs of each of the fifty-six short stories.

SOURCE NOTES

PRELUDE

My description of the theatrical stage set of 221B Baker Street owes to a visit to Portland's Artists Repertory Theatre and its production *Sherlock Holmes and the Case of the Christmas Carol,* a funny and effective combination of the Holmesian milieu and Charles Dickens's seasonal conceit, written by John Longenbaugh, a noted Seattle Sherlockian.

Smithsonian's website offered an intriguing and useful series of blog entries on the theme of "Design and Sherlock Holmes" in 2012, primarily authored by Jimmy Stamp. As of this writing, they remain digitally accessible.

CHAPTER I

Sidney Paget's illustrations for "A Scandal in Bohemia" make a splendid introduction to the lovely and lurid Victoriana captured in the Sherlock Holmes stories. The era is really too immense for comprehensive discussion in a book such as this one or perhaps even full comprehension by one individual. But for anyone seeking to create their own impressionistic, semi-imaginary Victorian period, I might recommend crosshatching

Conan Doyle, the contemporary writings of Oscar Wilde, the historical novels of Sarah Waters, and the online British Newspaper Archive, an extraordinary service that enjoys the support and participation of the British Library. I found the pages of the *Pall Mall Gazette* particularly rewarding. Operations like Google Books, Project Gutenberg, and Archive .org provide ready access to huge troves of Victorian writing, which the curious reader can find with moderately aggressive search-engine work; most period texts referred to in this book can be found online, in whole or in part. *The Night Side of London,* cited in a footnote in this chapter, offers a deliciously seamy take on the British capital as it would have been viewed from some angles during the era in which Sherlock Holmes gestated in young Arthur Conan Doyle's mind.

More full-length biographies of Arthur Conan Doyle exist than any sane person could profitably read. In the preparation of this book, two collections of Conan Doyle's correspondence proved the most essential: *Arthur Conan Doyle: A Life in Letters,* edited by Jon Lellenberg, Daniel Stashower, and Charles Foley (Penguin, 2007); *Letters to the Press: The Unknown Conan Doyle,* edited and introduced by John Michael Gibson and Richard Lancelyn Green (University of Iowa, 1986). Among the narrative biographies, Daniel Stashower's *Teller of Tales* (Henry Holt, 1999) is widely considered the reigning champ, and is particularly notable for its sympathetic but tough-minded treatment of Spiritualism. I also found Andrew Lycett's *The Man Who Created Sherlock Holmes* (Free Press, 2007), Richard Miller's *The Adventures of Arthur Conan Doyle* (Thomas Dunne, 2008), and Martin Booth's *The Doctor and the Detective* (Macmillan, 1997) useful. The mystery writer John Dickson Carr's 1949 effort, *The Life of Sir Arthur Conan Doyle,* written under the reportedly malign influence of Conan Doyle's son Adrian, is chiefly of novelistic rather than historical value but certainly informed some passages of this book. A curiosity: John Lamond's *Arthur Conan Doyle: A Memoir,* from 1931, was authorized — one might say fomented — by the Conan Doyle family and dwells heavily on Spiritualism.

And, of course, I made ample use of Conan Doyle's own *Memories and Adventures* — factually less than forthcoming, but in its own way a revealing cross-section of the man's mind, sensibility, and self-image. His collection of literary essays, *Through the Magic Door,* also provided several key insights to his intellectual development and outlook on his craft.

The two Sherlockian special-interest books I would recommend to any casual reader who loves the character are Vincent Starrett's *The Private Life of Sherlock Holmes* — a glimpse of the time of its own creation as much as of Holmesiana itself — and James Edward Holroyd's happy-go-lucky *Baker Street By-ways.* There are, of course, many to choose from, many excellent. Those two bring a rare delight and delicate touch to the subject. From more recent years, Roger Johnson and Jean Upton's *Sherlock Holmes Miscellany* is quite good.

CHAPTER 2

Paul Collins's identification of the author of *The Notting Hill Mystery* appeared in the *New York Times* on 7 January 2011. A belated birthday present to Sherlock, perhaps?

If you read one pre-Sherlockian Victorian detective work, make it *The Moonstone.*

Among Arthur Conan Doyle's many sporting endeavors, I particularly enjoy thinking about the Allahakberries, a cricketing side organized by his friend and collaborator J. M. Barrie, which featured an ever-shifting roster of Victorian-Edwardian literary luminaries. Wells, Kipling, Wodehouse, Milne, E. W. Hornung, George Cecil Ives, and many others took up their bats for the Allahakberries. The team is the subject of *Peter Pan's First XI,* by Kevin Telfer (Sceptre, 2010).

For a full-length biography of Joseph Bell — particularly valuable for its rich portrayal of the Edinburgh intellectual milieu that fostered Bell and, later, Conan Doyle — see Ely M. Liebow's *Dr. Joe Bell: Model for Sherlock Holmes* (Poplar Press, 1982). Bell and Conan Doyle feature as the detecting characters in a series of mystery novels by the English writer David Pirie, who also scripted a BBC series, *Murder Rooms,* on the same premise.

Matthew Sweet, author of the eye-opening *Inventing the Victorians,* has also written and spoken extensively on Sherlock Holmes, as an electronic search will reveal.

CHAPTERS 3 & 4

Again, the online British Newspaper Archive was essential to my humble efforts to form and convey impressions of Piccadilly and Baker Street circa 1881. Donald Serrell Thomas's *The Victorian Underworld* (New York University Press, 1998) makes a handy introduction to the criminal lore that underlies many of the Sherlock Holmes tales.

CHAPTER 5

Re Sherlockian societies, the definitive list has long been maintained by Peter E. Blau, an amiable legend among the cognoscenti. As of this writing, it can be accessed at sherlocktron.com. The Baker Street Babes maintain several digital ports of call, all of which can currently be found via bakerstreetbabes.com.

There are numerous and extensive writings on the history of the Baker Street Irregulars, many composed by members of that venerable society. Jon Lellenberg's BSI Archival History website, bsiarchivalhistory.org, provides an entrée and helped inform many of my descriptions of early Irregular proceedings. That era is also documented in newspaper reports of the period and afterward. Present-day Sherlockians produce quite a bit of digital material, naturally. The podcast series *I Hear of Sherlock Everywhere,* created by Scott Monty, is a reliable resource, as is the regular compendium of links and news at always1895.net, compiled by Matt Laffey.

For two biographical glimpses of the elusive William Hooker Gillette, see Doris E. Cook's *Sherlock Holmes and Much More* (Connecticut Historical Society, 1974) and *William Gillette: America's Sherlock Holmes,* by Henry Zecher (Xlibris, 2011).

CHAPTER 6

There has been, in recent years, some trumped-up controversy over Bertram Fletcher Robinson's precise role in the writing of *The Hound of the Baskervilles,* which I frankly preferred not to dignify in this book's narrative text. In 2005, Britain's *Telegraph* ran the juicy headline "Did Conan Doyle Poison His Friend to Cheat Him out of *The Hound of the Basker-*

villes?" and reported the intention of a team of "investigators" to exhume Fletcher's remains. A Church of England court tossed that request with extreme prejudice, and nothing more seems to have come of the matter. (One possible flaw in the theory: Robinson didn't die until 1907, six years after the *Hound* appeared, an awfully long time to stew over an authorship dispute and a chronological wrinkle that not even Watson would let slide.) Still, the *Hound* is a curiosity in that regard: the only Sherlock Holmes story for which Conan Doyle enlisted a formal collaborator. The chain of events would seem straightforward enough: Robinson and Conan Doyle worked together on some basic conceptual material, but once their "creeper" became a Sherlock Holmes story, Conan Doyle took over, with some mutually satisfactory agreement to terms. Not everything is a case for Sherlock Holmes.

Any reader interested in learning more about present-day Dartmoor would do well to start with the Dartmoor Preservation Association: dart moorpreservation.com.

CHAPTER 7

A couple of haphazard but fun compendia of Sherlockian press clippings, cartoons, posters, ads, and other ephemera helped with my various inventories of the character's image in popular culture, notably *The Sherlock Holmes Scrapbook,* edited by Peter Haining (Bramhall House, 1974), and *Sherlock Holmes in America,* by Bill Blackbeard (Harry N. Abrams, 1981).

The sprawling tradition of Sherlockian parody and imitation, in which the *Wipers Times* and other World War I soldiers' papers participated, is limned by *The Alternative Sherlock Holmes,* by Peter Ridgway Watt and Joseph Green (Ashgate, 2003).

CHAPTER 8

Again, for a sensitive and contextualized look at Conan Doyle's Spiritualist activities, look to Daniel Stashower's *Teller of Tales.*

A fairly devastating treatment of Conan Doyle's conduct toward his daughter Mary can be found in *Out of the Shadows: The Untold Story of Arthur Conan Doyle's First Family,* by Georgina Doyle (Calabash, 2004).

CHAPTER 9

Five really good Basil Rathbone–Nigel Bruce films (in my opinion):

The Hound of the Baskervilles (1939)
Sherlock Holmes and the Voice of Terror (1942)
The Spider Woman (1944; if only for the spectacle of Rathbone disguised as an Indian)
The Woman in Green (1945; summarize the plot if you can!)
Pursuit to Algiers (1945)

Some of my account of the genesis and production of the Rathbone-Bruce films relies on Bruce's memoirs, never wholly published. Extracts appeared in the *Sherlock Holmes Journal,* Winter 1998.

Most of the vintage Sherlock Holmes movies referenced in this chapter can be seen, in whole or in part, on YouTube. It's a great way to kill a day, or a week. Or longer.

For a king-size introduction and general guide to the Sherlockian Great Game, new and old, see Leslie Klinger's *New Annotated Sherlock Holmes.* Numerous anthologies and monographs offer more episodic entrées to the subject, several of which were reissued in paperback in the 1990s under the auspices of Otto Penzler's Sherlock Holmes Library; of these, *17 Steps to 221B,* a collection of vintage British essays edited by James Edward Holroyd, makes a jolly introduction to the Game as played in the grand old style. For more state-of-the-art Sherlockian scholarly fare, find Leslie Katz's self-published articles or the small but select online archive offered by the *Baker Street Journal.* For instance, Sonia Fetherston's "Shoscombe Through the Looking-Glass" examines textual and imagistic links between the final Holmes story and Lewis Carroll; Peter Calmai's "Despatches from the Moor" delves into references to newspapers in *The Hound of the Baskervilles,* et cetera. A subscription to the *Baker Street Journal* or membership in the Sherlock Holmes Society of London, which includes semiannual receipt of the *Sherlock Holmes Journal,* would naturally provide a deeper view.

There are many forms of Sherlockian scholarship and analysis that fit into neither the Great Game tradition nor "official" academic boundaries. For one instance, see *Holy Clues: The Gospel According to Sherlock Holmes,* by Stephen Kendrick (Pantheon, 1999), an analysis of religious affairs in the Holmesian Canon.

CHAPTER 10

YouTube currently provides a sumptuous feast of TV Sherlocks, including (but not limited to) the Sheldon Reynolds series, the one-offs featuring Alan Napier and John Longden, as much Jeremy Brett as you could want, Douglas Wilmer, Peter Cushing, Christopher Plummer's awesomely grainy *Silver Blaze,* the cartoon *Hound,* et cetera.

Some of my passages on Brett are based upon material in Terry Manners's *The Man Who Became Sherlock Holmes: The Tortured Mind of Jeremy Brett* (Virgin, 2001).

Elinor Gray's Sherlockian fanfic list for sherlockian.net currently stands (IMHO) as the most cogent introduction to the unwieldy (and very sweaty) field.

An interesting take on Sherlockian adaptation can be found in the 2011 American film *Cold Weather,* in which an aimless twenty-something young man drifts around Portland (my neighborhood, in fact) trying to put his boyish love of Holmes to use to solve a loose-limbed mystery. When I tracked down the director, Aaron Katz, for an interview, I discovered a Holmesian soul brother: a Portland native who grew up on William Baring-Gould's *Annotated Sherlock Holmes* and, at around ten years old, nurtured a healthy disdain for crass modernizers like Basil Rathbone. As for his use of the character in a decidedly unnatural habitat — the low-key film genre in which liberally educated young people mumble non sequiturs at one another — Katz noted: "The character seamlessly brings together that very scientific, modern outlook with the romantic sense that there might be more mystery to your life than you would suspect . . . I wanted to show two guys trying to cope with situations where they had literally no idea what to do. How do they handle it? They do what I would do: they try to act like and think like Sherlock Holmes. You can do worse. There's something very satisfying and reassuring about Holmes — he would never start a fight he wouldn't win. And it's not a stretch to bring elements of his character into a present-day setting. His method, his ethic, his sensibility — everything about Sherlock Holmes, at the core of the character, is modern."

INDEX